On the Fly Guide to™

THE NORTHWEST

A Traveler's Guide to the Greatest Fly
Fishing Destinations in Oregon & Washington

Titles Available in This Series

Saltwater Angler's Guide to Southern California

Saltwater Angler's Guide to the Southeast

Flyfisher's Guide to the Florida Keys

Flyfisher's Guide to Idaho

Flyfisher's Guide to Northern California

Flyfisher's Guide to Montana

Flyfisher's Guide to Michigan

Flyfisher's Guide to Wyoming

Flyfisher's Guide to Northern New England

Flyfisher's Guide to Washington

Flyfisher's Guide to Oregon

Flyfisher's Guide to Colorado

Flyfisher's Guide to Pennsylvania

Flyfisher's Guide to Minnesota

Flyfisher's Guide to Utah

Flyfisher's Guide to Texas

Flyfisher's Guide to New York

Flyfisher's Guide to Virginia

On the Fly Guide to™

THE NORTHWEST

A Traveler's Guide to the Greatest Fly
Fishing Destinations in Oregon & Washington

John Shewey

Wilderness
Adventures
Press, Inc.™

Belgrade, Montana

© 2002 by John Shewey
Photographs contained herein © 2002 John Shewey unless otherwise noted.

Cover photograph "North Umpqua River" and "Summer Steelhead from the
Sol Duc River" © 2002 John Shewey

Photo page 298, Darc Knobel

Maps, book and cover design © 2002 Wilderness Adventures Press, Inc.™
Flyfisher's Guide to™ Wilderness Adventures Press, Inc.™

Published by Wilderness Adventures Press, Inc.™
45 Buckskin Road
Belgrade, MT 59714
800-925-3339
Website: www.WildernessAdventuresBooks.com
Email: books@wildadv.com

First Edition
10 9 8 7 6 5 4 3 2 1

Printed in the United States of America

Library of Congress Cataloging-in-Publication Data

Shewey, John.
  Northwest on the fly : a traveler's guide to the greatest fly fishing
destinations in Oregon and Washington / by John Shewey.
      p. cm.
  ISBN 1-885106-96-3 (pbk. : alk. paper)
  1. Fly fishing–Oregon–Guidebooks. 2. Fly fishing–Washington
(State)–Guidebooks. 3. Oregon–Guidebooks. 4. Washington
(State)–Guidebooks. I. Title.
  SH539 .S539 2002
  799.1'24'09795–dc21
                                                          2002007669

TABLE OF CONTENTS

A TRAVEL INTRODUCTION 1

ON THE FLY GUIDE WATERS MAP 4

1 THE GRANDE RONDE RIVER 7
    Steelhead Paradise 7
    Fishing the Grande Ronde 12
    Restaurants and Accommodations 14
    La Grande, Oregon 16
    Grande Ronde and Imnaha Rivers 18
    Nearby Attractions and Activities 18
    Fast Facts 19
    Local Fly Shops, Guides, & Contacts 20

2 THE YAKIMA RIVER 23
    Washington's Blue-Ribbon Gem 23
    Fishing the Yakima 27
    Restaurants and Accommodations 28
    Nearby Fisheries 29
    Nearby Attractions and Activities 30
    Fast Facts 31
    Local Fly Shops, Guides, & Contacts 32

3 THE LOWER DESCHUTES RIVER 33
    The West's Most Remarkable River 33
    Stonefly Time 39
    Fishing the Deschutes 40
    Deschutes River Steelhead 41
    Deschutes River Access 42
    Restaurants and Accommodations 44
    Nearby Fishery: Washington's Klickitat River 46
    Nearby Fishery: The John Day River 48
    Fast Facts 54
    Local Fly Shops, Guides, & Contacts 57

4 THE WILLIAMSON RIVER AND KLAMATH COUNTRY 59
    Trophy Trout Waters Beyond Compare 59
    Fishing the Lower Williamson 63
    The Williamson River Club at Crystalwood Lodge 64
    Lonesome Duck 66
    The Upper Williamson 67
    Upper Klamath and Agency Lakes 69
    The Wood River 70
    Fast Facts 72
    Local Fly Shops, Guides, & Contacts 73

5 THE HOH, SOL DUC, AND BOGACHIEL RIVERS 75
Olympic Peninsula Steelhead. 75
Fishing the Hoh, Sol Duc, and Bogachiel 81
Restaurants and Accommodations 82
Nearby Attractions and Activities. 83
Fast Facts 85
Local Fly Shops, Guides, & Contacts 87

6 THE ELWHA RIVER 89
Backcountry Trout Close to Home 89
Fishing the Upper Elwha. 92
Restaurants and Accommodations 94
Port Angeles Lodging 94
Nearby Fisheries 95
Middle and Lower Elwha 95
Nearby Attractions and Activities. 95
Fast Facts 96
Local Fly Shops, Guides, & Contacts 97

7 POTHOLES RESERVOIR AND THE SEEP LAKES 99
Mixed-Bag Fishing in Eastern Washington 99
Fishing the Seep Lakes 104
Restaurants and Accommodations 108
Nearby Fisheries 108
Potholes Reservoir 108
Nearby Attractions and Activities 109
Fast Facts 110
Local Fly Shops, Guides, & Contacts 111

8 LENICE, NUNNALLY AND MERRY LAKES. 113
Wind, Waves, and Reel-Screaming Runs. 113
Restaurants and Accommodations. 115
Nearby Attractions and Activities. 115
Fast Facts 116
Local Fly Shops, Guides, & Contacts 117

9 MANN LAKE AND THE STEENS MOUNTAINS 119
Rugged Splendor in the Oregon High Desert. 119
Fishing Mann Lake. 122
Restaurants and Accommodations. 124
Nearby Fisheries: Juniper and Wildhorse Lakes, Blitzen River. 125
Nearby Attractions and Activities. 126
Fast Facts 129
Local Fly Shops, Guides, & Contacts 131

10 BROWNLEE RESERVOIR. 133
The Northwest at its Warmwater Best 133
Fishing Brownlee Reservoir 136
Restaurants and Accommodations. 139
Nearby Fisheries: Owyhee River 141

Nearby Attractions and Activities....................................141
Fast Facts 144
Local Fly Shops, Guides, & Contacts 145

11 THE METOLIUS RIVER 147
Central Oregon's Beloved Spring Creek 147
Fishing the Metolius 149
Restaurants and Accommodations.....................................152
Nearby Fisheries: Suttle Lake......................................153
Nearby Attractions and Activities..................................153
Fast Facts 154
Local Fly Shops, Guides, & Contacts 156

12 THE CROOKED RIVER 157
Year-Round Wild Rainbows 157
Restaurants and Accommodations.....................................162
Nearby Attractions and Activities..................................162
Fast Facts 163
Local Fly Shops, Guides, & Contacts 164

13 THE MIDDLE DESCHUTES RIVER 165
A Winter Treat Dry Flies and Brown Trout..........................165
Restaurants and Accommodations.....................................169
Fast Facts 170
Local Fly Shops, Guides, & Contacts 171

14 THE SKYKOMISH RIVER..173
Home Waters of the Legends 173
Fishing the Skykomish 175
Restaurants and Accommodations.....................................177
Nearby Attractions and Activities..................................178
Fast Facts 179
Local Fly Shops, Guides, & Contacts 180

15 THE NORTH FORK OF THE STILLAGUAMISH 181
Long-Time Haunt of the Great "Sasquatch of the Stilly" 181
Fishing the North Fork of the Stilly...............................184
Accommodations...184
Fast Facts 186
Local Fly Shops, Guides, & Contacts 188

16 THE SKAGIT AND SAUK RIVERS 189
March Madness for Native Steelhead.................................189
Fishing the Skagit and Sauk Rivers 194
Restaurants and Accommodations.....................................198
Nearby Attractions and Activities..................................199
Fast Facts 200
Local Fly Shops, Guides, & Contacts 202

17 CHICKAHOMINY RESERVOIR. 203
 The Archetypal Desert Trout Reservoir. 203
 The Chickahominy Experience 207
 Fishing Chickahominy. 209
 Love It or Hate It 210
 Nearby Attractions and Activities. 211
 Yellowjacket Lake and Moon Reservoir 212
 Restaurants and Accommodations 212
 Fast Facts 214
 Local Fly Shops, Guides, & Contacts 215

18 THE MALHEUR RIVER 217
 Remote Rainbows in the Oregon Desert 217
 Fishing the Malheur. 222
 Nearby Fisheries: Beulah Reservoir 224
 Restaurants and Accommodations. 224
 Fast Facts 225
 Local Fly Shops, Guides, & Contacts 226

18 CHOPAKA LAKE. 227
 Dry-Fly Action for Big Rainbows 227
 Nearby Fisheries: Blue Lake. 228
 Accommodations. 228
 Fast Facts 231
 Local Fly Shops, Guides, & Contacts 232

19 LAKE LENORE 233
 Trophy Cutthroat in the Desert. 233
 Fishing Lake Lenore. 235
 Restaurants and Accommodations. 237
 Area Lodging 237
 Fast Facts 239
 Local Fly Shops, Guides, & Contacts 240

20 DRY FALLS LAKE. 241
 Scenic Splendor and Hard-fighting Rainbows and Browns 241
 Restaurants and Accommodations. 244
 Area Lodging 244
 Fast Facts 245
 Local Fly Shops, Guides, & Contacts 247

21 THE NORTH UMPQUA RIVER 249
 Steelhead Water of Legend. 249
 Timing the Runs. 251
 Flies and Tackle 255
 North Umpqua Logistics. 256
 Steamboat Inn 256
 Restaurants and Accommodations. 258
 Nearby Fisheries: South and Middle Umpqua. 258

Nearby Attractions and Activities...................................259
Fast Facts 260
Local Fly Shops, Guides, & Contacts 261

23 THE KALAMA RIVER...263
A Northwest Fly Angling Tradition 263
Fishing the Kalama River 265
Accommodations..266
Fast Facts 267
Local Fly Shops, Guides, & Contacts 268

24 EAST FORK OF THE LEWIS RIVER 269
Elegant, Close-to-Home Steelhead Water 269
Accommodations..272
Fast Facts 273
Local Fly Shops, Guides, & Contacts 274

25 THE LAKES OF CENTURY DRIVE: HOSMER, CRANE PRAIRIE & DAVIS 275
The Stillwater Mecca of Central Oregon............................275
Fishing Hosmer Lake...277
Fishing Crane Prairie Reservoir...................................280
Fishing Davis Lake..283
Nearby Attractions and Activities.................................286
Nearby Fisheries 287
Restaurants and Accommodations....................................287
Fast Facts 289
Local Fly Shops, Guides, & Contacts 291

26 EAST LAKE...295
Float Tubing a Volcano 295
Accommodations..297
Nearby Attractions and Activities.................................298
Fast Facts 299
Local Fly Shops, Guides, & Contacts 300

27 THE ROGUE RIVER 301
Historic Steelhead Water in Southern Oregon.......................301
The Upper Rogue...302
The Middle Rogue..307
The Lower Rogue...308
Fishing The Rogue...312
Pulling Flies on the Rogue 313
The Holy Water 315
Morrison's Rogue River Lodge 315
Restaurants and Accommodations....................................318
Nearby Attractions and Activities.................................319
Fast Facts 320
Local Fly Shops, Guides, & Contacts 321

28 SAAK LAKE RANCH 323
    Private Waters on the High Plateau 323
    Fast Facts 326
    Local Fly Shops, Guides, & Contacts 326

29 GRINDSTONE LAKES 327
    Oregon's Premier Private Stillwater Fishery 327
    Fast Facts 329
    Local Fly Shops, Guides, & Contacts 329

30 THE MCKENZIE RIVER 331
    Western Oregon's Best Trout Water 331
    McKenzie Summer Steelhead 336
    Hatchery Success 338
    Fishing the Summer Run 338
    Restaurants and Accommodations 340
    Nearby Fisheries 341
    Nearby Attractions and Activities 342
    Fast Facts 344
    Local Fly Shops, Guides, & Contacts 345

FLY SHOPS OF THE NORTHWEST 346

SPORTING GOODS STORES 352

SOURCES OF INFORMATION 356

INDEX 359

FISHING DIARY 365

Mt. Index rises above the Skykomish River in Washington.

WASHINGTON *Major Roads and Cities*

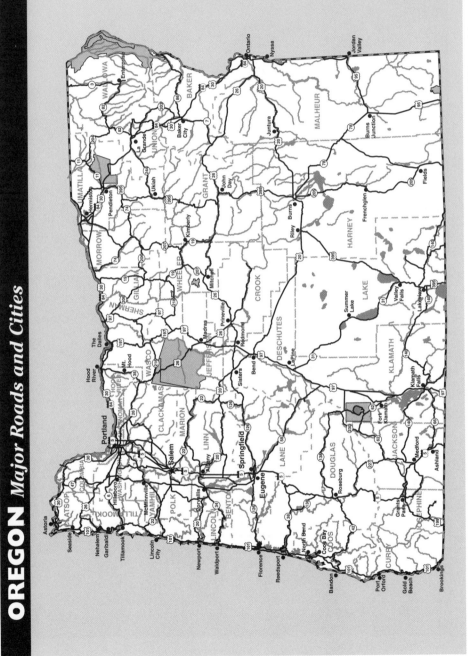

OREGON *Major Roads and Cities*

The beautiful North Umpqua provides steelhead waters of legend.

INTRODUCTION

NORTHWEST ON THE FLY

A Travel Introduction

The Deschutes. The North Umpqua. The Yakima. The Sol Duc. These are but a few of the legendary fly waters of the Pacific Northwest, a region blessed with superb fisheries as varied as the landscape itself. Indeed, if anything defines Northwest fly fishing it would be the word "diverse."

One day you swing flies on elegant pools for summer steelhead with towering conifers leaning out over the river like sentinels guarding the lush, verdant slopes of western Washington and western Oregon. The next day might find you casting from a float tube during the early morning calm on some distant high-desert reservoir, anticipating the vicious strike of a trophy-class rainbow.

The Northwest offers a little of everything and a lot of most things. Nowhere else do such superb trout fishing opportunities exist alongside exceptional fisheries for sea-run species ranging from steelhead and cutthroat to coho and king salmon. Beyond these traditional fisheries lies the realm of the so-called warmwater fishes, and the Northwest boasts tremendously productive waters teeming with smallmouth bass, crappie and other species.

The diverse nature of the waters in Oregon and Washington attracts equally diverse legions of fly anglers. Some live here or visit here just for steelhead, others for the great stillwaters and still others to meet the challenge of superb trout streams. The varied array of Northwest fisheries certainly renders subjective any attempt to list just the 40 or so best, as we have done with this guide.

Certainly all Northwest anglers would agree with many of the inclusions herein, but certainly we would expect some dissension along the way, for there are great fisheries out there that may not appear in any chapter of this volume. A few come to mind immediately, such as that wonderful eastern Washington steelhead river, the Wenatchee.

A few years ago, the Wenatchee would certainly have appeared near the top of my list of favorite Washington steelhead rivers, but as of this writing she enters her third straight year of being closed entirely for steelhead angling owing to concerns over dwindling runs of native fish in the upper Columbia tributaries. I hope the situation there reverses itself and in so doing forces me to include a Wenatchee River chapter in any future printings of this volume.

Likewise, as I write this, two of Oregon's premier trout lakes have all but gone dry. Nonetheless, both are featured herein simply because my 20 years of fishing these waters tells me that within one to two years both Davis Lake and Chickahominy Reservoir will regain their former glory. Both fisheries are cyclical: They enjoy half a decade or so of superb fishing and then a dry winter comes along to send the fisheries into a tailspin. They recover quickly, however, and often the first two years after recovery finds them at their best—which is exceptional.

The changing nature of those two waters, and of many others, certainly underscores the need for traveling anglers to obtain good, local information on the waters they intend to visit. This guide offers many insights that I've been lucky to collect over the course of many seasons living amid and enjoying these great waters. In addition to studying these chapters, however, anglers should consult local fly shops and guides for up-to-the-minute information.

To that end, I cannot overstate the importance of hiring a guide to help you learn the intricacies of waters entirely new to you. Throughout this book, where applicable, I have listed some of the best guides for specific waters. These are guides I know and trust—men who approach their job with a thorough sense of professionalism and who will heighten immeasurably your enjoyment of the waters in which they specialize.

In any event, while we might disagree over certain waters being included or left out of a book like this one, no angler familiar with Northwest waters would argue that Oregon and Washington don't enjoy uniquely varied and productive fly angling destinations. In this regard, I have striven to make this book useful to Northwest anglers and to those visiting from elsewhere. Herein you will find a vast store of tips and tricks and insights into the fisheries that make the Northwest such a remarkable fly angling destination.

John Shewey

WASHINGTON

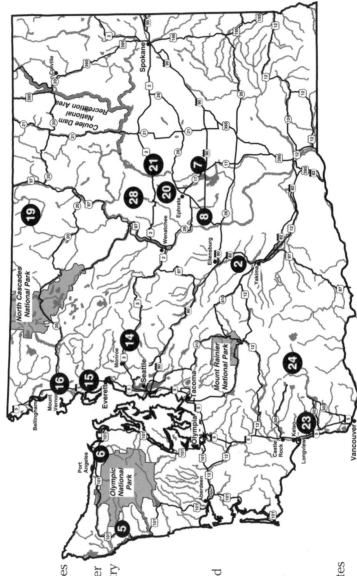

© Wilderness Adventures Press, Inc.

On the Fly Guide
Waters

1 The Grande Ronde River
2 Yakima River
3 The Lower Deschutes River
4 The Williamson River and Klamath Country
5 Hoh, Sol Duc and Bogachiel Rivers
6 Elwha River
7 Potholes Reservoir and the Seep Lakes
8 Lenice, Nunnally and Merry Lakes
9 Mann Lake and the Steens Mountains
10 Brownlee Reservoir
11 The Metolius River
12 The Crooked River
13 The Middle Deschutes River
14 Skykomish River

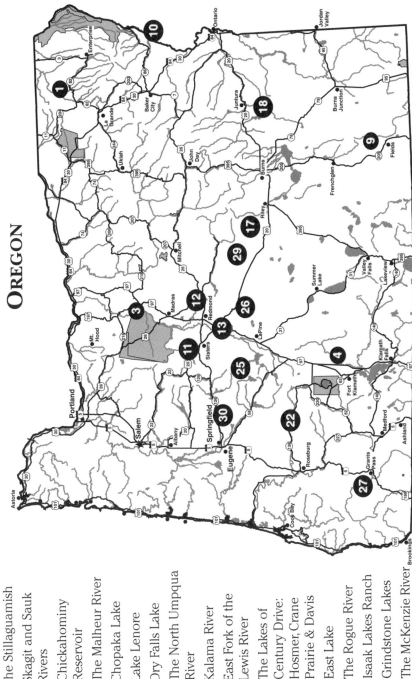

OREGON

© Wilderness Adventures Press, Inc.

15 The North Fork of the Stillaguamish

16 Skagit and Sauk Rivers

17 Chickahominy Reservoir

18 The Malheur River

19 Chopaka Lake

20 Lake Lenore

21 Dry Falls Lake

22 The North Umpqua River

23 Kalama River

24 East Fork of the Lewis River

25 The Lakes of Century Drive: Hosmer, Crane Prairie & Davis

26 East Lake

27 The Rogue River

28 Isaak Lakes Ranch

29 Grindstone Lakes

30 The McKenzie River

CHAPTER 1

THE GRANDE RONDE RIVER

Steelhead Paradise

I was just happy to be there, to be immersed in hip-deep water on the Grande Ronde under the most awesome conditions imaginable. Certainly they intimated an impending change of weather, but those high, hazy clouds now served mainly to dampen the sun's bright glow. Not even a wisp of wind blew through the canyon, where yellowing leaves hung bright and still along the banks, announcing October's arrival some days past. Seventy-degree comfort beckoned nothing more than an old T-shirt. The weather gods had been appeased. Now we'd see about those steelhead gods.

The Grande Ronde is a river of rapid change. A stiff desert wind can quickly dampen the enthusiasm of would-be fly casters and a shower in the mountains can turn the river brown, reducing visibility to less than a foot. Just as suddenly, October warmth can succumb to the nastiest kind of bone-numbing winter chill. One day you're fishing skated dry flies under ideal conditions; the next you're reduced to sinking lines and weighted flies to combat the suddenly high, cold water.

But this day bordered on perfection. I had only to choose my water, a task made all the more difficult by the near-complete lack of fishing pressure above Boggan's Oasis. I decided to fish something new, something I'd never fished before. That part would be easy, for this river offered miles of water that had thus far remained un-trodden by my cleated boots. Rounding a sweeping bend in the road, I spied a long, flat pool whose upper end offered the choppy, boulder-strewn water that draws my eye on sunny days.

I parked in the shade, strung a rod and attached my trusty Spawning Purple, the fly that for many seasons had delivered so many hook-ups. This was my confidence fly, the pattern I usually started with and always fell back on. I fished the pool well, but to no avail. The riffle above also looked inviting, so I walked up the bank to have a look only to discover a series of three, narrow stair-step runs all stacked together along my side of the river. The longest spanned a mere 40 yards or so. This was the kind of water frequently overlooked by other anglers. Not that it mattered now, with so few people on the water, but I'd remember this place to be sure. Some day it would likely serve as my refuge water when all the big runs were occupied.

For now, I'd be content to fish each of the three little runs just to learn them, to decipher their respective codes and figure out the "sweet spots." The first fished beautifully and tailed out in a slick, three-foot-deep glide that begged a resting fish. I guessed this lower end to be the garden spot, so to speak. The second run needed no such guesswork: A 6-pounder pounced on my fly in the choppy seam at mid-pool and tore the river to pieces before finally gaining a respectful release back to the river.

I watched this wild hen fin back to the opaque depths. Then I palmed the fly and gently stroked the wing, grooming it back into shape and squeezing the water back into the river.

The steelhead gods had smiled.

A Grande Ronde steelhead.

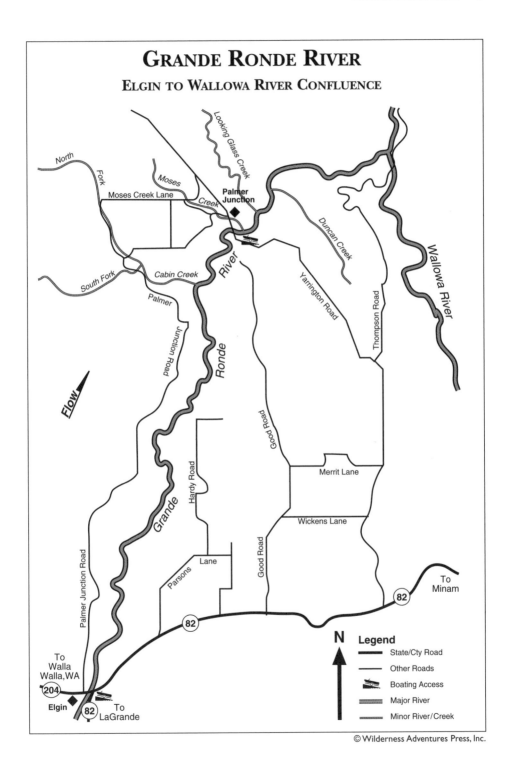

GRANDE RONDE RIVER
ELGIN TO WALLOWA RIVER CONFLUENCE

Looking Glass Creek

North

Fork

Moses

Moses Creek Lane

Creek

Palmer Junction

Duncan Creek

Wallowa River

South Fork

Cabin Creek

River

Palmer

Yarrington Road

Thompson Road

Junction Road

Ronde

Flow

Grande

Good Road

Hardy Road

Merrit Lane

Wickens Lane

Lane

Good Road

Parsons

To Minam

82

Palmer Junction Road

82

N

Legend

State/Cty Road

Other Roads

Boating Access

Major River

Minor River/Creek

To Walla Walla, WA

204

Elgin

82

To LaGrande

© Wilderness Adventures Press, Inc.

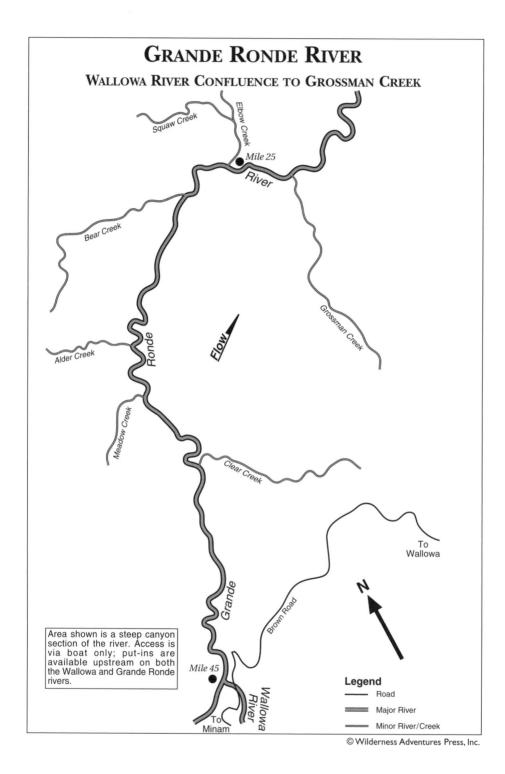

GRANDE RONDE RIVER
WALLOWA RIVER CONFLUENCE TO GROSSMAN CREEK

Squaw Creek

Elbow Creek

● *Mile 25*

River

Bear Creek

Grossman Creek

Ronde

Flow

Alder Creek

Meadow Creek

Clear Creek

To
Wallowa

N

Grande

Brown Road

Area shown is a steep canyon
section of the river. Access is
via boat only; put-ins are
available upstream on both
the Wallowa and Grande Ronde
rivers.

Mile 45 ●

To
Minam

Wallowa
River

Legend

——— Road

▬▬▬ Major River

▭▭▭ Minor River/Creek

© Wilderness Adventures Press, Inc.

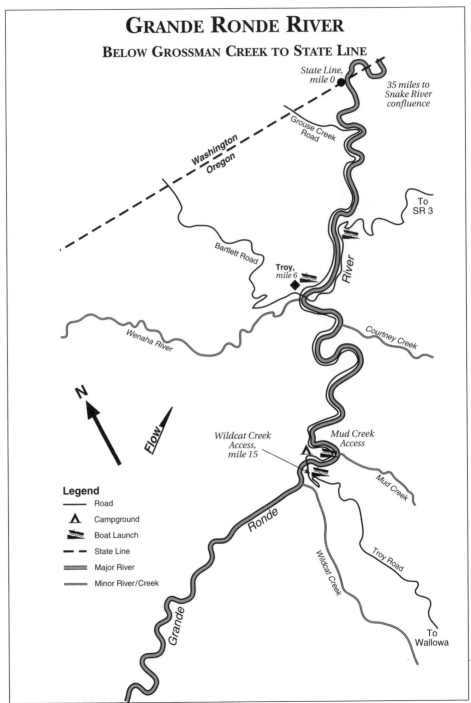

GRANDE RONDE RIVER
BELOW GROSSMAN CREEK TO STATE LINE

State Line, mile 0

35 miles to Snake River confluence

Grouse Creek Road

Washington
Oregon

To SR 3

Bartlett Road

Troy, mile 6

River

Wenaha River

Courtney Creek

N

Flow

Wildcat Creek Access, mile 15

Mud Creek Access

Mud Creek

Legend
— Road
▲ Campground
🛶 Boat Launch
- - - State Line
▓▓▓ Major River
▒▒▒ Minor River/Creek

Ronde

Wildcat Creek

Troy Road

Grande

To Wallowa

© Wilderness Adventures Press, Inc.

Throughout its run in Washington, the Grande Ronde fills the bottom of a spectacular canyon.

Fishing the Grande Ronde

When steelhead reach the mouth of the Grande Ronde, they find plenty of fly anglers there to greet them. In fact, the mouth of the river—two miles of road-accessible catch-and-release water—has in recent years become one of the Northwest's great fly angling circus environments. The place is literally swarming with fly rods when decent numbers of fish arrive between late September and mid-October. Luckily, however, the fly fishing crowd at the mouth is a well-behaved crowd. People understand and practice traditional steelhead fly fishing etiquette. So far. I've seen too much erosion in etiquette on other rivers to dare hope that the same thing won't soon occur on the Ronde.

That's not to say you shouldn't fish the mouth of the Grande Ronde. This short reach of the river offers not only Grande Ronde fish, but lots of Idaho fish that hold over for a time when the Grande Ronde is running a little cooler than the Snake River below. Don't expect to find any solitude and do expect to be on the water very early if you intend to fish through a run ahead of everybody else. The mouth offers easy-access, undeveloped camping sites.

When you visit the Grande Ronde, however, remember that the mouth of the river does not necessarily represent the fishery in general. You can escape the big crowds by fishing higher on the river. A lengthy roadless and inaccessible stretch of river separates the mouth from the many miles of easy-access water above and below the Washington/Oregon border. When the water cools enough to suit them, steelhead infiltrate the river and fishing picks up all along its course, from the public access at Shumaker all the way past the border to the little town of Troy. The one always-crowded spot in this long section is the Cottonwood site at the acclimation ponds (above Bogan's).

Wherever you fish on the Grande Ronde, you will find well-defined, easy-to-read steelhead water. When the water hovers around optimal levels (below 1000 cfs), the Grande Ronde is one of those streams that makes me think the river was expressly designed for fly anglers. As such, the Ronde is prime water for skated dry flies and all manner of classic wet flies. Unless the water gets so cold that the fish won't move, I see no point in insulting these long-distance travelers with ugly flies. I'll take fur, feather, and tinsel, matched with floating lines, over leadheads and flashy plastics. That's just my choice. All manner of flies do the job here.

Once the weather turns cold—usually in November—the Grande Ronde fish become far less inclined to chase flies with reckless abandon. Wintry weather necessitates using tactics more typical of fishing for winter-run steelhead along the coast. You must get the fly closer to the fish using sinking lines or heads and/or weighted flies. Fly choice matters far less than the depth at which you fish the fly (and far less than many anglers might care to believe). Most Grande Ronde regulars will suggest dark colors for late-season deep-running flies. Blacks and purples are most popular. I will only add that last season, late in the year, I fished only two patterns, both bringing equal success: My usual size 1.5 Spawning Purple and a size 2/0 Orange Heron, this latter fly hardly being a dark pattern.

The late-autumn fishing differs markedly from the September and October action. Cold water dictates a different approach. Likewise, weather conditions can deteriorate quickly. One day you enjoy 50-degree sunshine, and the next day you wake up shivering in three inches of snow. Luckily, when the perfect autumn weather of October disappears, so do most of the anglers.

Those wintry November days beckon you because of the softening effect of passing years. Later remembrances often fail to recall the shivering hands, frosty breath, and numb feet. You head for the Grande Ronde regardless because those fish and that canyon exert an influence inexplicable to all but the other initiates, who simply smile a knowing smile at the recounted tales of late-autumn steelheading on this remarkable river.

Restaurants and Accommodations

Once you're on the Grande Ronde, your restaurant options are limited to the café at Heller Bar near the mouth, to Bogan's Oasis near the border, and to Troy up on the Oregon side. But if you're heading through eastern Oregon on your way to or from the Ronde, you may want to stop in for a sample of some of the finest dining anywhere on the east side of the state. The small town of La Grande offers first-class dining options and I would be remiss not to describe them. Meanwhile, if your journey brings you through Pendleton in the evening, make time for dinner at Rafael's, one of the state's finest restaurants.

I might add that Terminal Gravity Brewery, located in the tiny town of Enterprise, is a required stop if you're in the neighborhood. Their beer rocks, the food is great, and the atmosphere relaxed and contagious. Oregonian newspaper writer John Foyston lauded Terminal Gravity IPA as the best beer around in 1998. Owned by Dean Duquette and Steve Carper, Terminal Gravity is located in an old yellow house at 803 School Street (541-426-0158). Should your route to the Grande Ronde take you through the Tri-Cities, make time (and reservations) for dinner at Sundance Grill in Kennewick (509-783-6505).

Heller Bar offers lodging in addition to its restaurant (509-758-4800). Otherwise, most anglers camp along the lower Grande Ronde, whose two-mile road-access stretch provides plenty of undeveloped BLM campsites. Likewise, the upper river, between Shumaker and Troy, offers several convenient, riverside camping areas. The little town of Asotin boasts a single four-room motel (Asotin Motel, 509-243-4888), while much larger Clarkston, Washington offers myriad restaurants and ample motel space. Clarkston lies about an hour from the mouth of the Grande Ronde, but staying in town allows you the option of crossing the bridge to Idaho for a crack at the Clearwater River or driving south to fish the Grande Ronde or the Snake.

Clarkston Lodging

Sunset Motel, 1200 Bridge Street, 800-845-5223
Motel 6, 222 Bridge Street, 509-758-1631
Best Western, 1257 Bridge Street, 509-758-9551
Golden Key Motel, 1376 Bridge Street, 509-758-5566
Astor Motel, 1201 Bridge Street, 509-758-2509
Hacienda Lodge Motel, 812 Bridge Street, 509-758-5583

The tiny community of Troy, meanwhile, offers the lodging and dining services of Shilo Inn (541-828-7741) and inexpensive rental cabins at Zeller's Resort (541-828-7786). Downstream on the Washington side, Bogan's offers a popular restaurant along with shuttle service (509-256-3372). Otherwise, you'll need to bring along your camping gear when you visit the Grande Ronde between Troy and the mouth. Plenty of undeveloped campsites are situated all along the river.

The author with a Grande Ronde hatchery fish taken during late October on the Oregon side of the border.

The Grande Ronde downstream of Troy on the Oregon side.

La Grande, Oregon

La Grande occupies a pastoral valley nestled beneath the Blue Mountains, whose timbered heights offer a geographic and psychological barrier between the dusty monotony of the intensely cultivated Columbia Basin to the west and the rugged beauty of northeastern Oregon. La Grande is the gateway to the mountains. The valley's rural economy assures a conservative agrarian outlook, yet a unique dichotomy exists owing to the presence of Eastern Oregon University, which draws students from many walks of life. On campus, you are almost equally likely to meet a transplanted Hawaiian or a homegrown college kid.

Because of the university, La Grande offers a palpable diversity that manifests itself partly in the city's downtown district. Spanning only a few blocks, downtown La Grande is home to several fine restaurants, the most impressive of which are ever-popular 10 Depot Street, which has become an icon of sorts, and relative newcomer Foley Station, which would just as easily be right at home in downtown Portland.

Ten Depot favorites include prime rib, the restaurant's specialty, which is seasoned and roasted to perfection in a large prime rib oven. Seafood offerings include grilled salmon served with a superb cucumber-dill sauce, jumbo marinated grilled shrimp, baked lobster and the popular "Oregon Caesar Salad," which features smoked halibut and bay shrimp along with Ten Depot's own Caesar dressing. Owner Sandy Sorrels garners from her garden the fresh herbs used in Ten Depot's sauces and dressings, including a pesto sauce of which the staff is justifiably proud and which parades its flavor best in fettuccine topped with filet of salmon.

Ten Depot attracts a loyal following of locals, many who visit on a weekly basis. Indeed, the community considers Ten Depot an old friend—weekends lure ranchers and farmers into town from throughout the valley (as does Sorrels' other restaurant, Mamacita's, located just down the street).

Meanwhile, at nearby Foley Station, chef Merlyn Baker delights in combining the elements of exquisite flavor, colorful presentation and perfect portions and his work is on display not only for lunch and dinner, but also for breakfast. So exceptional are the breakfasts at Foley Station that on a weekend morning seating is at a premium despite the restaurant's spacious design.

"I like to take people on a culinary journey where they don't need to go anywhere," says Baker, whose far-reaching experience allows him to navigate a delightfully broad spectrum of food from around the world. He has cooked from Alaska and the San Juan Islands to North Carolina and the Caribbean. His considerable experience in the Portland and Seattle fine-dining scenes includes a stay as executive head chef at Jake's. He and three partners moved to the quieter confines of eastern Oregon and opened Foley Station (541-963-7473) in 1997.

At Foley Station, diners with decision-making issues face a stressful dilemma. Everything sounds, looks, and smells great, forcing one to peruse the menu at length, pondering each offering. The unique entrées arrive with eye-catching flair. In many instances, cutting the first bite seems sacrilegious, but such concerns vanish instantly on the palate as the flavorful journey begins. The menus change with the season, but always force difficult choices: a waffle covered with fresh mango or the sumptuous country ham and red-eye gravy? Grilled vegetable sandwich featuring portabellas, eggplant, red pepper and provolone or classic Dungeness crab cakes bursting with flavor.

The remarkable dinner menu, which changes monthly, is comprised of tantalizing creations worth lingering over and absorbing with all the senses. Northwest cuisine is well represented. A recent menu included fresh Washington king salmon braised with roasted garlic and Scotch whiskey. Foley Station's world tour also includes Mediterranean dishes, Southwest fare, European flavors and other surprises. Arrive early for dinner and marvel over appetizers like herbed chicken breast paté with Dijon crème fraiche or Champagne batter-fried Camembert cheese.

Anglers heading through eastern Oregon should take time to explore downtown La Grande, home to several fine restaurants.

Downtown La Grande also offers several coffeehouses: Highway 30 Coffee, at the corner of Adams and Depot Streets, offers seating both at ground level and in the loft. You can kick back, put your feet up and stay a while. The drive-up favorite is Cowboy Cappuccino, located at the north end of downtown.

Nearby Fisheries

Grande Ronde and Imnaha Rivers

The Grande Ronde, especially in its upper half, offers fine fishing for wild rainbow trout. The 40-mile drift from Minam, Oregon to Troy covers remote, little-known trout waters densely populated with beautiful 8- to 14-inch natives (some larger). This scenic river canyon, floatable in any rugged craft, requires a trip of three or four days, at least if you intend to spend a lot of time fishing. Be wary, however, of low water conditions—the river floats best above 2,000 cubic feet per second. Check with the BLM (509-522-6290) for current conditions. At least 50 primitive campsites await along this reach of the river, available first-come, first-serve. No permits are needed, but the BLM requires parties to carry portable toilets and fire pans. The launch sites are located at the Minam River/Wallowa River confluence at the town of Minam or a mile-and-a-half downstream at Minam State Park.

Other area rivers offer similar trout fishing, including the Minam, Lostine, and Wallowa. The little Imnaha River, tucked away in the far eastern flank of the Wallowa Range, is a fine steelhead stream in its own right, yet so distant for most people that few anglers know of its charms. Great waters like the Grande Ronde, Imnaha and other area streams invariably attract great guides. Mac Huff of Eagle Cap Fishing Guides is the man if you need a guide for any of the waters of the beautiful Wallowa Mountains, which also hide dozens of fishable hike-in lakes.

Nearby Attractions and Activities

If not for a preponderance of private, leased land, the Grande Ronde would offer ample opportunity for chukar hunting. A few landowners still allow access, but you need time to knock on doors to seek permission. The Oregon Department of Fish and Wildlife operates its Wenaha Wildlife Management Area around Troy, with wild turkeys, blue grouse and ruffed grouse being the primary gamebirds available. Some chukars inhabit the area as well. Some of the guides, including Mac Huff, welcome their bird-hunting clients to bring along a shotgun, but he warns that chukar hunting leaves little time for steelhead angling and vice versa. I agree with him on that count, for on many occasions I have tried to combine steelheading and chukar hunting into a classic "cast-and-blast," but invariably I end up doing one or the other.

Author's Tip

The Grande Ronde probably vies with Oregon's North Umpqua as the best place in the region to take a steelhead on a skated dry fly. You can't accomplish that feat without giving it some effort. So tie on a skater and stick to your guns. Given decent water conditions and temperatures, you will get your dry-fly fish on this fabulous river. Sometimes I opt for a two-fly arrangement on the Grande Ronde, running a size 5 Spawning Purple two feet behind a Bomber.

Bomber

Favorite Fly
Bomber

HOOK	Light wire steelhead, No. 2-6
TAIL	White calftail or similar
BODY	Spun and clipped deer hair
HACKLE	Grizzly
WING	White calftail or similar

Fast Facts
Grande Ronde River

LOCATION	Northeastern Oregon/southeastern Washington
WATER TYPE	Rugged, free-flowing canyon-bound river
PRIMARY GAMEFISH	Summer steelhead; also rainbow trout
BEST TIME	Late September through November
BEST FLIES	Various classic wet flies and skated dry flies
EQUIPMENT	7- to 9-weight rod, floating and sink-tip lines, spiked boots or cleats.

CONDITIONS   Pleasant autumn weather turns cold—often bitter cold—
                            between early November and early December. Ample
                            unimproved camping along road-accessible reaches of
                            the river. When floating the roadless section, beware of
                            camping on private lands and be especially wary of the
                            "Narrows," a rock-lined gorge passable only by those with
                            experience and strong boating skill.

DRIVE TIME   From Seattle: 6-7 hours
                            From Portland: 5-6 hours
                            From Boise: 5-7 hours

DIRECTIONS   To reach the mouth of the Grande Ronde at Heller Bar on
                            the Snake River, follow Snake River Road south out of
                            Clarkston, WA (or south from Asotin if you are arriving
                            from Enterprise, Oregon). Asotin lies seven miles
                            south of Clarkston and the Grande Ronde reaches the
                            Snake River about 24 miles south of Asotin. The last eight
                            miles are gravel. To reach the Grande Ronde at the
                            border and the town of Troy, follow State Route 129 out of
                            Asotin or follow SR 3 north from Enterprise, Oregon.
                            When you reach the Grande Ronde River, Troy Road
                            (paved) leads 18 miles along the north bank to Troy.

Local Fly Shops

JOSEPH FLY SHOP
2-3 N. Main Street
Joseph, OR 97846
541-432-4343

FOUR-SEASONS FLY SHOP
Twin Rivers Anglers
534 Thain Street
Lewiston ID 83501
208-746-8946

FOUR SEASONS FLY SHOP
10210 Wallowa Lake Highway
La Grande, OR 97850
541-963-8420

CLEARWATER FLY SHOP
417 West First Street
Kennewick, WA 99336, 509-582-1001

BLUE MOUNTAIN ANGLERS
& FLY SHOP
1847 Westgate
Pendleton, OR 97801
800-825-1548

THE TRADITIONAL SPORTSMAN
814 Main Street
Lewiston, ID 83501
208-746-6688

Guides

EAGLE CAP FISHING GUIDES
(Mac Huff)
800-940-3688 or 541-432-9055

DEER CREEK GUIDE SERVICE
(Mike Kinney)
360-435-3778
www.mikekinney.com

LITTLE CREEK OUTFITTERS
541-963-7878

SCOTT ODONNELL
503-738-9022
www.scottodonnell.com

Contacts

WASHINGTON DEPARTMENT
OF FISH & WILDLIFE
Eastern Washington - Region 1 Office
8702 North Division Street
Spokane, WA 99218
509-456-4082

OREGON DEPARTMENT
OF FISH & WILDLIFE
Enterprise Field Office
65495 Alder Slope Road
Enterprise, OR 97828
541-426-3279

Fresh snow on the Yakima Canyon.

CHAPTER 2

THE YAKIMA RIVER

Washington's Blue-Ribbon Gem

The Yakima might just be the perfect trout stream. This fertile Washington river is home to a dense population of wild rainbow trout and its cold flows annually host tremendous hatches of myriad types of caddis, mayflies, and stoneflies. The river's hatches continue throughout the year, making the Yakima one of the West's great year-round destinations.

What's more, the Yakima offers fishing on every level, from the simplicity of pounding the banks with stoneflies or hoppers during their respective seasons, to the intricacies of casting fine tippets to large trout sipping size 22 Red Quill spinners at dusk on a smooth tailout. The river's rainbows typically span 10 to 18 inches and the Yakima yields a handful of huge fish, reaching 24 inches. These 20-plus-inch brutes are rare, but they're in there.

Upstream from Ellensburg, fishing pressure on the Yakima is far less, owing mostly to difficult access.

Offering about 60 miles of prime fly water, the Yakima's most popular reach is the "Canyon Section," which begins just south of Ellensburg where the river enters a deep, rimrock-lined desert canyon reminiscent of Oregon's Deschutes River Canyon. Canyon Road follows the river all the way through the canyon for almost 20 miles. Upstream from Ellensburg, access is more tenuous.

The Yakima follows a predictable schedule of water flow throughout the year—a schedule that might at first glance seem a little odd. The river runs high and fast all summer and doesn't drop into prime shape until fall and winter, when optimal flows drop below 1,000 cubic feet per second in the canyon. This arrangement stems from the river's omnipotent role for regional agriculture. Blocked by dams in its upper reaches, the Yakima's high summer flows are maintained to supply irrigation water to the valleys below. Once the irrigation season ends, the dams above are corked so the reservoirs can refill over the winter and spring.

The river's rainbows are comfortable with the water arrangement. They feed aggressively all summer, rising during the profuse hatches and hugging the banks to devour stoneflies, hoppers, and other insects. When the water drops during the fall, the Yakima displays a new personality. Gravel bars appear all over the river and the flow becomes far more defined and readable. Trout rise bank to bank during good autumn hatches.

This is the time I head for the Yakima. I enjoy this river most during late September and October. Certainly I make an occasional spring trip to the Yakima because the river's hatch of Mother's Day Caddis is as good or better than any caddis hatch in the West. Some years the caddisflies hatch so profuse that at times fishing becomes an exercise in futility—just too many naturals. Likewise, exceptional spring hatches of stoneflies, March Brown mayflies and other bugs create excellent dry-fly action.

But autumn on the Yakima is a special time. The low flows make her a more intimate river and the crowds of spring and summer are but a memory. Most significantly to me, however, is autumn's hatch of the colorful Pale Evening Dun mayflies. These bright yellow *Heptagenia* duns are large by autumn standards, requiring size 12 or 14 imitations. The trout love them and a strong hatch, though rare in some years, brings the river to life.

Usually the PEDs hatch alongside smaller and far more abundant Blue-Winged Olive mayflies. Both insects emerge around midday, making this one of the most pleasant times to fly fish the Yakima Canyon. The Blue-Winged Olives *(Baetis)* mayflies remain a staple on the river all year and are especially significant during autumn, winter, and early spring.

Even during the winter, the Yakima offers excellent fishing, especially for those adept at nymphing. The winter months offer occasional heavy hatches of midges and *Baetis* mayflies, but they tend to be fleeting, unpredictable affairs. Still, the Yakima Canyon is a remarkable wintertime destination for those willing to brave the cold. A light dusting of snow atop the steep slopes transforms the canyon into a vividly stunning landscape. During the cold months, bighorn sheep frequently graze just above the Yakima's banks and bald eagles often perch in trees or rest on the gravel bars.

An easily waded river during the fall and winter, the Yakima becomes a floater's river during the spring and summer when flows increase markedly. The canyon section offers an easy float, even for novice oarsmen. Don't try the upper river without first drifting it with an Upper Yakima veteran. Several good launch sites are scattered through the canyon reach.

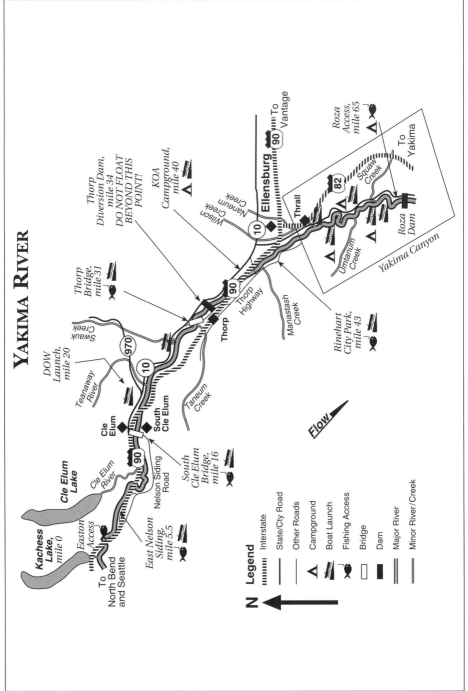

YAKIMA RIVER

Legend

:::::::	Interstate
	State/City Road
	Other Roads
△	Campground
	Boat Launch
🐟	Fishing Access
▯	Bridge
▮	Dam
	Major River
	Minor River/Creek

Flow

N

Kachess Lake, mile 0

Cle Elum Lake

Easton Access

To North Bend and Seattle

East Nelson Siding, mile 5.5

Nelson Siding Road

Cle Elum River

Cle Elum

South Cle Elum

South Cle Elum Bridge, mile 16

Taneum Creek

Teanaway River

DOW Launch, mile 20

Swauk Creek

Thorp Bridge, mile 31

Thorp Diversion Dam, mile 34 DO NOT FLOAT BEYOND THIS POINT!

KOA Campground, mile 40

Thorp

Thorp Highway

Manastash Creek

Rinehart City Park, mile 43

Wilson Creek

Naneum Creek

Ellensburg

To Vantage

Thrall

Umtanum Creek

Squaw Creek

Roza Access, mile 65

To Yakima

Roza Dam

Yakima Canyon

Fishing the Yakima

The Yakima rewards anglers who arrive armed with a full array of practiced fly fishing tactics. At high water, the fishing can be as simple as tossing stonefly dries or hopper patterns against the banks and watching fish boil for the fly. At its toughest, the Yakima's trout behave like seasoned veterans on Silver Creek or the Henry's Fork, demanding light tippets and delicate presentations.

One of my favorite times on the Yakima is during autumn when the daytime hatches of *Baetis* and *Heptagenia* mayflies yield to evening spinner falls. When both events arrive with a vengeance, the Yakima is an awesome place. The midday hatch itself offers prime dry-fly action, with trout rising from bank to bank. Then, when the little Red Quill spinners return in the evening, the autumn's most challenging fishing begins. Big trout move into quiet glides, sipping tiny spent mayflies from the surface. This is the time for 6X or even 7X tippets and size 20-22 dries.

That's just one face of the Yakima. Other anglers revel in her tremendous emergence of Mother's Day Caddis or in her reliable stonefly hatches. Throughout the season, the Yakima offers a continuing parade of predictable, fishable insect hatches.

Most angling pressure focuses on the canyon section below Ellensburg. The river above Ellensburg requires a lot more "figuring out" due to far less obvious access. Regardless of where you fish on the Yakima, expect to employ a full range of tactics, from dropping dry flies just inches from the bank to drifting weighted nymphs through deep, rock-studded runs.

If you are visiting the Yakima for the first time, by all means hire a guide for a day or two. Not only will the float itself prove worthwhile, but also your guide will eliminate any guesswork about where and how to ply the river for its beautiful rainbows. Jack Mitchell's Evening Hatch Guide Service ranks among the most highly respected on the river. Steve Worley, who owns the local fly shop in Ellensburg, likewise enjoys high regard as a Yakima guide. Both outfits enjoy lots of repeat business. So if they happen to be booked up, use my favorite ploy to find another excellent guide: ask them whom they would want to hire.

Restaurants and Accommodations

The Northwest's oldest continually operating microbrewery resides in the city of Yakima. Grant's Brewery Pub is located in the historic Yakima Train Depot at 32 North Front Street (509-575-2922). Yakima offers several other good restaurants, including Birchfield Manor (509-452-1960) and Greystone Restaurant (509-248-9801), located on Front Street in the old Lund Building (this entire area is part of the beautifully rejuvenated old Train Depot district). Italian enthusiasts should try Gasperetti's (509-248-0628) at 1013 North 1st Street or Deli De Pasta (509-453-0571), located at 7 North Front Street. One of the region's top Mexican restaurants, the popular Santiago's, is located at 111 E. Yakima Avenue (509-453-1644).

A little closer to the actual fishing, Ellensburg offers ample motel space and plenty of restaurants. Also, plenty of undeveloped camp space is available in the Yakima Canyon, but none of it offers much refinement. Still, many Yakima anglers simply load up the camping gear and stake out a spot at Umtanum or any of several other public recreation sites clearly marked along the river in Yakima Canyon. Privately owned campgrounds include Yakima River RV Park (509-925-4734) located at 794 Ringer Loop and Riverview Campground on Canyon Road (509-925-6043). The Ellensburg area boasts several nice B&Bs, including Wren's Nest (509-925-9061), Murphy's Country B&B (509-925-7986), and Leslie's Lazy B&B (509-968-3829).

Ellensburg Lodging

Best Western, 1700 Canyon Road, 509-925-9801
Comfort Inn, 1722 Canyon Road, 509-925-7037
Super-8, 1500 Canyon Road, 509-962-6888
Harold's Motel, 601 N. Water St., 509-925-4141
I-90 Inn, 1390 Dollarway Rd. N., 509-925-9844
Lighthouse Motel, 607 W. Cascade Way, 509-925-9744
Nite's Inn Motel, 1200 S. Ruby, 509-962-9600
Traveler's Regalodge, 300 W. 6th, 800-523-4972

Nearby Fisheries

Perhaps the best unknown smallmouth bass fishery in the Northwest, the lower half of the Yakima River meanders through eastern Washington's famous wine country on its way to meet the Columbia at the Tri-Cities. Possibly unknown is too strong a word, but certainly the Yakima's smallmouth fishery remains unheralded. In the 100-mile stretch between Yakima and Richland, access ranges from good to nonexistent. Anglers willing to knock on doors, drive the side roads and do a little hiking will find untouched pools harboring bass up to 18 inches (or more) in length. Interstate 84 follows the river's course, but often at a considerable distance, so I suggest obtaining a good county map and checking out the myriad local access roads. Also consult with Clearwater Fly Shop in Kennewick (509-582-1001).

The beautiful Pale Evening Dun offers excellent hatches during mid-autumn.

The Yakima Canyon is a great floating river. Here, anglers "pound the banks" with dry flies.

Nearby Attractions and Activities

The Yakima Canyon lies within half an hour of the west end of Washington's famous Yakima Valley wine country. Visit any of the wineries for a good tour map of the region's two dozen established wine producers. The valley is especially well-known for its red varietals, including Cabernet Sauvignon, Merlot, Cab Franc, Syrah, and others. Among my favorites on the west end of the valley are Bonair Winery, Horizon's Edge Winery, and Tefft Cellars. The Yakima Valley throws three big annual shindigs, the first being the Red Wine & Chocolate event, during which participating wineries combine chocolate confections with finely crafted red wines. This event is held President's Day weekend in February. Spring barrel tasting is next, held the last full weekend in April. Then, on Thanksgiving weekend, all the wineries throw open their doors for food, newly released wine samples, and an all-around grand time. For details on the wine country, contact the Yakima Valley Winery Association at 1-800-258-7270 or check out the association's website at www.yakimavalleywine.com.

Author's Tip

During non-hatch periods, most Yakima anglers revert to nymphs fished along the bottom under an indicator. Nymphing is very productive on the Yak, but so too are large streamers when fished properly in the right kind of water. In fact, some of the river's largest rainbows fall to streamer patterns. Look for deep runs with plenty of cover in the form of large rocks, steep banks, or sudden drop-offs. Fish a sculpin pattern on a high-density sink-tip, working the fly down and across and slipping line to maintain depth.

Favorite Fly

Stimulator

HOOK	Tiemco No. 200 or similar, No. 6-8
TAIL	Elk or deer hair
BODY	Orange or golden brown dubbing
HACKLE	Brown, short and palmered through body
RIB	Fine wire
WING	Fine deer or elk hair, natural
THORAX	Grizzly over yellow dubbing

Stimulator

Fast Facts

Yakima River

LOCATION	Central Washington, near Ellensburg
WATER TYPE	Freestone river
PRIMARY GAMEFISH	Wild rainbow trout and mountain whitefish
BEST TIME	Year-round
BEST FLIES	Dry Flies: X-caddis and Sparkle Duns to match particular caddis and mayfly hatches, respectively; Stimulator, No. 6-8 and other stonefly patterns; hopper patterns; streamers. Nymphs: dark stone fly nymph, Hare's Ear Nymph, Pheasant Tail Nymph and various others.
EQUIPMENT	4- to 6-weight rod with a floating line
CONDITIONS	The Yakima is a year-round fishery with the full complement of high-desert weather patterns. Camping areas can be very crowded on weekends. Easy floating in the canyon section, but advanced skills and local knowledge required on the upper river.
DRIVE TIME	From Seattle: 2-3 hours From Portland: 4 hours
DIRECTIONS	From Seattle, follow I-90 east over the Cascades until you reach Ellensburg, the hub city for the Yakima River. Take the main Ellensburg exit and head south to reach the Yakima Canyon. From Portland, head east on I-84 and cross the Columbia at Biggs on U.S. 97. Follow Highway 97 north past the city of Yakima to the Canyon Road Exit at SR 821.

Local Fly Shops

WORLEY-BUGGER FLY COMPANY
811 4th Parallel
Ellensburg, WA 98926
888-950-3474

GARY'S FLY SHOP
1210 West Lincoln
Yakima, WA 98902
509-457-3474

RED'S FLY SHOP
Yakima Canyon Rd., P.O. Box 186
Ellensburg, WA 98926
509-929-1802

CLEARWATER FLY SHOP
417 West First Street
Kennewick, WA 99336
509-582-1001

Area Fly Shops

SWEDE'S FLY SHOP
17419 139th Avenue NE
Woodinville, WA 98072
425-487-3747

CREEKSIDE ANGLING COMPANY
1660 Northwest Gilman Blvd. #C-5
Issaquah, WA 98027
425-392-3800

KAUFMANN'S STREAMBORN
1918 4th Avenue
Seattle, WA 98101
206-448-0601

PATRICK'S FLY SHOP
2237 Eastlake Avenue East
Seattle, WA 98102
206-325-8988

ORVIS SEATTLE
911 Bellevue Way NE
Bellevue, WA 98004
425-452-9138

AVID ANGLER FLY SHOP
17171 Bothell Way NE, Ste. A130
Lake Forest Park, WA 98155
206-362-4030

REI-SEATTLE
222 Yale Ave. N
Seattle, WA 98109
206-223-1944

REI-PORTLAND
1798 Jantzen Beach Ctr
Portland, OR 97217
503-283-1300

Guides

EVENING HATCH GUIDE SERVICE
509-962-5959
www.theeveninghatch.com

WORLEY-BUGGER FLY COMPANY
888-950-3474/509-962-2033
www.worleybuggerflyco.com

Contacts

WASHINGTON DEPARTMENT OF
FISH & WILDLIFE
South Central Washington
Region 3 Office
1701 South 24th Avenue
Yakima, Washington 98902-5720
509-575-2740

ELLENSBURG CHAMBER OF
COMMERCE
509-925-3137

CHAPTER 3

The Lower Deschutes River

The West's Most Remarkable River

Oregon's Lower Deschutes is unique. There exists not another comparable place and for that reason I rank this remarkable river as the single best freshwater fishery in the West. Nowhere else can you find a river that combines blue-ribbon angling for big, native trout with a world-class summer steelhead fishery. The Deschutes bundles both offerings into one muscular, magnificent river. Certainly there are trout streams that might prove superior to the Deschutes. I grew up on the Henry's Fork and would never dare suggest the Deschutes is a better trout river. But the Henry's Fork doesn't have summer steelhead. I love the North Umpqua for her remarkable steelhead, but she cannot match the Deschutes as a trout river. Quite simply, the Deschutes offers the best of both worlds.

Indeed, if I were in charge, we'd get two or three Septembers and Octobers every year, for autumn is the time when the Deschutes most prominently displays her best offerings. During the fall, trout anglers revel in a renewed wave of mayfly and caddis hatches and steelhead enthusiasts drop everything to head for the Deschutes as these great migratory fish file into the river.

LOWER DESCHUTES RIVER
LAKE BILLY CHINOOK TO WARM SPRINGS ROAD

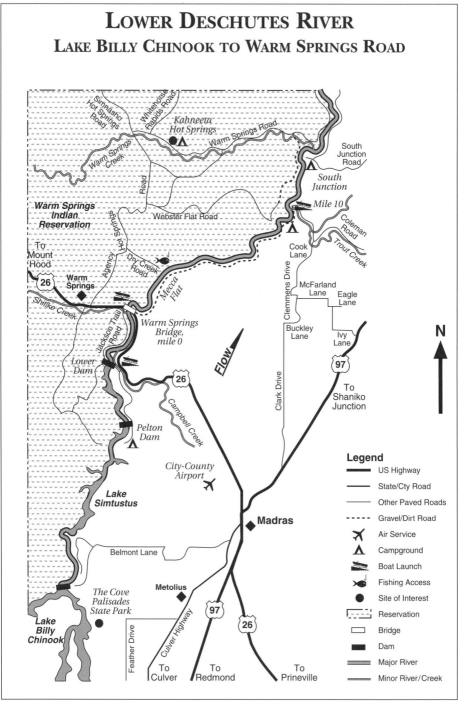

Simnasho Hot Springs Road

Whitehorse Rapids Road

Kahneeta Hot Springs

Warm Springs Road

South Junction Road

Warm Springs Creek

South Junction

Road

Mile 10

Warm Springs Indian Reservation

Webster Flat Road

Coleman Road

To Mount Hood

Hot Springs

Agency

Dry Creek Road

Cook Lane

Trout Creek

26

Warm Springs

Mecca Flat

McFarland Lane

Eagle Lane

Shitike Creek

Jackson Trail Road

Warm Springs Bridge, mile 0

Buckley Lane

Ivy Lane

Clemmens Drive

97

Lower Dam

Flow

26

To Shaniko Junction

Campbell Creek

Clark Drive

Pelton Dam

City-County Airport

Lake Simtustus

N

Legend

━━━ US Highway
──── State/Cty Road
──── Other Paved Roads
- - - - Gravel/Dirt Road
✈ Air Service
▲ Campground
Boat Launch
Fishing Access
● Site of Interest
Reservation
▢ Bridge
■ Dam
Major River
Minor River/Creek

Belmont Lane

Madras

Metolius

The Cove Palisades State Park

97

26

Lake Billy Chinook

Feather Drive

Culver Highway

To Culver

To Redmond

To Prineville

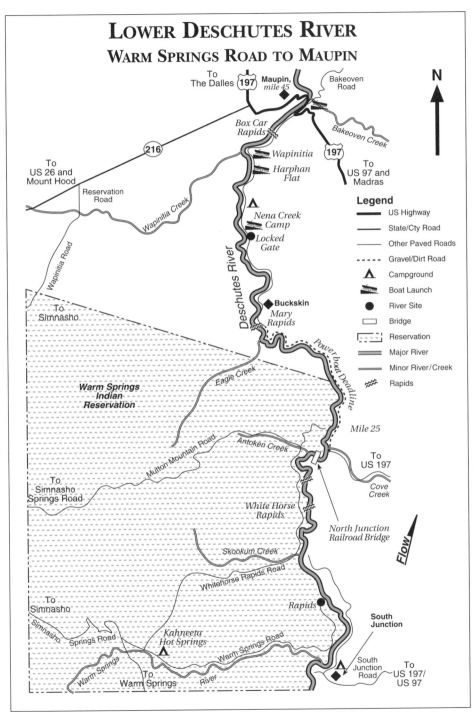

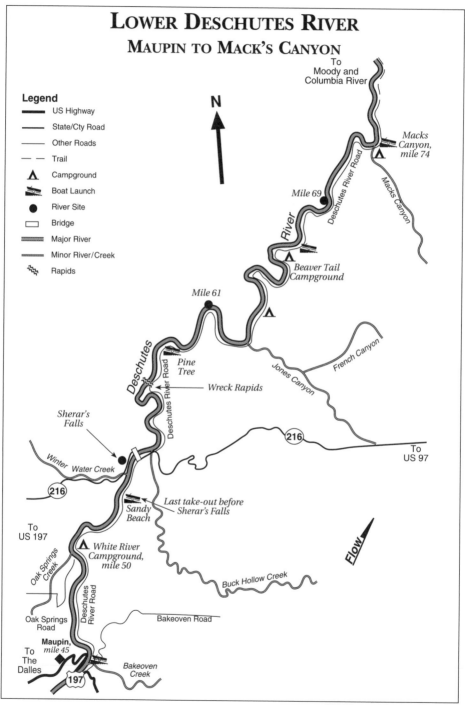

LOWER DESCHUTES RIVER
MAUPIN TO MACK'S CANYON

To
Moody and
Columbia River

Legend

▬▬▬	US Highway
─────	State/Cty Road
────	Other Roads
─ ─ ─	Trail
▲	Campground
⛵	Boat Launch
●	River Site
▭	Bridge
▓▓▓	Major River
═══	Minor River/Creek
≈≈	Rapids

N

Macks
Canyon,
mile 74

Mile 69

Deschutes River Road

Macks Canyon

River

Beaver Tail
Campground

Mile 61

French Canyon

Jones Canyon

Pine
Tree

Deschutes

Deschutes River Road

Wreck Rapids

Sherar's
Falls

216

To
US 97

Winter Water Creek

216

Last take-out before
Sherar's Falls

Sandy
Beach

To
US 197

White River
Campground,
mile 50

Oak Springs Creek

Buck Hollow Creek

Flow

Oak Springs
Road

Deschutes River Road

Bakeoven Road

Maupin,
mile 45

To
The
Dalles

197

Bakeoven
Creek

© Wilderness Adventures Press, Inc.

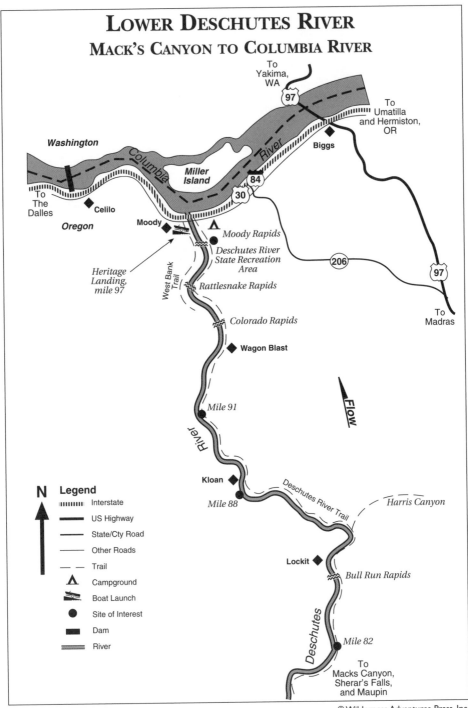

LOWER DESCHUTES RIVER
MACK'S CANYON TO COLUMBIA RIVER

To
Yakima,
WA

97

To
Umatilla
and Hermiston,
OR

Washington

Columbia

River

Biggs

**Miller
Island**

84

30

To
The
Dalles

Celilo

Oregon

Moody

Moody Rapids

Deschutes River
State Recreation
Area

Heritage
Landing,
mile 97

West Bank
Trail

Rattlesnake Rapids

206

97

To
Madras

Colorado Rapids

Wagon Blast

Mile 91

River

Flow

N Legend

||||||||| Interstate

US Highway

State/Cty Road

Other Roads

Trail

Campground

Boat Launch

Site of Interest

Dam

River

Kloan

Mile 88

Deschutes River Trail

Harris Canyon

Lockit

Bull Run Rapids

Deschutes

Mile 82

To
Macks Canyon,
Sherar's Falls,
and Maupin

© Wilderness Adventures Press, Inc.

The Deschutes River's native redsides typically run 13 to 16 inches.

Two or three months before the steelhead arrive, the Deschutes basks in her most popular trout extravaganza, the famed hatch of giant Salmonflies and Golden Stoneflies. Often I refer to late May and early June as the "stonefly carnival" on the Deschutes because it draws so many anglers from near and far. But in this sense I mean no negative connotation in choosing the word "carnival," for the river simply comes alive with bugs, rising trout, boats, and fly anglers. It is a joyous occasion for all involved.

The river's beautiful trout, called redsides, derive their genetic makeup primarily from the redband trout, essentially a variety of rainbow trout indigenous to the waters of central and eastern Oregon. Typical specimens range from 12 to 16 inches; heavyweights, of which there are many, reach 20 or more inches. They rank among the hardest-fighting rainbows in the West.

They thrive in this 100-mile-long river, which plunges headlong toward the Columbia in an ever-deepening rimrock-lined desert canyon. The canyon is home to coyotes, bobcats, cougar, mule deer, chukar partridge, eagles, falcons, hawks, waterfowl, and many other creatures. I once walked right up on two magnificent bull elk on the trail above the river's mouth and a friend once watched a black bear wade the river. Neither creature seems like the normal inhabitant for such an environment, but this river and its awesome canyon are full of surprises.

The river fairly rages over dozens and dozens of rapids, some of which require expert boating skills. The most famous of these is Whitehorse, the violent, mile-long Class IV rock garden that eats boats every year. Other spectacular rapids include Boxcar, Oak Springs, Rollercoaster, Washout, Colorado, and Rattlesnake. The river's whitewater splendor inevitably draws a huge summer crowd of splash-and-giggle enthusiasts, but by and large they focus on the stretch of river around Maupin. They disperse after Labor Day.

Countless articles and books have glorified the Deschutes and her trout. Certainly I could wax on about this magnificent river, but the bottom line is this: No matter where you live, if you have never fished the Deschutes, start making plans now to do so. If trout is your game, come for the stonefly hatch. If you wish to hook powerful summer steelhead and also experience the trout fishery, come during the fall. Unless you have lots of fly angling experience and plenty of time, hire a guide, at least for a day or two.

Stonefly Time

On the Deschutes, the season's most explosive dry-fly action arrives with the May and June hatches of Salmonflies and Golden Stoneflies. Nearly two inches long, the Salmonflies (*Pteronarcys californicus*) are the Goliaths of the river's insect world. Only slightly smaller, the brilliantly hued Golden Stoneflies hatch during the latter half of the Salmonfly emergence.

Sometime during early or mid-May the Salmonflies begin their annual emergence. The hatch begins on the lower reaches of the river and then marches upstream daily. The nymphs crawl shoreward, emerging during the early morning hours. Later, during the afternoon, adult stoneflies fly out over the river to deposit their eggs on the water. In any given locale, these ovipositing flights may feature thousands of airborne insects hovering over the river.

Trout gorge on the stoneflies, especially during the first week or so of the hatch. During the ovipositing fights, fish rise all over the river. During the actual morning hatch, however, most feeding trout stick close to shore where they can intercept migrating nymphs and chase down adults dropping off overhanging shrubbery. Virtually every fly shop between Portland and Eugene and between Bend and Hood River keeps up to date on the progress of the hatch, so one phone call will generally garner all the information you need to plan a trip.

Fishing the Deschutes

Once the stonefly carnival ends, the Deschutes settles into its pattern of offering less publicized but predictable hatches of every kind. Chief among the summer hatches are the evening caddis flights. They can be remarkably dense. This fertile river offers numerous genera and species of caddis, among them the abundant Green Rockworms (*Rycophila*) and Spotted Sedge (*Hydropsyche*). By autumn, the lower river offers strong hatches of the big, colorful October Caddis (*Dichosmoecus*), inch-long orange-bodied bombers that even bring squawfish up to the surface at dusk.

The Deschutes offers excellent mayfly hatches as well. Most significant are the Blue-Winged Olives, which hatch most profusely between March and May and again during autumn. Lucky be the angler who arrives on the Deschutes when inclement weather serves up a strong hatch of Pale Morning Duns (*Ephemerella*). The trout love them. Sporadic hatches of Green Drakes (*Drunella*) occur during stonefly season, generally on those precious few blustery, overcast days. By autumn, you may encounter localized hatches of Mahogany Duns (*Paraleptophlebia*) and Pale Evening Duns (*Heptagenia*).

A wild Deschutes steelhead.

The river's redsides see lots of anglers and lots of flies. They learn fast. Anglers can throw an Elk Hair Caddis at every rise and catch a few fish and have a fine day. However, more dedicated fly anglers soon learn that the Deschutes rewards those who adopt more refined tactics. This includes the ability to effectively present a dry fly or emerger pattern in the river's most difficult places. Big, cagey trout frequently feed in swirling back-eddies, under the cover of dense, overhanging foliage and in deep, cover-rich runs.

Many anglers switch back and forth between nymph patterns and surface flies, depending on hatches, specific water types, and observed trout behavior. Other anglers specialize in one form of fishing or the other because the Deschutes often offers two rivers for the price of one: You can seek runs and riffles where trout feed almost exclusively on subsurface foods or you can hunt for rising trout along the banks, in back eddies, and along current seams.

In either case, it pays to do your homework. Find out what bugs are hatching and when, and then be prepared to match the hatch. Or allow a qualified Deschutes River guide to dictate where and how you fish the many faces of the Lower Deschutes River.

Deschutes River Steelhead

Only a brief split second in actual time, that moment is like a snapshot for me. I'll never forget it. I wanted very badly to put my friend Ken Hanley onto a summer steelhead—he doesn't have ready access to such fish nor such rivers from his home near San Francisco. Besides, I had earlier tried very hard to kill both of us by coming within six inches of rolling my truck down 1,500 vertical feet into the Deschutes River Canyon in an aborted attempt to negotiate the one access road that plunges into the canyon several miles above the mouth.

After escaping that dilemma by chaining up the tires on my 4x4 and saying a few Hail Marys, we took the circuitous route back upriver to a favorite little run above Macks Canyon. From the road that follows safely along the river, I pointed out the little slot—the "garden spot"—where most of the hook-ups occur in this pool. I directed Ken into the head of the run and then I went below to fish the head of the pool immediately downstream.

I kept looking back, waiting. I had that feeling. This was late October. This was the Deschutes. This was a pool I knew intimately. Ken shot his floating line out over the gliding run, steering the fly between the boulders that marked the garden spot. With increasing frequency I looked back upriver. One of Ken's next few casts would hit the perfect spot. I turned back downriver to uncork a cast of my own and then looked back again at precisely the right moment.

I caught it all in one fleeting, memorable glance: A silver torpedo of about 10 perfectly-proportioned pounds was head to the sky like a launched rocket, completely out of the water. The fly line was throwing a glistening spray of mist, and Ken, 60 feet above it all, stood slack-jawed. That is the moment forever imbedded in my mind. Immediately thereafter the fish came unpinned, but Ken and I had just enjoyed the best part of steelhead angling—that instant when the line hauls tight with the heavy surge of a headstrong steelhead.

Such moments are played out time and time again on the Lower Deschutes between August and November when steelhead stack up in all the good holding water throughout the river. These are a mix of several steelhead strains, including Deschutes natives, Deschutes hatchery fish, and stray fish from many other Columbia and Snake River tributaries. Most weight 5 to 9 pounds, but some of the big Idaho-bound brutes run 12 to 20 pounds.

They respond readily to dry-line tactics when the sun is off the water. Their aggressiveness to the fly rivals that of the Grande Ronde fish far to the east. Covering the water effectively is far more significant than particular fly patterns, although certainly the Deschutes enjoys a litany of well-known patterns devised specifically for her fish. Among these are the Max Canyon and Freight Train.

Most anglers ply these waters with 8- and 9-weight rods. Two-handed rods have gained a considerable following, too. Regardless of their choice in rods, Deschutes steelheaders must learn to cast a fair length of line, often into the teeth of an upriver wind.

As with any large river system, the Deschutes rewards those who take the time to know her. If you don't have time to get acquainted, then by all means hire a guide. Some of the Northwest's best steelhead guides work the Deschutes during the fall. Among them are men such as Brad Staples, Dec Hogan, and Rich Youngers.

The lower 25 miles of the Deschutes, being essentially roadless, is the domain of the jet sleds. Jet sled guides help you cover a lot of productive water in a day's fishing—water you could not otherwise fish without an exhaustive hike or a multi-day float trip from Macks Canyon. I met Brad Staples, who operates Western Fishing Adventures, many years ago. He returns with his jet boat each fall, as he has done for two decades. Few men know the lower river better.

Deschutes River Access

Boaters have the advantage on the Deschutes simply because they can escape the oft-crowded bank-access areas, which on some reaches of the river are quite limited. Only experienced boaters should navigate the Deschutes, especially between Trout Creek and the mouth. All floaters must obtain and possess a valid boater's pass (available from fly shops).

River guide Tim Doherty lands a Deschutes steelhead.

The uppermost float on the Deschutes begins at Warm Springs, where Highway 26 crosses the river on the route connecting Portland and Madras. Most floaters take out at Trout Creek about 10 miles below, although multi-day floaters typically continue down to the take-outs near Maupin. The uppermost of these is sprawling Harpham Flats, six miles upstream from town and 30 miles below Trout Creek.

The river's best road access begins six miles above the town of Maupin at "Locked Gate" and stretches about 25 miles below Maupin. The eight-mile length from Maupin down to Sherar's Falls (unfloatable) is paved; everything else is gravel. Above town, the gravel road is fairly easy going, but the 17 miles of gravel from Sherar's to Macks Canyon will leave you checking your teeth for loose fillings. Just drive slow.

The Warm Springs Indian Reservation borders the upper end of the Lower Deschutes for about 30 miles on the west bank. Within the reservation, the west bank to midriver is strictly off limits except for a six-mile reach from Dry Creek Campground down to the bank opposite Trout Creek Campground. Anglers fishing the reservation side of this stretch must have a tribal permit to do so (as well as to camp at Dry Creek).

Trout Creek itself offers another of the drive-in access points. The long, rough gravel road heads west off Highway 97 north of Madras. Farther north is the only other drive-in access between Trout Creek and Locked Gate above Maupin. The road to South Junction heads west off Highway 97 after the highway tops out on the grade west of the little town of Shaniko. This is the so-called "Shaniko Junction," where SR 197 departs U.S. 97, heading northwest and eventually winding down into the canyon at Maupin.

Below Macks Canyon, the only drive-in access is a steep, rugged affair that drops down into the canyon from the west side at Klone, some 7½ miles above the mouth. A good regional map will show this route. Otherwise, the lower 25 miles of the Deschutes is accessible primarily by boat—jet boating up from the mouth or drifting down from Macks Canyon. Trails along both banks lead upriver for those willing to hike, and the east-side trail—an old service road—has become a popular route for mountain bikers.

Restaurants and Accommodations

The little community of Maupin straddles the Deschutes about halfway between the Columbia River and Pelton Dam. Maupin serves as the epicenter of activity for many Deschutes anglers. Float trips frequently begin or end here. The town even offers a full-service fly shop, owned by John Smeraglio. The little Oasis Resort & Restaurant is a popular stop for breakfast or a burger (541-395-2611); otherwise, dining options are limited. Nonetheless, Maupin offers everything you might need for a Deschutes River expedition. Lodging options are somewhat limited, but do include the popular C & J Lodge (541-395-2404) along with cabins at the Oasis and Deschutes Motel at 616 Mill Street (541-395-2626). For information on the town's other options, call the Chamber of Commerce at 541-395-2599.

If you are fishing the upper section of the Lower Deschutes, near Warm Springs, you might want to arrange lodging half an hour away at the town of Madras. This is especially true if you are meeting your guide at the Warm Springs put-in. The town, home to a fly shop called Numb-Butt Fly Company, straddles Highway 97 and is also conveniently located about an hour from the popular access/campground at Trout Creek and about an hour from Maupin via Highway 97 and SR 197.

Madras Lodging

All of these lodging options are located on or near either Highway 97 or Highway 26 heading to Warm Springs.

Relax Inn, 797 SW Hwy. 97, 541-475-2117
Royal Dutch Motel, 1101 SW Hwy. 97, 541-475-2281
Madras Hotel, 171 SW C Street, 541-475-2345
Juniper Motel, 414 NW Hwy. 26, 541-475-6186
Hoffy's Motel, 600 N Hwy. 26, 541-475-4633
Best Western, 12 SW 4th Street, 541-475-6141
Budget Inn, 133 NE 5th, 541-475-3831
Sonny's Motel, 1539 SW Hwy. 97, 541-475-3263

A few miles east from the mouth of the Deschutes lies the tiny but busy crossroads town of Biggs. Here U.S. 97—the major north-south artery through central Oregon—meets Interstate 84 about 100 miles east of Portland. Biggs offers lodging, gas stations and several truck-stop-style restaurants, as does the diminutive town of Rufus, five miles to the east. The Biggs motels include Dinty's Motor Inn (541-739-2596), Riviera Motel (541-739-2501), and Biggs Nu-Vu Motel (541-739-2525). Deschutes State Park, located at the mouth of the river on the east bank, features a nice, well-shaded campground.

Less than half an hour west of the Deschutes River's mouth, the larger community of The Dalles is home to one of the best restaurants east of the Cascade Mountains. Situated in an historical downtown building at First and Court Streets, Baldwin Saloon serves exceptional lunches and dinners. Call ahead to check hours and make dinner reservations (541-296-5666).

If you float the river, you will need camping gear. On multi-day guided trips be sure to ask your guide what gear you should bring. On busy weekends, prime riverside campsites are at a premium, so find one during the afternoon. The drive-in access sites (between Locked Gate above Maupin and Macks Canyon below) feature good, undeveloped campsites. The Bureau of Land Management operates a small information office at the west end of the bridge in Maupin. Stop in for advice and information about camping along the river.

Located in The Dalles about half an hour from the mouth of the Deschutes, Baldwin Saloon ranks among the very best restaurants in central and eastern Oregon.

Nearby Fishery

Washington's Klickitat River

Not all that long ago, on any given summer day, southwest Washington steelhead anglers enjoyed the prospect of choosing between any of five productive rivers within an hour of Vancouver. To the north the Kalama and East Fork still attract many fans, but east of the city, two long-time favorites have fallen on difficult times. The Washougal and Wind Rivers, while still fair fisheries, just don't support the runs they boasted several decades ago.

Those four rivers always enjoyed high repute, but the fifth is a lesser-known and far less appreciated river. The Klickitat River drains the southeast flank of Mt. Adams, its headwaters contained within the Yakima Indian Reservation. Each year this river boasts substantial returns of both native and hatchery steelhead, yet fly anglers remain uncommon. Part of the problem lies in the river's muddy waters. The Klickitat forms at a massive glacier of the same name so its water flows cold and gray-brown throughout the summer, save those brief early morning hours when it clears ever so slightly.

Come mid-autumn, however, the river clears substantially as Klickitat Glacier locks up in ice for the winter. You can wait for the autumn freeze or you can fish the early morning hours during summer. Either way, the Klickitat is certain to draw you back for many years to come. The river is perfectly designed for fly fishing: steep enough for well-defined pools and runs, large enough to allow long casts and classic presentations and small enough to cover with ease. Big, aggressive native steelhead frequently weigh 10 pounds or more. The plentiful hatchery steelhead are scrappy 5- to 10-pound fish.

Moreover, the Klickitat is far more accessible than her neighbor across the Columbia, the Deschutes. Klickitat River Road follows the river for almost 20 miles before yielding to a 10-mile reach offering only one drive-in access. Those seeking peace and quiet can head for the river where it flows through Klickitat Wildlife Area.

For any steelhead anglers who dread the autumn crowds on the Deschutes, the Klickitat is your savior. That's exactly how I discovered it. I had seen one too many boats at the mouth of the Deschutes and decided it was high time I explored the smaller, yet similar river across the Columbia. I now visit the Klickitat each fall, trying to gauge my trip to coincide with that magical time when the glacier refreezes and the river clears.

The Klickitat enters the Columbia east of Hood River and White Salmon. From the west side, just cross the Columbia at Hood River and head east on SR 14. Well-marked Klickitat River Road turns north at the town of Lyle. On your way up the river, stop at the Fisher Road Bridge (1½ miles from Lyle) and check out the awesome Klickitat Gorge, where the entire river gets funneled down into a narrow basalt gorge.

KLICKITAT RIVER

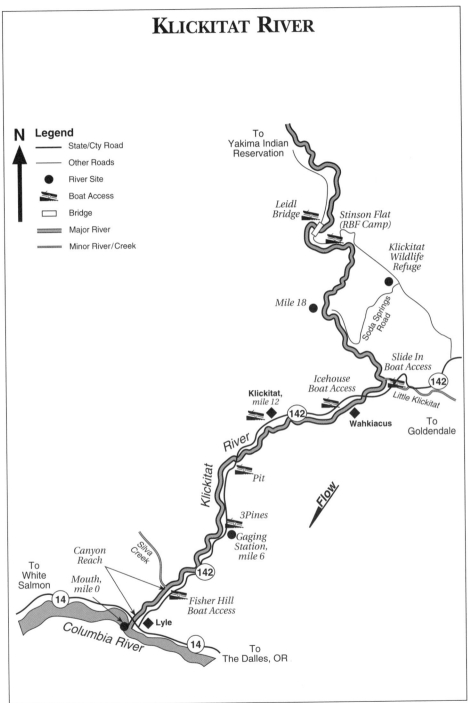

N

Legend

—— State/Cty Road

—— Other Roads

● River Site

Boat Access

▭ Bridge

═══ Major River

═══ Minor River/Creek

To
Yakima Indian
Reservation

*Leidl
Bridge*

*Stinson Flat
(RBF Camp)*

*Klickitat
Wildlife
Refuge*

Mile 18

Soda Springs Road

*Slide In
Boat Access*

142

*Icehouse
Boat Access*

Klickitat,
mile 12

Little Klickitat

142

Wahkiacus

To
Goldendale

River

Klickitat

Pit

Flow

3Pines

*Gaging
Station,
mile 6*

*Canyon
Reach*

*Silva
Creek*

142

To
White
Salmon

*Mouth,
mile 0*

14

*Fisher Hill
Boat Access*

◆ **Lyle**

Columbia River

14

To
The Dalles, OR

© Wilderness Adventures Press, Inc.

If you have a drift boat in tow, remind yourself to get out of the river before you reach the unfloatable gorge. (Otherwise the Klickitat is an easy drift.)

The Lyle Hotel & Restaurant offers well-appointed accommodations and good meals (509-365-5953). Another option is the Oakcrest Retreat (509-365-2533). The Lyle Country Café (509-365-2100) serves up a mean burger. Another restaurant, Huntington's (509-369-4371), is located upriver in the town of Klickitat.

Nearby Fishery

The John Day River

Oregon's longest free-flowing river, the John Day runs a scenic, remote and circuitous route through north-central Oregon, eventually surrendering to the Columbia just 20 miles east from the mouth of the Deschutes. Over the past decade or so, the John Day's smallmouth bass fishery has reached national prominence. The river literally teems with bass and under ideal summer conditions, fly anglers might hook 50 or more fish per day.

Most John Day smallmouth bass, like those on the faraway mainstem Umpqua, span 8 to 12 inches. Yet bass to 18 inches are reasonably common, and the magnificent desert scenery more than atones for the abundance of smaller bass. The John Day offers ample opportunity to rise bass to small popping bugs, especially during morning and evening. All the usual subsurface tactics work here as well.

Moreover, the John Day is an adventurer's river. Its best water requires a three- to six-day float, due both to the river's remoteness and to a preponderance of private property that makes drive-in access impossible in all but a few places. Bass fishing peaks between May and July when the river is high enough to float (1,200 to 2,000 cfs, typically) in rafts or drift boats, but low enough to offer good fishing prospects. Late summer leaves the river too low for easy passage.

The so-called "upper" river is popular with springtime rafters, but also with smallmouth enthusiasts. This 50-mile reach begins at the popular put-in at Service Creek on State Route 19 (or 10 miles downstream at the Twickenham Access) and ends at Clarno, where Highway 218 crosses the river. The "lower" John Day begins at Clarno and flows 70 miles down to the Cottonwood Access at the Highway 206 crossing southeast from Wasco. This lower drift is the more remote of the two and also offers the best bet for late fall steelhead when water conditions allow.

The John Day's summer steelhead run shows up any time between October and the following spring. During low-water years, most of the fish remain holed up down in the six-mile-long John Day Arm off the Columbia River. They head upriver when late-autumn rains begin between November and December, leaving little window of opportunity. During high-water years, when the irrigation season ends and the river

JOHN DAY RIVER

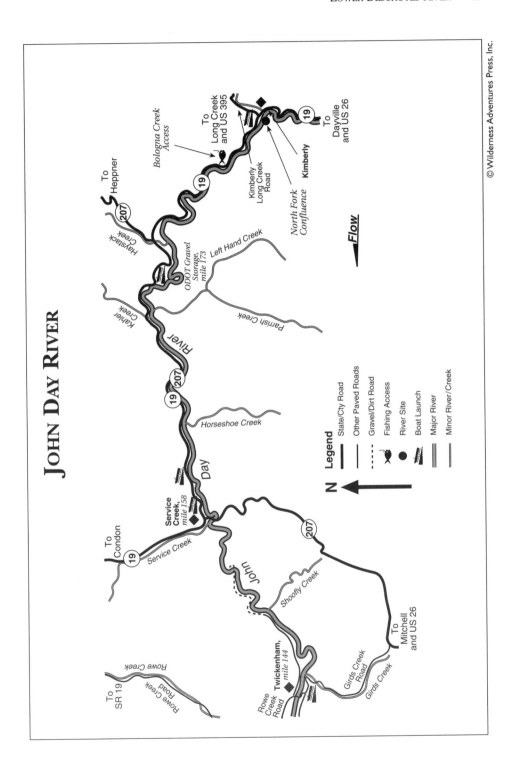

To Heppner

To Long Creek and US 395

Bologna Creek Access

19

207

Haystack Creek

ODOT Gravel Storage, mile 173

Left Hand Creek

Kahler Creek

Parrish Creek

River

19

207

Kimberly Long Creek Road

North Fork Confluence   **Kimberly**

19

To Dayville and US 26

Horseshoe Creek

Day

Service Creek, *mile 158*

To Condon

19

Service Creek

John

207

Shoofly Creek

To Mitchell and US 26

Rowe Creek

To SR 19

Rowe Creek Road

Twickenham, *mile 144*

Rowe Creek Road

Girds Creek Road

Girds Creek

Legend

State/Cty Road
Other Paved Roads
Gravel/Dirt Road
Fishing Access
River Site
Boat Launch
Major River
Minor River/Creek

N

Flow

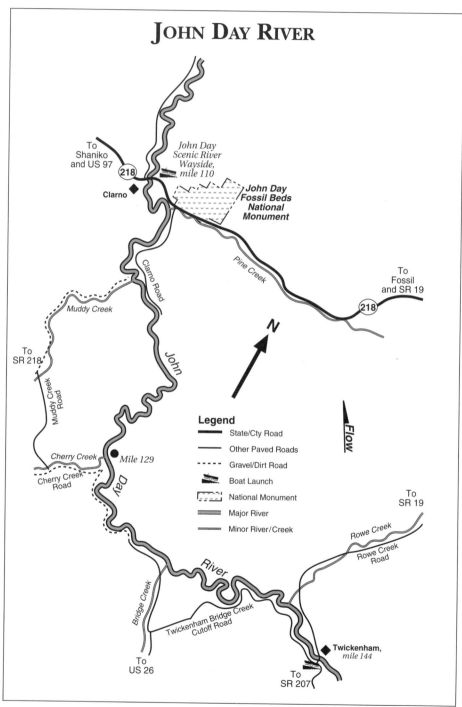

JOHN DAY RIVER

To Shaniko and US 97

218

Clarno

John Day Scenic River Wayside, mile 110

John Day Fossil Beds National Monument

Clarno Road

Pine Creek

To Fossil and SR 19

218

Muddy Creek

John

N

To SR 218

Muddy Creek Road

Flow

Cherry Creek ● Mile 129

Legend

State/Cty Road
Other Paved Roads
Gravel/Dirt Road
Boat Launch
National Monument
Major River
Minor River/Creek

Cherry Creek Road

Day

To SR 19

Rowe Creek

Rowe Creek Road

River

Bridge Creek

Twickenham Bridge Creek Cutoff Road

To US 26

Twickenham, mile 144

To SR 207

© Wilderness Adventures Press, Inc.

JOHN DAY RIVER

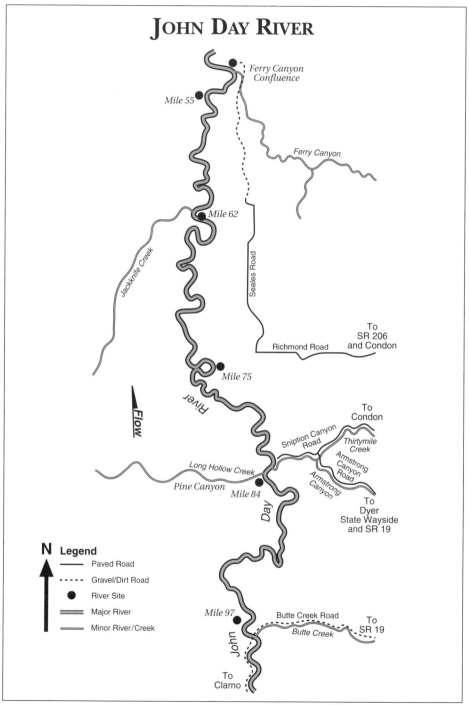

Ferry Canyon
Confluence

Mile 55

Ferry Canyon

Mile 62

Jackknife Creek

Seales Road

To
SR 206
and Condon

Richmond Road

Mile 75

Flow

River

To
Condon

Sniption Canyon
Road

Thirtymile
Creek

Armstrong
Canyon
Road

Long Hollow Creek

Armstrong
Canyon

Pine Canyon   Mile 84

To
Dyer
State Wayside
and SR 19

Day

N **Legend**

——— Paved Road

- - - - Gravel/Dirt Road

● River Site

Major River

Minor River/Creek

Mile 97

Butte Creek Road

To
SR 19

Butte Creek

John

To
Clarno

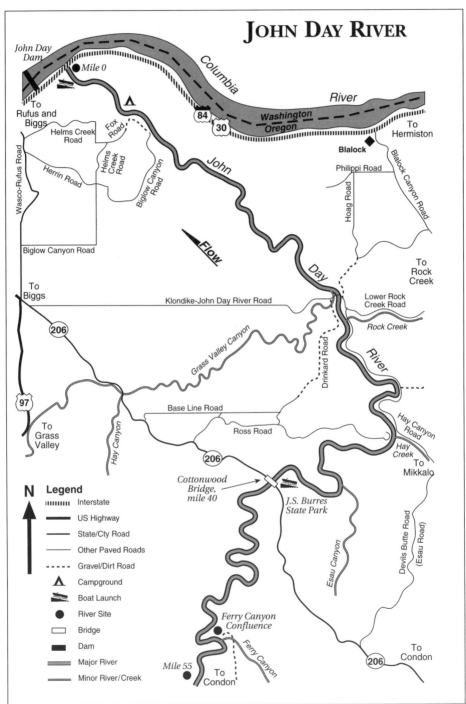

John Day River

John Day Dam

Mile 0

Columbia

River

Washington
Oregon

To
Rufus and
Biggs

84
30

To
Hermiston

Blalock

Philippi Road

Helms Creek
Road

Fox Road

Helms Creek Road

Herrin Road

Biglow Canyon Road

John

Hoag Road

Blalock Canyon Road

Flow

Day

To
Rock
Creek

Biglow Canyon Road

To
Biggs

Klondike-John Day River Road

Lower Rock
Creek Road

Rock Creek

206

Grass Valley Canyon

Drinkard Road

River

97

To
Grass
Valley

Base Line Road

Ross Road

Hay Canyon Road

Hay Canyon

206

Hay
Creek

To
Mikkalo

Cottonwood
Bridge,
mile 40

J.S. Burres
State Park

Devils Butte Road
(Esau Road)

N Legend

Esau Canyon

|||||||| Interstate

—— US Highway

— State/Cty Road

— Other Paved Roads

---- Gravel/Dirt Road

▲ Campground

🚤 Boat Launch

● River Site

▭ Bridge

▬ Dam

═ Major River

— Minor River/Creek

Ferry Canyon
Confluence

Ferry Canyon

Mile 55

To
Condon

206

To
Condon

© Wilderness Adventures Press, Inc.

refills, steelhead action picks up during October. In any season, the John Day is highly variable by nature. Unchecked by dams, its flows vary tremendously from year to year.

First-timers should consider a guided trip to learn the river's peculiarities. Owing largely to the river's superb smallmouth bass fishery, numerous outfitters now lead multi-day expeditions on the John Day. Among the highly regarded John Day guides are Steve Flemming (541-763-2277), Wild River Ranch Guides & Outfitters (541-468-2900), and Little Creek Outfitters (541-963-7878). Testifying to the John Day's popularity, many Oregon fly shops now book trips on the river. If you're looking for nice accommodations near the put-in site, try Service Creek Bed & Breakfast (541-468-3331).

Author's Tip

When heavily pressured Deschutes redsides get finicky about high-and-dry stonefly patterns, a "drowned adult" tactic often works wonders. Hold a dry pattern underwater and squeeze until it is thoroughly soaked; then fish the fly dead-drift, allowing it to sink just a few inches below the surface. The Bird's Stone, along with the locally popular Clark's Stone, are two patterns well suited to this duty. If they resist the urge to sink below the surface, trim them down some with your clippers.

Favorite Steelhead Fly

Black Max

HOOK	Steelhead wet fly, No. 2-4
TAG	Gold tinsel
TAIL	Dyed-orange golden pheasant crest or orange hackle fibers
BODY	Hot orange butt and then black wool yarn body
RIB	Oval gold tinsel
WING	Black bear hair or similar
CHEEK	Jungle cock

Black Max

Favorite Trout Fly

Maxwell's Jughead

HOOK	3XL light wire dry-fly, No. 4-10
TAIL	Stacked deer hair
BODY	Yellow or orange yarn
RIB	Clipped brown hackle
WING	Deer hair
HEAD	Spun and clipped deer hair

Maxwell's Jughead

Fast Facts

Lower Deschutes River

LOCATION	North-central Oregon
WATER TYPE	Large, canyon-bound freestone river
PRIMARY GAMEFISH	Redband trout; summer steelhead; mountain whitefish
BEST TIME	May through October
BEST FLIES	Match the hatch patterns or big attractors for trout; traditional steelhead flies
EQUIPMENT	5- to 6-weight rod; floating line for trout; 8- to 9-weight rod and floating line for steelhead.
CONDITIONS	Afternoon wind is common. Cold weather sets in by mid-November, often earlier.

DRIVE TIME	From Portland: 2-3 hours
	From Seattle: 6-7 hours
	From Eugene: 4 hours
	From San Francisco: 10 hours
	From Boise: 6-8 hours, depending on route
DIRECTIONS	The Lower Deschutes begins below Pelton Dam near Warm Springs and flows north, meeting the Columbia near Biggs. There are three major access points: the mouth of the river at I-84 west of Biggs, the town of Maupin about halfway up the river's 100-mile course, and the little town of Warm Springs, where Highway 26 from Portland arrives from the west.

Local Fly Shops

DESCHUTES CANYON
FLY SHOP
599 S. Highway 197
Maupin, OR 97037
541-395-2565

NUMB-BUTT FLY COMPANY
380 North Highway 26
Madras, OR 97741
541-325-5515

GORGE FLY SHOP
201 Oak Street
Hood River, OR 97031
541-386-6977

DESCHUTES ANGLER
504 Deschutes Avenue
Maupin, OR 97037
541-395-0995

Area Fly Shops

FIN-N-FEATHER FLY SHOP
785 W. Third Street
Prineville, OR 97754
541-447-8691

THE FLY FISHER'S PLACE
151 W. Main Avenue
Sisters, OR 97759
541-549-3474

FLY-N-FIELD
143 SW Century Drive
Bend, OR 97701
541-318-1616

THE PATIENT ANGLER
55 NW Wall Street
Bend, OR 97701
541-389-6208

THE FLY BOX
1293 NE 3rd
Bend, OR 97701
541-388-3330

DESCHUTES RIVER OUTFITTERS
61115 South Highway 97
Bend, OR 97702
541-388-8191

Area Fly Shops, continued

THE HOOK FLY SHOP
Sunriver Village Mall, Building 21
Sunriver, OR 97707
541-593-2358

SUNRIVER FLY SHOP
Sunriver Business Park
Sunriver, OR 97707
541-593-8814

THE FLY FISHING SHOP
67296 E. Hwy. 26
Welches, OR 97067
503-622-4607

NORTHWEST FLYFISHING
OUTFITTERS
17302 NE Halsey
Gresham, OR 97230
503-252-1529

STEWART'S FLY SHOP
23830 NE Halsey
Wood Village, OR 97060
503-666-2471

CLACKAMAS RIVER FLY SHOP
12632 SE McLoughlin, Ste. 200
Portland, OR 97222

BUFFALO CREEK OUTFITTERS
91 State Street
Lake Oswego, OR 97034
503-675-3082

RIVER CITY FLY SHOP
11429 Scholls Ferry Road
Beaverton, OR 97008
503-579-5176

VALLEY FLYFISHER
153 Alice Street S.
Salem, OR 97302
503-375-3721

CREEKSIDE FLYFISHING SHOP
345 High Street S
Salem, OR 97301
503-588-1768

FLY COUNTRY OUTFITTERS
3400 State Street, Ste. G-704
Salem, OR 97301
503-585-4898

NORTH COUNTRY OUTFITTERS
6175 NE Cornell Rd.
Hillsboro, OR 97124
503-615-0555

COUNTRYSPORT LTD.
126 SW 1st Ave.
Portland, OR 97204
503-221-4545

SCARLET IBIS FLY SHOP
2319 NW 9th Street
Corvallis, OR 97330
541-754-1544

THE CADDIS FLY ANGLING SHOP
168 West 6th
Eugene, OR 97401
541-342-7005

HOMEWATERS FLY SHOP
444 West 3rd
Eugene, OR 97401
541-342-6691

BLUE MOUNTAIN ANGLERS
& FLY SHOP
1847 Westgate
Pendleton, OR 97
800-825-1548

Guides

WESTERN FISHING ADVENTURES
(Brad Staples)
503-250-0558

CREEKSIDE FLY FISHING
(Rich Youngers)
503-588-1768
www.creeksideflyfishing.com

CARR'S WILD TROUT ADVENTURES
(Colin Carr)
541-548-0765

FISHING ON THE FLY
(Tim Doherty)
541-389-3252

JOHN SMERAGLIO
541-395-2565

JOHN JUDY FLY FISHING
541-595-2073

Contacts

OREGON DEPARTMENT
OF FISH & WILDLIFE
High Desert Regional Office
61374 Parrell Road
Bend, OR 97702
541-388-6363

Bank access is limited on the Williamson, so most anglers float the river.

CHAPTER 4

THE WILLIAMSON RIVER AND KLAMATH COUNTRY

Trophy Trout Waters Beyond Compare

In terms of sheer numbers of big trout, the Klamath country fisheries are virtually beyond compare. Outside of Alaska, you won't find a region whose waters are so densely populated with wild, trophy-class rainbows. Five-pound specimens won't raise any eyebrows among those who regularly ply the waters of the Williamson or Wood Rivers or of Upper Klamath or Agency Lakes. Moreover, any angler with a good guide and decent casting ability can catch the fish of a lifetime several times over on any given day on these waters.

The Williamson is a split-personality river. Its lower half, below Klamath Marsh, runs through pastoral farmlands and secluded housing tracts down to its confluence with Upper Klamath Lake. Without Klamath Lake and its huge wild rainbows, this "lower" Williamson River would hardly be worth your time. But the behemoth rainbows of the lake wander up the river like steelhead. By summer, the river is full of 3- to 15-pound redbands from Klamath Lake.

The Lower Williamson may be further divided into its upper section, below Collier Park and its lower section from the town of Chiloquin down to the mouth. The

*Jennifer Byers enjoys the view as Steve Bonner fishes the
upper end of the lower Williamson near Collier Park.*

upper reach, below Collier Park and the Spring Creek confluence is virtually inaccessible to the public so anglers wishing to ply its easily fished waters must hire one of the guides who have access to this section (see Crystalwood Lodge below). The remainder of the lower river offers better public access, but the water takes on a tea color that makes it less aquarium-like than the reach above.

In any event, the trout of the Lower Williamson are migratory fish. Sometimes they eat and sometimes they don't. That's the bottom line. They are quirky fish that, once in the river, often act more like steelhead than trout. On the Lower Williamson, a perfectly good mayfly hatch can go completely unmolested by hundreds of huge trout. Then the next day the same hatch arrives flush with rising trout. Float the river and you see pods of trophy trout. Catch them in an eating mood and you enjoy uncomplicated fishing for some of the biggest trout of your life. Otherwise you just see lots of big trout and maybe find a few willing to eat a wet fly quartered down and strip-retrieved.

Then there is the "other" Williamson River, the stretch above Klamath Marsh known as the Upper Williamson. Based on the tiny trickle of water emerging from the downstream end of Klamath Marsh, I hardly see much connection between the two rivers. The Lower Williamson is home primarily to potadromous rainbows—fish that reside in the lake but run up the river during summer, perhaps to escape the lake's rising water temperatures. The Upper Williamson, conversely, offers a healthy

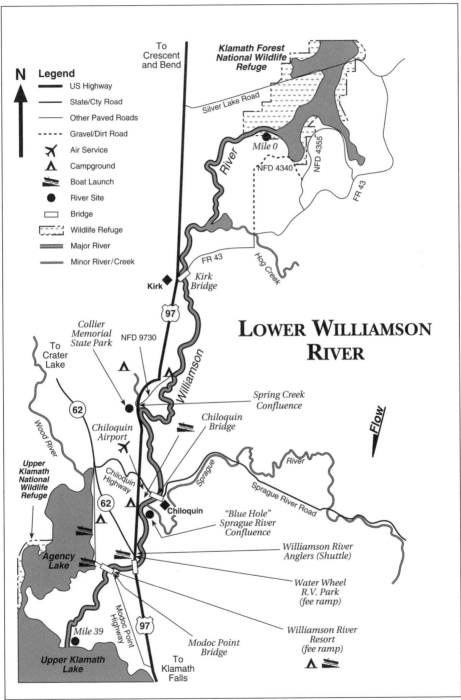

N

Legend
▬	US Highway
—	State/Cty Road
—	Other Paved Roads
- - - -	Gravel/Dirt Road
✈	Air Service
⛺	Campground
🛶	Boat Launch
●	River Site
▭	Bridge
⬚	Wildlife Refuge
▨	Major River
═	Minor River/Creek

To Crescent and Bend

Klamath Forest National Wildlife Refuge

Silver Lake Road

River

Mile 0

NFD 4340

NFD 4355

FR 43

Hog Creek

FR 43

Kirk

Kirk Bridge

97

Collier Memorial State Park

NFD 9730

To Crater Lake

62

Wood River

Williamson

Spring Creek Confluence

LOWER WILLIAMSON RIVER

Flow

Chiloquin Airport

Chiloquin Bridge

Upper Klamath National Wildlife Refuge

Chiloquin Highway

Sprague

River

Sprague River Road

62

Agency Lake

Chiloquin

"Blue Hole" Sprague River Confluence

Williamson River Anglers (Shuttle)

Water Wheel R.V. Park (fee ramp)

Mile 39

Modoc Point Highway

97

Modoc Point Bridge

To Klamath Falls

Upper Klamath Lake

Williamson River Resort (fee ramp)

© Wilderness Adventures Press, Inc.

population of native rainbows and wild brook trout. Being resident fish, these trout of the Upper Williamson act like respectable stream-born trout anywhere. They feed on the hatches and provide superb opportunities for enticing large fish on dry flies in crystal-clear, spring-fed waters.

The two Williamsons share a common characteristic other than name and big trout: Both abound in private property. You can float the Lower Williamson on your own, but unless you have lots of time to dedicate to the task, you are better off hiring a guide. Some pools hold pods of fish and some don't. As the season progresses, the fish often move to different locations and the pattern can change from year to year. You could spend half a season just figuring out where best to cast the fly. So unless you have a boat and lots of time on your hands, hire a guide.

Steve Bonner (Native Run Guide Service) is one such guide. He knows the Williamson and has been guiding the river for years. Yet he readily admits that with each passing season he understands these fish even less. Like I said, they are quirky fish and rules applied to typical river trout don't apply to these migratory beasts.

Good guides make the Williamson far more user-friendly.

Despite insisting that he has yet to figure out these fish, Bonner—by virtue of his countless hours on the river—has figured out the fishery. That's the more important figuring. Bonner, like a handful of other good Williamson River guides, knows where to find the fish and knows the best methods to coax them into eating a fly. And he knows how to cater even to the rank beginner, who, on this river, stands about as good a chance as anybody of hooking a 10-pound rainbow.

Fishing the Lower Williamson

The Lower Williamson offers several strong hatches during the summer and fall, the best known of which is the river's July *Hexagenia* or "Hex" hatch. These giant yellow mayflies (*Hexagenia limbata*) usually emerge at dusk. As with any hatch they are prone to witness, the Williamson's trout remain unpredictable in their reaction to the huge mayflies. Sometimes they rise and feed on the bugs and sometimes they don't. Sometimes a mile of river offers no rising fish and then you round a bend only to find a pool full of huge trout feeding at the surface.

When the river's trout feed on hatching insects at the surface you are treated to one of the West's great dry-fly treasures. You need good casting and downstream-presentation skills. In many instances, these rising giants act as spooky and finicky as a Henry's Fork or Silver Creek trout. Conversely, you find the occasional riser who abandons all caution and proves an easy mark.

More often than not, however, the river's hatches proceed unmolested by the trout. These migratory fish often seem entirely unaware of hatching insects. Moreover, they often disdain the idea of feeding at all. However, the Williamson's rainbows behave as individuals. Some feed actively while others don't. In places—especially later in the year upstream from Chiloquin—you can spot fish and then watch if and how they react to the fly. More often you must carefully approach the pools and cast a long line. By mid-summer, the pools all hold fish to one extent or another, so you can be reasonably certain that you are fishing over large trout.

In the absence of risers, the technique of choice is to cast streamers or nymphs on sinking lines. Quarter across and downstream, allowing enough dead-drift to sink the fly. Then allow the fly to swing back across in the manner of a steelhead fly, but add a "strip-pause-strip-pause" retrieve. Favorite flies include leech patterns, Woolly Buggers, and assorted nymph dressings.

Obviously this cast-swing-strip technique is easily mastered, so the Williamson's difficulty lies more in the nature of the river. The public section, from Chiloquin to Highway 97 can be especially tough on newcomers because you can easily float right over the best slots before you see them. That's why I'd suggest a guide for your first trip down the river—you can learn the pools and slots where the trout reside and learn where best to anchor to fish these places.

The Williamson River Club at Crystalwood Lodge

"How was the conversation around the dinner table last night?" inquired Rich Macintyre, ever attentive to even the most trivial details involving his guests at Crystalwood Lodge.

One of the West's most remarkable destination establishments, Crystalwood Lodge straddles a slight rise overlooking the Wood River Valley north by northwest from Klamath Falls. Since 1993, Crystalwood has provided its guests with the most remarkable of angling experiences on waters teeming with wild, trophy-class trout. The Macintyres strived to make the lodge's every aspect a memorable experience, a tradition now continuing with Liz Parrish and Peggy O'Neal, the new owners. The rare quality of the fisheries and of the natural surroundings demand equally rare meals and accommodations. No details remain unpolished.

And the conversation had been lively among the 10 diners that September evening, and tales of the day's fishing highlights had served only as the appetizer. Before the luxurious meal had concluded with a warm mixed-fruit cobbler, the eclectic collection of guests had solved half the world's problems. Eagerly emptied dessert plates and five spent bottles of thoughtfully chosen wine signaled a migration to the lodge's cozy sitting room, where talk returned once again to the remarkable local fisheries. Among these waters are lesser-known retreats like the lodge's own Crystal Springs, home to the same migratory rainbows that cast fame upon the Williamson and Wood Rivers.

Crystalwood Lodge attracts anglers who share an appreciation for detail and an enthusiasm for the fate and well being of the region's world-class fisheries. A first-rate guide staff—headed by Steve Bonner—knows every fishable inch of the Klamath Basin and caters to all levels of fly fishing aficionados. Given enough time, you can sample any of half a dozen remarkable fisheries, ranging from the giant hog-ponds of Upper Klamath Lake and adjacent Agency Lake to the intimate meanders of the Wood River. You can swing wet flies on the Williamson, cast small dry flies to active risers, or plop hoppers against undercut banks on the Wood. Or perhaps you will strip leech patterns or streamers for absurdly fat rainbows on the lakes or try the rough-and-tumble confines of the Klamath River. Regardless, the Crystalwood guides will put you on fish—big fish.

At day's end, Crystalwood's spacious deck begs late afternoon coffee and provides a restful overlook of the expansive Wood River wetlands. The 133-acre property abuts the marshlands, providing a diverse habitat rich in flora and fauna. Massive ponderosas cast long shadows over gentle wooded slopes and scenic aspen groves grace the edges of verdant meadows. Every species of owl found in Oregon has been found on the property, including rare great grey owls, which nest in the area. Likewise, the adjacent marsh attracts more than two million migrating waterfowl each season and many of these remain here to nest on the Upper Klamath National Wildlife Refuge and surrounding wetlands.

Long days yield to summer sunsets that leave the marsh awash in pastels. Accompanied by a serenade of coyote song, guests find themselves drifting off to sleep in comfortable, well-appointed rooms—but not before a memorable dinner and the customary recounting of the days' fishing tales, which are sure to feature wild trophy-class trout as a common theme.

Crystalwood Lodge requires reservations. The lodge is open year-round and is pet-friendly. Fishing opportunities and conditions change as the season progresses, but the fish are always abundant and always large. Consult with Liz to plan your stay to coincide with specific events, such as the *Hexagenia* hatch or the prime hopper fishing. To contact the lodge:

THE WILLIAMSON RIVER CLUB AT CRYSTALWOOD LODGE
P.O. Box 469
Fort Klamath, OR 97626
541-381-2322, www.crystalwoodlodge.com

Steve Bonner, owner of Native Run Fly Fishing, admires a Williamson rainbow.

Lonesome Duck

Located upstream from the Highway 97 Bridge on the south bank of the river, Lonesome Duck offers three classy rental cottages. One is the property's original cottage and the other two are newer, beautifully-designed cabins. Lonesome Duck, owned by Steve and Debbie Hilbert, offers packages that include meals or you can make your stay a do-it-yourself escape. Rental drift boats and canoes are available and the property borders some two miles of the river's best *Hexagenia* water. Lonesome Duck also employs one of the region's best guides (such as Marlon Ramp). Current rates are $225/night for the cabins or $160/night for the cottage, both with a two-night minimum stay.

LONESOME DUCK
800-367-2540
email: steveh@lonesomeduck.com

The Upper Williamson

The Williamson River emerges from lush springs in the Fremont National Forest. For its entire run down to sprawling Klamath Marsh it flows almost exclusively through private property. This classic spring creek is rich in aquatic life and in large native rainbows and wild brook trout.

What's more, the Upper Williamson offers an exceptional hatch of Black Drake or *Siphlonurus* mayflies. These huge mayflies rank as the number one attraction drawing anglers to the exclusive private fishing holdings found on the river. The well-known and highly regarded Yamsi Ranch, owned by the Hyde family, offers a top-flight all-inclusive fly angling experience on the ranch's extensive riverfront holdings. Meanwhile, Aspen Ridge Ranch opens its waters specifically for the Black Drake hatch during the summer.

YAMSI RANCH
P.O. Box 371
Chiloquin, OR 97624
541-783-2403
www.yamsiflyfishing.com

ASPEN RIDGE RANCH
HC 63, Box 315
Chiloquin, OR 97624
541-389-9452

Don Roberts explores Crystal Springs, behind Crystalwood Lodge.

Upper Klamath & Agency Lakes

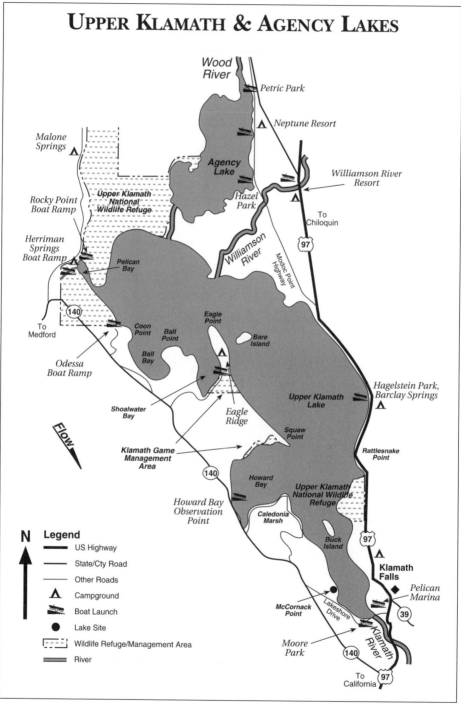

Wood River

Petric Park

Neptune Resort

Malone Springs

Agency Lake

Williamson River Resort

Rocky Point Boat Ramp

Upper Klamath National Wildlife Refuge

Hazel Park

To Chiloquin

Herriman Springs Boat Ramp

Williamson River

Modoc Point Highway

97

Pelican Bay

To Medford

140

Coon Point

Ball Point

Eagle Point

Bare Island

Odessa Boat Ramp

Ball Bay

Upper Klamath Lake

Hagelstein Park, Barclay Springs

Shoalwater Bay

Eagle Ridge

Squaw Point

Rattlesnake Point

Klamath Game Management Area

140

Howard Bay

Upper Klamath National Wildlife Refuge

Howard Bay Observation Point

Caledonia Marsh

Flow

Buck Island

97

Legend

N

	US Highway
	State/Cty Road
	Other Roads
▲	Campground
	Boat Launch
●	Lake Site
	Wildlife Refuge/Management Area
	River

Klamath Falls

Pelican Marina

McCornack Point

Lakeshore Drive

Klamath River

39

Moore Park

140

To California

97

© Wilderness Adventures Press, Inc.

Upper Klamath and Agency Lakes

Super-fertile and shallow, Klamath and Agency Lakes grow big trout in a hurry. Wild redband trout from 14 to more than 30 inches in length abound in these waters, along with some large brown trout found primarily in Agency Lake. Generally, the fishing is straightforward. You appeal to the voracious appetites of these large fish by casting and retrieving streamers and leech patterns. During early summer, damsel migrations occasionally cause selective feeding, but leeches and streamers reign as the most productive patterns.

Both lakes require a boat. These are big, open waters prone to high winds—no place to get caught in a float tube when the surface turns to whitecapped swells. Boat ramps are scattered around both lakes at various locations. Some are public, like the two ramps on Agency Lake's east shore, while resorts privately operate other ramps and marinas on Klamath Lake. Choose the ramp closest to your destination.

Upper Klamath Lake offers a few resort-type establishments, including well-known Rocky Point Resort, which offers lodging, a restaurant, guide service, rental boats and just about anything else you need. Make reservations well ahead of time during the peak season.

ROCKY POINT RESORT
28721 Rocky Point Road
Klamath Falls, OR 97601
541-356-2287

The Wood River

Large trout from Agency Lake ascend the lovely Wood River like those from Upper Klamath Lake running up the Williamson. But that is where the comparisons ends. The Wood River—which offers precious little public access—carves out a long meander on its north-to-south journey through the valley bearing its name. Its smooth glides hide deeply undercut banks where large rainbow and brown trout lurk.

The Wood River's trout start out at 14 or so inches, but 18- to 22-inch fish predominate. Lots of 5- to 8-pound fish inhabit the river during the summer and by August and September they often respond to hopper patterns.

If you have your own boat, you can launch at Petric Park on Agency Lake and motor up the lower end of the Wood River. Otherwise, you're remaining access option is to do the bridge-to-bridge floats in a small craft of some kind. I'd recommend against this latter option. The best alternative is to hire one of the local fly fishing guides that have access to private property on the river. Horseshoe Ranch near Fort Klamath is a good choice as they offer lodging, meals, and a guide service, with six miles of private bank access to the Wood (541-381-2297).

Accommodations

The little riverside town of Chiloquin offers several motels ideal for visiting anglers, all of which are located along the highway: Melita's Motel & Café (541-783-2401), Sportsman's Motel (541-783-2867), Spring Creek Ranch Motel (541-783-2775) and Winema Rapids Motel (541-783-2271). Waterwheel Campground, located at 200 Williamson River Road, includes ample space for RVers (541-783-2738), and Agency Lake Resort is conveniently located at 37000 Modoc Point Road (541-783-2489).

Author's Tip

When fishing the Williamson, keep two rods handy at all times. One rod should be rigged with a clear intermediate line for fishing wet flies and the other with a floating line and long leader so you can be ready when you find trout feeding at the surface.

Favorite Fly

Mohair-Marabou Leech

HOOK	3XL wet-fly hook, No. 6-8
TAIL	Brown, black or olive marabou
BODY	Brown, black or olive mohair (or dubbing), picked out
HEAD	Metal bead (optional)

Mohair-Marabou Leech

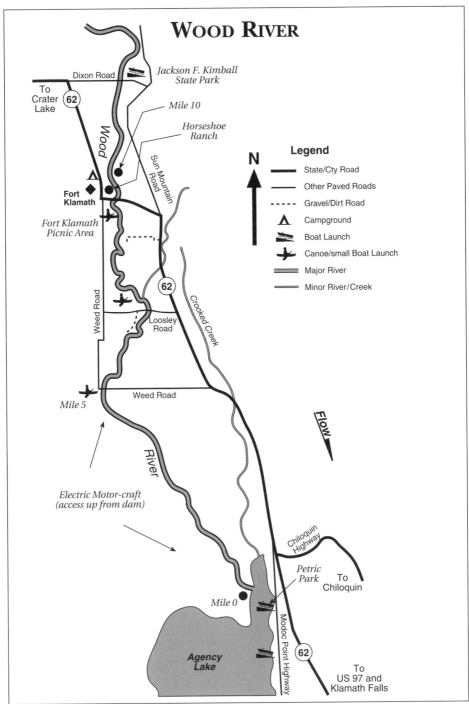

WOOD RIVER

Dixon Road

Jackson F. Kimball
State Park

To
Crater
Lake

62

Mile 10

Wood

Horseshoe
Ranch

Sun Mountain Road

N

Legend

State/Cty Road

Other Paved Roads

Gravel/Dirt Road

Campground

Boat Launch

Canoe/small Boat Launch

Major River

Minor River/Creek

**Fort
Klamath**

*Fort Klamath
Picnic Area*

Weed Road

62

Crooked Creek

Loosley
Road

Weed Road

Mile 5

River

*Electric Motor-craft
(access up from dam)*

Chiloquin Highway

Flow

Petric
Park

To
Chiloquin

Mile 0

Modoc Point Highway

62

*Agency
Lake*

To
US 97 and
Klamath Falls

© Wilderness Adventures Press, Inc.

Fast Facts

Lower Williamson and Klamath Country

LOCATION	South-central Oregon
WATER TYPE	Large, shallow, fertile lakes and spring creeks
PRIMARY GAMEFISH	Rainbow (redband) and brown trout
BEST TIME	Spring, summer and fall
BEST FLIES	Match-the-hatch patterns to terrestrials, wet flies and streamers
EQUIPMENT	Generally you will need a boat for these waters; 5- to 7-weight rods; floating, sink-tip and stillwater intermediate lines.
CONDITIONS	This part of Oregon enjoys great summer and fall weather, sometimes bordering on uncomfortably hot. Afternoon winds common.
DRIVE TIME	From Portland: 5 hours
	From San Francisco: 7 hours
	From Boise: 7 hours
	From Seattle: 9 hours
DIRECTIONS	From Bend, follow Highway 97 south. You will reach the Williamson River first, crossing the river near Chiloquin, afterwhich you will reach the north end of Upper Klamath Lake. Agency Lake and the Wood River Valley are both located a few miles to the west.

Local Fly Shops

TROPHY WATERS
FLYFISHING SHOP
800 Klamath Avenue
Klamath Falls, OR 97601
541-850-0717

WILLIAMSON RIVER ANGLERS
Highway 97/62 Junction
Chiloquin, OR 97624
541-783-2677

Area Fly Shops

NATIVE RUN FLY SHOP
324 Redwood Highway
Grants Pass, OR 97527
541-474-0090

MCKENZIE OUTFITTERS
1340 Biddle Road
Medford, OR 97504
800-704-5145

ASHLAND OUTDOOR STORE
37 North Third Street
Ashland, OR 97520
541-488-1202

Guides

NATIVE RUN FLY FISHING
(Steve Bonner)
541-474-0018
www.nativerunflyfishing.com

WILD WEST FLY FISHING
(Marlon Rampy)
541-245-4314
www.flyfishoregon.com

Contacts

OREGON DEPARTMENT OF
FISH & WILDLIFE
Klamath Watershed
District Office
1850 Miller Island Road
Klamath Falls, OR 97603
541-883-5732

Jennifer Byers works a summer steelhead run on the Sol Duc.

CHAPTER 5

THE HOH, SOL DUC, AND BOGACHIEL RIVERS

Olympic Peninsula Steelhead

Jennifer waded carefully into position up and across from a huge steelhead that we had spotted from the bridge. A late-summer sun lit up every stone on the bottom of the elegant Sol Duc River, whose gentle August flows could hardly portend its bold and muscular wintertime pace.

I watched from the bridge. This summer-run steelhead remained starkly visible, holding in four feet of gin-clear water well downstream of a large, rounded boulder. I hadn't expected to find a double-digit fish, but this steelhead easily weighed 12 pounds. Waiting for Jen to gain the proper casting station, I studied the bottom, counting several small trout scattered about the run beneath the bridge.

She made her first cast, down an across with a size 4 Skunk. Too short. I spread my arms, indicating to her to strip four more feet of line off the reel. She lengthened out and again quartered down and across. The fly landed in the soft water opposite her and then hooked around as the line came tight in the current. I watched the little Skunk swing past the fish, but still too far upstream. Again I signaled Jen to

HOH RIVER

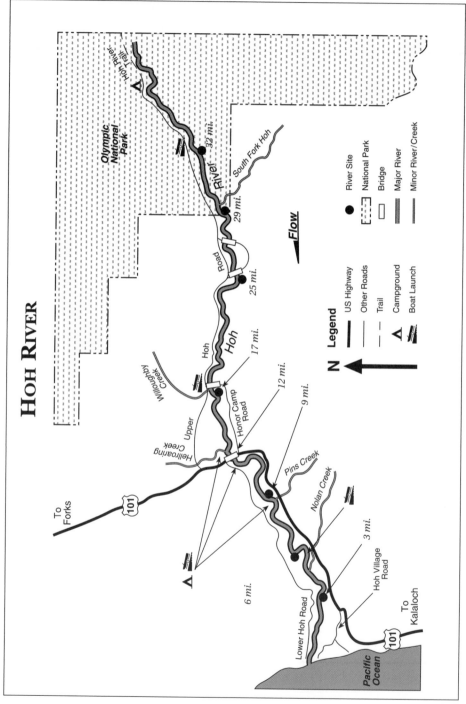

The spectacular Hoh River.

lengthen her cast. This time she hit it perfectly. The fly swam slowly across the flow ahead of and above the fish.

No reaction. She tried the same cast several times. I signaled her to switch flies. After two such changes we still couldn't move the fish. Some steelhead are biters; some are not. This one seemed uninterested. Jen tried one more fly, my trusty old Spawning Purple. The fly hit a little too far over in the slow water on the far side of the river, so the line bellied badly forcing the fly into a rapid downstream dash. Suddenly a shadow darted from beneath a slab-shaped boulder, headed straight downstream and creamed the fly. You just gotta love those searun cutthroat.

The ensuing frenzy spooked the steelhead out of the pool, and Jennifer soon landed a beautiful fresh-run cutthroat of 16 inches. This was the first of three searuns we caught that afternoon. We never touched a steelhead, a fact that concerned us not in the least. The Sol Duc had cast her spell upon us. She ranks among the region's most beautiful rivers and so strong is her magic that even now, as September wears on, I feel the pull to drop everything and head north to the Olympic Peninsula.

The Sol Duc is but one of several great rivers located on the west side of Washington's Olympic Peninsula. Her equally famous sister, the Bogachiel, converges with her near Forks, as does the lesser-known Calawah, to form the Quillayute River. The entire Quillayute system—the Sol Duc, Calawah and "Bogy"—is well-known for its runs of winter steelhead. Lesser known are the anadromous fish of summer and fall, the summer-run steelhead and migratory cutthroat.

To the south flows the Quillayute's sister system, the famous Hoh River, home to equally impressive runs of steelhead and salmon. There are other great rivers on the Pacific side of the peninsula—the Queets for example—but it is the Hoh, Bogachiel, and Sol Duc that occupy the hearts and minds of so many steelhead anglers.

I'm an Olympic Peninsula dabbler. I find myself wandering that direction once or twice each year, usually when the North Umpqua runs high and brown during March or during the fall, when hot weather delays the start of my chukar hunting.

Each time I leave the Hoh, Bogy, or Sol Duc I find myself wanting more—how easily the truck heater and dark highway soften the immediate memory of chilled fingers and rain-soaked clothes. By the time I'm halfway home, I've likely begun to second-guess myself. Should I have wandered north for a day on the Sol Duc? Did I make the right decision in sticking with the Upper Hoh despite the rising water? With so many choices available, I suppose such musings are a natural outcome of the "post-peninsula" depression, if you will.

Yet my dabblings have earned me some fine fish on the Sol Duc, Bogachiel, and Hoh. I've put in enough time to deserve a few hook-ups. Perhaps I will never know these waters intimately, but from time to time they nonetheless reward my fumblings. Each visit I face a dilemma: fish the places I know best or strike out and explore something new. Some years ago I decided on a system. Each trip to the peninsula I would explore, fish, and learn at least one new pool or section of river. I've stuck with that plan.

Each of these rivers has its own peculiarities, its own personality. The Sol Duc rises slowly and clears quickly. During winter her boulder-strewn runs and brush-clad banks make her a river best done by boat. But the Sol Duc is no water for inexperienced boaters. In fact, no one should row this river without first drifting with an experienced Sol Duc oarsman. The Bogy draws big crowds when the winter fish are in, yet fly fishers willing to walk her soggy trail find their reward in the form of artistically designed steelhead pools devoid of other interlopers. The Calawah, the third river of the Quillayute system demands precise timing to intercept (in the main fork) those native winter steelhead bound for the two forks, both of which are closed to fishing during the winter and spring.

The Hoh, meanwhile, boasts an entirely different scenario. This emboldened river draws her headwaters from the glaciers of the Olympic peaks. The river bears the signature of her sources in the form of gray-green water. During cold, dry weather, the water drops and clears; ensuing rains stir up the glacial silt and raise the river into an off-color leviathan. During summer, the glaciers dump their gray till into the river until freezing weather reclaims the high country. Those with precise timing can find autumn mornings when the Hoh runs not only low, but also comparatively clear.

Despite the Hoh's appearance, it is probably the most fly-rod friendly of all these waters in terms of accessibility, wadability, and floatability. Her cobblestone runs are easily negotiated by foot and easily covered with single-hand or double-hand rods. You can drive along the river east of Highway 101 and find several well-defined steelhead pools adjacent to the road. The river's only downfall is its color, yet her fish seem unaffected in their willingness to take a fly. Certainly the river fishes best when the water clears to some extent, but even when cloudy, anglers can draw summer-run fish to classic wet flies fished on floating lines.

The Quillayute system rivers demand more intimate knowledge. The Sol Duc in particular requires some "figuring out." It fishes best for those who drift and fish the best water. Without a boat, anglers must simply drive from place to place and fish productive pools. Access is earned through exploration. The same holds true on the Bogachiel, except that the easily accessible trail on the north bank offers access to several miles of good water.

All of these rivers offer a similar steelhead pattern. Hatchery fish arrive first, usually pushing into the rivers beginning in December. They dominate the runs through February. By late February and on through early April, native winter steelhead arrive, many of them ranging from 10 to 14 pounds and a few pushing or exceeding 20 pounds.

Casting over gin-clear water on the Sol Duc in July.

Sol Duc and Bogachiel Rivers

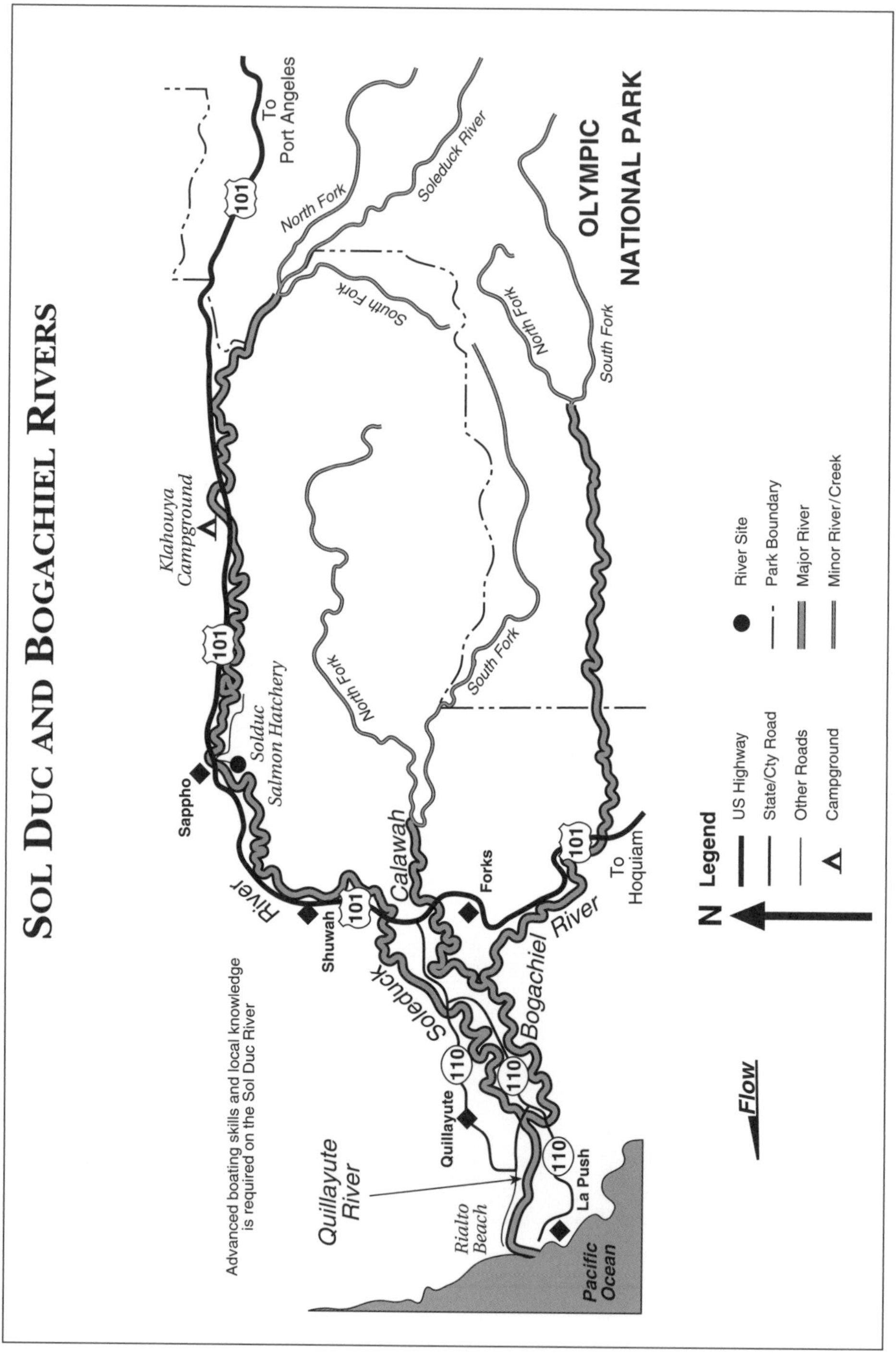

OLYMPIC
NATIONAL PARK

Klahowya Campground

Soleduc Salmon Hatchery

Sappho

Shuwah

Forks

Quillayute

La Push

Rialto Beach

Pacific Ocean

Quillayute River

Soleduck River

Bogachiel River

Calawah

North Fork

South Fork

Soleduck River

North Fork

South Fork

To Port Angeles

To Hoquiam

Advanced boating skills and local knowledge is required on the Sol Duc River

Flow

N Legend

	US Highway
	State/Cty Road
	Other Roads
△	Campground

●	River Site
-·-	Park Boundary
	Major River
	Minor River/Creek

© Wilderness Adventures Press, Inc.

Fishing the Hoh, Sol Duc, and Bogachiel

During winter and spring, the steelhead rivers of the Olympic Peninsula demand one of two approaches, and sometimes both. Match your tackle and tactics to your water or seek water to match your favorite methods. I'm a dedicated swinger, so to speak. I pursue steelhead with classic flies, fished down and across. Hence, I seek water suited to my methods. Such water abounds on all these rivers and is the rule on the Hoh. Conversely, the Sol Duc offers abundant steelhead water of every description. One pool might boast a bottom of fine cobble while just around the bend lies a boulder-studded run suited only to floating lines and weighted flies.

Many anglers have adopted the two-handed Spey-casting rods for these waters. The long rods allow for better line control in many situations. Moreover, the Sol Duc and to a lesser degree the Bogy feature many pools where anglers must cast with their backs against a screen of alders and cottonwoods. Here the Spey-caster enjoys a decided advantage. In contrast, the Hoh offers ample backcast room and affords me the luxury of fishing the head systems I have long employed for winter steelhead. I fish these lines on single-handed rods and have for many years espoused the art of line control and fly control through angle of presentation. The Hoh offers a perfect proving ground for such methods.

As for flies, you would be hard-pressed to find something that wouldn't work. Fly fishers employ everything from artistically dressed Spey-style flies to lures more akin to jigs. Classic hair-wing flies enjoy a substantial presence, as do marabou flies. Personally, I prefer to pay homage to the late Syd Glasso by fishing flies dressed in the style he perfected and popularized during his days living at Forks and fishing these great rivers. My favorite is Glasso's Orange Heron and like many Northwest steelhead anglers, I subject this fly to numerous variations.

The particulars of fishing winter steelhead are well covered in the exhaustive body of fly fishing literature. I will only add that flexibility pays dividends on the peninsula rivers. Figure out the relative rates of rising water and falling water of each river and adjust your plans accordingly.

Moreover, hire a guide for your peninsula trip if you really want to learn something. Specifically, get hold of J.D. Love or Gordon Gracey. If those two are booked, call Waters West Fly Shop in Port Angeles. For anglers visiting from outside the region, this latter tactic is a virtual necessity. You could spend your entire trip just trying to figure out where and when to fish. The peninsula's best guides have long since done that homework for you.

Restaurants and Accommodations

In addition to the numerous area campgrounds (some of which are closed during winter), the tiny community of Forks offers a dozen or so motels and nearly as many bed & breakfast establishments. Among the latter is the highly regarded Brightwater House, which boasts 3,500 feet of frontage on the Sol Duc (360-374-5453). Sol Duc River Lodge B&B (360-327-3709) and Three Rivers Resort (360-374-5300) both offer first-class accommodations along with in-house guide service. North of Forks, the little riverside community of Beaver features Hungry Bear Motel, Café & RV Park, situated on the Sol Duc (360-327-3660). Also located in Beaver are the more upscale Sol Duc Guest House (360-327-3373) and Eagle Point Inn (360-327-3236).

If you are interested in nice accommodations on the Hoh River, check out Hoh Humm Ranch B&B (360-374-5337). Likewise, Hoh River Resort (360-374-5566) offers RV spaces, campsites and some basic sportsmen's cabins. Additional lodging options are listed below and a complete detailed brochure of area accommodations is available from the Forks Chamber of Commerce at 360-374-2531.

Forks offers myriad dining options. The food ranges from decent to good, especially considering the relatively remote location of this tiny old logging town. On the highway just north of town is the ever-popular Smokehouse Restaurant, an enjoyable stop for a hearty dinner, which generally includes fresh seafood choices. Expect a crowd during the summer and on any given weekend during the winter steelhead season. At those times, reservations will save you a long wait (360-374-6258).

The main drag through town is lined with the remaining dining establishments. I've tried about half of them, including Plaza Jalisco, which offers good Mexican fare and Pacific Pizza, whose delivery service comes in handy when you're too lazy or too tired to leave the motel room (360-374-6258). Vagabond Café and Raindrop Café both make good breakfast stops and the former offers a nightly selection of guilt-inspiring desserts. I've yet to stop at Sully's Drive-In, but the burgers must be as good as they claim based on the usual crowd that assembles at the place.

Speaking of burgers, the Hard Rain Café serves up a great one, and they just happen to be located mere minutes from the Hoh River. Drive east on the Hoh River Road and you will pass Hard Rain on your right. In addition to burgers, Hard Rain offers a well-stocked little mercantile, RV hook-ups, camping sites, and hot showers (360-374-9288). Fishing advice is free.

Forks Area Lodging

Bagby's Motel, 1080 S.Forks Ave., 360-374-6231

Dew Drop Inn, 100 Fernhill Rd., 360-374-4055

Far West Motel, 251 N. Forks Ave, 360-374-5506

Forks Motel, 351 S.Forks Ave, 360-374-6243

Mill Creek Inn, 1061 S. Forks Ave., 360-374-5873

Pacific Inn Motel, 352 S. Forks Ave., 360-374-9400

Bear Creek Homestead B&B, 2094 Bear Creek Road, 360-374-6231,
www.bearcreekhomestead.com

Fisherman's Widow B&B, 31 Huckleberry Lane, 360-374-5693,
www.northolympics.com/fw

Huckleberry Lodge B&B, 1171 Big Pine Way, 360-374-6008,
www.huckleberrylodge.com

Miller Tree Inn B&B, 654 E. Division St., 360-374-6808,
www.millertreeinn.com

Misty Valley Inn B&B, 194894 Hwy. 101, 360-374-9389,
www.mistyvalleyinn.com

River Inn B&B, 2596 Bogachiel Way, 360-374-6526

Shadynook Cottage B&B, 81 Ash St., 360-374-5497,
www.shadynookcottage.com

Nearby Attractions and Activities

Winter and early spring is no time to drag the non-angler along to the peninsula, although the nearby Pacific coastline offers dramatic scenery any time of year and spring (and autumn) brings a flood of migratory fowl. During the summer and fall, however, the Olympic Peninsula offers many alternatives for those not content to spend the day casting flies across beautiful rivers.

The Clallam Bay/Seiku area, on the strait north of Forks, features the Makah Cultural Museum along with some of the area's best diving, kayaking, and birding. Farther west lies the tiny town of Neah Bay, home to the Makah Cultural & Research Center. Included therein is the country's most extensive collection of pre-contact artifacts from the Northwest coastal tribes. Nearby Cape Flattery ranks among the region's top bird-watching areas during the spring and fall migrations, and Neah Bay is an excellent place to book a saltwater charter-fishing excursion. Even if the salmon aren't in season, these waters teem with rockfish, lingcod, cabezon, halibut, and other bottomfish. Several charters operate out of this quaint little Makah village: Raven Charters (360-645-2121), Big Salmon Resort Charters (360-645-2374), and Farwest Resort (360-645-2270).

Lake Ozette, located northwest of Forks, offers the well-maintained Lake Ozette Trail Loop, a nine-mile system that reaches the beach at Sand Point and then travels up the beach to the 300-year-old petroglyphs at Wedding Rocks. North of here, the trail arrives at Cape Alava, near the sight of an ancient Makah village that was buried by a mudslide some 500 years ago. The village site is closed to the public, but the Macah Museum in Neah Bay houses and displays artifacts recovered during the excavation in the 1970s.

The Hoh Rain Forest is worth a visit, especially during the summer or fall when you rarely need worry about experiencing some of those 200-odd inches of annual rainfall. Upper Hoh Road ends at the visitor's center. Several short, well-maintained trails lead you on tours of the surrounding forest. Much of this region, of course, is included in the 922,000-acre Olympic National Park. Visit the park headquarters at Port Angeles for information and tips about activities and sights in the park.

Author's Tip

Even though these waters are revered for their winter steelhead, my favorite time on the peninsula begins when the first autumn freshets raise the river just an inch or two. Such rainfall often occurs first during late September and seems to awaken the rivers, bringing in unheralded waves of searun cutthroat and enlivening the summer steelhead already in the Quillayute and Hoh systems.

Favorite Fly

Orange Heron (Syd Glasso)

HOOK	Long-shank salmon iron, No. 4/0-2
TAG	Flat silver tinsel (optional)
BODY	2/3 orange silk and 1/3 hot orange dubbing
RIB	Flat silver tinsel with small silver oval as a counter-rib binding down the hackle stem
HACKLE	Blue eared pheasant rump hackle, palmered along the rib
THROAT	Teal flank
WING	4 matched, hot-orange hackle tips

Orange Heron

Fast Facts

Hoh, Sol Duc and Bogachiel Rivers

LOCATION	Pacific side of the Olympic Peninsula in Washington
WATER TYPE	Free-flowing rivers; the Hoh is glacial-fed
PRIMARY GAMEFISH	Winter and summer steelhead; also salmon and searun cutthroat
BEST TIME	February-March and September-October
BEST FLIES	A wide range of patterns will take steelhead and cutthroat
EQUIPMENT	For steelhead: 7- to 9-weight rod (Two-handed Spey-casting rods are increasingly popular); floating line for summer; sinking heads or tips for winter fishing.
CONDITIONS	The Olympic Peninsula enjoys spectacular summer and fall weather to balance with the extremely wet winters and springs.
DRIVE TIME	From Seattle: 3 hours From Portland: 6-7 hours
DIRECTIONS	Study the ferry routes from the metro area and choose a route that puts you in Port Angeles. From Port Angeles, head west on Highway 101. Several miles west of scenic Lake Crescent, the highway crosses the Sol Duc and then follows the river on its westerly journey. Just north of Forks, the highway crosses the Calawah. South of town, 101 provides fleeting glimpses of the Bogachiel, finally crossing the river at Bogachiel State Park. To find the Bogy trail, turn left off the highway (before you cross the river) on Undie Road and head a few miles upriver to the parking area. To find the Hoh River, continue south on Hwy. 101 another six or seven miles to a well-marked left turn to the Hoh Rain Forest (Upper Hoh Road). Three miles in, the road swings close to the river and eventually leads up to the Hoh Rain Forest Visitor's Center

Local Fly Shops

WATERS WEST
219 North Oak Street
Port Angeles, WA 98362
360-452-6521

OLYMPIC SPORTING GOODS
190 North Forks Ave.
Forks, WA 98331
360-374-6330

QUALITY FLY SHOP
2720 E. Highway 101
Port Angeles, WA 98363
360-452-5942

THE PORT TOWNSEND ANGLER
940 Water Street
Port Townsend, WA 98368
360-379-3763

Area Fly Shops

NORTHWEST ANGLER FLY SHOP
18830 Front Street
Poulsbo, WA 98370
360-697-7100

PATRICK'S FLY SHOP
2237 Eastlake Avenue East
Seattle, WA 98102
206-325-8988

HAWK'S POULSBO SPORTS CENTER
19424-C 7th Avenue NE
Poulsbo, WA 98370
360-779-5290

SALMON BAY TACKLE
5701 15th Avenue NW
Seattle, WA 98107
206-789-9335

KITSAP SPORTS
10526 Silverdale Way NW
Silverdale, WA 98383
360-698-4808

WARSHAL'S SPORTING GOODS
1000 1st Avenue
Seattle, WA 98104
206-624-6550

FLY SMITH
1515 5th Avenue
Marysville, WA 98270
360-658-9003

ORVIS SEATTLE
911 Bellevue Way NE
Bellevue, WA 98004
425-452-9138

GREYWOLF ANGLER
275953 Highway 101
Gardiner, WA 98368
360-797-7177

REI-SEATTLE
222 Yale Ave. N
Seattle, WA 98109
206-223-1944

KAUFMANN'S STREAMBORN
1918 4th Avenue
Seattle, WA 98101
206-448-0601

REI-PORTLAND
1798 Jantzen Beach Ctr.
Portland, OR 97217
503-283-1300

Area Fly Shops, continued

AVID ANGLER FLY SHOP
17171 Bothell Way NE, Ste. A130
Lake Forest Park, WA 98155
206-362-4030

FLY FISHER
5622 Pacific Ave. SE #9
Lacey, WA 98503
360-491-0181

MORNING HATCH FLY SHOP
3640 South Cedar, Ste. L
Tacoma, WA 98409
253-472-1070

STREAMSIDE ANGLERS
4800 Capital Blvd. SE
Tumwater, WA 98501
360-709-3337

Guides

J.D. LOVE
360-327-3772

GORDY GRACEY
360-374-4188/374-6300

Contacts

WASHINGTON DEPARTMENT
OF FISH & WILDLIFE
Coastal Washington - Region 6 Office
48 Devonshire Road
Montesano, WA 98563
360-249-4628

FORK CHAMBER OF COMMERCE
360-374-2531

CHAPTER 6

THE ELWHA RIVER

Backcountry Trout Close to Home

Heading north on Highway 101, I relished the summer breeze rippling Hood Canal. Never before had I ventured to the Olympic Peninsula during mid-summer. My previous visits had been timed to intercept the native winter steelhead that ascend the peninsula's famed rivers, the Sol Duc, Hoh, and Bogachiel. Late winter attracts hordes of anglers to the peninsula; the town of Forks makes a living off them.

So I braced to encounter the typical too-damn-close-to-Seattle crowds on my inaugural trout fishing adventure to the upper Elwha River. Jennifer and I arrived in Port Angeles late that day and our first discovery was a dinner house called Michael's, located downtown on First Street. We snuck in the back door and weaved our way through gracefully set tables and into a deeper, darker, and busier enclave where the host greeted us. After a day-long drive, the extravagant and varied menu

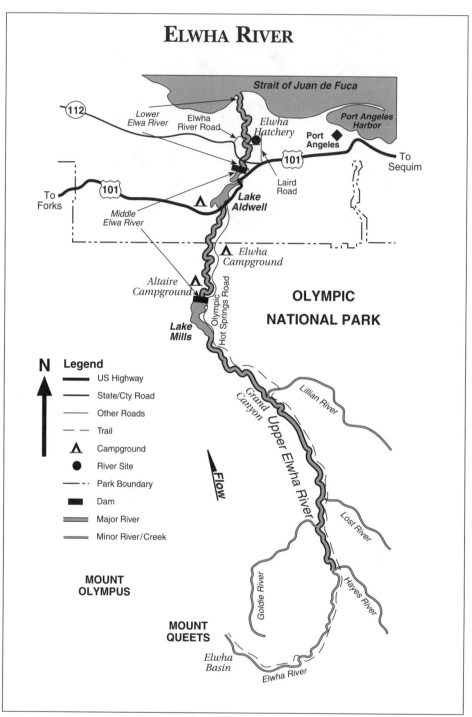

ELWHA RIVER

Strait of Juan de Fuca

112

Lower
Elwa River

Elwha
River Road

Elwha
Hatchery

Port Angeles
Harbor

Port
Angeles

101

To
Sequim

Laird
Road

To
Forks

101

Middle
Elwa River

Lake
Aldwell

Elwha
Campground

Altaire
Campground

Lake
Mills

Olympic
Hot Springs Road

OLYMPIC

NATIONAL PARK

Lillian River

Grand Canyon Upper Elwha River

Flow

Lost River

N

Legend

	US Highway
	State/Cty Road
	Other Roads
	Trail
⛺	Campground
●	River Site
	Park Boundary
▬	Dam
	Major River
	Minor River/Creek

MOUNT
OLYMPUS

Goldie River

Hayes River

MOUNT
QUEETS

Elwha
Basin

Elwha River

© Wilderness Adventures Press, Inc.

demanded a careful perusal, especially for a fly fishing bum whose taste in fine food far exceeds his budget.

Self-made, work-your-way-up Michael Lynch, the owner and our waiter that evening, walked us through an impressive selection of Northwest wines, of which we chose an Adelsheim Pinot Noir. Our entrées would have been perfectly at home in a trendy restaurant in downtown Seattle. I waded through a superb pastina pescatore served with fresh prawns and calamari. Still, I longingly hoped Jennifer's appetite would prove no match for a generous Caldeirada seafood stew with saffron rice and Spanish cazuela. Indeed, despite her best efforts, I enjoyed the remnants of her entrée as well. Food, wine, and service were first class and soon we sipped coffee and studied the maps, assembling our battle plan for the forthcoming hike into the Elwha watershed.

We planned to make quick work of the first few trail miles, then descend to the pack bridge at the bottom of the Elwha's "Grand Canyon." After that, we would return to the trail and head for the Elkhorn area far upstream. We expected plenty of company. After all, the hotels were crowded with summer tourists and weekenders from Seattle and its surrounds. What we found was a river entirely devoid of fellow anglers. The fishing was good. Not great, but good, and we took several nice rainbows, a few cutthroat and two bull trout.

A beautiful little bull trout from the Elwha River.

In some pools, we spotted fish from above and then tried tempting them with a dry fly. Most would move to the fly once, but failing a solid hook-up on the first try, they seemed disinclined to rise again. Before our little adventure came to an end, we had taken fish on dry flies, on nymphs, on soft hackles, and on streamers. I remember thinking that this was a river for anglers of every persuasion, but only for individuals willing to lace up the hiking boots and cover a lot of trail miles. We hiked the last few miles of trail well after dark.

I kept track of the birds we encountered along the journey. We stumbled into a brood of young Williamson's sapsuckers and all three of the junior birds seemed overtly curious, so much so that they scrambled about on tree trunks just a few feet above our heads while their parents called from the safety of a higher perch. The woodpecker list alone, by day's end, boasted pileated, hairy and downy woodpeckers along with red-naped sapsuckers and flickers. Olive-sided flycatchers, usually somewhat secretive, made a surprise appearance on an alder limb above the trail and an excited chirping led us to a baby western tanager that had apparently fallen from the nest. Unable to render any aid, we elected to leave the parents to the task of tending their nestling. Both parents, brilliantly bejeweled in orange, yellow, black and white, flitted about nervously in the overhead canopy.

The next day we sampled the Middle Elwha, where roadside access makes for an easy excursion for modest-sized rainbows that seem eager if not abundant. We caught some handsomely marked natives, but we longed for the wilder confines of the upper Elwha. Alas, aching knees and worn-out muscles reminded us that our longings would remain just that, for the previous day's 20-some-mile hiking and fishing marathon had taken its toll. The price of admission had been amply justified by the scenic and lonely confines of the upper Elwha, and as any Seattle-area angler can attest, the combination of good fishing and solitude is an increasingly rare treat in western Washington.

Fishing the Upper Elwha

The Upper Elwha is a hiker's refuge. The good fishing begins at the end of the so-called Grand Canyon and extends deep into the heart of the drainage well back in the mountains. The lower end of the Grand Canyon is but an hour's walk or so. A pack bridge spans the mouth of the canyon, marking the beginning of the best water. Now here's the catch: For several miles thereafter, the river is virtually inaccessible. You'll need a modest death wish and a mountain goat's fortitude to fish the Grand Canyon reach. It can be done in places, but study your topo map carefully and use all care. This is steep country, with sheer rock cliffs leading down to the water.

Because the canyon reach is so inaccessible, the most viable option is to stay up on the main trail rather than descend to the river at the pack bridge. The main trail, high above the Elwha, continues on a southerly course deeper into the national park, skirting wide of the canyon. Eventually, the trail leads back to the river and when you reach Elkhorn (the trail is signed all along its length), you have reached the beginning of the best water. Obviously, the distances involved (about 12 miles to Elkhorn) dictate that a multiple-day trip is the best way to fish the upper Elwha.

The Elwha is fine dry-fly water and hosts seasonal emergences of Golden Stoneflies, caddisflies, Pale Morning Duns, Blue-Winged Olives and even a few Green Drakes. The stoneflies and the drakes hatch by June, at which time the river still runs fairly high with snowmelt. Thus they are less significant to anglers than are the hatches of late summer and fall, when the upper Elwha is at its best. Caddis hatches occur daily and a few Little Yellow Stoneflies appear during August.

Rarely does the fishing get too technical on the upper Elwha. A selection of basic dry flies in a wide range of sizes will cover all the bases. Nymphs, soft hackles, and streamers are equally effective. Summer weather is generally dry and mild. However, this is western Washington, so rain can occur at any time. The water is superbly cold, but nonetheless inviting to wet-wading during August and September. But beware the slippery rocks. I'd suggest a pair of cleated and felted wading sandals or boots.

Most of the Elwha's natives range from 8 to 12 inches, but a few reach 20 inches. All are beautifully marked.

Restaurants and Accommodations

The aforementioned Michael's Divine Dining (360-417-6929) sits on the north side of the street at 117B E. First Street in Port Angeles. Another top-notch restaurant is 8th Street Bistro (360-457-9581). Located well out on the west end of 8th Street, this little lunch and dinner house might just be the town's best-kept secret. Everything about the bistro is unassuming with the exception of the sensational dinners, which include selections of local fresh seafood. If you're looking for a fast, friendly, and tasty lunch stop, try Bonnie's Bakery (360-457-3585) on the east side of Lincoln Street as you head out towards the west side of town. Two blocks farther south, and on the opposite side of Lincoln Street, sits Hacienda Del Mar, the town's best Mexican restaurant (360-452-5296). The Port Angeles Brewing Company (360-417-9152) serves up a superb dinner and beefy beer at 134 W. Front Street.

Olympic National Park offers two campgrounds along the Elwha River Road. Both can accommodate camp-trailers up to 21 feet in length. The national park office is located at 600 East Park Avenue in Port Angeles (360-452-0330). Shadow Mountain Campground, situated a mile east of Lake Crescent west of Port Angeles, is conveniently located for anglers visiting during the summer to fish both the Elwha and the Sol Duc. Shadow Mountain features both RV sites and tent sites (360-928-3043). Port Angeles boasts numerous upscale B&Bs, including Tudor Inn (360-452-3138), B.J.'s Garden Gate (360-452-2322) and Elwha Ranch B&B (360-457-6540).

Port Angeles Lodging

Aircrest Motel, 1006 E. Front, 360-452-9255
All-View Motel, 214 E. Lauridsen, 360-457-7779
Chinook Motel, 1414 E. First St., 360-452-2336
Fairmount Motel, 1137 Hwy. 101, 360-457-6113
Flagstone Motel, 415 E. First St., 360-457-9494
The Pond Motel, 1425 W. Hwy. 101, 360-452-8422
Port Angeles Inn, 111 E. Second St., 360-452-9285
Port Side Inn, 1510 E. Front St., 360-452-4015
Red Lion Hotel, 221 N. Lincoln, 360-452-9215
Royal Victorian Motel, 521 E. First St., 360-452-2316
Ruffles Motel, 812 E. First St., 360-457-7788
Sportsmen Motel, 2909 E. Hwy. 101, 360-457-6196
Super-8 Motel, 2104 E. First St., 360-452-8401
Traveler's Motel, 1133 E. First St., 360-452-2303
Uptown Inn, 101 E. Second St., 360-457-9434

Nearby Fisheries

Middle and Lower Elwha

The Middle Elwha offers fair fishing for rainbows up to 16 inches, though most seem to average about 9-10 inches. Mid-summer through early autumn is the best time and access is good along Elwha River Road. Below Lake Aldwel, the Lower Elwha attracts seasonal runs of salmon and steelhead. The winter steelhead runs peak between January and early March. A few summer steelhead arrive between June and September. These summer fish, less publicized than their winter brethren, comprise a modest little fishery for those who enjoy fishing skated dry flies between mid-summer and mid-autumn. Each autumn, the lower Elwha also welcomes a small but fishable run of searun cutthroat.

Nearby Attractions and Activities

A visit to the Port Angeles area would hardly be complete without taking in the spectacular view from Hurricane Ridge, just south of town. A 17-mile paved route leaves town and winds its way up to the top of the mile-high ridge, which commands a 360-degree vista of the surrounded country.

Wine enthusiasts can find just enough wineries in the area to fill up a day of touring. Four established wineries are spread out around Sequim and Port Angeles. The easiest to visit is Olympic Cellars, whose tasting room is situated in a big barn alongside Highway 101 nine miles west of Sequim. If you're heading west from the metro area, start your tour at Lost Mountain Winery at 3174 Lost Mountain Road in Sequim (360-683-5229). Then head for Olympic Cellars. While there, ask for directions to Black Diamond Winery. Those three wineries have regular visitor's hours. The fourth, Camaraderie Cellars, asks that you call ahead to schedule a visit (360-417-3564).

Author's Tip

The Upper Elwha generally serves up its trout without too many technicalities. However, should the fish prove slow to respond to the normal tactics, try swinging flies in the manner of steelhead flies. To do this, rig up with a black, No. 6 or 8 beadhead or conehead Woolly Bugger and attach a small soft hackle or a standard nymph pattern, such as a Pheasant Tail or Hare's Ear, two feet below. Beginning at the upstream end of the pools and runs, cast up and across to get enough dead-drift to sink the flies, as the current picks up the line, allow the flies to drag back to your side of the flow. In deep water, feed a little line during the swing to help the flies maintain depth. At the end of (or even during) the swing, strip line in short, quick bursts. Then just hold on.

Favorite Fly
Olive Parachute

HOOK	Dry-fly, No. 12-14
TAIL	Grizzly or dun hackle fibers
BODY	Olive dubbing
WING	Closed-cell foam or Poly yarn as a post
HACKLE	Grizzly or dun, tied parachute-style

Olive Parachute

Fast Facts
Upper Elwha River

LOCATION	Olympic Peninsula, near Port Angeles
WATER TYPE	Swift freestone river
PRIMARY GAMEFISH	Wild rainbow trout, cutthroat trout, and bull trout
BEST TIME	July through September
BEST FLIES	Attractor dry flies (Royal Wulff, Stimulator, Elk Hair Caddis, Madam-X), stonefly nymphs, Hare's Ear Nymph, Pheasant Tail Nymph, conehead Woolly Buggers.
EQUIPMENT	4, 5, or 6-weight rod and floating line.
CONDITIONS	Excellent, well-maintained trail system leads into the Elwha backcountry. Generally ideal summer weather, although storms can gather during the afternoons.
DRIVE TIME	From Seattle: 3 hours to the trailhead From Portland: 5-6 hours to the trailhead
DIRECTIONS	From Olympia, follow Highway 101 north to Port Angeles. From the Seattle area, take the Edmonds Kingston Ferry to SR 104. Cross the Hood Canal Bridge and continue on SR 104 to Highway 101, leading west to Port Angeles. Follow 101 through Port Angeles about five miles to a left turn on Elwha River Road, which leads to the National Park entrance ($10). A signed gravel road leads up to the Elwha trailhead.

Local Fly Shops

WATERS WEST
219 North Oak Street
Port Angeles, WA 98362
360-452-6521

QUALITY FLY SHOP
2720 E. Highway 101
Port Angeles, WA 98363
360-452-5942

OLYMPIC SPORTING GOODS
190 North Forks Ave.
Forks, WA 98331
360-374-6330

NORTHWEST ANGLER FLY SHOP
18830 Front Street
Poulsbo, WA 98370
360-697-7100

HAWK'S POULSBO SPORTS CENTER
19424-C 7th Avenue NE
Poulsbo, WA 98370
360-779-5290

KITSAP SPORTS
10526 Silverdale Way NW
Silverdale, WA 98383
360-698-4808

FLY SMITH
1515 5th Avenue
Marysville, WA 98270
360-658-9003

GREYWOLF ANGLER
275953 Hwy. 101
Gardiner, WA 98368
360-797-7177

PORT TOWNSEND ANGLER
695 Schwartz Road
Nordland, WA 98368
800-435-4410

KAUFMANN'S STREAMBORN
1918 4th Avenue
Seattle, WA 98101
206-448-0601

PATRICK'S FLY SHOP
2237 Eastlake Avenue East
Seattle, WA 98102
206-325-8988

SALMON BAY TACKLE
5701 15th Avenue NW
Seattle, WA 98107
206-789-9335

WARSHAL'S SPORTING GOODS
1000 1st Avenue
Seattle, WA 98104
206-624-6550

ORVIS SEATTLE
911 Bellevue Way NE
Bellevue, WA 98004
425-452-9138

AVID ANGLER FLY SHOP
17171 Bothell Way NE, Ste. A130
Lake Forest Park, WA 98155
206-362-4030

REI
222 Yale Ave. N
Seattle, WA 98109
206-223-1944

Contacts

WASHINGTON DEPARTMENT
OF FISH & WILDLIFE
Coastal Washington - Region 6 Office
48 Devonshire Road
Montesano, WA 98563
360-249-4628

OLYMPIC NATIONAL PARK
360-452-0330

PORT ANGELES
CHAMBER OF
COMMERCE
360-452-2363

OLYMPIC NATIONAL FOREST
360-956-2300

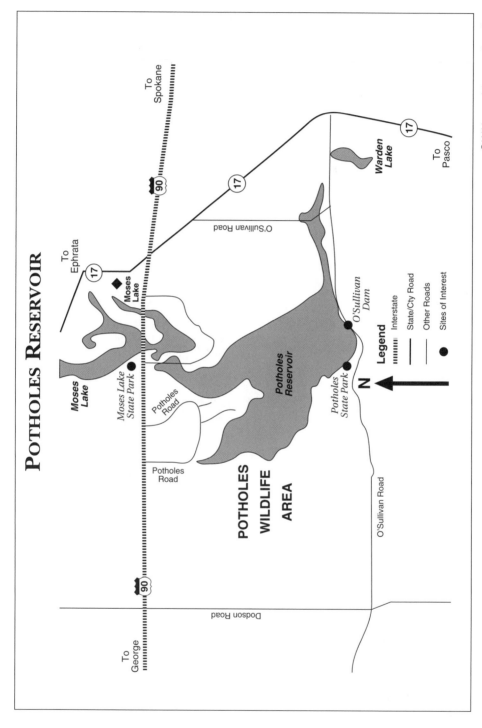

POTHOLES RESERVOIR

POTHOLES RESERVOIR AND THE SEEP LAKES

Mixed-Bag Fishing in Eastern Washington

Interstate 90 plows a rapid course through the Cascades, abandoning the metropolitan sprawl of Seattle and delivering fly anglers to the vast expanses and trout-rich lakes of eastern Washington. Lenice, Nunnally, Lenore, Dry Falls, Chopaka: You know the names; you probably know the waters. Visit these destination fisheries often and you also know the hordes of anglers that assemble on them, especially during the spring. Traffic signals for float tubes seem a reasonable idea during any given May weekend on Dry Falls or Chopaka, but you tolerate the crowds because the trout run large and the arid surroundings loom vast and unimpeded by the trappings of man.

Some years ago I sat afloat on Dry Falls, admiring the immensity of the place and imagining the ancient torrents cascading into roaring waterfalls, now evident only from the massive basalt escarpments looming stark and dry above the lake. Soon a thoroughly modern torrent began, for this was a Friday morning in May. The dusty

A western rattler in the Seep Lakes area.

access road sprang suddenly to life as a seemingly endless river of vehicles flooded the lake's parking lot. I had enjoyed fine fishing for three days, but this was too much. For the first time in my life I had to await an opening at the tube launch site before I could disembark. Three fly fishing clubs had scheduled spring outings at Dry Falls— all on the same weekend.

I would find other waters. Visions of *Callibaetis* mayflies and big, splashy rainbows turned my thoughts to Quail Lake, a small walk-in lake in the so-called Seep Lakes chain south of Potholes Reservoir and immediately northwest of Othello. I would reacquaint myself with lovely little Quail Lake, for I had not finned its fertile waters for half a dozen years. Little did I know that Quail had entered a down-cycle and would soon be rehabilitated to remove unwanted sunfish and rough fish populations. No wonder I couldn't find a rising trout to save my life.

I gave up the chase after a time and pondered my options. I'd heard the stories about the myriad other lakes and ponds that comprise the Seep Lakes: some managed for warmwater species, others planted with trout. Until that day, all my ventures into the Seep Lakes had been specifically to fish Quail Lake, which had long been managed for catch-and-release fly angling. So I explored other waters, and by trip's end I'd had decent fishing for trout, crappie, sunfish, and bass in half a dozen lakes, all new to me and all unique in their particular characteristics.

Quail Lake eventually recovered. I visited her again on two or three occasions. Then one day I took a call from magazine editor Steve Probasco.

"John, I need a Washington trout piece and I'm thinking about doing the Seep Lakes—you want the assignment?"

That was a no-brainer. Both Steve and I knew what we were getting into with this one because Quail Lake, the only special-regulations fishery in the bunch, was once again on a down-cycle. That left the prospects of reporting on a bunch of general-regulations lakes whose fast-growing stocked trout often end their days dangling from a stringer. Yet we also knew the Seep Lakes made for good copy because they simply don't attract the crowds that so often assemble on Washington's famed stillwater fly fishing destinations.

Moreover, with several dozen lakes available, the seeps below Potholes Reservoir comprise the perfect environment for adventurous, exploration-minded anglers who don't need their fishing holes served on a platter. Any given year the many Seep Lakes will boast a few waters harboring trophy-size rainbows. At the same time, many of the lakes offer first-rate action for bass, crappie and sunfish. Potholes Reservoir itself ranks among the region's best destinations for largemouth bass and smallmouth bass, with enough walleye and fat rainbows about to keep things interesting.

Then the other shoe dropped.

"Tell me when you want to do the photography, John, and I'll meet you over there," suggested Steve. Add up all the fly fishing waters in the Northwest and Probasco and Shewey, fishing bums till the bitter end, have collectively fished about all there is to fish. Yet so far we'd managed to avoid each other for a couple decades. One fly fishing writer is bad enough, but gather two of them in the same place and you might as well just walk under a ladder behind a couple black cats on Friday the 13th.

Our appointed May weekend arrived and I scouted a couple locations, hoping to find a few holdover rainbows, which grow fat in the food-rich Seep Lakes. My first stop was Mar-Don Resort, whose owners keep an up-to-the-minute account of what's happening. They suggested I have a look at the Blythe-Chukar Lake Chain, just minutes from the resort. I'd never fished this chain of lakes, whose four members are connected by a thread of water filling a small channel between each of the lakes.

I soon met Steve and Dan Eerkes at the resort and we hurried over to Blythe Lake, whose green depths revealed prolific concentrations of *Chironomids*, *Callibaetis* mayflies, scuds, snails and damsels. Armed with all manner of heady equipment and bearing the confidence born of countless hours spent doing this very thing all over the West, we launched our little flotilla and shifted into fish-finding mode (translation: trolling).

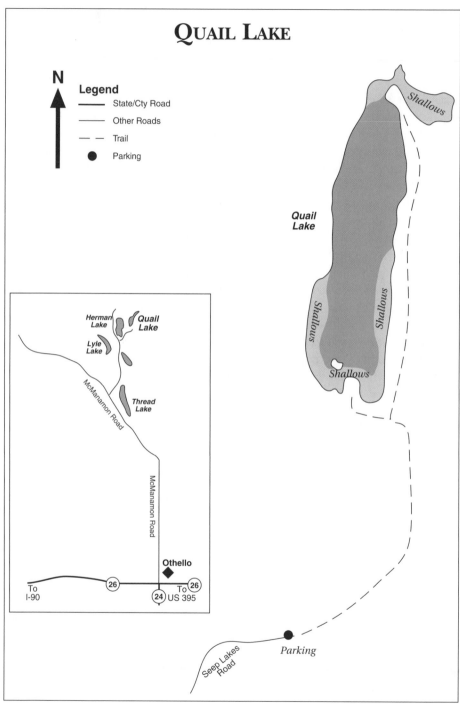

QUAIL LAKE

N

Legend
— State/Cty Road
— Other Roads
– – Trail
● Parking

Shallows

Quail
Lake

Shallows

Shallows

Shallows

Herman
Lake

Quail
Lake

Lyle
Lake

McManamon Road

Thread
Lake

McManamon Road

Othello

26

To
I-90

26

To
24 US 395

Parking

Seep Lakes
Road

© Wilderness Adventures Press, Inc.

Huge *Chironomids* hatched profusely while swarms of damsels danced over the shallows. Mayflies joined the party and soon drifted about all over the lake. A complete lack of rising trout could hardly dampen our enthusiasm because within minutes I had a solid yank. Then Dan nearly hooked up in the same area. I should have known that was just a tease, for we spent half an hour trolling up the narrow lake and never touched another fish. The deep end of the lake yielded to extensive shallows, lush with aquatic vegetation. Had we been here a couple weeks earlier, before the hot weather arrived, we might well have found feeding trout cruising the shallow-water weed beds.

Before I could ponder that thought at any length, I noticed a faint hissing sound emanating from my float tube. That's not the sound you want to hear a quarter-mile from the launch. Sure enough, the innertube had sprung a leak so I began a rather vigorous retreat.

Despite my imminent swamping, I did manage enough presence of mind to beg a couple of big leech patterns from Steve. If I was forced to head for shore I could at least fish my way there. As I approached the launch, I made a few crude calculations, trying to determine how fast I could either paddle a deflated and waterlogged tube back to the bank, or extricate myself from said tube and swim to the bank. Satisfied that I could rescue myself from 50 yards out, I began casting and retrieving Steve's big leech pattern, which he lovingly refers to as the Night Leech, but which I'd say resembles a miniature road-kill raven.

Stripping the fly slowly along the bottom in 15 feet of water, I soon met with a solid grab and was fast to the day's first fish. Road-kill raven or not, the Night Leech did the trick. The ensuing tussle soon yielded a porker of a rainbow, some 20 inches or so in length and more than that in girth. Now I was really wishing we had planned this outing for cooler weather. After all, if we could yank a lunker like that out of Blythe Lake under 85-degree midday sunshine, who knows what might happen on a cloudy, cool evening.

Such an evening proved elusive when an hour later we hauled our watercraft over the quarter-mile trail to Upper Hampton Lake, rumored to have produced some huge rainbows earlier in the month. An incessant wind whipped Upper Hampton into froth. Undaunted, Dan soon paddled completely out of sight on his adventure to the far corners of this 60-acre lake while Steve and I decided on a more conservative strategy of fishing close to the crude launch area. A deep channel seemed an ideal place to dredge leech patterns, but a classic desert sunset guilted us into working our cameras more than our fly rods. Dan bailed us out, though, for after exploring the extensive weedy shallows across the wide expanses of Upper Hampton, he hooked a 21-inch rainbow on his way back to shore.

The wind never died that night. In eastern Washington, you learn to live with the wind. We camped at Soda Lake, but not before Steve nearly bled himself out by slamming his head into an overhanging tin picnic-table shelter. That was a nice touch on Steve's part and uncommonly generous, for my sense of superstition about fly fishing writers gathering at the same fishery had manifested itself in a deep sense of foreboding. Something bad had to happen. Fortunately it didn't happen to me. Besides, I learned some new words from Steve that evening as blood trickled down his face. I guess that's why he's the editor—superior vocabulary.

Fishing the Seep Lakes

Recent additions to Washington's desert, the Seep Lakes sprang to life during the middle of the last century upon completion of Grand Coulee Dam. The Columbia Basin Project, designed and completed to make farmland out of desert throughout the region, caused dramatic changes in the water table. Rising water formed lakes in low-lying areas and desert canyons; then the subsequent damming and channeling of the seepages and springs created additional lakes and ponds.

The newly formed wetlands proved a magnet for wildlife. In conjunction with the irrigation project, the federal government created the Columbia National Wildlife Refuge to manage a 23,200-acre tract of the Seep Lakes. Washington Department of Fish & Wildlife manages additional acreage (Seep Lakes Wildlife Area).

The Seep Lakes lay hidden amid rolling grassy hills and rugged rimrocks. In some places, tremendous columns of basalt rise abruptly from water's edge while distant, sheer buttes maintain a lonely vigilance over the rugged scrublands. Sunset paints vibrant color across the rocky expanse. Wildlife abounds in this oasis, including more than 200 recorded bird species. Migrating waterfowl assemble in staggering numbers during the fall. Rattlesnakes abound as well, so hiking anglers must remain vigilant.

More than 50 fishable Seep Lakes contain a wide range of gamefish. Rainbow trout, stocked by WDFW, occupy most of the lakes and many lakes are managed specifically for these stocked rainbows. District biologist Jeff Korth plants most of the lakes with about 400 fingerlings per acre. The fish grow rapidly in these super-fertile waters.

Each new season unveils a new scenario at the Seep Lakes. Last year's hot trout waters might be relegated to second-tier prospects this season and so on. Many of the trout lakes must be rehabilitated periodically by WDFW after infestations of sunfish or other warmwater fish—infestations that result from illegal plantings. Korth wages the ongoing battle against undesirable species, but the fertility of these lakes allows for rapid recovery of the numerous fisheries. "I don't have a problem creating good fisheries out here," says Korth, "just give me some Rotenone."

The typical Seep Lakes stocking pattern works something like this: WDFW dumps fingerlings into a given lake. Cormorants enjoy a feeding frenzy, eating a third of the

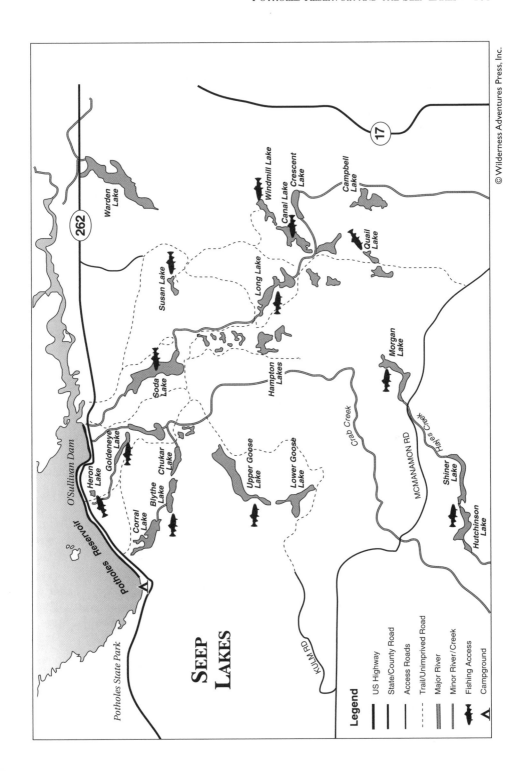

© Wilderness Adventures Press, Inc.

Legend

US Highway	
State/County Road	
Access Roads	
Trail/Unimprived Road	
Major River	
Minor River/Creek	
Fishing Access	
Campground	

fresh plants. As yearlings, the remaining rainbows span 13 to 14 inches and the catch-and-keep anglers take many. In most lakes, fair numbers of trout survive such perils and reappear as deep-bodied 18-inch carryovers the following season. Those that survive yet another year average five to six pounds, and although these are few in number, they occupy all of the good trout lakes in the Seeps.

The hike-in Seep Lakes generally offer the best fishing, especially for fly anglers looking for solitude and large fish. The quarter- to one-and-a-quarter-mile routes discourage all but the more adventurous souls. District Biologist Korth sees little need for additional special-regulations fisheries in the Seeps. Such regulations attract fly anglers in droves. Korth—along with many Seep Lakes regulars—prefers to maintain quality fishing at the hike-in lakes by virtue of human nature: most anglers simply don't want to hike.

Among these walk-in lakes are those in the Pillar-Widgeon Chain located within the federal refuge. The nine productive trout lakes in this group are open only during the months of March and September. Park at the trailhead adjacent to the south end of Soda Lake and walk south or head east from the parking area along the north end of Morgan Lake Road, southwest of Soda Lake. Other productive walk-in lakes include Janet Lake, located in a scenic canyon visible from nearby Katy Lake, along with the cluster of lakes between Windmill Lake and Warden Lake on the east edge of the state wildlife area. Seep Lakes Road runs north-south through the area and signs point the way to most of the drive-in waters.

Though often not always as productive as the walk-in waters, the road-accessible Seep Lakes nonetheless offer lots of variety. You can fish brown trout and rainbows at the south end of sprawling Warden Lake, boat the irregular shoreline of Canal Lake, spend an easy morning tubing scenic Susan Lake, or perhaps sneak into under-fished Heron or Goldeneye Lakes, both in plain sight of the road atop O'Sullivan Dam. Keep an open mind when you visit the Seep Lakes—if the first lake doesn't pan out, try another and another.

These super-fertile lakes teem with trout foods. *Chironomids* abound, including huge specimens requiring No. 10-12 pupa patterns. By mid-spring, profuse *Callibaetis* hatches occur daily; heavy damsel emergences begin during May. Equally abundant are scuds, snails, dragonflies, caddis, and leeches. Seep Lakes trout often feed selectively on *Callibaetis* and *Chironomids* during the spring, but attractor-type patterns account for most of the action day in and day out. Leech patterns and Woolly Buggers, along with Carey Specials and Zug Bugs suffice most of the time. Both spring and fall expect late-evening *Chironomid* rises.

When you arrive at a new lake, take a few moments to locate the transition zones between the shallows, shoal, or shoreline areas and the adjacent depths. In the absence of surface action, such transition zones make logical starting points. Cast and retrieve or troll such areas, experimenting with different depths. On Blythe Lake, both Dan and I hit fish in the same location by trolling parallel to the shore in about

15 feet of water. We later stopped there and fished leeches slowly along the bottom— a tactic that soon yielded a fat three-year-old rainbow.

You will certainly need watercraft when you fish these waters. On many lakes you can catch trout from shore, but overall a float tube or pontoon offers a distinct advantage. Rocky shorelines provide the best launch sites; beware the gooey mud on gently sloping dirt banks.

Carry a full complement of fly lines. An intermediate, such as the Scientific Anglers Stillwater Line, fishes perfectly over shallow weed beds, while a high-density full-sinking line allows you to fish deep. When trout key on *Chironomid* pupae or larvae, try the classic eastern Washington indicator rig consisting of a floating line, long leader, strike indicator and one to three flies. What the method lacks in excitement it often atones for in effectiveness. Personally I'd rather take a beating than bore myself to tears drifting about watching an indicator, so whenever possible I prefer to cast and retrieve.

In addition to trout, the Seep Lakes offer ample opportunity for warmwater species ranging from bass to crappie. Largemouth bass abound in certain waterways; smallmouth in others. In fact, Potholes Reservoir itself offers opportunity for both species. Try the rocky areas along the dam for smallies or explore the "dunes"

Signs pointing the way to two of the many seep lakes below Potholes Reservoir.

comprising the north end of the reservoir. Pumpkinseed sunfish abound in the Seep Lakes and are often the culprit when trout lakes require rehabilitation. Crappie, bluegill, yellow perch, and walleye occur in many lakes. In fact, a few of the lakes offer smorgasbord fishing. Fish a black Woolly Bugger and see how many species you can notch in Soda, Crescent, Goose, Hutchinson or Long Lake. Adventurous bass anglers might try exploring the unnamed ponds and sloughs along Crab Creek, Coyote Creek, Hays Creek and Shiner Lake, all located within the southwest corner of the federal refuge.

Restaurants and Accommodations

Mar-Don Resort, situated at the west end of Potholes Reservoir Dam, offers lodging, camping, a store, licenses, and advice. An air hose for float tubes is located on the west side of the blue shed across the road from the resort, alongside the access road to Corral and Blythe Lakes. Mar Don offers lodging and camping just minutes from the Seep Lakes. Call 509-346-2651 or 1-800-416-2736 for information. Rough camping is available at numerous designated sites throughout the Seep Lakes Wildlife Area and at Soda Lake on the Columbia National Wildlife Refuge (for a fee). Other than Soda Lake, no camping is allowed on refuge lands.

The closest full-fledged towns are Moses Lake to the north and Othello to the south. Motel space is available at both towns, along with some decent if not world-class dining options. Othello's motels are the Best Western Lincoln Inn (800-240-7865) at 1020 E. Cedar Street and Cabana Motel (509-488-2605) at 665 E. Windsor Street.

Nearby Fisheries

Potholes Reservoir

Potholes Reservoir ranks as perhaps the region's best and most under-utilized largemouth bass fishery. Access is the tricky part. Getting to the water is easy. Negotiating the "sand dunes" on the north side of the reservoir is far more challenging. The best advice I can give is to pick a summer or autumn day and hire Levi Meseberg, the guide at Mar-Don. He grew up there and knows the dunes as well as anybody alive. The Mar-Don guides aren't necessarily fly angling experts, but they are certainly bass experts and Potholes Reservoir experts. So brush up on your bass tactics and use your guide to put you on the fish. If largemouths up to five or six pounds leave you wanting for more, suggest to your guide that you might want to try for the reservoir's fat rainbows, hard-fighting smallmouth, or even bluegill up to a pound in size and eager to eat poppers.

Nearby Attractions and Activities

Potholes Reservoir and the Seep Lakes are a major stopover for migrating birds and an important nesting ground for many water birds and songbirds. Much of the area falls within the Columbia National Wildlife Refuge. Birdwatchers should be out on the roads early in the morning to find the many uncommon species that utilize the area. The headquarters for the national wildlife refuge is located a short distance away in Othello at 735 East Main Street. You can pick up a checklist refuge birds.

Speaking of birds, Washington Department of Wildlife has a large wildlife management area on the seeps and bordering the refuge. The area offers excellent waterfowl hunting opportunities, and the Mar-Don guides can arrange waterfowling trips.

Author's Tip

If you're looking for smallmouth bass and walleye on a fly, try the rock piles near the face of O'Sullivan Dam. You will need a boat or pontoon craft. Small craft can be launched off the dam (SR 262 runs along the top of the dam); larger craft can be launched down at Mar-Don resort on the west end of the dam. The rock piles, usually partially visible from the dam, offer ideal structure for bass and during the spring and fall, walleye often cruise along the channels nearby. Try fast-sinking lines and high-density sink-tips and fish Woolly Buggers, Zonker patterns or similar flies.

Favorite Fly

Night Leech (Steve Probasco)

HOOK	3XL streamer hook, No. 2-4
BODY	Black plastic chenille or similar
WING	Black rabbit strip
THROAT	Black hackle
HEAD	Red

Night Leech

Fast Facts

Potholes Reservoir and the Seep Lakes

LOCATION	Eastern Washington, south of I-90 near Moses Lake
WATER TYPE	Fertile seep lakes of varying sizes along with sprawling Potholes Reservoir
PRIMARY GAMEFISH	Rainbow trout, largemouth and smallmouth bass, crappie, bluegill, walleye
BEST TIME	Spring and fall
DRIVE TIME	From Seattle: 2¾ hours From Portland: 5 hours From Tri-Cities: 1½ hours From Boise: 6 hours
BEST TROUT FLIES	Basic selection of stillwater flies; including: Chironomid Pupa, No. 10-16; Callibaetis Gulper Special, Callibaetis CDC Dun, Pheasant Tail Nymph, Night Leech, Beadhead Zug Bug, Green Marabou Damsel Nymph, Scud (olive-gray), Woolly Bugger (black, olive), Peacock Carey Special.
BEST BASS FLIES	Poppers, divers, and leech patterns; large Woolly Buggers and Zonkers for walleye.
EQUIPMENT	4- to 6-weight rods; floating, intermediate and fast-sinking lines. Float tube or pontoon boat; a lightweight craft is ideal for the hike-in lakes. Bring at least one extra tire for your vehicle.
CONDITIONS	Cold early spring weather yields to hot summers and pleasant autumns. Gravel roads in the area are rough and dusty. Occasionally, cars are vandalized at trailheads. Rattlesnakes are common; ticks abound during the spring.
DIRECTIONS	From Seattle, follow I-90 east to Moses Lake or I-90/SR 26 to Othello. From Moses Lake, follow SR 17 south to a right turn on SR 262, which leads seven miles to O'Sullivan Dam. From Othello, follow McManamon Road north out of town about six miles to the entrance to Seep Lakes Wildlife Area. A network of rough gravel roads traverses the state wildlife area and the federal refuge. From Portland, follow I-84 east to Biggs and cross the Columbia on Highway 97. Follow Highway 97 north, past Yakima, to I-90 and proceed east as above. From the Tri-Cities, head north on U.S. 395 until you reach SR 17. Follow SR 17 north to Othello or to the turn-off for O'Sullivan Dam.

Local Fly Shops

BLUE DUN FLY SHOP
960 Valley Mall Parkway, Suite A
East Wenatchee, WA 98802
509-884-4070

WORLEY-BUGGER FLY COMPANY
811 4th Parallel
Ellensburg, WA 98926
888-950-3474

Area Fly Shops

BLUE DUN FLY SHOP
135 South Sherman
Spokane, WA 99202
509-884-4070

CLEARWATER FLY SHOP
417 West First Street
Kennewick, WA 99336
509-582-1001

SILVER BOW FLY SHOP
1003 East Trent Avenue
Spokane, WA 99202
509-483-1772

GARY'S FLY SHOP
1210 West Lincoln
Yakima, WA 98902
509-457-3474

Guides

LEVI MESEBERG
800-416-2736
www.mardonresort.com

Contacts

WASHINGTON DEPT.
OF FISH & WILDLIFE
North Central Washington
Region 2 Office
1550 Alder Street NW
Ephrata, WA 98823-9699
509-754-4624

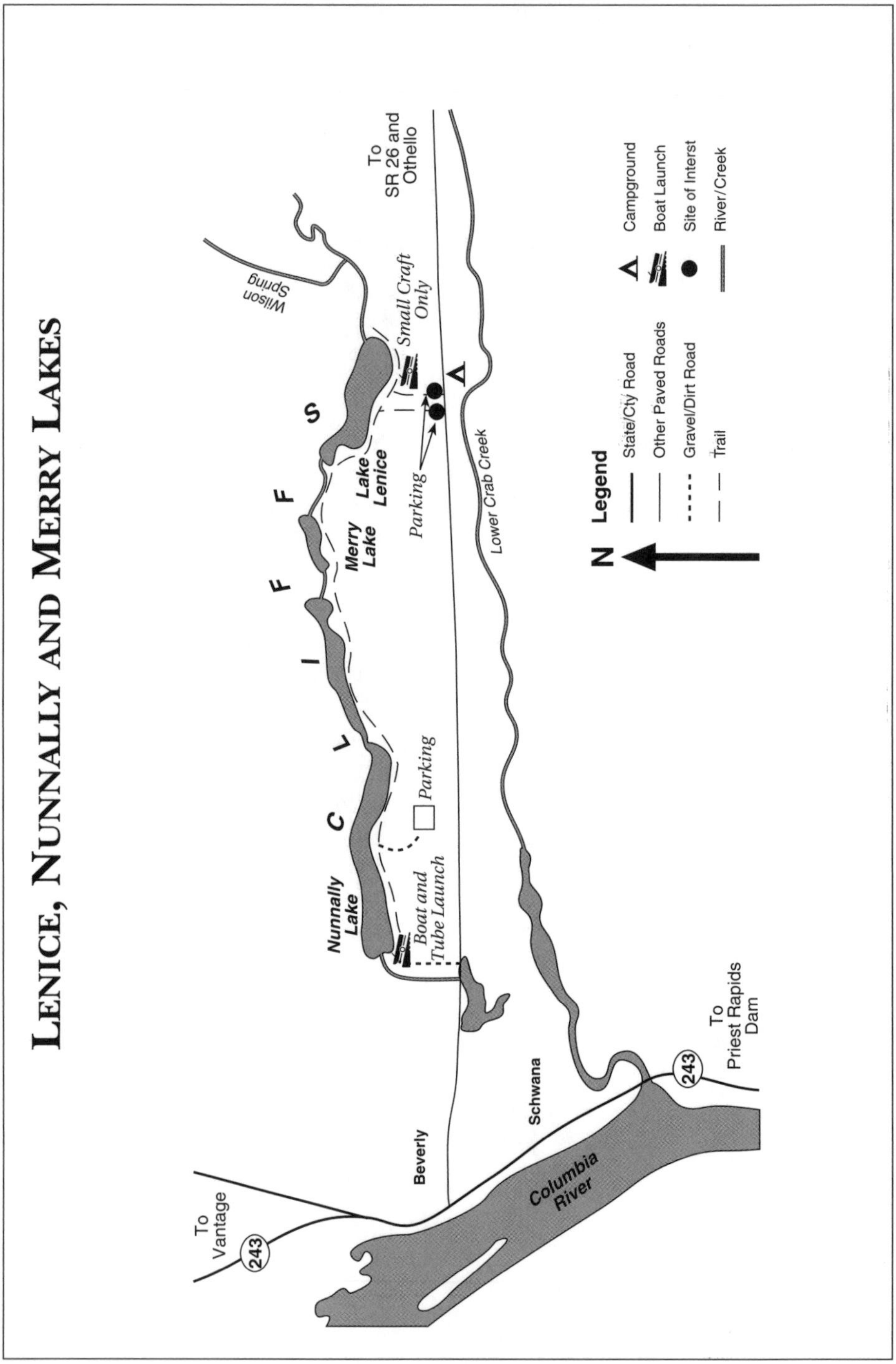

Lenice, Nunnally and Merry Lakes

To
SR 26 and
Othello

Wilson
Spring

Small Craft
Only

C   L   I   F   F   S

Merry
Lake

Lake
Lenice

Parking

Nunnally
Lake

Boat and
Tube Launch

Parking

Lower Crab Creek

Beverly

Schwana

To
Priest Rapids
Dam

To
Vantage

243

243

Columbia
River

Legend

N

——	State/Cty Road
·····	Other Paved Roads
- - -	Gravel/Dirt Road
– – –	Trail

Campground

Boat Launch

Site of Interst

River/Creek

© Wilderness Adventures Press, Inc.

CHAPTER 8

LENICE, NUNNALLY AND MERRY LAKES

Wind, Waves, and Reel-Screaming Runs

Surely my eyes deceived me. Nunnally Lake was completely and utterly deserted. That doesn't happen often when the fishing is good at Nunnally. Granted, it was late summer and an 85-degree sun bore into the sandy scablands. If ever you will find Nunnally devoid of anglers, this is the time. I had wandered over only because I was in the neighborhood en route northward to Chopaka Lake.

Having never seen Nunnally under such conditions, I could only imagine that late summer equated to poor fishing. Such was not the case. I had trudged through the sand just to have a look, and what I found at Nunnally was gin-clear water, big trout cruising the shoreline, and *Callibaetis* mayflies drawing lazy, splashy rises. Not an angler anywhere in sight. I literally ran back to the parking area and strung up a rod with a floating line.

I made the return hike to the lake, found a narrow break in the shoreline shrubbery, and targeted rising trout with a dry *Callibaetis* pattern. The big, rising trout tested my patience, but eventually I found a willing dance partner. We parted company in short order as three or four pounds of rainbow trout overwhelmed my 5X tippet.

Nunnally Lake

I hooked a second fish in the same manner, rising her to a dry fly under a hot desert sun. She likewise dove for the weeds and snapped my tippet.

So hastily had I retrieved my fly rod that I had only stuffed one small fly box into my shirt pocket. I decided Chopaka could wait. Again I trudged back to the truck and this time I drove the dozen-odd miles back to the little town of Vantage on the banks of the nearby Columbia. I found a gas station and filled the float tube; then I checked into the motel for the night. Having secured comfortable lodging, I drove back out to the Nunnally Lake parking lot. Still no cars.

Again I trudged through sand, this time toting a float tube and full complement of tackle. Mid-afternoon and not a lick of wind. That fact alone seemed rather remarkable, for rarely had I enjoyed windless days on these waters during those spring and late-autumn treks.

These waters are revered among Washington's stillwater fanatics. So fertile are the seep lakes that the planted rainbows and browns grow ridiculously fast on a diet rich in all the typical trout foods. Dense hatches of mayflies offer superb action throughout late spring; *Chironomids* hatch throughout the year. Many anglers fish these waters specifically to hook big trout on surface flies. Others relish the violent after-dark strikes on big leech patterns. In any case, anglers headed for Lenice (the most popular of the three lakes), Nunnally, or Merry Lake had better come armed with all the appropriate flies and a float tube or pontoon. And don't expect to have these superb waters to yourself.

That's why my late-summer visit was a new experience. Never before had I fished Nunnally, or its sister lakes, at the end of summer. I had simply never considered the idea, and I couldn't imagine that good fishing and an empty parking lot could possibly occur simultaneously at Nunnally.

These lakes had long proved to me their lofty reputations for producing excellent fishing for big trout. Like most anglers, I had always visited this out-of-the-way country between March and May or during mid-autumn. Yet before day's end I vowed to make an annual pilgrimage here during late summer. That afternoon I hooked a half-dozen more big, deep-bodied rainbows, and as darkness arrived I struck two more trout on a big, black leech pattern.

Not a single angler joined me on Nunnally Lake that day. I felt as if I had gotten away with something. After all, this was Labor Day weekend, a time when virtually all great trout waters in the Northwest are inundated with anglers. The cat's out of the bag now. Next Labor Day I'll no doubt have company and that's fine with me. I need someone to pinch me and tell me I'm not dreaming this stuff.

Restaurants and Accommodations

The nearby town of Vantage offers all necessary services, including Vantage Motel (509-856-2800) and three restaurants, along with a general store and two service stations. Considering the windblown desolation of the Crab Creek area and the 15-minute commute, I prefer to stay at the motel rather than camp near the lakes. Seven miles south of the turnoff to the lakes, the tiny town of Mattawa offers the Desert Aire Motel (509-932-4300).

Nearby Attractions and Activities

Located near the town of Vantage, Ginkgo Petrified Forest State Park offers a glimpse of the region's prehistoric past. During the 1930s, highway-construction crews unearthed a fossilized forest, which included rare petrified ginkgo trees. The area is now a 7,500-acre state park featuring a museum that displays cut and polished petrified wood, live ginkgo trees and petroglyphs. A trail system explores a prehistoric lake bed. Open year-round, the state park offers plenty of camp space. Take Exit 136 off I-90. As you drive south on SR 243 heading towards the turnoff to Lenice Lake, you will parallel the Columbia River and soon arrive at Wanapum Dam. The Wanapum Dam Heritage Center Museum houses an outstanding collection of stone points and tools collected from the local area. The museum is free and open daily 9:00-4:30. Fish windows allow an opportunity to watch migrating salmon and steelhead.

Author's Tip

For starters, don't leave any valuables in your vehicle. Car break-ins seem to be a recurring theme here. As for fishing, bear in mind that these lakes are open to night fishing. So take along a headlamp, a sinking line, and some big, black leech patterns. The after-dark action sometimes surpasses the daytime entertainment.

Favorite Fly

Nevada Leech (John Shewey)

HOOK	Long-shank streamer hook, No. 2-4, bent slightly upward at mid-shank
TAIL	A few strands of Krystal Flash and then a short, sparse strip of rabbit
BODY	Mohair with spun rabbit on head
COLORS	Black (for night fishing)

Nevada Leech

Fast Facts

Lenice, Nunnally, and Merry Lakes

LOCATION	Eastern Washington
WATER TYPE	Fertile desert seep lakes
PRIMARY GAMEFISH	Rainbow and brown trout
BEST TIME	Spring and fall
BEST FLIES	*Callibaetis* and *Chironomid* patterns; damsel nymphs; leech patterns.

EQUIPMENT	6- to 7-weight rod; floating line and two or three different sink-rate sinking lines.
DRIVE TIME	From Seattle: 3 hours From Portland: 5 hours From Boise: 6 hours
CONDITIONS	Expect high winds. You will need a float tube or pontoon, but bear in mind you must carry your float craft a quarter to a half-mile to the lakes. Don't leave valuables in the car.
DIRECTIONS	From Seattle, follow I-90 east past Ellensburg until you cross the Columbia at Vantage (all services). On the east bank of the river, take the Highway 26 off-ramp heading south. After about a mile, turn right SR 243, heading down the east bank of the Columbia. Six or seven miles from the turn-off, watch for a left hand turn to the Crab Creek Wildlife Area. Lenice Lake's parking area is located about five miles in; Nunnally's about two miles in and Merry's in between. From Portland, follow I-84 east to Biggs and cross the Columbia River on Highway 97. Follow Highway 97 all the way to I-90, turn east and then follow instructions as above. From Boise and points south, head for the Tri-Cities and then follow Highway 395 and then SR 17 to Othello. At Othello, head west on SR 26. When you reach the Columbia, turn south on SR 243.

Local Fly Shops

WORLEY-BUGGER FLY COMPANY
811 4th Parallel
Ellensburg, WA 98926
888-950-3474

CLEARWATER FLY SHOP
417 West First
Kennewick, WA 99336
509-582-1001

BLUE DUN FLY SHOP
960 Valley Mall Parkway, Suite A
East Wenatchee, WA 98802
509-884-4070

GARY'S FLY SHOP
1210 West Lincoln
Yakima, WA 98902
509-457-3474

Contacts

WASHINGTON DEPARTMENT
OF FISH & WILDLIFE
North Central Washington -
Region 2 Office
1550 Alder Street NW
Ephrata, WA 98823-9699
509-754-4624

MANN LAKE

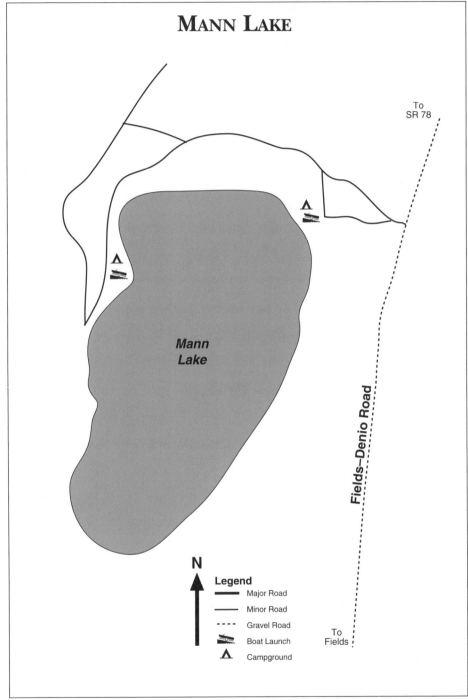

To
SR 78

*Mann
Lake*

Fields–Denio Road

N

Legend
—— Major Road
—— Minor Road
- - - Gravel Road
🚤 Boat Launch
⛺ Campground

To
Fields

© Wilderness Adventures Press, Inc.

CHAPTER 9

MANN LAKE AND
THE STEENS MOUNTAINS

Rugged Splendor in the Oregon High Desert

Regardless of one's taste in fly fishing pursuits, Mann Lake certainly counts among the region's "must-do" fisheries. This natural desert lake offers a remarkable and rare combination of extreme remoteness, great fishing prospects, and stunning scenery. The nearest sizeable community, Burns, lies nearly 100 miles distant; otherwise, the tiny desert oasis of Fields—nearly an hour south by gravel road— serves as the only source of supplies, fuel, and sometimes even human contact.

Mann Lake is wild in many respects: Some years ago I was settling into a lazy afternoon of sitting out the midday wind at Mann Lake when overhead arrived a rapidly flying green blob. Completely puzzled, I shaded my eyes against the sun and soon identified the strange object as a two-man tent, no doubt having taken flight from the other end of the lake. Tie everything down when you visit Mann Lake. The frequent winds pick up speed off the towering and spectacular east face of the Steens Mountains and then howl unimpeded down the narrow valley occupied by Mann Lake, one of Oregon's most remote destination fisheries.

Mann Lake is home to planted Lahontan cutthroat.

Oregon Department of Fish & Wildlife stocks the 200-acre lake with Lahontan cutthroat trout, native to the Lahontan Basin in Nevada. Perfectly adapted to high-alkaline Great Basin waters, these beautifully marked cutthroat grow rapidly in Mann Lake's shallow, fertile broth. Within three seasons a cutthroat from Mann Lake spans 18 to 22 inches. The large average size of these fish makes for an unforgettable fishing experience. Most years the average fish runs 16 to 19 inches and these, along with good numbers of 20- to 24-inch cutthroat, assure that Mann Lake continually ranks as a favorite spring destination for many Northwest fly anglers.

I made my first excursion to Mann Lake around 1983 when record precipitation levels were unleashing a fury of water on the region, resulting in severe flooding of ranchlands and basin areas. Mann Lake nearly doubled in size and the fishing reached unparalleled heights. I remember one April morning when Tim Blount and I stood on opposite sides of a narrow bay and caught big cutthroat so fast that we lost count somewhere around 50 fish. Even back in the "high water" days, however, the geography of the place always competed for my attention no matter how fast and furious the fishing.

Indeed, a major part of Mann Lake's attraction is the remarkable scenery afforded by the looming Steens Mountains, a huge fault-block range rising gently from the west but dropping thousands of near-vertical feet on its east face. The steep slope dominates the skyline above Mann Lake. Between March and May—the most popular time for fishing Mann Lake—broad sheets of snow gleam ivory-white high on the Steens and frequent storm clouds gather over the rugged crags.

The lake itself occupies a narrow sagebrush basin seasonally occupied by native peoples for thousands of years. Today several large ranches scratch out a lonely existence up and down the valley, including Mann Ranch, whose cattle graze above the lake's south end and through which flows Mann Lake's only feeder creek. Meanwhile, pronghorns often graze the slopes to the west and north of Mann Lake. The entire region typifies the basin-range environment of Oregon's least populated corner. Coyotes get so noisy at times as to disrupt one's sleep. Other wildlife common in the area includes jackrabbits, bobcats, burrowing owls, sage grouse, chukar partridge, valley quail, myriad raptors, abundant waterfowl and even the unique and striking little desert swift fox. To see a swift fox, wait until well after dark and then drive the road towards Fields. Keep your eyes peeled for a cat-sized fox with giant ears.

In addition to its more observable wildlife, this arid region is home to many species of snakes and lizards. Herpetologists travel here for a chance to find such creatures as the collared lizard and western whipsnake among more common desert regulars such as the fence lizards, skinks, horned lizards, and rattlesnakes. Among the abundant rodents are the striking kangaroo rats, which can only be described as perfectly cute.

Most anglers who visit Mann Lake simply hunker down at the camping areas on both sides of the lake. I've done my share of that and occasionally do so today, sleeping in the back of the truck and setting up a tarp for shade. More often these days, I seek more sheltered accommodations. About six miles north of Mann Lake lies a giant dry (or almost dry) lake bed called Tudor Lake and across the road from Tudor Lake a tiny little stream runs down past a small mesa called Stonehouse Butte. Follow the dirt road up to the entrance of Stonehouse Canyon and you find a couple of nice camping spots offering some protection from the wind and sun.

I'm also somewhat partial to the pleasant campground over on the Blitzen River near the town of Frenchglen (Page Springs Campground). The drive from Frenchglen to Mann Lake takes about two hours so often I will pull into Frenchglen on the way to Mann Lake, grab a bite to eat at the Buckaroo Room or Frenchglen Hotel, spend the night at Page Springs, and then head out at dawn for Mann Lake.

Fishing Mann Lake

The sight-fishing opportunities keep me coming back to Mann Lake. Imagine stalking quietly around the shoreline in search of 20-inch trout cruising along in a foot of water and then delivering a delicate cast far enough ahead of your target that the fly has time to sink to the bottom before the fish gets there. Then you hold your breath for a beat or two before twitching the fly as the trout approaches to within a couple of feet. The fish turns slightly and you see the white flash of its open mouth signaling you to raise the rod tip. Fish on!

The best sight-fishing opportunities occur during calm spring mornings and again during calm mornings or evenings during the fall. I prefer a clear intermediate line for this kind of work. Typically, I'll cast a size 12 or 14 Zug Bug or size 14 olive scud pattern. Get out early, just after sunrise, and walk slowly along the west bank looking for cruising cutthroat.

These fish find plenty to eat in Mann Lake, which is densely populated with every imaginable stillwater trout food. *Chironomids* provide an important year-round food source for the cutthroat. Represented by numerous species, the *Chironomids* come in many sizes and colors, including the big "bloodworm midges," whose hemoglobin-laden larvae typically span half an inch or more in length. The first midge hatches begin soon after the ice cover melts in February. By mid-March *Chironomids* hatch every day and these emergences, typically at mid-morning, last throughout the spring.

By April, water beetles, backswimmers, and boatmen become increasingly evident, and Mann Lake features many varieties, from the inch-and-a-half-long giant diving water beetle to miniscule whirligig beetles and boatmen. Beetles, along with plentiful olive and olive-gray scuds, are especially abundant in shallow water and draw trout into the shoreline margins. This is when I enjoy the best sight casting.

April also brings the first damsel and *Callibaetis* mayfly activity, which increases during June. Neither the damsels nor mayflies produce super-dense hatches, but both abound and trout feed heavily on them. The damsels range from bright green to brown. Try an imitation fished on a floating or intermediate line and stripped slowly along over the weed beds.

Mann Lake likewise abounds in leeches, so Woolly Buggers and other leech patterns usually produce fish. Sometimes, in fact, when shoreline fishing slows down, float tubers dragging or stripping leech patterns continue to enjoy consistent success. Black, olive, and brown are top colors.

By far the most popular time at Mann Lake, the spring fishing extends from March through May, after which desert heat slows things down until autumn. Few anglers venture to Mann Lake during late September and October, yet superb fishing awaits those willing to brave unpredictable autumn weather. The water tends

Fish on at Mann Lake.

towards gin-clear and the trout, long past their spring spawning urges, are bright, fat, and hungry.

Shallow throughout and wadeable around its edges, Mann Lake is float-tube optional. Certainly a boat or tube comes in handy from time to time, but you don't need watercraft to catch fish here. Ferocious winds blow through the basin with regularity, so beware the "high seas" on Mann Lake. In direct contrast to most Mann Lake anglers, I prefer to be in a float tube when the wind blows across Mann Lake. I'd rather brave the wind by drifting and trolling a fly from a tube than attempting any sort of cast in the face of a 20- or 30-mile-per-hour gust.

Bear in mind that Mann Lake offers no immediate amenities. Camping space is available on both sides of the lake and a BLM-installed outhouse and launch adorns the west side. Otherwise, this is bring-your-own country: bring your own shade, water, firewood and shelter.

An hour south of Mann Lake, the tiny oasis of Fields is a required stop for milkshakes, burgers or breakfast.

Restaurants and Accommodations

If you don't mind the hour-long drive, the quaint little diner at Fields is a required stop for homemade milkshakes and burgers. During the spring, expect to share the tiny restaurant with bird-watchers arriving from far-flung corners of the state. By mid-autumn, anglers can swap stories with chukar hunters and deer hunters over a big breakfast. The adjacent store offers basic supplies and gasoline, along with a photographic record of the many record-book and near-record desert bighorn sheep taken by hunters in the Steens, Pueblos and Trout Creek Mountains.

Twenty miles farther south, the Denio Restaurant offers a fine and hearty meal. Both Denio and Fields are located on the same side of the Steens and Pueblo Mountains as Mann Lake and both remain open during the winter. If you make the two-hour drive around the Steens Mountains, you will be amply rewarded by a hearty meal in Frenchglen at the Frenchglen Hotel (see below under Nearby Attractions and Activities).

Despite the distances, any of the above-mentioned restaurants are well worth the stop. The memorable family-style dinner at the Frenchglen Hotel will make a regular Steens Mountain visitor out of anybody with a taste for fine food and unique surroundings. Be sure to make reservations here (541-493-2825). Seating for dinner is at 6:30.

Getting to Mann Lake via Frenchglen takes longer than the Highway 78 route. But Frenchglen and Fields act like magnets for me so I always time my departure and arrival so that I can enjoy a dinner at Frenchglen and a breakfast or lunch at Fields.

Mann Lake itself offers little in the way of luxury unless you count pit toilets, a decent boat launch and a few fire rings. Most anglers arrive with campers or RVs for shelter against wind and weather. The closest motel is at Fields about an hour south and offers three rooms. Burns lies 90 miles away—a long commute but certainly an option if you intend only a day or two of fishing. On the west side of the Steens Mountains, two hours from Mann Lake, the little village of Frenchglen offers the historic Frenchglen Hotel along with the Frenchglen Guest House, whose two well-appointed rooms go for $65 per night (owned by the Litchys). Both establishments close for the winter. Page Springs Campground (BLM) and the Camper Corral are located just outside of Frenchglen.

Nearby Fisheries

Juniper and Wildhorse Lakes
Blitzen River

Juniper Lake, a few miles north of Mann Lake, offers fair to good action for 12- to 20-inch cutthroat. Anglers adept at traveling the desert backroads might wish to explore the Trout Creek Mountains and the tiny streams found therein, but check the current fishing regulations synopsis as many of these waters are now closed to protect rare populations of redband trout. The west slope of the Steens offers drive-in Fish Lake and stunning hike-in Wildhorse Lake, both teeming with small trout. Wildhorse Lake occupies a broad cirque below the 9,700-foot Steens Mountain summit. The two-mile-long trail dives steeply off the rim. Despite the return climb, you won't be sorry for making the descent—last time I visited, Wildhorse Lake writhed with small but willing and beautiful trout. All major creeks on the Steens' west slope offer fair to good fishing for native redband trout and a unique opportunity to explore these waters is offered by Steens Mountain Packers (541-495-2315). Using a helicopter, owner John Witzel flies anglers into and out of remote creeks rarely visited by other anglers.

Also located on the west slope of the Steens, High Desert Redband Trout Cowboy Camp offers private access to several trout-filled streams and a 75-acre lake whose wild redband trout average a fat 18 inches and reach 10 pounds or more. The camp package includes all the amenities: exceptional "cowboy camp" meals, fishing guides, pontoon boats, tackle, and more. For details on this rare opportunity, contact Steve Beyerlin or Chuck Messner at 800-348-4138. The camp is open from April through October.

All streams on the west slope of the Steens Mountains feed into the Donner & Blitzen River, more commonly known simply as the Blitzen River. The Blitzen offers wild redband trout, some of which reach 20 inches in length, and is especially suited to anglers willing to hike far into its more out-of-the-way canyon reaches. The fishing begins at Page Springs Campground, where trails lead up the Blitzen Canyon. Or you can drive the south extension of the Steens Loop Road to reach Blitzen Crossing and hike up or down this diminutive and physically demanding river.

Nearby Attractions and Activities

Located half an hour south of Mann Lake, Alvord Hot Springs attracts tub soakers from all around the area. You never know with whom you will share the warm, steamy, open-air confines of this small, informal hot springs located just off the east side of the road to Fields. I'll never forget sitting through a late-night October blizzard in the cozy comfort of Alvord Hot Springs. When the storm finally abated, the clouds parted to reveal a bright full, midnight moon and as if on cue a pack of coyotes serenaded the lonely desert.

Alvord Hot Springs derives its name from the adjacent Alvord Desert, a gleaming white expanse of alkali flats and sand that stretches for miles across the desert. This hot springs, and most of the other natural features in the region are represented on the BLM's *Steens Mountain Recreation Map*, available from the BLM headquarters in Burns. Another nearby hot springs—Mickey Hot Springs—is located in an area under study for possible inclusion in a designated wilderness area.

The tiny town of Fields offers a store, motel, gas station and restaurant, the latter of which is a must-stop affair known for its fresh-made milkshakes, grilled burgers, and hearty breakfasts (541-495-2275). Across the street from Fields stands a dense grove of willows and cottonwoods perennially inhabited by great horned owls. During the spring, walk quietly through the grove and keep an eye peeled for young owlets perched in a row on a sturdy branch. Numerous other birds inhabit this little spring-fed oasis, so expect to share the grove and the town with birdwatchers arriving from the far corners of the Northwest.

Should you feel the urge to plug the slot machines, head south from Fields about 20 miles to the tiny border town of Denio, Nevada. Owned by Lance Litchy—who also own the Mercantile and Buckaroo Room in Frenchglen—Denio offers motel space, a full bar, supplies, and roadhouse-style meals. Both Fields and Denio remain open all year.

Across the Steens—or rather around the Steens Mountains—lies the hamlet of Frenchglen, whose historic, state-owned Frenchglen Hotel (541-493-2825) offers quaint accommodations and fine meals. Managed by John Ross, the hotel features nine rooms that rent via reservation for around $60 per night. The hotel opens March 15 and closes November 15.

Just down the street, the Frenchglen Mercantile and Buckaroo Room (541-493-2738) offers necessary supplies, souvenirs, and its own Pronghorn Pale Ale, a microbrewed beer made exclusively for the Litchys by Norwester Brewing of Portland.

During June, the Litchys throw a big bash called the Frenchglen Brew Fest, attracting Steens Mountains fans from all over the state. During the weekend-long event, the Buckaroo Room expands to include ample outdoor seating on the patio or on stacked hay bales surrounding a small stage where area musicians ply their craft during the evening. The Merc and Buckaroo Room open during April and close during November.

Frenchglen more or less closes down for winter, so check ahead to see when the town re-opens before driving there in search of lodging or meals.

The wildlife refuge deserves further comment: Bird watching enthusiasts can expect a wide variety of migratory and resident species, especially during April and May. State Route 205 from Burns to Frenchglen passes through a sizeable chunk of the refuge. Also, the fields near Burns and around the first 10 miles of SR 205 host large flights of migrating geese, ducks, cranes, and shorebirds.

Much of the land now designated as the Malheur Refuge once belonged to the P Ranch, where cattle baron part-owner Peter French ran some 45,000 cattle on about 200,000 acres. French arrived in the Blitzen Valley in 1872 but was gunned down in 1897 for reasons still debatable. The little town of Frenchglen was named for French and his partner. A few of the ranch buildings remain, including the unique French Round Barn, located just off the road to New Princeton.

Located in the tiny town of Frenchglen on the west side of the Steens, historic Frenchglen Hotel offers comfortable lodging and fine meals.

Mann Lake as viewed from the 9,100 foot summit of the Steens Mountains.

Author's Tip

The Fields-Denio Road, which leads to Mann Lake, eats quite a few tires, so make sure your spare is in good condition. Also, carry an extra can of gas if you intend to explore the country.

Favorite Fly

Beadhead Pheasant Tail

HOOK	Tiemco #200 or similar, No. 12-14
TAIL	Pheasant tail fibers
BODY	Pheasant tail fiber
THORAX	Peacock herl
WINGPAD	Pheasant tail fibers
HEAD	Metal bead

Beadhead Pheasant Tail

Fast Facts

Mann Lake

LOCATION	Southeastern Oregon, below the east face of the Steens Mountains
WATER TYPE	Fertile, shallow, alkaline natural desert sump lake, often turbid
PRIMARY GAMEFISH	Lahontan cutthroat trout, 14 to 24 inches; planted as fingerlings by ODFW
BEST TIME	March-May and late September through October
BEST FLIES	Chironomid pupa patterns, No. 12-18; Griffith's Gnat, No. 14-20; Zug Bug, No. 10-18; Woolly Bugger, No. 6-8; Olive Damsel Nymph, No. 10-12; scud patterns, No. 16-18; Peacock Carey Special, No. 6-10.
EQUIPMENT	5- to 7-weight rod; floating line; sink-tip or slow-sinking line. Float tube or boat optional. Waders and cold-weather clothing.

CONDITIONS	Frequent winds; rapid weather changes. No fresh water or firewood.
DRIVE TIME	From Bend: 4 hours From Portland: 7 hours From Eugene: 7 hours From Boise: 5 hours From Burns: 2 hours
DIRECTIONS	Follow U.S. Highway 20 to Burns, Oregon, which lies about two hours east of Bend and about three hours west of Boise. At Burns, follow Highway 78 south out of town. Just outside of Burns a right turn (Highway 205) leads to Frenchglen, which lies about an hour from Burns. To reach Mann Lake from Frenchglen, continue south on Highway 205, which leads through Catlow Valley and eventually crosses over the foothills and meets the Fields-Denio Road just north of Fields. Turn left towards Mann Lake, which lies another hour or so north.

The faster route from Burns continues straight on Highway 78, past the tiny towns of Crane and New Princeton and eventually up the comparatively gentle northern extension of the Steens Mountains. As the road winds down the back side of the range, watch for a right turn onto Fields-Denio Road (gravel), which leads some 25 miles to Mann Lake, which will be on your right. Along the way you will pass 10-cent, 15-cent, and Juniper Lakes—all on your right—but don't mistake these for Mann. Past Juniper Lake you will skirt the edge of a broad lake bed (sometimes with water) called Tudor Lake, mount a small rise and then descend toward Mann Lake. Watch for the signed right turn into the lake. The access road wraps around the lake's north shore.

Local Fly Shops

KIGER CREEK FLY SHOP
120 NW Circle Drive
Hines, OR 97738
541-573-1329

B & B SPORTING GOODS
Highway 20 & Conley Avenue
Hines, OR 97720

Area Fly Shops

THE IDAHO ANGLER
1682 S. Vista
Boise, ID 83705
208-389-9957

STONEFLY ANGLER
625 Vista
Boise, ID 83705
208-338-1700

INTERMOUNTAIN ARMS & TACKLE
900 Vista Village Center
Boise, ID 83705
208-345-3474

BEAR CREEK FLY SHOP
5521 West State Street
Boise, ID 83703
208-853-8704

Contacts

OREGON DEPARTMENT OF
FISH & WILDLIFE
Malheur Watershed District Office
237 S. Hines Blvd., P.O. Box 8
Hines, OR 97738
541-573-6582

The author with a fine smallmouth bass from Brownlee Reservoir.

CHAPTER 10

BROWNLEE RESERVOIR

The Northwest at its Warmwater Best

Survey a group of Oregon fly anglers about the state's best smallmouth destination and most will cite the Mainstem Umpqua River and the John Day River. Bass abound in both rivers, providing excellent fly rod opportunities. But far to the east, out of sight and out of mind for most fly fishers, flows the Snake River, backed up by Brownlee, Oxbow, and Hells Canyon Dams. Remote by Northwest standards, the Snake River's combination smallmouth bass/crappie fishery ranks among the most prolific warmwater destinations in the region.

These borderland impoundments are no secret to the angling world in general: Gear anglers have taken several state record crappies from Brownlee Reservoir. However, in a region where trout, steelhead, and salmon reign supreme in the hearts and minds of fly anglers, the Snake's warmwater offerings remain little appreciated. In other words, you won't see many other fly fishers.

So why would you travel that far for smallmouth? For starters, these waters teem with big fish; 14- to 18-inch bass are common and crappie typically span 10 to 12 inches. Better yet, if you spend a little time on Brownlee, you stand a fair chance of hooking a 20-inch smallmouth. The fish are big by Northwest standards—bigger on average than the bass in the John Day or Umpqua—and there are lots of them.

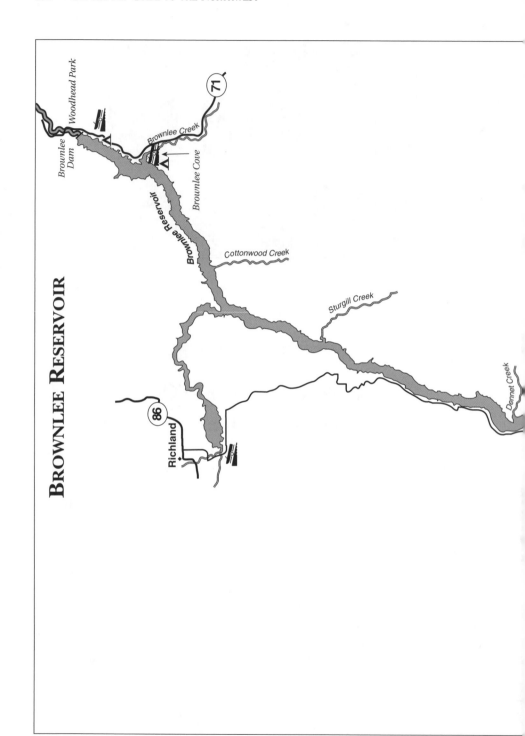

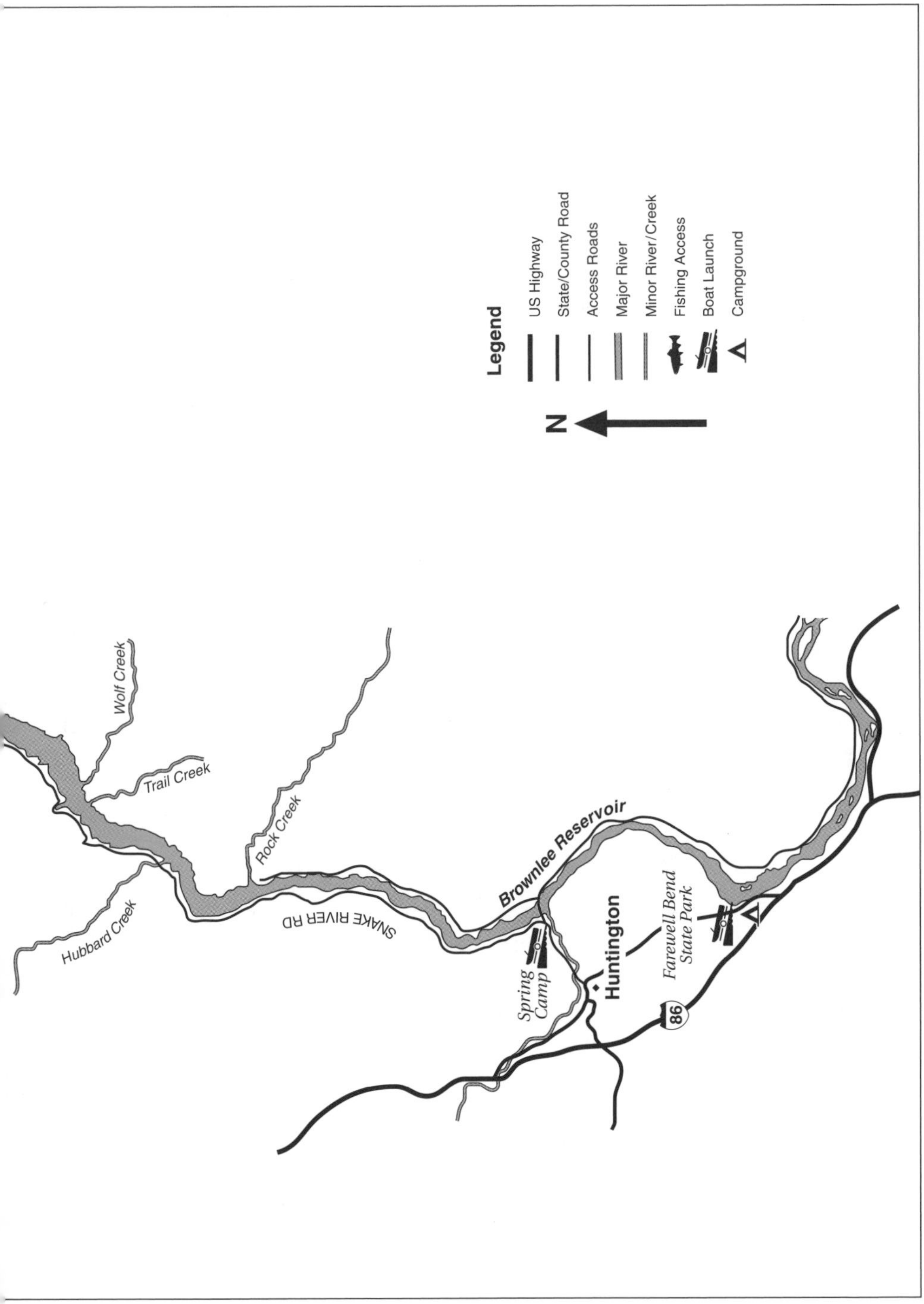

Legend

US Highway
State/County Road
Access Roads
Major River
Minor River/Creek
Fishing Access
Boat Launch
Campground

N

Wolf Creek

Trail Creek

Hubbard Creek

Rock Creek

SNAKE RIVER RD

Brownlee Reservoir

Spring Camp

Huntington

Farewell Bend State Park

86

Located upstream, or south, of Hells Canyon, Oxbow and Brownlee Reservoirs form a 70-mile-long portion of the Idaho/Oregon border. Towering canyon slopes clad in sagebrush, rabbitbrush, and cheatgrass rise precipitously from the rocky shorelines along these arid-country reservoirs. Fifty-mile-long Brownlee Reservoir lies far from just about everywhere save the border town of Ontario and a few tiny hamlets strung through the region. Interstate 84 leaves Portland and travels some 340 miles before reaching Exit 345, which leads through the small community of Huntington and then down to the southern reaches of Brownlee's 14,000 acres. Between Huntington on the south and Richland on the north, Snake River Road (gravel) follows the reservoir for almost 30 miles through the canyon, making Brownlee the most accessible portion of the Snake River.

Even farther off the beaten path, Oxbow Reservoir hides deep in the Snake River Canyon south of famed Hells Canyon and east from the scenic community of Halfway. Interstate 84 delivers you to Baker City, where Exit 302 leads to State Route 86. SR 86 heads east, picking up the Powder River, itself a fine smallmouth stream in its lower reaches. At Richland, where the Powder River Arm of Brownlee Reservoir offers fine prospects for crappie and bass, SR 86 swings northeasterly and climbs over the hill to Halfway and then turns east again, leading a dozen or so miles down to Oxbow Dam. After the long descent to the river, the road swings abruptly south and follows Oxbow Reservoir to Brownlee Dam before crossing over to the Idaho side as Highway 71.

No roads access the lower third of Brownlee Reservoir, but anglers wishing to ply the waters of Oxbow and Brownlee would be well served to head for the town of Richland. From Richland you can follow SR 86 to Oxbow or turn south on Snake River Road, climb over the rim, and wind your way down to Brownlee.

Fishing Brownlee Reservoir

Fishing picks up during late spring, when crappie, smallmouth bass and bluegill congregate in channels, off steep points, and in deep coves. When warm weather arrives during late May or June, spawning crappies invade the shallows and bass follow along feeding on crappie fry. You needn't worry too much about disturbing spawning crappies because their spawning season extends for several weeks with some fish spawning early and others later.

During the spawning period, look for gently sloping shorelines dominated by shale beds and slack water. Crappies abound in these areas. Among them are active spawners, but these are always in the minority. Bass occupy these same places, feeding heavily on juvenile crappies and on just about any fly pattern that looks remotely edible.

June offers the best mixed-bag fishing with both crappies and bass abundant in the shallows. Foot-long bass are common and 18- to 20-inch tackle-busters comprise at least a small portion of the catch for anglers who learn their way around the reservoirs. Crappies grow big here as well, with fish of 10-12 inches quite abundant. In fact, a 1995 sampling by Oregon Department of Fish & Wildlife (ODFW) determined an average Brownlee Reservoir white crappie to span 10 inches in length.

During July, crappies again seek deeper water during much of the day, but often feed in the shallows around dusk. Throughout the summer, steep, rocky drop-offs and creek channels remain prime areas to find both species. Also, look for wood structure in the form of rotting trees anchored in place by ODFW, dead snags lying in shallow water, stick-ups in the creek channels and coves and flotsam drifted into floating piles. These structures attract schools of crappies, especially during the post-spawn period lasting from late June through September. Water levels fluctuate rather wildly on these Snake River impoundments, so you may luck into a chance to study the reservoirs at low drawdown levels. If so, record the locations of structures that will hold fish at higher water levels.

A quiet morning on Brownlee Reservoir.

Brownlee Reservoir offers a variety of species, including some large sunfish.

Smallmouth bass grow large in Brownlee.

Straightforward tactics prevail on the Snake River impoundments, especially between May and July when lots of bass and crappie occupy shallow-water areas. The combination of a floating line, long leader, and weighted fly allows you to fish a relatively vertical retrieve, which crappies often find irresistible. Simply drop the fly into likely water, allow it to sink, then begin an erratic, darting retrieve interspersed with frequent pauses. Often the take occurs as the fly drops during a pause in the retrieve.

Smallmouth fall for this same tactic and are also easily lured into striking streamers and nymphs fished on sinking or sink-tip lines, where the retrieve is more horizontal. Smallmouth love to follow flies, sneaking along behind as if they can't quite decide whether to strike. You can force their hand simply by altering the retrieve speed and cadence. Try several different retrieves in each precise area. In other words, cast three times to the same place and depth, but each time change the pattern of your retrieve. Try a quick, non-stop hand-over-hand retrieve on one cast and on the next allow the fly to settle to the bottom after each series of strips.

In the Snake River system, whether it be the relatively still waters of the impoundments or the faster water below the dams, smallmouth bass tend to eat just about anything that doesn't eat them first. Rarely are they finicky about fly patterns. You'll get plenty of action with a basic selection of weighted Woolly Buggers, Marabou Muddlers, Clousers and nymphs. Small poppers and diving bugs often elicit wild strikes from bass in shallow water, especially morning and evening. Likewise, a Muddler or Woolly Bugger fished just under the surface tempts bass into slashing takes, especially during the crappie spawn when the smallies are on the prowl for fry along the shallow shelves and shale beds. Dawn and dusk always prove the best times for surface tactics.

Crappies eat the same kinds of flies. In fact, a No. 8 Woolly Bugger, dressed with lead barbell eyes, a metal cone or a bead, is ideally suited for "combo" fishing in areas where bass and crappie coexist. Certainly you can target either species at any time, but most regulars spend lots of time fishing flies that either species will take. Uncertainty is half the fun: you never know what might grab the fly next. In fact, while crappie and smallies predominate, big bluegill, yellow perch, largemouth bass, fat rainbow trout, and catfish all grab the same flies from time to time, so surprises occur regularly.

On a great day in May or June, you might hook several dozen crappies, a couple dozen bass and a few incidentals; even an average day amounts to half of that number once you learn your way around the reservoirs. That's the kind of action that keeps me coming back to the dry and dusty confines of Oregon's version of the sprawling Snake River.

Restaurants and Accommodations

Brownlee Reservoir offers a few nice camping areas located along the access road. Because the access road is rather rough and dusty, I generally pack along a tent and cooler rather than run back and forth from Huntington to my favorite fishing spots. Still, you can find motel space in nearby Huntingon at Farewell Bend Motor Inn (541-869-2211) or to the north in Richland at Hitching Post Motel (541-893-6176). Also, Farewell Bend State Park, located near the freeway 25 miles north of Ontario, features dozens of campsites and RV sites. To the west, Baker City is well worth more than a brief stop when you are in the area. The quaint, old downtown area includes the remarkable Geyser Grand Hotel, whose beautifully appointed rooms and stunning décor recall the inn's regal past. The recently restored Geyser Grand also features superb dinners served in elegant courses in the hotel's spacious dining room. Reserve rooms and dinners ahead by calling the Geyser Grand at 888-434-7374.

Despite its location way out in eastern Oregon, Baker City offers yet another "Portlandesque" dining experience in the form of Roger and Shirley Ivie's Phone Company Restaurant located downtown on First Street (541-523-7997). The Phone Company derives its name from its old brick building that once housed the local phone company.

The Phone Company Restaurant is just one of several fine restaurants in downtown Baker City.

The Ivies make everything from scratch and their menu features an accommodating variety of perfectly prepared entrées along with nightly seafood specialties. Among the unique Phone Company dishes is an "Apple Hazelnut Chicken," featuring tender chicken breasts grilled with an apple-hazelnut glaze. The smoked prime rib, slow-cooked over apple and hickory wood, ranks as a local favorite, but arrive early to enjoy the privilege. The prime rib is available Friday and Saturday "while it lasts."

Superb homemade salad dressings and soups are a must. The delectably creamy clam chowder ranks among the best of its kind in eastern Oregon, and the creamy roasted garlic parmesan dressing shines as a perennial favorite with local patrons. The Phone Company's reputable desserts include a delicious French silk pie and a sensational fresh cobbler. Roger and Shirley are generally on hand to graciously receive the inevitable compliments from customers who appreciate the experience required to create such perfect homemade fare.

Nearby Fisheries

Owyhee River

Any time you're in or near Ontario, you are well within reach of the lower section of the Owyhee River, a fine little tailwater fishery below Owhyee Dam. Stocked by ODFW with rainbows and brown trout, the Owyhee's fertile waters take but a year or two to turn the little hatchery fingerlings into fat, lengthy adults. Both species typically run 14 to 20 inches and bigger fish are certainly available.

The Owyhee is especially popular with the large fly angling community in and around Boise. They live a lot closer to this river than most Oregon fly anglers. Proximity counts on the Owyhee because her flows largely define the quality of the fishery. With no minimum-flow requirements, the Owyhee often falls on hard times during dry years. During ideal years, however, high spring flows yield to stable summer flows and ultimately to the low water of autumn—the time favored by most Owyhee regulars.

Some fine hatches occur on the Owyhee, including dense caddis hatches, March Brown and *Baetis* mayflies and winter stoneflies. Often, however, fishing takes the form of probing slow-moving pools with nymphs and streamers, both of which are fished with an active retrieve. At its best—when you catch the water level just right— the Owyhee might offer up a brown trout pushing six or seven pounds.

The fishable reach of the Owyhee spans only about 10 miles, beginning at Owyhee Dam and extending down to the vicinity of Snively Hot Springs. Below Snively, the flow slows even more and private property abounds. To get there, head south out of Ontario, but instead of taking the Vale turn at Highway 20, continue south toward Nyssa and Owyhee and then turn right at Owyhee River Road.

Oregon's Snake River border country offers several other fisheries of note. Northeast from Baker City, to the east of I-84, lies Thief Valley Reservoir whose 12- to 20-inch rainbows provide good fly angling during the spring and fall. You will need a boat or float tube. Take the North Powder exit from I-84 and head east to a right turn at Government Gulch Lane. After two miles turn right again, crossing the railroad tracks, and then follow the gravel up and over a low summit before descending to the reservoir. On the south side of the Wallowa Mountains, near the attractive little community of Halfway, flows Pine Creek. The upper portions are easily accessible while the lower reaches require permission from landowners.

Nearby Attractions and Activities

You won't find much in the way of entertainment around Brownlee Reservoir itself, but those willing to spend a day or two exploring the nearby countryside might find their reward to be a stunning view from high in the Elkhorn Range above Baker

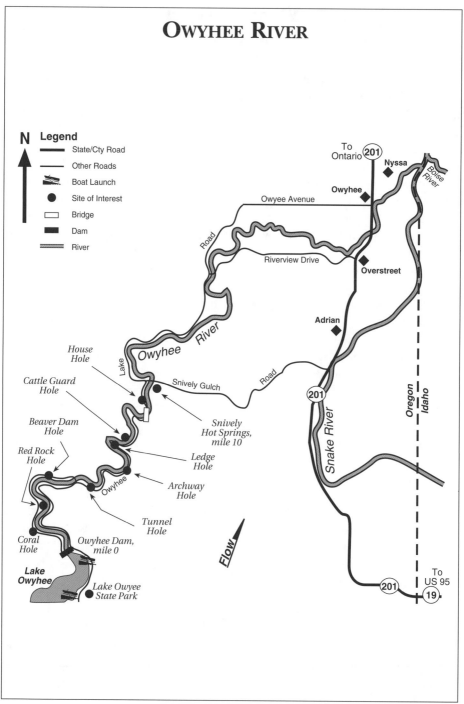

OWYHEE RIVER

N

Legend
—— State/Cty Road
—— Other Roads
Boat Launch
● Site of Interest
▢ Bridge
▪ Dam
River

To Ontario (201)
Nyssa
Boise River
Owyee Avenue
Owyhee
Riverview Drive
Overstreet
Road
Adrian
Owyhee River
Lake
Snively Gulch
Road
House Hole
Cattle Guard Hole
Snively Hot Springs, mile 10
Beaver Dam Hole
Ledge Hole
Red Rock Hole
Owyhee
Archway Hole
Tunnel Hole
Coral Hole
Owyhee Dam, mile 0
Flow
(201)
Snake River
Oregon / Idaho
Lake Owyhee
Lake Owyee State Park
To US 95
(201) (19)

© Wilderness Adventures Press, Inc.

City or the Wallowa Range above Halfway. Both of these towns are worth a visit. Baker City revels in its elegant historic downtown district, which comes complete with the Geyser Grande Hotel, Phone Company Restaurant, several other unique eateries and a brewpub. Halfway lives a much quieter existence, but its quaint old downtown area offers testimony to the towns out-of-sight, out-of-mind beauty. From Halfway, Hells Canyon is but a stone's throw away (at least by eastern Oregon standards).

Author's Tip

Don't linger too long in one place when searching for Brownlee's crappie. Instead, fish each location thoroughly, making sure to fish all depths. If you don't hit crappie within a reasonable number of casts, move on to another location.

Favorite Fly

Carey-Bugger

HOOK	3XL streamer hook, No. 4-6
TAIL	Marabou, short
BODY	Peacock herl ribbed with fine wire
COLLAR	Pheasant rump
HEAD	Metal bead

Carey-Bugger

Fast Facts

Brownlee Reservoir

LOCATION	Eastern Oregon on the Snake River, forming the Oregon/Idaho border
WATER TYPE	Semi-turbid reservoir
PRIMARY GAMEFISH	Black & white crappie, smallmouth bass, yellow perch. Also bluegill, rainbow trout, catfish, large-mouth bass.
BEST TIME	May and June; September and October
BEST FLIES	A variety of streamers will take fish. Poppers and divers work well under the right conditions.
EQUIPMENT	5- to 7-weight rod. Floating and sink-tip or sinking line. Float tube or boat optional, but certainly useful.
CONDITIONS	Hot weather is difficult to escape, so scout out the few groves of willow trees for afternoon fishing. Take plenty of fresh water. Access road is rough gravel.
DRIVE TIME	From Portland: 6 hours From Bend: 5 hours From Boise: 2 hours
DIRECTIONS	Follow I-84 north from Ontario or south from Baker City to the Huntington exit, then head through town and follow the signs down to the reservoir.

Area Fly Shops

FOUR-SEASONS FLY SHOP
10210 Wallowa Lake Highway
La Grande, OR 97850
541-963-8420

THE IDAHO ANGLER
1682 S. Vista
Boise, ID 83705
208-389-9957

INTERMOUNTAIN ARMS & TACKLE
900 Vista Village Center
Boise, ID 83705
208-345-3474

STONEFLY ANGLER
625 Vista
Boise, ID 83705
208-338-1700

BEAR CREEK FLY SHOP
5521 West State Street
Boise, ID 83703
208-853-8704

Contacts

OREGON DEPT. OF FISH & WILDLIFE
Baker City Field Office
2995 Hughes Lane
Baker City, OR 97814
541-523-5832

OREGON DEPT. OF FISH & WILDLIFE
Ontario Field Office
3814 Clark Blvd.
Ontario, OR 97914
541-889-6975

BAKER COUNTY
CHAMBER OF COMMERCE
541-523-5855

HUNTINGTON
CHAMBER OF COMMERCE
541-869-2019

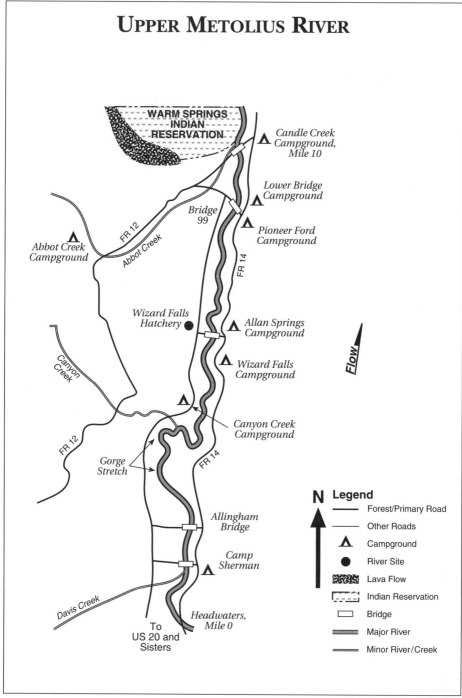

UPPER METOLIUS RIVER

WARM SPRINGS
INDIAN
RESERVATION

Candle Creek
Campground,
Mile 10

Lower Bridge
Campground

Bridge
99

Pioneer Ford
Campground

FR 12

Abbot Creek
Campground

Abbot Creek

FR 14

Wizard Falls
Hatchery

Allan Springs
Campground

Wizard Falls
Campground

Flow

Canyon
Creek

Canyon Creek
Campground

FR 12

Gorge
Stretch

FR 14

Allingham
Bridge

Camp
Sherman

N

Legend

———— Forest/Primary Road

——— Other Roads

▲ Campground

● River Site

▨ Lava Flow

▭ Indian Reservation

▭ Bridge

▰ Major River

▰▰ Minor River/Creek

Davis Creek

To
US 20 and
Sisters

Headwaters,
Mile 0

© Wilderness Adventures Press, Inc.

CHAPTER 11

THE METOLIUS RIVER

Central Oregon's Beloved Spring Creek

A long-favored destination of fly anglers from the Northwest, Oregon's beautiful Metolius River bubbles to life from springs that emanate from porous subterranean lava flows beneath verdant ponderosa forests. A tame, meadow-clad glide in its upper reaches, the Metolius soon gathers momentum from its increasingly steep gradient. It rushes headlong through remote, precipitous canyons on its 28-mile journey to a sprawling three-pronged reservoir that also captures the Deschutes and Crooked Rivers.

For decades the Metolius was heavily stocked with catchable-sized rainbow trout, their presence no doubt forcing the river's native redband trout into a subservient role. The hatchery program largely defined the fishery on the Metolius. For many more years anglers grew accustomed to fast action on a river filled to the brim with pen-raised trout.

Always mixed among the weekend warriors—to whom the Metolius-area businesses catered—were the more practiced and refined anglers whose skills and dedication allowed them to shun the easy-access, heavily stocked campground waters and seek the elusive native redbands and bull trout. They discovered the river's natural beauty, hatchery trout notwithstanding, and dreamed of a watershed managed for wild fish.

In 1996 they got their wish. Management of the Metolius River was redirected to focus on native fish populations and the decades-old program of filling the river with hatchery rainbows was discontinued. This decision followed the river's designation as a Wild & Scenic River in 1988.

With the hatchery fish gone from the river, the Metolius entered a brave new world and a lot of old-time Metolius regulars were disgruntled at the change. No longer could they enjoy the 30-fish days of old, for initial fish surveys in the late '90s found less than 80 adult redband trout per river mile. Gone was the use of bait; catch-and-release was made mandatory.

The change to the Metolius has been a profound one. Success is now measured in single digits or perhaps one or two large fish. As Bend-based writer Keith Ridler noted, "True, it is harder today to be successful on the Metolius, fishing for wary natives rather than the hatchery trout of a decade ago. But aren't truly worthwhile endeavors always more challenging, and the rewards of success commensurately greater?"

The Metolius may never again boast the density of trout it tolerated during the days when ODFW planted nearly 20,000 fish per summer. The river simply cannot support such numbers. The Metolius's fertility assures abundant trout food, but her steep gradient and limited prime habitat remain the significant limiting factors. Still, fishing for the redbands seems to improve with each passing season. Fish densities seem to be edging up ever so slightly, especially as instream improvement projects broaden the selection of good holding areas for trout.

So what can a fly angler expect from this "new" Metolius? First and foremost, the river's spectacular scenery remains unchanged and also remains the prime reason to visit the river for many anglers. If put to a vote, this unique spring creek would certainly win the title of Oregon's most beautiful trout stream.

As for the fishing, we must to some extent wait and see. Still, these past few years since the management change on the Metolius, the river has proven increasingly productive for practiced anglers, but not so good for the part-time fly fisher who dabbles with a Royal Wulff in a pool next to a campground—the same pool that once held a continually replenished supply of hatchery drones.

Most Oregon fly anglers applaud the new Metolius. In fact, the river has slowly earned the respect of fly fishers who used to shun its crowded summer campgrounds and cookie-cutter hatchery fish. The ever-talented fly dresser and artist Richard Bunse once created quite a local stir with his "popcorn fly," which looked for all the world like a piece of popcorn and which often rose hatchery rainbows better than an Elk Hair Caddis. That fly won't work here any more. These wild redbands are a different breed, a better breed.

Fishing the Metolius

These days, success on the Metolius comes to those who understand and practice classic Western spring-creek techniques, including downstream slack-line casts and the use of sparsely dressed flies during heavy hatches. The Metolius gets plenty such hatches. Golden Stoneflies, for example, hatch all summer. Myriad caddis and mayflies make seasonal appearances. Among the latter are the Green Drakes (*Drunella*), which emerge during May and June.

Despite the river's abundant hatches, Metolius River trout don't always feed at the surface with great vigor. Often, only scattered risers respond to good hatches. The reasons for their lack of interest in surface foods might stem from several sources. For starters, most angling effort has traditionally been concentrated around the campgrounds and roadside pools of the upper river—waters that have historically been dominated by hatchery trout. Anglers who explore the river's remote reaches, namely in "the Gorge" upstream from Wizard Falls Hatchery and in the lower river, below Bridge 99, will find wild trout working the surface with a little more enthusiasm.

The headwaters of the Metolius provide a splendid view of Mt. Jefferson.

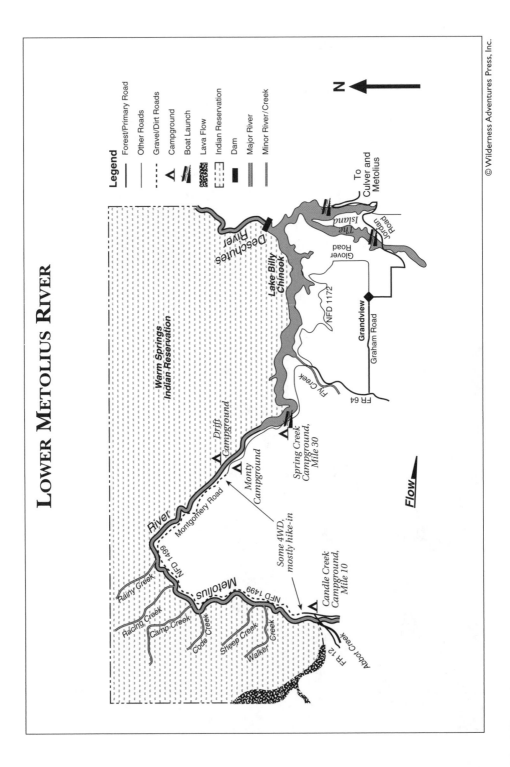

LOWER METOLIUS RIVER

© Wilderness Adventures Press, Inc.

Second, many anglers simply don't recognize the best dry-fly water and don't fish those places during the good hatches. Swift riffles and runs dominate the Metolius—water that doesn't lend itself to dry-fly action during mayfly and caddis hatches. Instead, look for rising fish in the river's slow tailouts and around deep current seams. Also, fish those places where structural elements provide a break in the current. Fish the right water during a good hatch (or even a modest one) and you'll wonder what all the fuss is over hatches with no rising trout.

Naturally, the Metolius is superb water for those anglers adept at nymph fishing. However, even nymphing presents unique challenges on this river. Flies and tactics must be designed to fish deep in fast water. At the same time, anglers must be proficient in the art of long-line nymphing. Many good pools simply allow no close approach, either owing to deep and/or swift water or the spooky nature of the larger native redbands.

The Metolius offers a secondary fishery for large bull trout—one of the West's healthiest populations of these native char. All must be carefully released. They typically range from two to six pounds, but double-digit fish fall to fly anglers each year. The highly gregarious bull trout prey heavily on other fish, so streamer patterns are the ticket when pursuing these brutes. Some anglers fish Deceivers or similar saltwater flies while others prefer large Marabou Muddlers, sculpins or Zonkers. The fish seem far less selective than the anglers. Mostly it's a matter of using a high-density line to keep the fly deep and then working the streamer through deep seams, runs, and pools.

Large bull trout are common residents of the Metolius system.

Restaurants and Accommodations

A visit to the Metolius would hardly be complete without a dinner reservation at Kokanee Café, which could easily compete with the many fine Bend restaurants for the best cuisine in central Oregon. Located across the bridge and down the street from Camp Sherman Store, the café draws crowds on summer evenings, so make reservations (541-595-6420).

Accommodations on the Metolius range from some half-dozen nice camp-grounds to well-appointed rental cabins. The campgrounds rank among the state's best. For starters, they border the river. Also, they are shaded by towering ponderosas in a park-like setting. Among the rental units are the cabins owned by Metolius River Lodge (800-595-6290) and those operated by Metolius River Resort (800-818-7688). Camp Sherman Store & Fly Shop also offers a rental cabin (541-595-6711). The store and fly shop carries everything you might need, from gasoline to fishing advice. House on the Metolious has 200 acres with private bank access on the river (541-595-6620).

The nearby town of Sisters has exploded into a tourist trap of the highest order. The growth virtually sickens me, yet I still enjoy a sandwich from Depot Deli or a pastry and coffee from Sisters Bakery. Sisters also includes one of central Oregon's best fly shops, The Fly Fisher's Place owned by Jeff Perin (541-549-3474). Sisters also provides a valuable service for many anglers by offering a pleasant, shopping-rich diversion for non-fishing family members.

Sisters Lodging

Sisters Motor Lodge, 511 W. Cascade Ave., 541-549-2551
Comfort Inn, 540 Hwy. 20, 541-549-7829
Conklin Guest House B&B, 69013 Camp Polk Rd., 541-549-0123
Rags to Walkers B&B, 17045 Farthing Lane, 541-548-7000

Sisters includes numerous small restaurants of every description. The ever-popular Hotel Sisters Restaurant, in the middle of town, serves fine dinners in a beautifully preserved 1900-vintage hotel (541-549-7427). The Gallery Restaurant, while nothing special in culinary terms, is a long-time favorite with locals and visitors. Located on the main drag at 171 W. Cascade (541-549-2631), The Gallery always draws a crowd during peak travel periods (summer and again during ski season). A relative newcomer, Royal Thai Café (291 E. Cascade, 541-549-3025) offers exceptional, genuine Thai food.

Nearby Fisheries
Suttle Lake

Suttle Lake, located alongside Highway 20 just west of the Metolius River Road, offers a chance at big brown trout during late spring and fall. They are never particularly plentiful, but they run two to eight pounds and will hit streamers in shallow water at low light. You'll need watercraft. Little Three Creeks Lake, a pleasant and scenic little hike-in brook trout fishery, lies south of Sisters. Check it out on the map and then spend a morning or afternoon sampling its lightly-fished waters.

Nearby Attractions and Activities

When you visit the Metolius, drive up to the headwaters (called "Head of the Metolius") and walk the short, easy trail down to the observation deck at the river's source. The Metolius literally springs from the ground here under a commanding view of Mt. Jefferson, Oregon's second highest peak. Black Butte, which rises to more than 6,000 feet above the Head of the Metolius, makes for a nice, steep morning hike and offers a superb view of central Oregon and the stunning volcanic peaks of the Cascades. To reach the trailhead, turn north off the highway at Indian Ford, east of the Metolius River turn-off. Head north a few miles to a signed left turn that winds most of the way up the mountain.

The Camp Sherman Store offers anything you might need while visiting the Metolius River.

Author's Tip

Only the hardy adventurous type need apply, but for those willing to brave her rugged waters, the lower Metolius offers ample opportunity to escape the crowds. A gravel road, closed to vehicle traffic runs along the east bank for several miles below Bridge 99. Also, you can access the lower river from below, above the Metolius Arm of Lake Billy Chinook. Consult a Forest Service map for specific directions.

Favorite Fly
X-Caddis

HOOK   Dry-fly, No. 12-18
TAIL   Antron strands
BODY   Olive or brown dubbing
WING   Elk or deer hair, short

X-Caddis

Fast Facts
Metolius River

LOCATION   Central Oregon, west of Sisters

WATER TYPE   Spring creek

PRIMARY GAMEFISH   Native redband trout and bull trout

BEST TIME   Year-round

BEST FLIES   Dry Flies: X-Caddis and Sparkle Duns to match particular caddis and mayfly hatches, respectively; Stimulator, No. 6-8; Griffith's Gnat, No. 20; Green Drake Paradrake, No. 10. Nymphs: Golden Stonefly Nymph, Hare's Ear Nymph, Pheasant Tail Nymph and various others. Use streamers for bull trout.

EQUIPMENT	4- to 6-weight rod with a floating line.
CONDITIONS	Campgrounds are very pleasant and well-maintained. Summer and fall weather is typically ideal.
DRIVE TIME	From Portland: 3 hours From Boise: 6-7 hours
DIRECTIONS	From western Oregon, follow any of the highways east across the Cascade Range, heading toward the town of Sisters. If you arrive from the north or south, continue west through Sisters on Highway 20/126 until you reach a right turn at the well-marked Camp Sherman/Metolius River turn-off. If coming from the west, you will reach the turn-off before reaching Sisters.

Local Fly Shops

CAMP SHERMAN STORE & FLY SHOP
P.O. Box 638
Camp Sherman, OR 97730
541-595-6711

THE FLY FISHER'S PLACE
151 W. Main Avenue
Sisters, OR 97759
541-549-3474

Area Fly Shops

FLY-N-FIELD
143 SW Century Drive
Bend, OR 97701
541-318-1616

THE PATIENT ANGLER
55 NW Wall Street
Bend, OR 97701
541-389-6208

THE FLY BOX
1293 NE 3rd
Bend, OR 97701
541-388-3330

DESCHUTES RIVER OUTFITTERS
61115 South Highway 97
Bend, OR 97702
541-388-8191

THE HOOK FLY SHOP
Sunriver Village Mall, Building 21
Sunriver, OR 97707
541-593-2358

SUNRIVER FLY SHOP
Sunriver Business Park
Sunriver, OR 97707
541-593-8814

CREEKSIDE FLYFISHING SHOP
345 High Street S.
Salem, OR 97301
503-588-1768

VALLEY FLYFISHER
153 Alice Street
Salem, OR 97302
503-375-3721

FLY COUNTRY OUTFITTERS
3400 State Street, G-704
Salem, OR 97301
503-585-4898

Guides

JOHN JUDY FLY FISHING
541-595-2073
(Judy guides for guests of House on
the Metolius and is the only commercial fishing guide on the river, but only
for guests of the lodge on its private
water.)

Contacts

OREGON DEPARTMENT
OF FISH & WILDLIFE
High Desert Regional Office
61374 Parrell Road
Bend, OR 97702
541-388-6363

SISTERS CHAMBER OF COMMERCE
541-549-0251

CHAPTER 12

THE CROOKED RIVER

Year-Round Wild Rainbows

Central Oregon's Crooked River emanates from Bowman Dam and Prineville Reservoir. Due to the cold flows from the reservoir, this diminutive river boasts an estimated density approaching 2,000 redband trout and as many as 5,000 whitefish per mile. All of these fish are crammed into a river that often flows at a meager 100 cubic feet per second. The catch rate is astounding for anglers of even modest experience.

We used to refer to the Crooked River as the region's best nine-inch trout fishery. Over the past few seasons, however, increasing numbers of larger trout have earned this popular fishery a more serious reputation as a top-flight wild trout stream. Brett Hodgson, the assistant district biologist with ODFW, confirms that larger trout seem increasingly common on the Crooked, but he admits not knowing the reasons for the river's apparent turnaround.

Hodgson points to the fierce competition between mountain whitefish and red-band trout—both natives—as a major dynamic in the river ecosystem. Whitefish numbers have exploded over the past half-decade, probably owing to ideal spawning conditions. They now outnumber the trout two or three to one, competing for space and food. Whether the dynamic relationship between trout and whitefish somehow explains the increasing numbers of 12- to 18-inch trout, Hodgson can't say. He readily acknowledges that angling pressure on the Crooked has increased markedly during the past couple of seasons.

Perhaps the influx of people on the water explains the increase in larger trout being reported. New, more restrictive regulations partially explain the rise in angler-use days on the Crooked, but the more significant factors are the explosive population growth in central Oregon and the Crooked's unique, well-publicized status as one of the state's most consistent winter/spring trout destinations. In any case, central Oregon fly anglers flock to the Crooked River, especially between December and May when few other rivers in the region offer such productive fishing.

From just below Bowman Dam, the Crooked River meanders through a precipitous desert canyon with towering rimrocks throwing long shadows across the stream. About 10 miles of public-access water offers room to spread out, yet anglers tend to congregate within the first two miles below the dam. The road to Prineville Reservoir follows closely along the river and numerous short, gravel sideroads provide parking. Nice BLM camping facilities await those who decide to spend the night.

At low water, the Crooked River is a small, shallow, easily-waded stream, replete with rocks and boulders of all sizes. Slippery algae cover the rocks, making for less than perfect footing. Cleated wading boots help and many anglers opt for a wading staff to negotiate the river's murky waters. Nonetheless, this is small water, barely 20 yards wide in any given stretch. The best fishing occurs when water levels drop below 200 cfs. Still better are those frequent occasions when the flows hover around 100 cfs, making the Crooked an intimate, easily readable, wadeable and fishable river.

With the river running low, many anglers make the decided mistake of assuming that only the pools hold trout. Certainly the deeper confines of the Crooked offer prime habitat for the native fish, but so too do the shallow, rocky riffles and glides that predominate. The trout seem perfectly contented to feed in water just one to two feet deep. On a trip last April, for example, Brent Snow and I spent two hours hooking perhaps two dozen trout from knee-deep water located between two of the large, deep pools. Meanwhile, the two anglers who had ventured upstream ahead of us spent a fruitless hour fishing the deep water before heading back down the trail to their car.

They had made the common mistake of not choosing the best water for fishing the inevitable pre-hatch feeding binge and then not sticking around long enough to

CROOKED RIVER

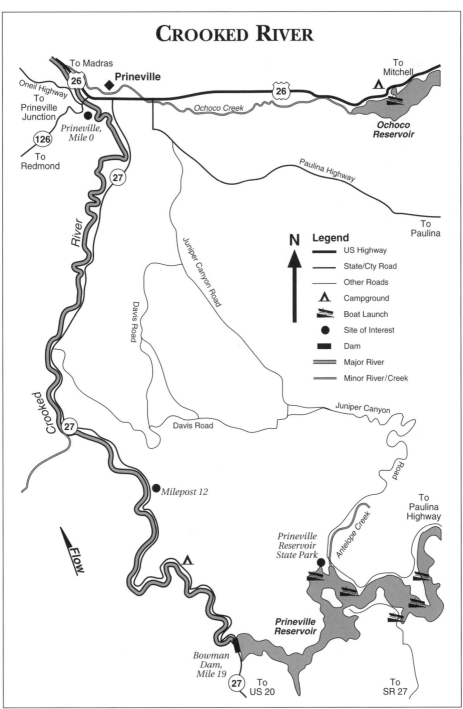

To Madras

Prineville

To Mitchell

26

Oneil Highway

To
Prineville
Junction

26

Ochoco Creek

Ochoco
Reservoir

Prineville,
Mile 0

126

To
Redmond

Paulina Highway

27

To
Paulina

N **Legend**

US Highway

State/Cty Road

Other Roads

⚊ Campground

Boat Launch

● Site of Interest

▬ Dam

Major River

Minor River/Creek

Juniper Canyon Road

Davis Road

River

Juniper Canyon

Davis Road

Crooked

27

● Milepost 12

Flow

Road

To
Paulina
Highway

Antelope Creek

Prineville
Reservoir
State Park

⚊

Prineville
Reservoir

Bowman
Dam,
Mile 19

27

To
US 20

To
SR 27

© Wilderness Adventures Press, Inc.

The Crooked River is a wild trout fishery for all seasons.

enjoy the hour-long *Baetis* hatch that ensued shortly after their departure. So think in terms of fishing all the good water, not just the pools. Any reach of the Crooked offering knee-deep water, a smooth, gliding surface and a channel littered with boulders will prove to be loaded with trout. Moreover, such habitat is ideally suited to non-indicator sight-nymphing when the river drops to its lowest levels.

The pools also offer plenty of trout, although in places you must fish your way through a school of whitefish before finding the redbands. Often the river's pools fish best during a strong hatch. In fact, these pools can come alive with rising trout when the *Baetis* or *Chironomids* emerge on warm spring days. Summer brings searing heat to the Crooked River Canyon, but those who wait till dusk often enjoy swarming caddis hatches. The caddis hatches continue into mid-autumn. Autumn also presents renewed *Baetis* activity.

During non-hatch periods, the Crooked River's trout don't pay much attention to the surface, so most anglers fish with scud patterns, Hare's Ear Nymphs, Pheasant Tail Nymphs, and small egg patterns. Especially popular are orange scud patterns, tied on size 12 through 16 hooks and weighted with a bead and/or a little lead wire; a close second is a similar pattern dressed in natural gray or tan. Indicator nymphing is the method of choice, but at low flows, the Crooked is perfectly suited to non-indicator nymphing and at times even sight-nymphing, despite the fact that the water never flows particularly clear.

At its lowest flows, the Crooked clears up just enough so that you can stalk carefully through the shallows casting nymph patterns to small pockets and seams among the rocks. Such tactics reward those who concentrate on carefully studying the fly's drift and watching diligently for visible trout. The Crooked River, at low flows, is the perfect training ground for those who desire to add a new challenge to their nymph fishing by eliminating the strike indicator.

Without question, spring offers the best hatches on the Crooked, with *Chironomid* and Blue-Winged Olive mayfly emergences beginning during February and gaining momentum through May. Both tend towards the ridiculously tiny side; expect to fish surface patterns ranging from size 18 down to size 24. The spring hatches follow a banker's hours schedule. Generally, the first bugs appear around noon and then the full-blown hatch occurs between 1 p.m. and 3 p.m.

Even the winter months offer the occasional hatch of midges or Blue-Winged Olives, but most of the winter action is limited to nymphs. Between November and February, the Crooked River ranks with the best off-season trout fisheries in the Northwest. Unlike rivers farther east, the Crooked enjoys a comparably mild winter climate. That's not to say you won't freeze your tail off from time to time, but sunny, 40-degree afternoons occur frequently during December, February, and March.

Truly, the Crooked River is a wild trout fishery for all seasons. Its dense population of wild redbands is virtually beyond compare for such a small river, and catch-and-release regulations from November through May protect these native gems during a time of the year that has proven most attractive to fly fishers. Indeed, despite the rapidly increasing popularity of this fishery, it remains one of Oregon's best wild trout waters. With larger trout becoming increasingly common, the future looks bright for the Crooked River and its beautiful native redbands.

Restaurants and Accommodations

After following the river up to Bowman Dam, Crooked River Road climbs up to Prineville Reservoir and a large, convenient state park campground. The campground includes RV spaces, tent sites and five reasonably priced rental cabins. For information, call 541-447-4363 or to make reservations, call 800-551-6959. Some nice but largely undeveloped campsites are strung along the river in various places. Just look for the pull-offs and BLM signs.

Just 20 minutes from the action, the little town of Prineville has six motels and many restaurants. Ranchero Mexican Restaurant, on the highway at 969 NW 3ʳᵈ, offers good lunches and dinners (541-416-0103), or try the new Panda Restaurant (555 N. Main, 541-447-8288) for excellent Chinese food.

Prineville Lodging

Stafford Inn, 1773 NE 3ʳᵈ, 541-447-7100
City Center Motel, 509 NE 3ʳᵈ, 541-447-5522
Little Pine Motel, 251 NW Deer Street, 541-447-3440
Ochoco Inn, 123 NE 3ʳᵈ, 541-447-6231
Rustler's Inn, 960 NW 3ʳᵈ, 541-447-4187
Rodeway Inn, 1050 E. 3ʳᵈ, 541-447-4152

Nearby Attractions and Activities

The Crooked River Dinner Train offers a unique dining experience in the Prineville area. The three-hour trips run a scenic route through central Oregon, taking in pastoral rangelands and desert canyons. The train offers various 19th century western themes with its dinners and brunches with prices ranging from $60 to $70 per adult. For information or reservations, call 541-548-8630.

Author's Tip

When fishing a two-nymph set-up on the shallow pools and runs of the Crooked River, space the flies just eight inches apart using 4X or even 5X tippet. Coupled with proper line-management, this arrangement allows the flies to fish near the bottom without the need for a large, heavily weighted fly, making the entire rig easier to cast.

Favorite Fly

Beadhead Scud

HOOK	Scud hook, No. 12-16
BODY	Orange or olive-gray dubbing
RIB	Fine wire
HEAD	Metal bead

Beadhead Scud

Fast Facts

Crooked River

LOCATION	Central Oregon, near Prineville, northeast of Bend
WATER TYPE	Tailwater
PRIMARY GAMEFISH	Wild redband trout and mountain whitefish
BEST TIME	All year unless water levels are unusually high
BEST FLIES	Scuds, Pheasant Tail Nymphs, Hare's Ear Nymph, and other similar flies, with bead heads, No. 12-18; dry patterns to match Blue-Winged Olive mayflies, small *Chironomids* and small caddis.
EQUIPMENT	3- through 6-weight rod and floating line
CONDITIONS	The road is paved and provides ready access. Several nice camping areas. Summers are very hot; spring varies from bitter cold to pleasantly warm. River flows through a juniper-clad box canyon.
DRIVE TIME	From Portland: 3 hours From Eugene: 3½ hours From Boise: 6 hours From Bend: 45 minutes
DIRECTIONS	From the town of Redmond, head east on Highway 20 towards Prineville; once in Prineville, turn right at the stop light at the signed turn-off for Bowman Dam and Prineville Reservoir. The best fishing is in the first eight miles below Bowman Dam.

Local Fly Shops

THE FLY FISHER'S PLACE
151 West Main
Sisters, OR 97759
541-549-3474

FIN-N-FEATHER FLY SHOP
785 West Third Street
Prineville, OR 97754
541-447-8691

NUMB-BUTT FLY COMPANY
380 North Highway 26
Madras, OR 97741
541-325-5515

FLY-N-FIELD
143 SW Century Drive
Bend, OR 97701
541-318-1616

THE PATIENT ANGLER
55 NW Wall Street
Bend, OR 97701
541-389-6208

THE FLY BOX
1293 NE 3rd
Bend, OR 97701
541-388-3330

DESCHUTES RIVER OUTFITTERS
61115 South Highway 97
Bend, OR 97702
541-388-8191

THE HOOK FLY SHOP
Sunriver Village Mall, Building 21
Sunriver, OR 97707
541-593-2358

SUNRIVER FLY SHOP
Sunriver Business Park
Sunriver, OR 97707
541-593-8814

Guides

Arrange through local fly
shops listed above.

Contacts

OREGON DEPARTMENT
OF FISH & WILDLIFE
High Desert Regional Office
61374 Parrell Road
Bend, OR 97702
541-388-6363

PRINEVILLE CHAMBER
OF COMMERCE
541-447-6304

CHAPTER 13

THE MIDDLE DESCHUTES RIVER

A Winter Treat, Dry Flies and Brown Trout

You've heard of the Deschutes River, but you may never have heard about the Middle Deschutes River. The famous lower Deschutes offers everything a fly angler could want: 100 miles of prime wild trout and steelhead water amid stunning scenery. The Middle Deschutes, meanwhile, lives a less glamorous existence, quietly cutting a canyon through central Oregon between Bend and Lake Billy Chinook.

During the summer, its flows decimated by the demands of regional agriculture, the Middle Deschutes barely escapes central Oregon with so much as a trickle. But after the irrigation season ends during the fall, the canals are corked and the Middle Deschutes regains its substantial presence. The high flows continue through the winter and into the spring—the time when the Middle Deschutes shines as the state's best off-season dry-fly river.

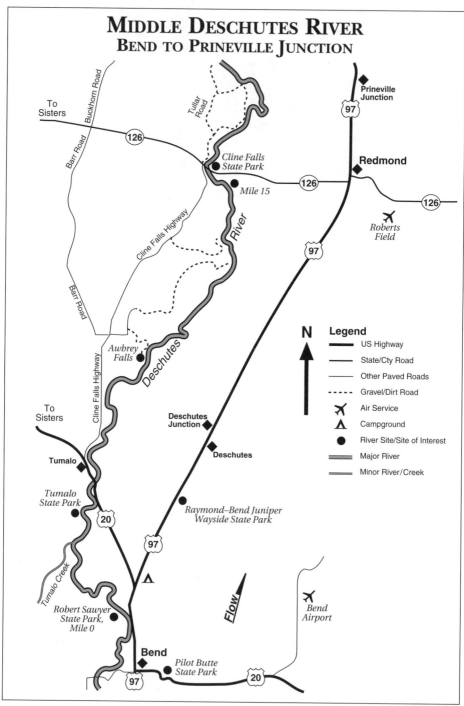

MIDDLE DESCHUTES RIVER
BEND TO PRINEVILLE JUNCTION

Prineville
Junction

To
Sisters

Buckhorn Road

Tullar
Road

Barr Road

126

Cline Falls
State Park

Redmond

126

Mile 15

126

River

Cline Falls Highway

Roberts
Field

97

Barr Road

Deschutes

N

Legend

Awbrey
Falls

Cline Falls Highway

To
Sisters

Deschutes
Junction

Deschutes

Tumalo

US Highway

State/Cty Road

Other Paved Roads

Gravel/Dirt Road

Air Service

Campground

River Site/Site of Interest

Major River

Minor River/Creek

Tumalo
State Park

20

Raymond–Bend Juniper
Wayside State Park

97

Tumalo Creek

Flow

Bend
Airport

Robert Sawyer
State Park,
Mile 0

Bend

Pilot Butte
State Park

97

20

© Wilderness Adventures Press, Inc.

MIDDLE DESCHUTES RIVER
PRINEVILLE JUNCTION TO LAKE BILLY CHINOOK

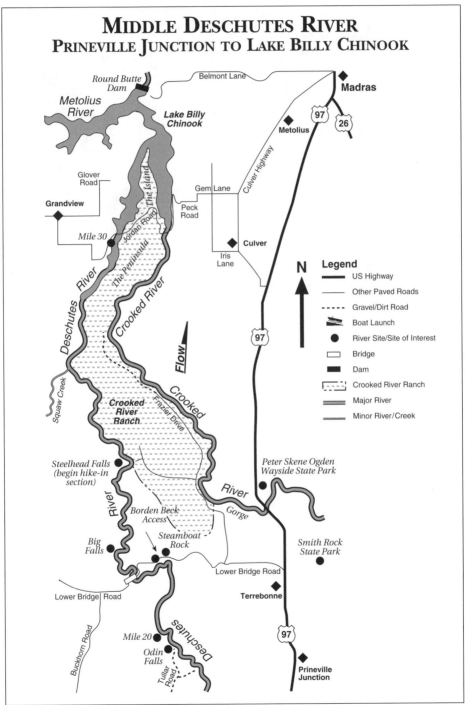

© Wilderness Adventures Press, Inc.

A large brown trout from the Middle Deschutes.

The action begins around the last day of January when the first tentative hatches of Little Black Stoneflies occur. The bugs always hatch at mid-afternoon and the stonefly action lasts through the month of February. By mid- or late February, *Baetis* mayflies begin sporadic hatches, which become more predictable during March. Then, around the end of March, the much larger March Brown mayflies (*Rithrogenia*) begin hatching. All three insects—the little stoneflies and both mayflies—prompt the river's trout to feed at the surface. Many a time I've stood hip-deep in the Middle Deschutes rising brown trout rising to dry flies while softly falling snow obscured the canyon walls.

Golden Stoneflies and some Salmonflies emerge during April and May. These huge insects need not be dense—trout are sure to notice even a few such bugs drifting down the river. Many fly anglers abandon the Middle Deschutes by the end of March, but those who know of the large stoneflies often hook the river's larger browns during late spring.

These brown trout, all wild, span 8- to 20-plus inches. An average day of good dry-fly action yields a dozen or so browns, most of which run 10 to 13 inches. Each season I get a few of those beautiful 16- to 20-inch fish. Wild rainbows share the river with the brown trout and in places the "redsides" predominate.

The Middle Deschutes takes some figuring out, so to speak. You must first learn the access points: places like Lower Bridge and the Foly Waters. The Bend and Sisters

MIDDLE DESCHUTES RIVER — 169

fly shops can help you with that part of the equation. Then you must embrace the physical demands of this river. The best fishing arrives at the price of climbing around and exploring the canyon and then wading through flooded brush, trees, and cattail stands.

Restaurants and Accommodations

During the late winter and early spring, when the Middle Deschutes delivers its best fishing, most traveling anglers opt for motel space rather than suffering bitter-cold nights in the outdoors. The best sections of the Middle Deschutes lie virtually equidistant from the towns of Sisters to the west and Redmond to the east. Sisters lodging options are covered in the Metolius River chapter of this guide. Unless the Metolius is also on your fishing menu, Redmond is the better choice because of its proximity to both the Middle Deschutes and the Crooked River—the area's top two wintertime fisheries. By staying in Redmond you can reach either river within half an hour.

With a portion of the Middle Deschutes flowing past the property, Inn at Eagle Crest offers the area's most exclusive lodging about five miles west of Redmond. Eagle Crest—a popular golf destination during the summer—features 75 lodge rooms plus rental condos (541-923-2453). Most of Redmond's motels are conveniently situated along Highway 97 and include Redmond Hub Motel (541-548-2101), Redmond Inn Motel (541-548-1091), Motel 6 (541-923-2100), and Village Squire Inn (541-548-2105).

A variety of restaurants serve this small but rapidly growing community. One of my favorites is a relative newcomer, Seventh Street Brewhouse at 855 SW 7th (541-923-1795). You can't go wrong for lunch or dinner. Perhaps the best restaurant in town is another fairly recent addition, Harris Wine Cellars (541-923-9849) at 541 SW Harris. Redmond boasts several good Mexican restaurants, including Cisco & Pancho's at 343 NW 6th (541-923-5042) and Cinco de Mayo at 1309 SW Highland (541-548-7737). I often find myself making the quick trip from Lower Bridge due east to Highway 97 and the little town of Terrebonne, a few miles north of Redmond. The draw is a quick, tasty lunch or dinner at La Siesta, on the east side of the highway (541-548-4848).

Author's Tip

Unbeknownst to most anglers, the Middle Deschutes hosts one of the state's most prolific hatches of March Brown mayflies. The hatch peaks during April and is best on the reach from Eagle Crest near Redmond downstream toward the Foly Waters (Lower Bridge is located about halfway through this section). Warm, cloudy days are best and often produce hatches of near-epic stature. Look for deep, choppy riffles that feed into slower pools.

Favorite Fly

Quigley Stonefly (Bob Quigley)

HOOK	Dry-fly, 2XL, No. 12-14
TAIL	Black deer hair
BODY	Black floss, alternately with red butt
WING	Black deer hair with butt ends forming head
HACKLE	Black, clipped

Quigley Stonefly

Fast Facts

Middle Deschutes River

LOCATION	Central Oregon, east of Sisters and west of Redmond
WATER TYPE	Canyon-bound freestone stream with radical seasonal water-level fluctuations
PRIMARY GAMEFISH	Wild brown trout, rainbow trout, and whitefish
BEST TIME	February through May
BEST FLIES	Black Quigley Stonefly, Floatin' Fool and black Elk Hair for the winter hatch of Little Black Stoneflies, other significant hatches are Blue-Winged Olives and March Brown mayflies, brown Willow Flies, Golden Stoneflies, and Salmonflies.
EQUIPMENT	4- to 6-weight rod and floating line; wading staff
CONDITIONS	January offers cold, sunny weather most days. February and March are transition months when anything from bitter cold and snow to bright, warm and sunny is possible. The river flows through a box canyon. Trails

lead along the banks. Expect difficult wading and physically demanding fishing because the winter water levels are so much higher than the summer levels.

DRIVE TIME

From Bend: ½ hour
From Portland: 3-4 hours
From Eugene: 3 hours

DIRECTIONS

From Sisters or Redmond, follow Highway 126 to a north turn on Buckskin Road (a gravel road a few miles west from the bridge crossing over the river. Follow Buckskin Road to a right turn at Lower Bridge Road, which leads down to the bridge and the public access. For additional access points, consult the central Oregon fly shops in Sisters or Bend.

Local Fly Shops

THE FLY FISHER'S PLACE
151 West Main
Sisters, OR 97759
541-549-3474

FIN-N-FEATHER FLY SHOP
785 West Third Street
Prineville, OR 97754
541-447-8691

FLY-N-FIELD
143 SW Century Drive
Bend, OR 97701
541-318-1616

THE PATIENT ANGLER
55 NW Wall Street
Bend, OR 97701
541-389-6208

THE FLY BOX
1293 NE 3rd
Bend, OR 97701
541-388-3330

DESCHUTES RIVER OUTFITTERS
61115 South Highway 97
Bend, OR 97702
541-388-8191

THE HOOK FLY SHOP
Sunriver Village Mall, Building 21
Sunriver, OR 97707
541-593-2358

SUNRIVER FLY SHOP
Sunriver Business Park
Sunriver, OR 97707
541-593-8814

Contacts

OREGON DEPARTMENT
OF FISH & WILDLIFE
High Desert Regional Office
61374 Parrell Road
Bend, OR 97702
541-388-6363

REDMOND CHAMBER
OF COMMERCE
541-923-5191

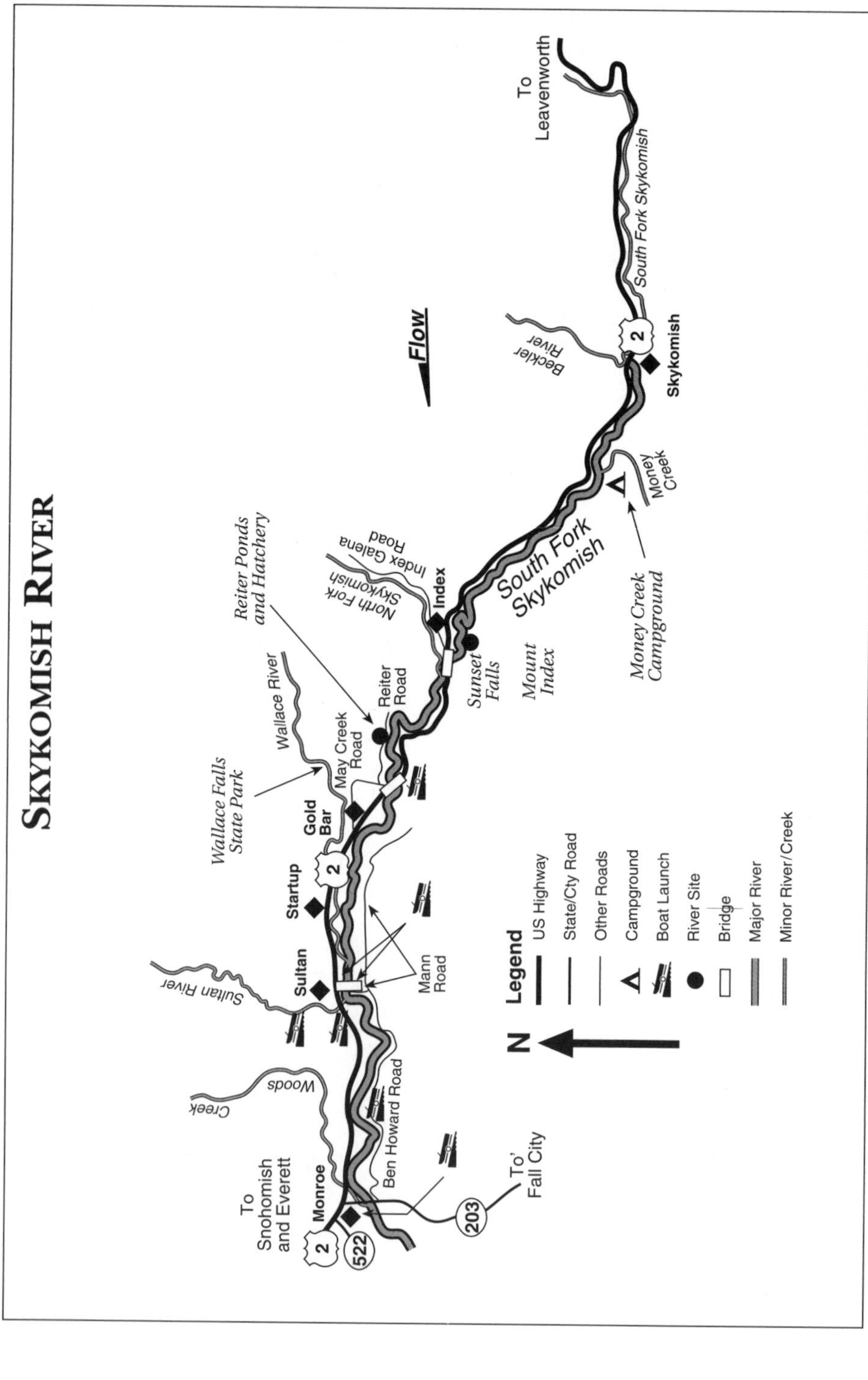

SKYKOMISH RIVER

Flow

To Leavenworth

South Fork Skykomish

Beckler River

2 Skykomish

Money Creek

Money Creek Campground

Reiter Ponds and Hatchery

Index Galena Road

North Fork Skykomish

Index

South Fork Skykomish

Mount Index

Sunset Falls

Reiter Road

Wallace River

May Creek Road

Wallace Falls State Park

Gold Bar

2

Startup

Sultan

Sultan River

Mann Road

Woods Creek

To Snohomish and Everett

Monroe

2 522

Ben Howard Road

203 To' Fall City

N

Legend
- US Highway
- State/Cty Road
- Other Roads
- Campground
- Boat Launch
- River Site
- Bridge
- Major River
- Minor River/Creek

CHAPTER 14

THE SKYKOMISH RIVER

Home Waters of the Legends

A stone's throw from the Northwest's most populous region flows one of her most productive and prestigious steelhead rivers. Within an hour of fleeing the city, Seattle fly anglers find themselves swinging flies through cobblestone runs on the Skykomish River, a stream revered by several generations of steelhead enthusiasts. The Sky, in fact, more than any other metro-area river, embodies the area's steelhead fly-fishing history.

At times these days, the Sky's convenient proximity to the metro area is also the river's downfall in the form of crowded conditions. Yet fly fishers who fish mid-week and who are willing to work at it a little can find elegant steelhead pools devoid of other anglers. Indeed, the scenic Skykomish beckons me more than any other Seattle-area river because this historic stream abounds in steelhead water, from the long, slow cobblestone expanses of the lower river to the glassy, boulder-studded chutes, tailouts and pockets of the upper reaches.

A summer steelhead from the Skykomish River.

A few years ago I found myself daydreaming amid a sea of show-goers at a sports expo in Seattle. My thoughts had drifted away to the green February flows of the Skykomish, only an hour distant. The crowded aisles at the show reminded me that a sports show weekend is a great time for fishing in the Seattle area—especially if a little rain falls to further convince the average outdoorsman of the need to see what's new at the show rather than don a slicker for a soggy day on the water. I had to get out on the river.

I was "showed out," so to speak.

Turned out to be a wise choice, for nothing at the sports show could equal the elation of having that sea-bright fish grab a Spawning Purple above the bridge at Sultan. Nothing except perhaps the ensuing tug-o-war, wherein this fish departed for greener pastures below the bridge, taking most of my backing with her. I never saw the fish, though I'm sure she barely scratched 10 pounds. But she was excitable to say the least, and we parted company soon after she vacated the pool.

The story doesn't quite end there. Later that same year I found myself wandering down Highway 2, taking the long way home from the Wenatchee. Late September had cast its colorful spell on the maples and alders along the South Fork of the Sky. I played that dangerous game with which we are all familiar: One eye longingly study-ing the river below, the other tracking the oncoming log trucks. The water looked too good to leave unmolested, but I was already late getting home to Bend—still many hours away. The long route had beckoned for a reason: I was fishing the Sky. Duties at home be damned.

Between the falls, a promising looking pool lured me in for a look. The low water of late summer had yet to feel the refreshing deluge of September freshets, so I chose a long leader and a size 2 Spawning Purple. The steelhead gods were on my side this time around—apparently my two fishless days on the Wenatchee had appeased their sense of appropriate sacrifice. Within a dozen casts I was cradling a seven-pound hatchery fish, his flanks brightly lit with a wide wash of crimson.

I returned him to the river, retired the fly to its clip in the Wheatley and stowed the rod. I'd make it home on time. I fished two pools on the Sky that year, one during the winter and one in the fall. The river had granted me two hook-ups. Truly, she is a magical river.

Fishing the Skykomish

The Skykomish runs a steep, direct course, joining the Snoqualmie near the town of Monroe. Its lower 15 miles braid and meander, but the Sky's character changes quickly upstream from Gold Bar. In a span of about 20 miles, anglers find a tremendously varied river. This elegant free-flowing river, along with its stark, bold backdrop of precipitous crags and timbered slopes, has inspired countless fly anglers. One of the sport's most beautiful classic steelhead flies—the Skykomish Sunrise—was created by George McLeod, at his father Ken's request, and named for this magnificent stream.

The Skykomish hosts both summer and winter steelhead, the latter comprising the more numerous runs. The December-through-February run of one-salt fish, most of hatchery origin, attracts swarms of meat hunters. But on March 1, the Sky goes to catch-and-release regulations for the big native "spring" steelhead (check current regulations). The hordes disassemble and the lower river is purged of assorted bank anglers and drift-boaters pulling plugs through every inch of good water. March 1 signals the arrival of the fly anglers and of the remaining gear anglers who enjoy the hard pull of a mammoth steelhead destined for release.

Despite its impressive proportions, the lower Skykomish is easy water for fly anglers because its cobblestone/gravel bottom is quite free of the boulders and ledges that steal deep-swung flies on many other winter steelhead streams. The low-gradient channel offers easy wading and the river's wide pools beg long casts with the increasingly popular two-handed rods, along with the more traditional single-handed rods used to good effect by the river's pioneering anglers. Should your fly snag bottom at the end of the swing, a little slack line will usually free it from the small, rounded stones comprising the riverbed.

Like the Skagit to the north, the Skykomish offers ideal conditions for artfully devised flies. The flies need not bounce off the bottom, but simply swing deep in the flow, a task made possible through line choice and line control. This latter element—line control—explains the popularity of two-handed Spey rods on the Sky and other Washington rivers. Likewise, Spey-style flies have gained an ardent following in the region, as have the marabou steelhead flies. Weighted leeches and other such patterns take plenty of fish, yet their use seems unbefitting to a river of such beauty and a fish of such wonder.

The lower river braids in places, its channel shifting slightly with heavy flows; yet nearby mountains offer the protection of freezing weather to hold in check the effects of sudden snowmelt and torrential rains in the valley. In fact, the Sky often drops into fishable condition when other area rivers are blown out.

The popular stretch of the lower river extends from the town of Sultan down to Monroe, a distance of about nine river miles. Highway 2 connects both towns from the river's north bank while Ben Howard Road follows the south bank, providing bank access in places and accessing the boat ramp upstream from Monroe (turn south across the bridge at Sultan or turn north on Ben Howard Road just south of the 203 Bridge in Monroe). The other take-out lies just below the river bridge on Highway 203 in Monroe, on your right as you pass over the bridge. The short drift between these two cement ramps gives access to some productive fly water and allows anglers to pick one or two runs to fish thoroughly.

Another launch (the Two-Bit Hole) is located on private property off Ben Howard Road below Sultan. The landowner charges a nominal fee for access (look for the mailbox with the name Gwilt). This fee ramp will save you about two miles on the drift down to Monroe. Otherwise, the launch at Sultan serves as the starting point for trips downriver. One additional option is to launch up at Big Eddy, about nine miles above Sultan; this drift takes you through lots of fly water and through a Class II rapid. You can also float from Monroe down to the mouth of the Skykomish, taking out at a very crude launch below the Highway 522 Bridge (four miles).

Although better known for its big native winter steelhead, the Skykomish hosts a decent run of hatchery and native summer fish from June through September. Following the snowmelt, the Sky drops and clears quickly, and summer fish migrate rapidly through the lower river. They can be intercepted below Sultan, but the better holding water awaits upriver and into the forks.

The Sky's South Fork unfolds in a hurry, tumbling headlong down the Cascades from Stevens Pass through a deep canyon heavily laden with cobble and boulders. Highway 2 follows its course. The North Fork draws its headwaters from equally awesome country in the heart of the high Cascades. The two forks converge about eight miles upstream from the town of Gold Bar on Highway 2. Both forks produce summer and winter fish in good numbers and the river below the forks has historically ranked among the state's most productive steelhead rivers.

The North Fork flows unobstructed as far up as Deer Creek Falls, allowing anadromous fish unfettered access to the upper reaches. The South Fork, meanwhile, features a series of waterfalls that block upstream fish passage. However, the Washington Department of Fish and Wildlife traps and trucks fish over the falls opening more than 100 additional river miles to steelhead, salmon, trout, and char. The trucking begins around July and lasts until about the end of the season, typically totaling 700 to 1,000 steelhead. Thus, anglers can enjoy summer steelheading at its scenic best, with some of the most productive water flowing from the town of Skykomish down to Halford.

The Skykomish is a steelhead river for all seasons and one easy to reach from the Seattle area. And despite the crowds that assemble all too often, Washington's well-mannered steelhead fly angling community assures plenty of elbow room most of the time during the spring and summer. Should you arrive at a steelhead pool already occupied by other fly anglers, simply wait your turn and start in at the top of the run. The majority of the Sky's fly anglers will welcome you, and the river's legendary runs and pools may provide the beginning of new angling friendships.

Restaurants and Accommodations

The town of Monroe is the hub for anglers heading for the Skykomish, especially during the winter/spring season when some of the best pools lie just minutes from town. Monroe, a town of 7,000 people, boasts a fairly wide array of restaurants and lodging options. The requisite brewery is Twin Rivers at 104 N. Lewis Street (360-794-4056), and I often find myself sitting down to Mexican fare at Monroe's Ixtapa Restaurant, located right along the main drag (360-794-8484).

The town of Sultan—situated along prime steelhead water seven miles upriver from Monroe—offers a single motel, the Dutch Cup (360-793-2215). The Dutch Cup is ideally situated and offers nice, clean accommodations, including two kitchenette units. Call ahead for reservations, especially on prime weekends during the winter-run season.

Monroe Lodging

Best Western Baron Inn, 19233 Hwy. 2, 360-794-3111
Brookside Motel, 19930 Hwy. 2, 360-794-8832
Fairground Inn, 18950 Hwy. 2, 360-794-5401
Holiday Inn Express, 19103 Hwy. 2, 360-863-1900
Monroe Motel, 20310 Old Owen Rd., 360-794-6751
Sky River Inn, 333 River Drive E., 360-677-2261

If you are visiting the Sky during summer or fall for summer-run steelhead, you should stay farther upstream, closer to the prime water between Gold Bar and the tiny town of Skykomish. The Dutch Cup Motel in Sultan remains a good, inexpensive option, though you'll be driving upstream each morning. Money Creek Campground offers riverside sites a few miles west of Skykomish and the town itself offers Skykomish Motel (360-677-2477) and Casedia Motel (360-677-2390). More luxurious lodgings include several rental cabins (call Mt. Index Properties, 360-793-7616), Sky River Inn on the river near Skykomish (360-677-2261), and the beautiful new Wallace Falls Lodge near Gold Bar (360-793-8784).

Nearby Attractions and Activities

Steven's Pass Ski Area ranks among Washington's best and most popular ski areas and is located east of the little community of Skykomish, 80 miles from Seattle. The winter steelhead season on the Skykomish River coincides perfectly with the season's best skiing conditions. For information and tickets, call 206-812-4510 or go online at www.stevenspass.com.

While you're on the Skykomish, check out impressive, 265-foot-high Wallace Falls near Sultan. A large state park offers trails and camp space. Wallace Falls is at its best during the wet months when seasonal rains and spring snowmelt swell the falls to awesome proportions.

Author's Tip

While I can offer no personal anecdotes on the matter, several of my angling friends inform me that during low-water periods, late-winter steelhead often congregate on the Snohomish River below the mouth of the Sky. The stretch below the mouth, they tell me, can be productive, oft-overlooked water under such conditions.

Favorite Fly

Skykomish Sunrise (George McLeod)

TAG	Flat silver tinsel
TAIL	Mix of red and yellow hackle fibers
BODY	Red chenille
RIB	Silver oval tinsel
HACKLE	Mix of red and yellow hackle
WING	White bucktail, calftail or polar bear
EYES	Jungle cock (optional)

Skykomish Sunrise

Fast Facts

Skykomish River

LOCATION	Northwest Washington
WATER TYPE	Large freestone steelhead river
PRIMARY GAMEFISH	Winter and summer steelhead; salmon, searun cutthroat
BEST TIME	February-April for winter steelhead; June-September for summer steelhead
BEST FLIES	A wide variety of steelhead flies are employed on the Skykomish River, including some of the classic patterns invented decades ago by well-known Skykomish anglers (e.g. Purple Peril, Skykomish Sunrise).
EQUIPMENT	8- to 9-weight rod; floating line for summer fish; sinking heads or tips for winter fishing.
CONDITIONS	The Sky offers lots of big water during the winter, so two-handed rods have become especially popular for their ability to throw long lines easily. Wading is easy on the lower river; more difficult in the boulder-strewn water higher upstream.
DRIVE TIME	From Seattle: 1 hour From Portland: 5 hours
DIRECTIONS	From the south, follow I-5 to Seattle and then take the I-405 Exit, following 405 around the east side of the metro area. Continue north, through Bellevue and Redmond, to the SR 522 Exit (Woodinville/Monroe). Follow SR 522 to Monroe, From Monroe, take Highway 2 upriver along the Skykomish. If you are coming from the north, follow I-5 south to Everett and then exit eastbound on SR 2. From the east side of the Cascades, head for Leavenworth from Wenatchee or Ellensburg and then follow Hwy. 2 over Stevens Pass or follow I-90 over the Cascades to Seattle and I-405 northbound.

Local Fly Shops

THE FLYSMITH
1515 5th Avenue
Marysville, WA 98270
360-658-9003

SWEDE'S FLY SHOP
17419 139th Avenue NE
Woodinville, WA 98072
425-487-3747

KAUFMANN'S STREAMBORN
1918 4th Avenue
Seattle, WA 98101
206-448-0601

PATRICK'S FLY SHOP
2237 Eastlake Avenue East
Seattle, WA 98102
206-325-8988

ORVIS SEATTLE
911 Bellevue Way NE
Bellevue, WA 98004
425-452-9138

REI
222 Yale Ave. N
Seattle, WA 98109
206-223-1944

AVID ANGLER FLY SHOP
17171 Bothell Way NE, Ste. A130
Lake Forest Park, WA 98155
206-362-4030

FLY FISHER
5622 Pacific Ave. SE #9
Lacey, WA 98503
360-491-0181

NORTHWEST ANGLER FLY SHOP
18830 Front Street
Poulsbo, WA 98370
360-697-7100

HAWK'S POULSBO SPORTS CENTER
19424-C 7th Avenue NE
Poulsbo, WA 98370
360-779-5290

KITSAP SPORTS
10526 Silverdale Way NW
Silverdale, WA 98383
360-698-4808

SALMON BAY TACKLE
5701 15th Avenue NW
Seattle, WA 98107
206-789-9335

WARSHAL'S SPORTING GOODS
1000 1st Avenue
Seattle, WA 98104
206-624-6550

MORNING HATCH FLY SHOP
3640 South Cedar, Ste. L
Tacoma, WA 98409
253-472-1070

STREAMSIDE ANGLERS
4800 Capital Blvd. SE Ste. B
Tumwater, WA 98501
360-709-3337

Guides

DEER CREEK GUIDE SERVICE
(Mike Kinney) 360-435-3778
www.mikekinney.com

Contacts

WASHINGTON DEPARTMENT
OF FISH & WILDLIFE
North Puget Sound - Region 4 Office
16018 Mill Creek Boulevard
Mill Creek, WA 98012-1296
425-775-1311

MONROE CHAMBER OF COMMERCE
360-794-5488

SULTAN CHAMBER OF COMMERCE
360-793-2565

CHAPTER 15

THE NORTH FORK
OF THE STILLAGUAMISH

Long-Time Haunt of the
Great "Sasquatch of the Stilly"

I asked Walt Johnson if he remembered what fly pattern accounted for his first steelhead. "Sure," he replied, "I'll run upstairs and get it."

In a matter of minutes he was back in the cozy confines of his living room. Walt handed me a small box, in which lay a delicately dressed little steelhead fly boasting an orange body highlighted by a tail of red hackle fibers and a red collar. The wing featured white bucktail and a pair of long jungle cock eyes. "We used to call that the orange shrimp," Walt informed me, "and that right there is the very fly that took my first fly-rod steelhead."

All of this might sound rather pedestrian until I relate that Walt was about 80 at the time he showed me his orange shrimp and that he had taken that first fly-caught steelhead during the summer of 1938. All this time Walt had saved the precise fly that nearly six decades earlier had indoctrinated him into the small and exclusive club of steelhead fly anglers.

Walt went on to attain legendary status as a steelhead fly angler of the highest repute, an honor he earned through his many seasons fishing his beloved home river, the North Fork of the Stillaguamish. But with such recognition came the legions of devoted fans and admirers, whose ranks have always discovered in Walt Johnson a man profoundly humble about his status and acutely passionate about his fishery and his sport, which in his case more often resembles art.

In the early days, before the crowds from Seattle inundated the "Stilly," Walt learned to outfox those anglers who tried to decipher his secrets by following him around on the river. He developed a habit of suddenly appearing and disappearing from a favorite run, pool, or riffle. He knew every trail, every road and every access point and used them all to outmaneuver those who wished to circumvent the Stilly learning-curve by hounding him. After a few years, Walt had earned the nickname "The Sasquatch of the Stilly."

Walt also took an active role in making the North Fork the world's first fly-only steelhead river. Thanks to laborious effort on the part of the Washington Fly-Fishing Club and its litany of revered steelhead anglers, in 1949 the North Fork earned this unique designation as a refuge for fly anglers during the summer steelhead season. This elegant river and its famous tributary Deer Creek were also refuges for one of the region's best runs of wild summer steelhead.

With the demise of the Deer Creek watershed, however, the fishery nearly collapsed. Years of aggressive logging took a heavy toll on the steep, timbered slopes above Deer Creek. The unchecked timber harvest so denuded the canyon of its stabilizing ground cover that the outcome was inevitable—years of siltation finally culminated in a series of catastrophic slides that doomed the Deer Creek natives to near extinction. Despite marginally improved modern timber harvest methods, the unmitigated watershed damage of the mid-20th century essentially wiped out the fishery that Walt Johnson and other pioneering anglers fought so hard to protect.

The natives still return to the North Fork and to Deer Creek, their numbers bolstered by the addition of hatchery stocks. But the Stilly's steelhead dreams of old are but a pleasant and distant memory to the few surviving legendary anglers who built tiny fishing cottages and camps all along the Deer Creek/North Fork confluence. Many of the little fishing cabins survive, tucked away out of sight at the village of Oso, but the bountiful run of native steelhead survives only as a trickle compared to its former glory.

Still, the North Fork remains on the list of must-do fisheries for any die-hard steelhead angler with a sense of appreciation for the sport's history. To cast a dry line and well-tied fly over these elegant waters is to tread upon hallowed ground. Before his death in 2002, the always-amiable Walt Johnson increasingly found reason for

STILLAGUAMISH RIVER

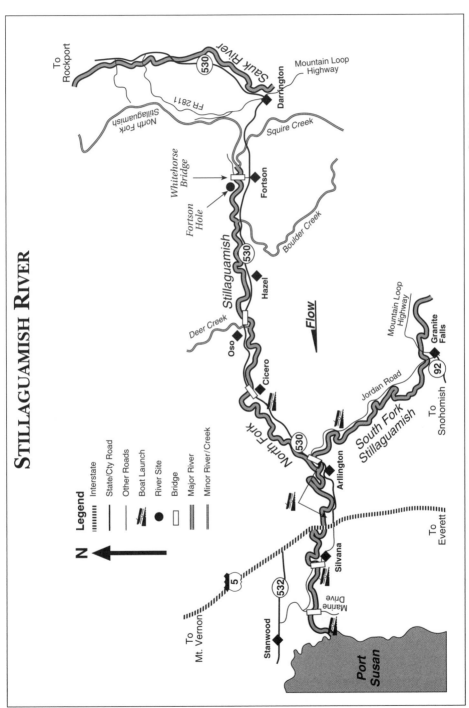

Legend

|||||||	Interstate
———	State/Cty Road
———	Other Roads
	Boat Launch
●	River Site
▢	Bridge
	Major River
	Minor River/Creek

N

To Rockport

Sauk River

530

FR 2811

Darrington

Mountain Loop Highway

North Fork Stillaguamish

Squire Creek

Whitehorse Bridge

Fortson

Fortson Hole

Boulder Creek

530

Stillaguamish

Hazel

Deer Creek

Flow

Oso

Cicero

Mountain Loop Highway

Granite Falls

92

Jordan Road

To Snohomish

South Fork Stillaguamish

North Fork

530

Arlington

To Everett

5

Silvana

532

Marine Drive

To Mt. Vernon

Stanwood

Port Susan

© Wilderness Adventures Press, Inc.

occasional bouts of anger at the ever-popular nymph-and-indicator anglers dredging the Fortson Hole, the Deer Creek confluence, and other summer-run havens on the Stilly. "They have no respect for the fish nor the river," Walt intoned. I'm with Walt on this one: A steelhead from the Stilly is simply too fine a gamefish to be insulted with ugly tactics.

Fishing the North Fork of the Stilly

Summer steelhead enter the North Fork between May and mid-autumn. The Deer Creek natives find safe haven once they enter their natal stream, for Deer Creek is closed to angling. Often, however, they hang out at the confluence, waiting for a freshet or some other mysterious sign to move upstream. Hatchery-produced steelhead arrive simultaneously and provide most of the sport in the upper river. June offers fresh-run, aggressive fish, but as the summer wears on and the water drops, the North Fork becomes increasingly difficult.

This is small water any time, but especially during August and September. Low, clear water often equates to spooky and/or dour fish. They seek the cover of deep, fast water, boulders, cut banks, logjams, and heavy shade. A fish holding in prime fly water is easily spooked by anglers who carelessly walk upriver on the cobble immediately adjacent to the run, or by too much line splash caused by sloppy casting.

Late summer fishing is a game of delicacy. Smaller flies often produce better results and long leaders help prevent the aforementioned line splash from spooking the fish. With the first good freshets of autumn comes renewed enthusiasm among the steelhead. Their ranks swollen by a few fresh, late-season arrivals, the Stilly's steelhead become increasingly aggressive for a short time.

Throughout the summer and fall, the North Fork offers excellent prospects for rising steelhead to skated dry flies. Otherwise, classic wet flies are in order. Most anglers fish larger flies in June and smaller flies during later summer.

The Stilly hosts a decent run of winter fish as well, and the river's easily waded cobblestone pools are perfectly suited to swinging flies for winter-run steelhead. The Stilly swells and discolors rather quickly with the onset of heavy rains, so local anglers certainly enjoy the advantage of simply waiting out the high water. In any event, take several fly lines (or heads) for winter fishing and then match your tackle to the conditions. The Stilly's winter fish—especially the March natives—often react aggressively to the fly, so you needn't bounce the bottom. Just choose a line system that will allow you to swing the fly a foot or two off the riverbed and cover the pools thoroughly.

Accommodations

The Mt. Higgins House (888-296-3777), located in Arlington, offers a very nice B&B option for visitors to the region. Located at 29805 SR 530, the well-appointed house looks out over a 70-acre historic farm and a small trout pond. Rates range from $115 to $135 per night. Arlington boasts a couple of motels as well: Smokey Point Motor Inn (360-659-8561) and Arlington Motor Inn (360-652-9595). The pretty little crossroads town of Darrington lies thirty miles upriver. Darrington's lodging options include Stagecoach Inn at 1100 Seaman (360-436-1776) and Sauk River Farm B&B at 32629 SR 530 (360-436-1794). RVers can stay at Cascade Trout Farm & RV Park, 1240 Darrington Street (360-436-1003).

Author's Tip

The North Fork Stilly, during late summer and early autumn, is a fine river to try for a steelhead on a dead-drifted dry fly. Countless fly patterns, when coupled with a great deal of persistence will do the trick. I like the old Soldier Palmer, a Wulff pattern, an Evening Coachman, or a Yellow Stimulator. No. 8 hooks are perfect. My favorite tactic for dead-drift fishing is to begin at the downstream end of the run and fish up and across just like trout fishing. I stay well off the bank when possible and cast a 12-foot leader. Often, I will make a second pass through the run with a down-and-across approach, allowing the dry fly to skate across current at the end of each drift.

Favorite Fly

Evening Coachman (Walt Johnson)

HOOK	Steelhead dry-fly, No. 2-8
TAG	Flat silver tinsel and flat red floss
TAIL	Golden pheasant crest
BODY	Peacock herl with band of flat red floss
RIB	A counter of fine wire
HACKLE	Grizzly hackle

Evening Coachman

Fast Facts

North Fork of the Stillaguamish River

LOCATION	Northwestern Washington, east of Arlington
WATER TYPE	Small- to medium-sized free-flowing river
PRIMARY GAMEFISH	Summer and winter steelhead; also searun cutthroat, king, and chum salmon
BEST TIME	June through October and January through March
BEST FLIES	Many classic patterns; Bombers and October Caddis as skaters; Spey flies for winter fish.
DRIVE TIME	From Seattle: 1 to 1½ hours
EQUIPMENT	For summer fish, a 6- to 8-weight rod and a floating line; many anglers also use sink-tip lines. For winter steelhead, a 7- to 9-weight rod and a selection of sinking lines to address varying heights and speeds of water.
CONDITIONS	Compared to the Sky or Skagit, the Stilly is a small, intimate river, easily waded. Access is tight in places, but look for the bridges and ask for local directions.
DIRECTIONS	Follow I-5 north to the Arlington exit (SR 503) and head east through Arlington and up the North Fork.

To cast a dry line and well-tied fly over the Stilly's elegant waters is to tread upon hallowed ground.

Local Fly Shops

THE FLY SMITH
1515 5th Avenue
Marysville, WA 98270
360-658-9003

AVID ANGLER FLY SHOP
17171 Bothell Way NE, Ste. A130
Lake Forest Park, WA 98155
206-362-4030

PATRICK'S FLY SHOP
2237 Eastlake Avenue E.
Seattle, WA 98102
206-325-8988

SWEDE'S FLY SHOP
17419 139th Avenue NE
Woodinville, WA 98072
425-487-3747

KAUFMANN'S STREAMBORN
1918 4th Avenue
Seattle, WA 98101
206-448-0601

ORVIS SEATTLE
911 Bellevue Way NE
Bellevue, WA 98004
425-452-9138

FLY FISHER
5622 Pacific Ave. SE #9
Lacey, WA 98503
360-491-0181

REI-SEATTLE
222 Yale Ave. N
Seattle, WA 98109
206-223-1944

NORTHWEST ANGLER FLY SHOP
18830 Front Street
Poulsbo, WA 98370
360-697-7100

HAWK'S POULSBO SPORTS CENTER
19424-C 7th Avenue NE
Poulsbo, WA 98370
360-779-5290

KITSAP SPORTS
10526 Silverdale Way NW
Silverdale, WA 98383
360-698-4808

SALMON BAY TACKLE
5701 15th Avenue NW
Seattle, WA 98107
206-789-9335

WARSHAL'S SPORTING GOODS
1000 1st Avenue
Seattle, WA 98104
206-624-6550

MORNING HATCH FLY SHOP
3640 South Cedar, Ste. L
Tacoma, WA 98409
253-472-1070

STREAMSIDE ANGLERS
4800 Capital Blvd. SE, Ste. B
Tumwater, WA 98501
360-709-3337

REI-PORTLAND
1798 Jantzen Beach Ctr
Portland, OR 97217
503-283-1300

Guides

DEER CREEK GUIDE SERVICE
(Mike Kinney)
360-435-3778
www.mikekinney.com

DENNIS DICKSON
360-435-6499
www.flyfishsteelhead.com

Contacts

WASHINGTON DEPARTMENT
OF FISH & WILDLIFE
North Puget Sound - Region 4 Office
16018 Mill Creek Boulevard
Mill Creek, WA 98012-1296
425-775-1311

ARLINGTON CHAMBER
OF COMMERCE
360-435-3708

DARRINGTON CHAMBER
OF COMMERCE
360-436-1177

*The author fishes the
North Fork for summer
steelhead.*

CHAPTER 16

THE SKAGIT AND SAUK RIVERS
March Madness for Native Steelhead

Most of my visits to the Skagit and Sauk Rivers have resulted in no steelhead on the bank. That's probably true for most anglers who frequent these rivers. You put in your days hoping for a handful of connections with big, bright, native winter steelhead. A few times each winter, after some degree of suffering, the line surges tight with that sudden, magnificent pull that separates the wet-fly swing from all other forms of steelhead angling. On the wide expanse of the Skagit or on the frigid waters of the Sauk River, that sudden, heavy surge generally yields immediately to the powerful reel-testing runs of a wild late-winter steelhead. These fish commonly weight 10 to 15 pounds and a few surpass 15 pounds.

As I write this, I notice my pulse racing just a little in memory of March 1997. I was wading and fishing down through a rock garden on the Sauk; the water had dropped into fine condition the previous day and cold, sunny skies welcomed my return to northern Washington after a three-year hiatus from the Skagit drainage.

This particular run, beset with all manner of fly-grabbing rocks and boulders, had yielded several hook-ups over past seasons. It was a comfortable, familiar run. The rest of the Sauk River remained a trial-and-error fishery for me.

This particular run reminded me of some of my favorite wintertime pools on the North Umpqua. Its highly structured arrangement appealed to me more than the typical long, flat, comparatively featureless cobblestone pools far more typical of the Skagit and Sauk Rivers. I had hooked and beached a 12-pound hen here the first day I fished the place. Ever since, I had stumbled around the Sauk, fishing a few places that looked good and watching where other anglers cast their lines. Over the course of eight or ten trips I had hooked two or three fish in other locales on the Sauk. I had hooked as many or more from this one run and always returned here, usually two or three times per excursion. This was my confidence pool.

That day back in '97 I had fished away the morning without a touch. So I soon headed for my confidence pool. A lone bald eagle, magnificent in the wintry sunlight, sat perched atop a snag on the far bank. I worked down through the top of the run, diligently steering my fly away from the worst of the boulders. With the water on the drop, it soon became apparent that I had chosen too heavy a fly line for this duty. Towards the end of each swing the fly would hang up on the rocks and several times I had to wade ashore, march downriver and free the fly, then walk back up to where I left off and begin again.

Naturally, the tedium of doing this became a little frustrating, so I began stripping line at the end of each swing, trying to swim the fly a little higher in the water column. This trick succeeded for a time in keeping my 4/0 Orange Heron off the rocks. But soon I stripped right into an unseen boulder and the fly held fast. A second or two passed as I gently pulled, trying to free the fly and then all hell broke loose. Boulders don't generally race to midriver, roll at the surface, and then bulldog downstream. My boulder turned out to be an awfully large steelhead. With little choice in the matter, I gave chase for a while, but the fish reached the corner a hundred yards below and broke 12-pound Maxima with the efficiency of a tarpon.

To this day I have no idea how much that fish weighed. I caught a brief glimpse when her back broke the surface; perhaps 15 pounds, perhaps 18, maybe more. I don't know. I do know that those are the type of encounters that prompt my occasional trips up to the Skagit and Sauk Rivers in northwest Washington.

Yet even in recounting such a tale I am saddened by what has transpired since. Concerned over low returns between 1998 and 2001, the Washington Department of Fish & Wildlife elected to close the traditional March catch-and-release season on the Skagit and Sauk Rivers. They did so even while allowing the catch-and-kill season to continue through February. It is the March catch-and-release season that is so coveted by fly anglers, but for two years running, the season has been closed. I can't predict the future, but I hope the spring season is again open by the time my words here reach their audience.

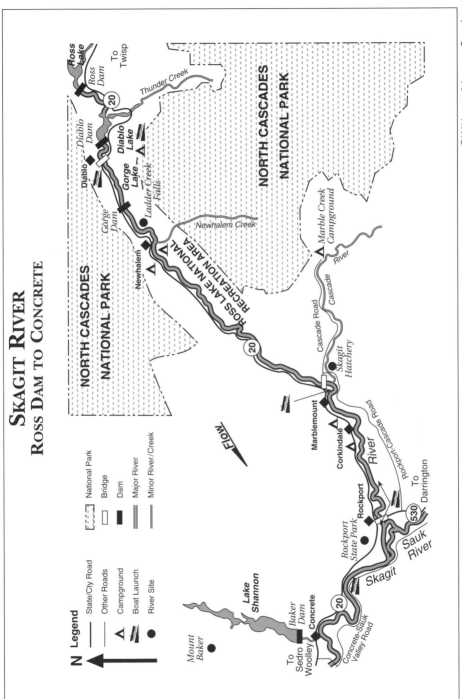

SKAGIT RIVER
ROSS DAM TO CONCRETE

Legend

State/Cty Road
Other Roads
Campground
Boat Launch
River Site

National Park
Bridge
Dam
Major River
Minor River/Creek

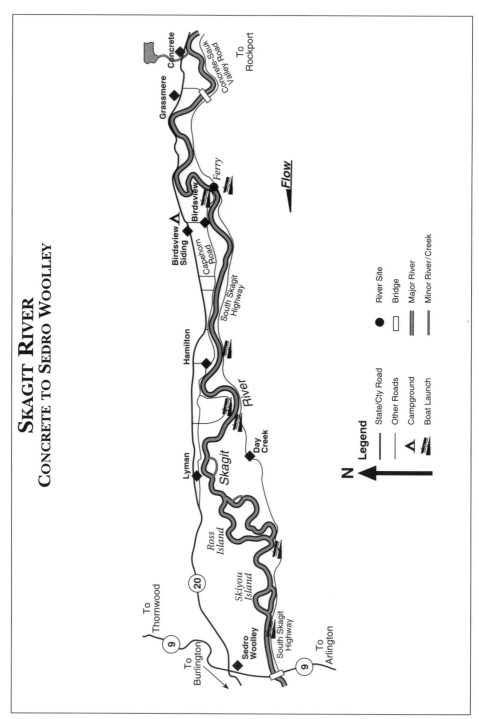

Skagit River
Concrete to Sedro Woolley

© Wilderness Adventures Press, Inc.

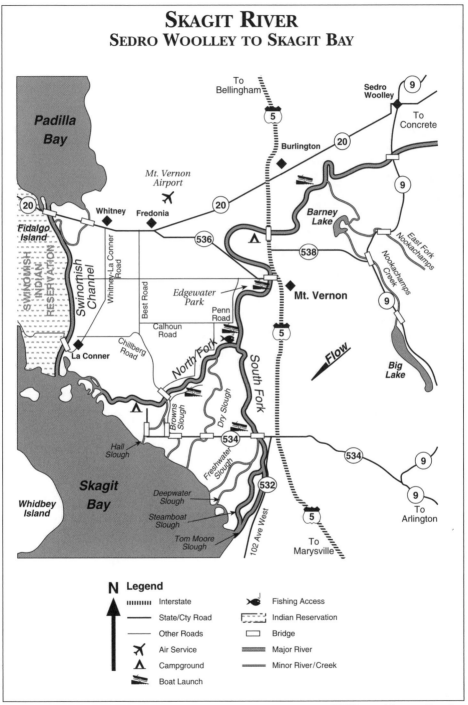

SKAGIT RIVER
SEDRO WOOLLEY TO SKAGIT BAY

To
Bellingham

Sedro
Woolley

9

To
Concrete

5

Burlington

20

9

Padilla
Bay

Mt. Vernon
Airport

Barney
Lake

East Fork Nookachamps

20

Whitney Fredonia

20

Fidalgo
Island

536

Nookachamps Creek

538

Mt. Vernon

9

SWINOMISH INDIAN RESERVATION

Swinomish Channel

Whitney-La Conner Road

Best Road

Edgewater
Park

Penn
Road

5

Flow

Big
Lake

Calhoun
Road

North Fork

South Fork

La Conner

Chillberg Road

Browns Slough

Dry Slough

Hall
Slough

534

Freshwater Slough

534

9

Skagit
Bay

Deepwater
Slough

532

9

Whidbey
Island

Steamboat
Slough

102 Ave West

5

To
Arlington

Tom Moore
Slough

To
Marysville

N **Legend**

▓▓▓▓ Interstate	🎣 Fishing Access
—— State/Cty Road	Indian Reservation
—— Other Roads	▭ Bridge
✈ Air Service	▬▬ Major River
△ Campground	▬ Minor River/Creek
Boat Launch	

© Wilderness Adventures Press, Inc.

*The Skagit
River in June.*

Fishing the Skagit and Sauk Rivers

Experienced steelhead anglers won't need this warning, but I'll offer it for the sake of those new to the sport: Steelhead angling on any river begins with an adjustment of expectations. This isn't trout fishing and with the exception of those waters teeming with small steelhead—the Rogue for example—steelhead simply don't behave like resident trout. They are different. Winter steelhead are especially different because they don't feed, at least not in any manner comparable with trout.

You might hook a steelhead on your very first cast into the wide waters of the Skagit. Or you might not hook a fish until your cast count reaches a thousand or more. Either event is as likely as the other. One thing is certain: You don't visit the Skagit or Sauk expecting to count fish. You fish these rivers to enjoy one of the Northwest's most remarkable watersheds.

Experienced steelhead anglers read the water carefully, fish the best water diligently, and employ an unshakable sense of confidence that instills in them the belief that the next cast is sure to connect with a huge steelhead. No matter how many fruitless casts add up over the course of days or weeks or seasons, the veteran steelheader never loses faith. Instead, the veteran immerses himself or herself in the river, enjoying the taut "snap" at the end of each good cast. He feels duty-bound to fish well; to fish with complete control over each cast and each swing. At the end of the day, the seasoned steelhead fly angler wants to be able to say, "I fished well today."

A steelhead hooked and perhaps landed on the Skagit or Sauk simply rewards the angler's desire to fish well and to treat the river, its angling traditions, and its inhabitants with a sense of reverent awe. Day in and day out, hooking a native winter steelhead on these waters is the exception not the rule. Adjust your expectations accordingly. Likewise, beware the Skagit's reputation for producing 20-pound steelhead. Most of the natives range from 10 to 14 pounds, although 20-pounds-and-up fish certainly dwell here. Regardless of their size, these Skagit and Sauk River natives are awesome, sea-bright steelhead so perfectly proportioned that their equals are few and far between on other rivers.

When you first visit the Skagit you might feel a slight sense of foreboding at the river's immensity and seeming lack of defining character. But soon you will learn to dissect the river. You will learn to fish what lies within reach and ignore that which does not. On water such as the Skagit and on many parts of the Sauk, you are looking for those subtle characteristics that clearly indicate good steelhead water. Look for exposed cobble bars forcing the current into a slight bend and creating slower seams along the inside. Also, seek current seams where fast water borders slower water, even if only a few yards in width. Find cobblestone covered by three to five feet of the right kind of current.

Learn to fish these areas diligently. Winter steelhead rarely move far to take a fly, so deliver the fly to them by matching your tackle to the water. Most anglers opt for carrying several different sinking heads or tips, each one a different density. You want that perfect pairing of line, water characteristics, and fishing techniques that allow you to swing the fly slowly across the flow just a foot or two off the bottom. Clean, gravel-bottomed runs allow some leniency in line choice as you can fish a line that virtually drags bottom without snagging the fly. Change the bottom from gravel to cobble and you must adjust your tackle and tactics to assure that the line swings above the bottom.

On the opposite extreme is the fly that fishes too shallow. If you are not occasionally snagging rocks at the end of your swing (when the fly slows over shallow water below your position), you probably need to fish deeper. You can do so by changing to a heavier line and/or by adjusting your tactics. I could write a dissertation here about line control and fly control in relation to depth of presentation, but much has already been written on the subject. If you need a refresher course, I would suggest rewarding yourself with a Skagit River trip with one of the river's highly respected guides. Some of Washington's best fly fishing guides live near here and

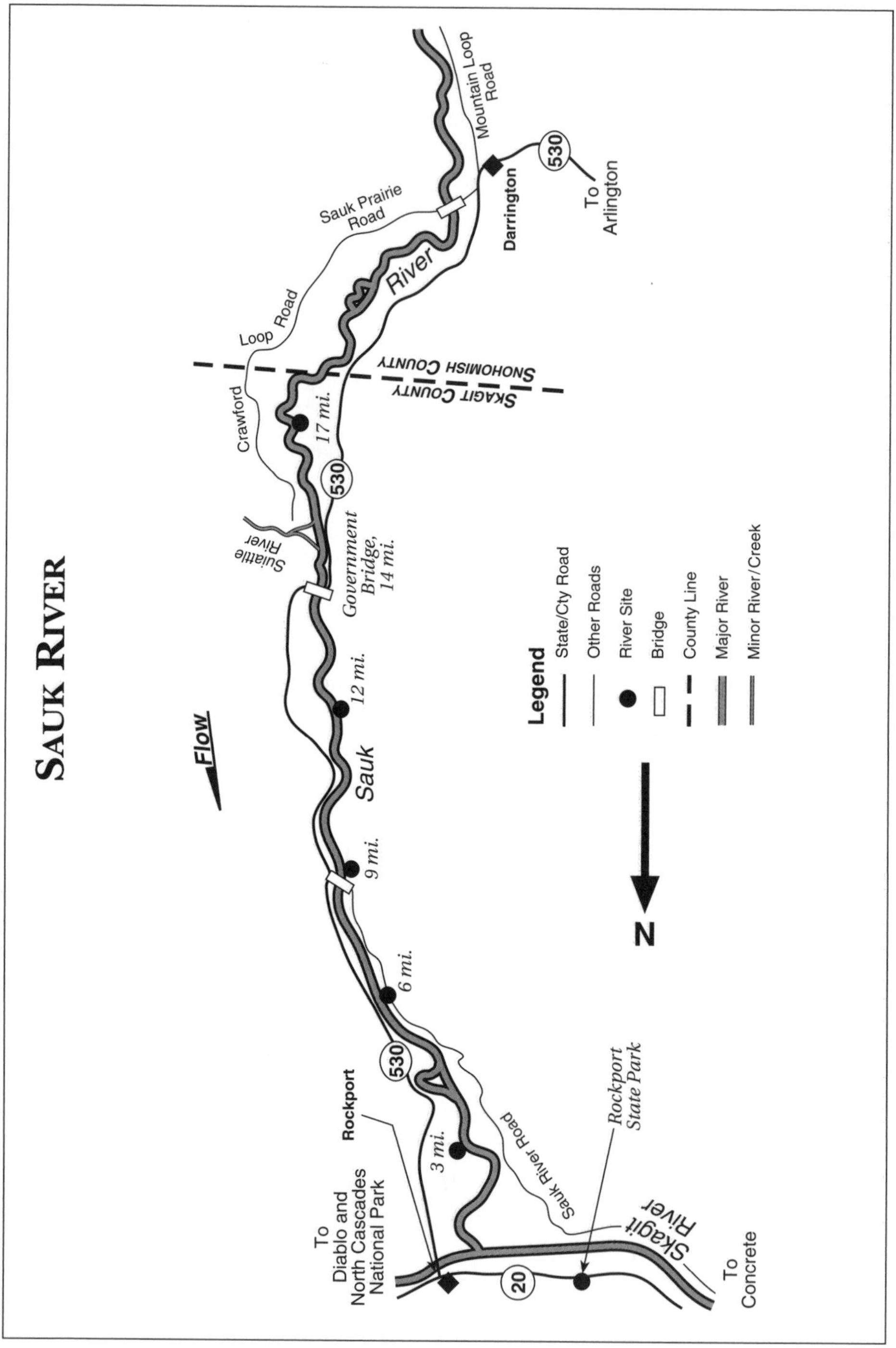

SAUK RIVER

© Wilderness Adventures Press, Inc.

Legend

——	State/City Road
—	Other Roads
●	River Site
▭	Bridge
—— ——	County Line
▬▬	Major River
▥	Minor River/Creek

N

Flow

To Arlington

Darrington

Mountain Loop Road

Sauk Prairie Road

Loop Road

Crawford

SKAGIT COUNTY
SNOHOMISH COUNTY

17 mi.

Suiattle River

Government Bridge, 14 mi.

12 mi.

Sauk

9 mi.

6 mi.

Rockport

3 mi.

To Diablo and North Cascades National Park

Sauk River Road

Rockport State Park

Skagit River

To Concrete

specialize in winter steelheading on the Skagit and Sauk. I am lucky to count some of these men among my friends.

Certainly, the Skagit and Sauk enjoy those occasional days when some fish, in very particular places, behave like summer steelhead by aggressively chasing down the fly. On Oregon's North Umpqua, I hunt these fish by first anticipating the perfect water conditions and then fishing the fly in the correct water. I don't know the Skagit and Sauk well enough to find these places there. I would bet, however, that Skagit River regulars could offer a short list of places where a big Spey fly fished on a floating line enjoys a better than average chance under the right conditions.

What I do know about the Skagit is that easy access seems more fleeting with each passing season. The best way to enjoy the river is by boat. Easy day-long floats run from Marblemount to Rockport and from Rockport to Concrete. The Sauk is likewise floatable, but I suggest you run this river with a guide before trying it solo.

On the Skagit, the Marblemount-to-Rockport drift lies upstream of the mouth of the Sauk River. This fact is paramount to your trip planning because the Sauk frequently discolors the Skagit below the confluence. The Sauk draws its headwaters from the ice sheets on Glacier Peak, giving the river a glacial till. Even more of an influence at times is the amount of silted rainwater that dumps into the Sauk from the timber-denuded slopes above. The upper portion of the Skagit, conversely, flows from dams on Ross Lake and most of its watershed lies within the confines of North Cascades National Park, whose timber-clad steeps remain intact enough to ensure better water quality.

Beware of the restrictions placed on the river to protect wintering bald eagles. Some of the gravel bars and islands are closed during the winter and spring to create refuge for several hundred eagles that over-winter in the Skagit Valley.

Both the Skagit and the Sauk hosts runs of summer steelhead between June and mid-autumn. These runs are rather sparse most years, but fishable nonetheless and without the pressure seen during the peak of the winter-run season. During odd-numbered years, pink salmon invade the Skagit, providing a popular fishery during late summer. Chum, chinook and silver salmon run the river as well, alongside searun cutthroat and a strong population of Dolly Varden.

If you're in the area, stop in at the U.S. Forest Service office in Sedro-Woolley and purchase a copy of the map, *Skagit and Sauk Wild & Scenic River System.*

Restaurants and Accommodations

On its journey through the Skagit Valley, Highway 20 passes through several small communities, including Hamilton, Concrete, Rockport and Marblemount. Various lodging arrangements are available throughout the valley. Known by long-time Skagit regulars as "Clark's Cabins" or affectionately as the "Bunny Farm," Clark's Skagit River Resort (360-873-2250) offers cabins, a lodge, RV hookups, camp space and a fine restaurant called The Eatery. Tootsie Clark is known far and wide for her delicious pies, served at the restaurant. Rooms and cabins range from $54 to $119 per night. Clark's is located near milepost 104 on Highway 20 between Rockport and Marblemount. Tent and RV sites are available year-round at Howard Miller Steelhead Park in Rockport (360-853-8808/7315) and at 670-acre Rockport State Park at milepost 97 (open only between May and October).

Area Lodging

Additional convenient lodging options include the following, most located right along Highway 20:

Three Rivers Inn, 210 Ball Street, Sedro-Woolley, 360-855-2626
Skagit Motel, 1977 Hwy. 20, Sedro-Woolley, 360-856-6001
North Cascade Inn, Concrete, 360-853-8771, 800-251-3054
Eagle's Nest Motel, Concrete, 360-853-8662
Cascade Mountain Inn, Concrete, 360-826-4333
Steelhead Landing Lodge, Rockport, 360-853-9819
Ovenell's Heritage Inn, 46276 Concrete-Sauk Valley Rd., 360-853-8494
Log House Inn, Marblemount, 360-873-4311
Salmonberry Way B&B, Marblemount (milepost 108), 360-873-4016

Restaurants in the Upper Skagit Valley range from quick-stop cafés that are closed during the winter to sit-down dinner houses. The old Log House Inn (360-873-4311), which dates back to 1889, features a cozy dining room, while the Buffalo Run Restaurant, also located in Marblemount, features buffalo burgers and steaks (360-873-2461). The summer-only restaurants usually close during October and open again in April, so call ahead. In Rockport, Fish Inn Café (360-853-9309) offers decent food and Pleasant View Inn Tavern (360-853-7043) overlooks Steelhead Park. On your way up the river, you might want to stop in for an early breakfast at Sunrise Café (360-855-1299) at 815 State Street or at the Sedro-Woolley Bakery & Café at 823 Metcalf (360-855-1888).

Well downstream, adjacent to I-5, the town of Mt. Vernon offers ample dining options, including Skagit River Brewing Company—a great place to relax over food and microbrewed beer after a day on the river. The Brewery resides at 404 S. 3rd Street (360-336-2884). You'll also find a good pizza place, called Pacioni's, at 606 S. 1st Street (360-336-3314).

Nearby Attractions and Activities

Highway 20, which follows the length of the Skagit River, crosses the North Cascades at Rainy Pass. Closed during the winter, this route over the mountains is a required traverse for anyone who appreciates awesome scenery. I've driven virtually every highway in the Pacific Northwest and I would be hard-pressed to select a more stunning vista than that afforded by Highway 20 as it connects eastern Washington to western Washington atop the Cascade Range.

North Cascades National Park includes much of this region, its borders stretching from Lake Chelan in the south to the Canadian border and extending west to within a few miles of Marblemount. If you visit the Skagit during the summer or fall, plan on spending a day to take in the awesome scenery of the national park. Wildlife abounds, including the pure-white mountain goats, which are fairly easy to find with a good pair of binoculars.

Well below the east side of Rainy Pass lies the little tourist trap of Winthrop. Nearby is the famous Sun Mountain Lodge, highly regarded not only for its many well-appointed amenities, but also for its fine dining (509-996-2211). A little farther south lies the hamlet of Twisp, home to Methow Valley Brewing Company. The beer is first-rate, the food better than the usual brewpub fare and the atmosphere relaxed and friendly. Across the street is the beautiful Methow Valley Inn, an elegant bed & breakfast originally built in 1912 (509-997-2253).

The Skagit Valley serves as wintering grounds for the largest concentration of bald eagles in the lower 48 states. As many as 300 eagles annually over-winter here, feeding on fish carcasses from the river's salmon runs. The prime season for eagle viewing runs from December through February. Several outfitters specialize in guided winter float trips to view the birds along this beautiful waterway. Call Eco Orca Northwest Float Trips (360-856-5224) or Chinook Expeditions (360-793-3451).

Visitors to the Skagit River will find all services and amenities in the downriver communities of Sedro-Woolley, Burlington, and Mt. Vernon.

Author's Tip

September weather in the Skagit Valley has few equals. Pleasantly warm afternoons yield to crisp nights. Early morning arrives with enough chill to beg a warm shirt or sweater. This is my favorite time to search for summer-run steelhead on the Sauk, because when high-mountain weather dips below freezing, the glaciers lock up just enough to allow a window of fishable water, especially early in the morning. This isn't the Deschutes or the Grande Ronde, but persistent anglers will find a willing fish here and there without much competition from other anglers.

Favorite Fly

Brad's Brat

HOOK	Salmon/steelhead, No. 2/0-4
TAG	Flat silver or gold tinsel
TAIL	Orange hackle fibers or dyed golden pheasant crest
BODY	Half orange, half red; wool or dubbing
RIB	Gold or silver oval
HACKLE	Brown
WING	White with orange over; bucktail, calftail or similar
CHEEKS	Jungle cock (optional)

Brad's Brat

Fast Facts

Skagit and Sauk Rivers

WATER TYPE	Large, freestone steelhead rivers
PRIMARY GAMEFISH	Winter steelhead; also summer steelhead; searun cutthroat; chum, pink, silver, and chinook salmon.
BEST TIME	February-April; June-September for summer steelhead
BEST FLIES	Many anglers prefer classic Spey flies, marabou flies and General Practitioners
EQUIPMENT	Two-handed Spey-casting rods are especially popular. Full complement of sinking heads or tips.
CONDITIONS	Both rivers rise quickly during heavy winter rains. The Sauk often runs off-color and thus discolors the Skagit below the confluence. Under these conditions, fish above the confluence.

DRIVE TIME   From Seattle: 1-1½ hours
                 From Portland: 5-6 hours

DIRECTIONS   Follow I-5 north to the U.S. 20 exit at Burlington and
                 head east.

Local Fly Shops

SKAGIT ANGLERS
315G Main Street
Mt. Vernon, WA 98273
360-336-3232

MAZAMA FLY SHOP
48 Lost River Road
Mazama, WA 98833
509-996-3674

H & H ANGLERS & OUTFITTERS
814 Dupont Street
Bellingham, WA 98225
360-733-2050

THE GUIDES FLY SHOP
6934 Guide Meridian
Lynden, WA 98264
360-398-2155

THE FLYSMITH
1515 5th Avenue
Marysville, WA 98270
360-658-9003

Area Fly Shops

SWEDE'S FLY SHOP
17419 139th Avenue NE
Woodinville, WA 98072
425-487-3747

KAUFMANN'S STREAMBORN
1918 4th Avenue
Seattle, WA 98101
206-448-0601

PATRICK'S FLY SHOP
2237 Eastlake Avenue East
Seattle, WA 98102
206-325-8988

ORVIS SEATTLE
911 Bellevue Way NE
Bellevue, WA 98004
425-452-913

AVID ANGLER FLY SHOP
17171 Bothell Way NE, Ste. A130
Lake Forest Park, WA 98155
206-362-4030

FLY FISHER
5622 Pacific Ave. SE #9
Lacey, WA 98503
360-491-0181

NORTHWEST ANGLER FLY SHOP
18830 Front Street
Poulsbo, WA 98370
360-697-7100

HAWK'S POULSBO SPORTS CENTER
19424-C 7th Avenue NE
Poulsbo, WA 98370
360-779-5290

KITSAP SPORTS
10526 Silverdale Way NW
Silverdale, WA 98383
360-698-4808

SALMON BAY TACKLE
5701 15th Avenue NW
Seattle, WA 98107
206-789-9335

Area Fly Shops, Continued

WARSHAL'S SPORTING GOODS
1000 1st Avenue
Seattle, WA 98104
206-624-6550

MORNING HATCH FLY SHOP
3640 South Cedar, Ste. L
Tacoma, WA 98409
253-472-1070

STREAMSIDE ANGLERS
4800 Capital Blvd. SE Ste. B
Tumwater, WA 98501
360-709-3337

REI
222 Yale Ave. N
Seattle, WA 98109
206-223-1944

Guides

DEC HOGAN
360-856-0108

Check with local and area fly
shops for other guides opportunities.

Contacts

WASHINGTON DEPARTMENT
OF FISH & WILDLIFE
North Puget Sound - Region 4 Office
16018 Mill Creek Boulevard
Mill Creek, WA 98012-1296
425-775-1311

Highway 20 provides spectacular views of the North Cascades.

CHAPTER 17

CHICKAHOMINY RESERVOIR

The Archetypal Desert Trout Reservoir

Nash needed a shore-break, a chance to pee on some sagebrush. He'd been in the boat a long time that morning on Chickahominy Reservoir.

Forrest fished from the front of the boat, I fished from the back of the boat and Nash wandered back and forth between us. This was the usual arrangement: Forrest's little homemade wooden drift boat painted light blue with each of us standing atop our respective seats, casting and retrieving all morning long with Nash maintaining constant vigilance over his domain.

Nash's domain began with his boat, his fishing partners, and his lake and extended to any living creature worthy of his attention. Nash, after all, is a German shorthaired pointer and a bird dog of the highest caliber. But this was fishing season

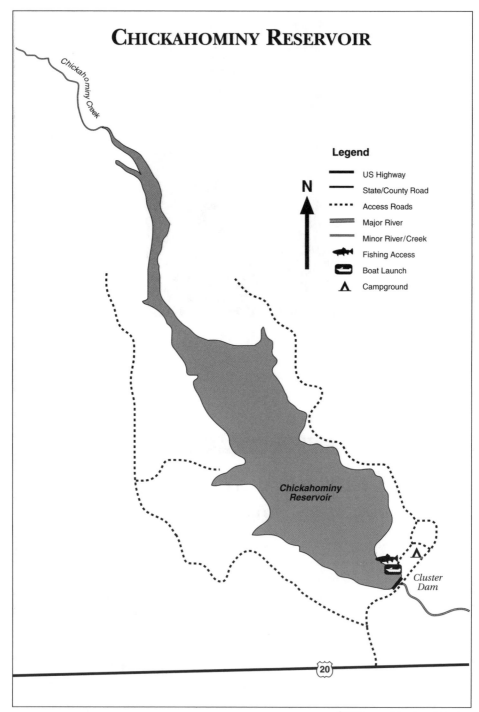

CHICKAHOMINY RESERVOIR

Chickahominy Creek

Legend

N

— US Highway
— State/County Road
---- Access Roads
▬ Major River
— Minor River/Creek
🐟 Fishing Access
⛴ Boat Launch
▲ Campground

Chickahominy Reservoir

Cluster Dam

20

and Nash was doing what he always does: Staring intently at Forrest's fly line at precisely that point where the line enters the water. Nash's front paws gripped the gunwale, his rear paws braced on the boat's front seat. Nash would give Forrest about 10 casts before he'd wander back to my end of the boat and hope for some action out of me. He'd stare at my fly line for about 10 more casts and if no trout were forthcoming, he'd give up on me and reclaim his position at Forrest's side.

Should either of us hook one of Chickahominy Reservoir's fat rainbows, Nash would lean out over the boat, eager to lend a hand with the landing and releasing process. Nash was a busy dog that morning on Chickahominy because rarely could either of us make 10 casts without hooking a fish. This was "Chick" at its best.

A colorful April sunrise had slowly disposed of the desert chill and the slightest breeze now blew a gentle chop against the side of the boat. We had 600 acres of shallow, fertile trout water all to ourselves—the benefit of fishing mid-week 90 miles from the nearest sizable city. We had embarked early, motivated by the fear that a late start would mean confronting Chickahominy's nasty midday wind—often a forcible brute that whips the barren reservoir into a whitecapped sea.

But on this spring morning, the desert weather dawned quiet and bright. The usual Chickahominy birds busied themselves with bouts of feeding interspersed with all manner of courtship displays, from the splashy hide-and-seek game of the common goldeneyes to the raucous, flashy displays of the willets, avocets and black-necked stilts.

Given a chance at firm ground, Nash would happily harass all manner of shorebirds, but for now he'd have to remain on trout patrol, for the fishing was simply too good to consider quitting. Every few minutes Forrest or I would hook one of Chick's fat rainbows on a Zug Bug or Pheasant Tail Nymph fished on an intermediate line. Most of the fish spanned 14 to 18 inches and seemed fat nearly to the point of absurdity. Healthy, fast-growing trout, even though not one among them was born here. Chick's trout derive entirely from hatchery stock and are planted as fingerlings. Within months they reach legal size and look like wild fish, with white-tipped fins and perfect proportions.

After two hours, we'd released a dozen fish apiece and the action showed no signs of abating any time soon. But Nash was acting more and more squirrelly. Adrift all morning, he needed to relieve himself. He'd been holding it a long time. We decided he'd have to wait until the action subsided; Forrest and I could hardly justify heading for shore with such great fishing.

About the time we steeled ourselves to ignore Nash's admonitions to take him to shore, we noticed a pickup headed our way. Given the road—a rutted-out two-tracker through the rocky desert scrub—they'd be a while in finding their way over to this side of the reservoir. Chickahominy offers ample room to spread out and likely the newcomers would stop at the first of the two "fingers" that reach out to the west, forming narrow bays on Chick's southwest corner.

Some time later the truck reappeared from behind a slight rise where the access road dips down to cross the depression at the head of the first finger. Then, finding better road, our new company made quick work of reaching the end of the peninsula on which Forrest and I had set up camp.

We cursed them under our breath for choosing such close proximity when the entire west side of this sprawling reservoir remained devoid of other anglers. But our fear of encountering a float-tube flotilla proved unfounded when the newcomers revealed themselves to be shore-bound bait anglers. Four good-ole-boys unloaded folding chairs, forked sticks, spinning rods, a cooler for beer and another for trout. Chickahominy, after all, offers no special regulations. The reservoir's fishery was created for put-and-take angling, but its remarkable fertility supports so many fast-growing trout that plenty remain for the fly angling crowd.

Another hour passed, during which Forrest and I hooked and released a dozen more trout while the Power-baiters on shore landed but a single fish. Nash had taken to occasional bouts of whining—not at all unusual on those days when he was forced to tolerate our ineptitude as anglers, but today the trout fed eagerly and Nash's song-and-dance act could only be attributed to a dire need to hike a leg somewhere.

Finally, we relented. I pulled the anchor and Forrest manned the oars. Quickly we covered the few hundred yards to the shoreline shallows, but Nash couldn't wait any longer. He bailed out in a foot of water, ran ashore toward the bank anglers and made a beeline for the first tall object on which he could relieve himself. Now bear in mind that Chickahominy's west shore is devoid of sagebrush for the first 30 yards or so. That left but one object tall enough for Nash, and sure enough he lifted his leg and peed all over the nearest tackle box.

Bad enough that Forrest and I had punished the bait anglers by hooking fish out in front of them all morning. So as Nash finished his job on the first fellow's tackle box—amid awestruck, jaw-dropped stares from all six onlookers—Forrest and I figured things were about to deteriorate in a hurry. Fortunately, however, the look of extreme relief on Nash's face and the incredulity of what just occurred struck the three unaffected bait anglers as rather amusing—or so we judged by the fact that they all burst into uncontrolled fits of laughter.

Despite the obvious humor in the situation, Forrest and I fought back our own chuckles, at least until one of the boys regained his composure just long enough to announce, "Apparently your dog holds the same opinion of Bob's fishing prowess as we do!"

The Chickahominy Experience

I've read from time to time that the word "pretty" has precious little in common with Chickahominy Reservoir. The turbid expanse this lake spreads across a barren depression in the middle of a sprawling sagebrush basin. Often a cold, dry desert wind howls across the plain unimpeded by so much as a single tree, hill, or even a high spot.

A veteran of many seasons on Chick, I've arrived at a simple conclusion regarding the reservoir's scenic attributes or lack thereof: A 4-pound trout pretty much atones for whatever else Chickahominy fails to offer. Indeed, the reservoir's planted rainbows grow quickly in a fertile soup rich in all forms of fish foods, from scuds and snails to leeches and damsels. Yearling rainbows span a fat 14 inches and those that survive another year reach 18 or more inches.

Certainly the beefy rainbows provide the primary attraction, but Chick does offer its memorable moments. From time to time, stunning desert sunsets paint a vivid wash of color across gathering storm fronts; other times the wind evaporates during the evening and the water springs to life with dimpling trout chasing *Chironomids* and water beetles. On many occasions I have stood knee-deep in the shallows casting wet flies through a whitewash of soft snowflakes, the enveloping winter chill swallowing every sound save the *swish-swish* of the fly line and the splashy struggles of trout close at hand.

Some years ago, Forrest hit the pickup brakes so hard that I nearly cracked the dashboard with my forehead. We were driving slowly along the shoreline on Chick's west edge while the sun melted into the horizon. Simultaneously, both of us gasped at the sight unfolding before us: dozens of trout, podded up like bonefish, slowly and deliberately working their way down the bank in a foot or two of water, likely in search of scuds and water beetles. We bailed out, grabbed our rods out of the bed of the truck, crept into casting range and enjoyed fast and furious action for half an hour before the pod of trout finally disbanded. Only then did we look back and realize that the truck's engine was still running and that both doors stood wide open.

Indeed, angling tales from Chick flow often and freely in the fly shops and brewpubs in Bend, especially during the spring when the fishery peaks. Typically, Chick's ice cover dissipates by mid-February. Often, cold water makes for slow fishing early on, but many fly anglers are drawn to the reservoir by the chance to stalk 16- to 24-inch carry-over rainbows in a foot or two of water. By April, the water hovers at ideal temperatures while all manner of aquatic trout foods provide ample forage for the fish. I've cleaned a few Chickahominy trout and found some to be stuffed with snails or *Chironomids* or water beetles while others are stuffed with a smorgasbord of everything the lake offers.

Hot, windy weather and dense algae blooms shut down the fishing during the summer, but the cool of autumn brings resurgence. Some of Chick's largest trout, fattened to near obesity, fall to anglers who venture out during October. Autumn is definitely the time to hunt the 6-pounders.

Now the downside: Chickahominy gathers its waters from Oregon's arid southeast sage-basin range where moisture is always in short supply. During the so-called wet years, there is plenty of water to go around. Stack several wet or even normal water years together and Chickahominy thrives. Conversely, the dry years exact a heavy toll on the fishery as water levels drop. If Chickahominy sounds like a place you might want to visit, be sure to check current conditions first by calling any of the regional fly shops or by contacting ODFW in Hines.

What's more, Chickahominy is afforded no special angling regulations. It exists essentially as a put-and-take affair, and in any such fishery there are only so many fish to go around. Gear anglers harvest lots of Chick's trout, and in some years slow fishing seems directly related to the number of fish remaining in the reservoir.

A pleasant early spring morning on Chickahominy.

Luckily, Chick lies a long distance from any major population center, so classic angling mob scenes rarely occur. Frankly, I'd rather see several dozen bait anglers than a like number of fly anglers. It is easier to compete for space with guys content to sit in chairs and watch a bobber.

At 600 acres, however, Chickahominy offers lots of room to spread out. The main entrance turns north off Highway 20 at a signed access road (the reservoir lies in plain sight of the highway) and proceeds a quarter-mile to the earthen dam. The road continues across the dam to the east side of the reservoir and several BLM-installed wind shelters and outhouses draw RV-campers to this side. A primitive dirt road wraps around the west side of the reservoir and several spurs lead off this road and out to two peninsulas that project into the lake, forming two narrow bays popular with fly anglers. Other than the main gravel access road, all of Chick's access spurs are prone to deep rutting and gooey mud during wet weather. Be especially careful on these roads during spring when they seem perfectly solid early in the morning when the ground is frozen. Later, when the temperature rises and the subterranean frost melts, those same solid roadbeds are quite capable of sucking a 4x4 down to its axles in the worst kind of mud.

Fishing Chickahominy

Because the reservoir is uniformly shallow, most fly anglers fish Chick by simply wading along the shoreline casting wet flies on sink-tip or intermediate lines. A float tube or boat is handy when the wind arrives or to access slightly deeper water where weed beds attract feeding trout. Along with the aforementioned lines, bring along an extra rod rigged with a floating line. Spring offers both *Chironomid* and water beetle action for the dry-fly enthusiast. Also, the floating line is the best choice for casting wet flies to trout cruising along the banks.

The *Chironomid* hatches begin early, typically before the middle of March and can vary from sparse and insignificant to super-dense and frustrating due to sheer numbers of naturals. Big "bloodworm" midges hatch during March and April. Wade into shallow water with a sampling net, stir up the bottom with your foot and take a couple swipes with the net. You will likely find dozens of half-inch-long bloodworms in the sample, along with small olive and brown midge larvae, scuds, beetles, and other trout foods.

A typical spring "midge" hatch begins by mid-morning. Cool mornings—which are certainly the norm at Chick—force the adult *Chironomids* to sit on the water while their wings dry. Trout begin to rise for them and anglers can employ a cast-and-wait tactic or target individual rising fish. My favorite tactic is to fish a midge pupa pattern on the tip with a Griffith's Gnat or "buzzer" pattern as a dropper. I cast the flies, allow them to sit for a time, and then begin a very slow retrieve, just stripping enough line to slowly skate the dry fly. By late spring, expect heavy *Chironomid* hatches to occur around dusk, at least when the wind stays down.

Chickahominy abounds in water beetles, including backswimmers, boatmen, and whirligig beetles. Beetle activity begins mid- to late spring. Sometimes the shallows come alive with beetles flying around, diving underwater, skimming about on the surface and generally driving trout crazy. On any given day between late April and early June, good beetle flights may create a rare dry-fly opportunity. Watch for trout cruising in shallow water, lead them with a dry fly, and then skate the fly on the surface. Or cast a wet fly, such as a Zug Bug, to trout feeding along the banks. Often this tactic resembles bonefishing in that you are stalking wary fish in shallow water and trying to lead the fish just right without spooking your quarry.

Because fishable "beetle flights" remain rather uncommon on most trout lakes, applicable tactics are little-known among anglers. One such tactic is to fish a buoyant fly using a light leader and high-density sink-tip line. The idea is to allow the beetle pattern, typically tied with floating foam or deer hair, to sit on the surface until the sinking line has settled to the bottom. Then make several quick strips to sink the fly and make it dive during the retrieve. When you stop stripping line the fly slowly ascends toward the surface. This method often proves both effective and entertaining.

During late April, damsels and *Callibaetis* mayflies appear, but only on rare occasions does either hatch become significant enough to cause selective feeding by Chick's rainbows. In fact, most of the time Chick anglers cast-and-retrieve searching patterns in shallow water. Favorites include the Zug Bug, Prince Nymph and Pheasant Tail Nymph, all with or without a bead head. Woolly Buggers are equally popular. The same flies work during the fall, when hardy anglers fish until ice begins to form around Chick's edges.

Isolated by its location, Chickahominy has no neighboring fisheries. Therefore, anglers are advised to check conditions ahead of time by calling ODFW, Kiger Creek Fly Shop or B & B's Sporting Goods, all located in Burns/Hines.

Love It or Hate It

Chickahominy is one of those love-it or hate-it fisheries. You love it when fat rainbows come easily to the fly and you hate it when brutal cold dampens your enthusiasm to the point that you question your sanity. I was suffering one of those hate-it days last spring while fishing with a friend from back east. The water was so cold that even my thick neoprene waders bought me only five minute spells of comfortable fishing between which I would stomp around on the bank hoping to regain feeling in my toes.

Meanwhile, an indecisive wind tried its hand at all directions before finally settling on just plain nasty cold regardless of its origins. I'd about had enough suffering. The action was so slow that my general sanity was being called into question. But then Paul hooked his first Chickahominy fish and his first Western stillwater fish. An immense rainbow—close to two feet long—rocketed skyward after a slashing take in two feet of water. The ensuing battle favored this awesome rainbow, which soon broke free. I stood nearby with a smile on my face, thinking, "I love this place."

Nearby Attractions and Activities

Chickahominy is a long way from anywhere—the nearest town is Riley, which qualifies more as a wide spot in the highway. Riley's U.S. Post Office Branch, located along the highway in a tiny brick building, assures that this little old stage stop remains alive and functioning. Across the street from the post office is Riley's only other establishment in the form of a store/gas station that is open from time to time but subject over the years to going out of business until new owners take a swing at attracting highway travelers. A giant billboard reminds you: "Whoa! Ya Missed Riley!"

About 30 miles east of Riley, the Harney County Seat of Burns serves as the hub city for the entire region. Some 4,000 residents reside in and around this historic town. The town itself offers only modest scenic value, but Old West history buffs will revel in the discovery that this seemingly quiet desert hamlet once ranked as a classic Wild West venue. Check out the Harney County Museum downtown. Likewise, take the hour trip south to Frenchglen and discover the valley that once served as the headquarters for the sprawling P Ranch and its part owner and cattle baron, Peter French. The P Ranch story, complete with the murder of Peter French, is required reading and is told in any of several narratives.

These days, few reminders of the old P Ranch exist, but among those that survive are the remarkable French Round Barn located east of the little village of Diamond. Here, Peter French trained horses indoors during the brutal winters of southeastern Oregon. Meanwhile, the tiny town of Frenchglen attracts visitors from all quarters for its easy access to the splendid Steens Mountains (see Mann Lake).

Much of the old P Ranch property is now contained within the Malheur National Wildlife Refuge, one of Oregon's most popular birding sites. Malheur Lake, along with adjacent Harney Lake, ranks as the state's largest body of water, at least during wet years when the two are unarguably joined at The Narrows. Staggering numbers of birds migrate through the area and nest within the refuge boundaries. During the spring, Burns caters to the birding crowd, which arrives to find thousands of birds occupying wetlands all around town: snow geese, Canada geese, white-fronted geese, sandhill cranes, ibis, and long-billed curlews along with countless species of ducks, shorebirds, raptors, and songbirds.

For that matter, Chickahominy Reservoir itself, along with nearby Silver Creek Valley, hosts tremendous numbers of wetland birds. During the spring, anglers can expect the company of willets, avocets, black-necked stilts, yellowlegs, killdeer, and other shorebirds while Chick's shallow bays attract gadwall, widgeon, cinnamon teal, mallards, pintail, bufflehead, goldeneye, and other waterfowl. Tim Blount and I once enjoyed watching a peregrine falcon hunt ducks, and during a February trip one year I stopped alongside the highway to watch five bald eagles and two golden eagles feasting on road-kill deer during a time of year when carrion supports many such predators.

Harney County holds an annual Bird Festival early each April. Interested parties can pay a nominal fee to join any of numerous birding tours. For more information, contact the Harney County Chamber of Commerce. Meanwhile, during the drive across the desert to Chickahominy, keep your eyes peeled for pronghorns, mule deer, coyotes, bobcats, and badgers.

Nearby Fisheries

Yellowjacket Lake and Moon Reservoir

Yellowjacket Lake, a 20-acre reservoir located in the Malheur National Forest north of Burns, offers good fishing for 10- to 16-inch rainbows. They grow fat on myriad food sources. Bring a float tube or small boat and follow FR 47 north out of Hines (signed) until you reach the turn-off on FR 41, which leads to the reservoir. Camping space is available. Moon Reservoir, on the Silver Creek drainage southeast from Chickahominy and south of Highway 20, offers fair to good action on bass and bream, depending on water conditions. Check with ODFW in Hines before going. Take the 00 Ranch Road south off Highway 20 (west of Burns) and watch for the dirt access roads. Don't go without a county or BLM map and don't go during wet weather. Also, try the small streams in the Malheur and Ochoco National Forests north of Burns. Get a Forest Service map, strap on the hiking boots and enjoy the process of discovery. Farther east, 18 gravel-road miles northeast from Juntura, Beulah Reservoir offers good action for rainbows during years of good water supply. Check with ODFW for current conditions.

Restaurants and Accommodations

This is beef country. Try The Pine Room on West Monroe Street in Burns for a steak of generous proportions (541-573-3201). For good, authentic Mexican food, try El Toreo on Broadway. For a smoke-free breakfast, head for the Apple Peddler on Highway 20 across from the Sentry Market. Several other restaurants are easily located along the main strip through Burns (Monroe and Broadway Streets). The campground at Chickahominy offers space for RVs and tents (no hook-ups), bathrooms and sun shelters.

Nearest Lodging (Burns and Hines)

Sage Country Inn Bed & Breakfast, 351½ W. Monroe, 541-573-7243
Horton House Guest House, 191 West C Street, 541-573-1687
Days Inn Ponderosa, 977 W. Monroe, 541-573-2047
Royal Inn, 999 Oregon Avenue, 541-573-5295
Best Western, 534 Highway 20, 541-573-5050
Silver Spur Motel, 789 North Broadway, 800-400-2077
Bontemps Motel, 74 West Monroe, 800-229-1394
City Center Motel, 73 West Monroe, 541-573-5100
Orbit Motel, Highway 20 West and Highway 395 North, 541-573-2034

Author's Tip

During the spring, try a two-fly combination with a size 4 or 6 black Woolly Bugger in the lead trailed by a size 12 beadhead Pheasant Tail, Zug Bug or Prince Nymph. Most trout take the smaller fly, but it seems the larger fly gets their attention. This combination often results in a higher catch rate.

Favorite Fly

Beadhead Prince Nymph

HOOK	2XL wet fly, No. 8-12
TAIL	2 white biots
BODY	Peacock herl ribbed with fine oval tinsel
HACKLE	Brown
WINGPAD	2 white biots
HEAD	Metal bead

Beadhead Prince Nymph

Fast Facts

Chickahominy Reservoir

LOCATION	90 miles east of Bend and immediately north of Highway 20 in Lake County
WATER TYPE	Large desert reservoir, usually turbid to varying degrees and subject to severe seasonal water-level fluctuations
PRIMARY GAMEFISH	Rainbow trout, 12 to 24 inches
BEST TIME	March-May and late September-November
BEST FLIES	Woolly Buggers, Prince Nymph, Zug Bug, Chironomid pupa, peacock Carey Special, red beadhead Pheasant Tail Nymph
EQUIPMENT	5- to 7-weight rod; floating line; sink-tip or slow-sinking line. Float tube or boat optional. Waders and cold-weather clothing.
CONDITIONS	Frequent high winds; very cold mornings through March; no fresh water or shade.
DRIVE TIME	From Bend: Less than 2 hours From Portland: 4½-5 hours From Eugene: 4½ hours From Boise: 3½ hours From Burns: 45 minutes

Chickahominy's planted rainbows grow quickly in this fertile reservoir.

Local Fly Shops

KIGER CREEK FLY SHOP
120 NW Circle Drive
Hines, OR 97720
541-573-1329

B & B SPORTING GOODS
Highway 20 & Conley Ave.
Hines, OR 97720
541-573-6200

Area Fly Shops

FLY-N-FIELD
143 SW Century Drive
Bend, OR 97701
541-318-1616

SUNRIVER FLY SHOP
Sunriver Business Park
Sunriver, OR 97707
541-593-8814

THE PATIENT ANGLER
55 NW Wall Street
Bend, OR 97701
541-389-6208

IDAHO ANGLER
1682 S. Vista Ave.
Boise, ID 83705
208-389-9957

THE FLY BOX
1293 NE 3rd
Bend, OR 97701
541-388-3330

INTERMOUNTAIN ARMS & TACKLE
900 Vista Village Center
Boise, ID 83705
208-345-3474

DESCHUTES RIVER OUTFITTERS
61115 South Highway 97
Bend, OR 97702
541-388-8191

STONEFLY ANGLER
625 Vista
Boise, ID 83705
208-338-1700

THE HOOK FLY SHOP
Sunriver Village Mall, Building 21
Sunriver, OR 97707
541-593-2358

BEAR CREEK FLY SHOP
5521 West State Street
Boise, ID 83703
208-853-8704

Contacts

OREGON DEPARTMENT
OF FISH & WILDLIFE
Malheur Watershed District Office
237 S. Hines Blvd., P.O. Box 8
Hines, OR 97738
541-573-6582

BURNS/HARNEY COUNTY
CHAMBER OF COMMERCE
541-573-2636

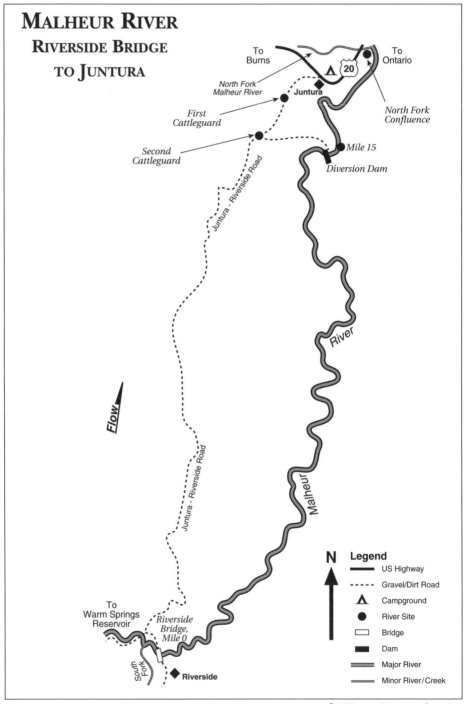

Malheur River
Riverside Bridge
to Juntura

To Burns

To Ontario

North Fork Malheur River

Juntura

North Fork Confluence

First Cattleguard

Second Cattleguard

Mile 15

Diversion Dam

Juntura - Riverside Road

River

Flow

Juntura - Riverside Road

Malheur

N

Legend

— US Highway

---- Gravel/Dirt Road

Λ Campground

● River Site

▢ Bridge

■ Dam

══ Major River

── Minor River/Creek

To Warm Springs Reservoir

Riverside Bridge, Mile 0

South Fork

Riverside

© Wilderness Adventures Press, Inc.

THE MALHEUR RIVER

Remote Rainbows in the Oregon Desert

Below Warm Springs Reservoir, the Malheur River might just be Oregon's best trout stream. And most anglers will never discover that fact because the river's great fishing lasts just a few weeks each year. Arrive at the right time and you find fat 14- to 20-inch rainbows eager to devour dry flies. Arrive at the wrong time—which is most of the time—and you find a river running high and muddy and virtually unfishable.

In part, geography assures that the Malheur remains among the region's best trout streams. This eastern Oregon desert river flows through a deep canyon many hours distant from the state's population centers.Only anglers possessing a stout sense of adventure need apply, for the Malheur reveals her secrets only to those willing to travel long miles at the drop of a hat and then explore by foot the river's canyon-bound roadless section.

The Malheur's best fishing occurs during spring and fall when desert weather patterns lack predictability. You can enjoy 75-degree sunshine one day and brace against a wind-driven snow the next. The autumn fishing is most predictable. The spring fishing lasts from a few days to a few weeks.

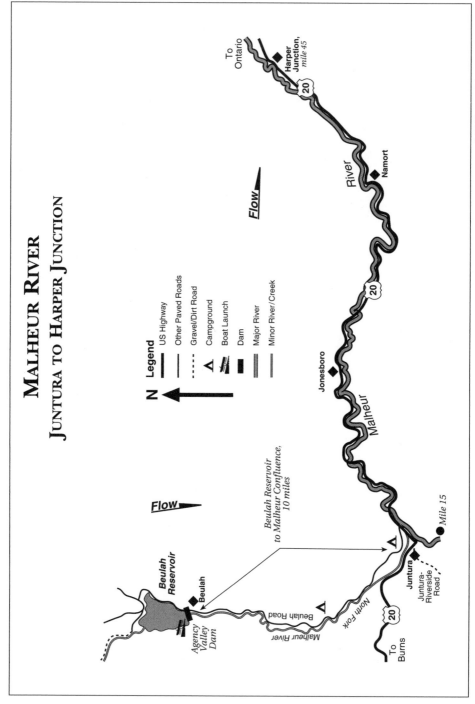

Malheur River
Juntura to Harper Junction

Legend

N

	US Highway
	Other Paved Roads
	Gravel/Dirt Road
▲	Campground
	Boat Launch
■	Dam
	Major River
	Minor River/Creek

Flow

To Ontario

Harper Junction, mile 45

Namort

River

20

20

Jonesboro

Malheur

Flow

Beulah Reservoir to Malheur Confluence, 10 miles

Mile 15

Juntura

Juntura-Riverside Road

Beulah Reservoir

Beulah

Agency Valley Dam

Beulah Road

North Fork

Malheur River

20

To Burns

Counting its three forks, the Malheur is eastern Oregon's second longest river system. The north and middle forks drain an expansive area of the Blue Mountains northeast of Burns. After leaving the mountains, the beautiful North Fork is finally captured by Beulah Reservoir, a fine stillwater fishery located 20 miles northwest of Juntura. The Middle Fork, meanwhile, departs the mountains above the tiny town of Drewsey and then meanders through private lands before reaching Warm Springs Reservoir southwest of Juntura.

Below the reservoir, the Middle Fork is known simply as the Malheur. A few miles below Warm Springs Dam, the South Fork contributes its meager flows. Offering little in the way of fishing, the South Fork Malheur originates in the arid, desolate mountains to the southwest. All told, the Malheur offers some 30 miles of prime trout water downstream from Warm Springs Reservoir with the tiny hamlet of Juntura located about halfway through that stretch of river. The upper 10 miles of this section offer the best fishing for deep-bodied rainbows.

One of those blink-and-you-miss-it towns, Juntura serves as the gateway to the Malheur and the town's towering old cottonwoods offer welcome shade during the desert summers. Just east of town, the North Fork joins the main stem, which is then followed east by U.S. 20. Juntura's Oasis Motel & Café are well named, offering the only semblance of civilization for many miles. Above Juntura, the Malheur flows through a roadless canyon, beginning a dozen river miles south of town at Riverside Wildlife Management Area, which is operated by Oregon Department of Fish & Wildlife (ODFW).

Each year, ODFW plants 90,000 fingerling rainbows in the Malheur River from Riverside downstream to Gold Creek. Supplementing these stocks is a native population of redband trout. The Malheur's trout grow rapidly due to the river's diverse and fertile food base. Fingerlings planted during the spring reach 8 to 10 inches by their first autumn. A year later they reach a fat 14 to 16 inches. During normal years of good water supply, the river boasts plenty of 18- to 20-plus-inch three-year-olds.

A tailwater fishery, the Malheur derives its nutrient base from the outflow of Warm Springs Reservoir. The flush of cold water from the reservoir promotes growth of algae and other aquatic vegetation, providing abundant habitat for aquatic insects. According to ODFW biologist Wayne Bowers, the diminutive South Fork, which joins the Middle Fork at Riverside, also contributes a substantial nutrient load, chiefly from agricultural runoff.

The Malheur serves the needs of regional agriculture in an arid part of Oregon where water ranks as the most coveted resource. Beginning with the spring irrigation season, the Malheur flows high and fast out of Warm Springs Reservoir. These high flows continue all summer. The river is floatable during summer, but not nearly so fishable as during the autumn, when water levels finally drop. Beginning in early

The author enjoys a rare and brief period of low water on the Malheur River.

October, the river begins to drop and by the middle of the month it reaches its perfect autumn flows. At low water, the Malheur is a small river, easily waded.

The autumn fishing continues until the river locks in ice, usually during early December or thereabouts. Spring offers a second season on the Malheur, primarily from late February through early April, but sometimes lasting into June and sometimes lasting only a few days. Summer fishing ranges from nearly impossible to fair, depending entirely on river flows any given year. Normally, the river runs high and off-color from mid-spring through September.

During these high flows, one can float the Riverside-to-Juntura stretch rather easily in a drift boat or raft. Large, sharp rocks demand that boaters remain vigilant. Otherwise, the diminutive Malheur requires only modest boating skills. The float requires a long day on the water so the better option is to split the adventure into two days to allow plenty of time for fishing. The river offers no formal launches, but you can drop the boat in at Riverside and take out above Allan Diversion Dam upstream from Juntura. There are camping spots along the river.

While the higher summer flows allow for an easier float on the Malheur, the low water of spring and autumn equates to better fishing. The first mile or so of river downstream from the bridge at Riverside no doubt ranks second in popularity only to the water below Juntura, where U.S. Highway 20 parallels the Malheur for miles. The Riverside reach is encompassed within the ODFW's Riverside Wildlife Management Area. Otherwise, BLM lands predominate, allowing for ample public access with one notable exception: Between Riverside and Juntura, the old railroad grade belongs to a private landowner. Anglers can hike the riverbanks and wade the river, but the narrow strip of private land is posted.

Other parcels of private property abut the river in places, especially downstream from Juntura. Stop in or call the BLM office in Hines/Burns and buy a copy of the district map that shows land ownership. Not only will the map help steer you away from private lands, but it will reveal the little-known hike-in access points between Riverside and Juntura.

Below Juntura the Malheur picks up the flows from the North Fork and then immediately enters a steep-sided canyon, but this time the highway follows right along the river's banks, affording easy access. Private land is generally posted, but public property abounds. Highway 20, the only east-west highway cutting across Malheur and Harney Counties, serves as a major trucking route, so watch your rearview mirror as you negotiate the winding curves along the river in search of a pullout.

The river's trout fishery extends down to the Gold Creek area about 15 miles downstream from Juntura. You won't find any signs announcing Gold Creek, as this seasonal tributary is but one of many such intermittent feeder creeks draining the side canyons.

Despite the highway immediately above, this reach of the Malheur draws only modest angling pressure. During the low-water periods of early spring and autumn, try wading across the river and fishing from the far bank. Few anglers go to such trouble and anglers possessed of an adventurous spirit always fare best on this river.

In fact, most highway travelers see the Malheur during summer, when heavy flows lend the river a flood-like appearance. Come October, however, the Juntura-to-Gold Creek reach offers easy wading and easy access. The adventure then derives from the fickle nature of eastern Oregon's autumn and spring weather.

Bear in mind also that the Malheur is largely climate controlled. Occasional periods of drought devastate the fishery, leaving little water in which to plant trout. Likewise, high-water years restrict the ideal low-water period during the spring. In fact, if the Malheur freezes early, say during late November, and then runs flush with surplus water in the spring, the fishable season lasts but a mere two months or so. The

Malheur fishes okay during high water, but only if the river flows green rather than muddy brown.

Obviously you can drive a long way for nothing on the Malheur, which explains the necessity of a pre-expedition phone call to the ODFW office in Hines (541-573-6582). Ask about water levels and water color. Autumn is usually a sure bet after mid-October, but spring is a toss-up. You might find wadeable, fishable water all the way through April or you might be limited to just a brief low-water period during February or early March.

A do-it-yourself adventure, the Malheur River isn't for everybody. But if fat rainbows, long walks and rugged desert splendor sound appealing, then fill the tank, check the spare tire and head for one of the Northwest's best remote trout streams.

Fishing the Malheur

Fishing tactics for the Malheur vary according to the water levels and conditions. During low-water periods of spring and fall, regular hatches allow for dry-fly angling. Midges emerge as early as February, but the March hatches are more likely to tempt the rainbows into surface feeding. By early March, expect hatches of caddisflies and Blue-Winged Olive mayflies. The Blue-Winged Olives (*Baetis*) require size 18 and 20 imitations. Try an olive-bodied comparadun or any appropriately sized parachute-style fly such as a Parachute Adams or Gulper Special. Even March Brown mayflies (*Rithrogenia*) appear on certain reaches of the Malheur.

During low-water years, springtime dry-fly action peaks during March and April when the typical morning dawns bright and chilly over the sage-cloaked heights of the Malheur River Canyon. The hatches gain momentum as the late-morning sun bathes the river in warmth. Sunny spring weather often equates to midday and evening caddis hatches. The spring mayflies—Blue-Winged Olives and March Browns—prefer muggy, overcast weather. Under such conditions, profuse hatches erupt from time to time.

The Malheur's rainbows might prove easy dry-fly marks one spring day and then the most challenging of trout the next. A lot depends on the water you fish and the particular conditions. The river runs rather slow during the low-water periods and the trout often reside in quiet, glassy pools. Study the pools and watch for subtle rises. Then stalk carefully into casting range. The Malheur's flat-water rainbows often require 12-foot leaders and 6X tippets.

On the other hand, you might find fat trout feeding in a seam along a boulder-strewn run where a choppy, broken surface allows for less finesse in your approach. In any case, bear in mind that a seemingly unimpressive rise might well be a 3-pound trout.

During non-hatch periods, try attractor-style dry flies or nymphs. Of the former, I prefer a size 8 or 10 Royal Trude or Stimulator. Both are good floaters and are large enough to attract attention from skyward-looking trout even when the river runs green. As for nymphs, choose the typical assortment of Hare's Ears, Pheasant Tails and other time-tested favorites. Better still—at least in many of the river's pools—are Woolly Buggers fished as streamers, which brings us to the late spring-through-summer fishing on the Malheur.

By mid- to late spring, the Malheur fairly roars down its canyon, bearing two or three times its late-autumn flow. Between July and September you may find opportunity to cast hopper patterns to bank-hugging rainbows, but only when the water flows green rather than brown. Regardless, the low-water, stalk-your-trout dry-fly action is but a fond memory that won't recur until October.

Instead, mid-spring is streamer time on the Malheur. The river's rainbows love big Woolly Buggers fished down and across. You can use a floating line, although a sink-tip line works better. Either line can be coupled with one of the new high-density leader butts made by AirFlo and available in many fly shops. A 3- to 4-foot leader and a size 4 weighted black Woolly Bugger rounds out the gear. The fly must sink quickly and maintain depth under tension, so use conehead or lead-head Buggers.

The tactic requires skill in line and fly control. Cast across stream and then mend up to allow a drag-free drift until the fly begins to track across the current. Now use the rod tip to "jig" the fly around and in front of large boulders and current

A hefty rainbow from the Malheur.

seams. Meanwhile, use your free hand to alternately retrieve and release line. In short, bring the fly to life and fish it in the right water. During high flows, the Malheur's trout seek refuge around boulders, in rock gardens, under cut banks, and along current seams. Fish these places thoroughly and keep the faith. You may not hook many fish, but you will hook fish and most will span a hefty 14 to 20 inches in length.

If such action sounds appealing, then you're a prime candidate for a late spring/early summer adventure to the Malheur. You won't have any company, save a few locals who like to keep things a secret when it comes to the Malheur and its big rainbows. Otherwise, plan your trip for late October to enjoy the best water conditions of the year or arrive early during spring to cast dry flies over fine hatches.

Nearby Fisheries

Beulah Reservoir

Beulah Reservoir, 18 miles northwest of Juntura, offers fast-growing stocked rainbows along with a few wild redbands that drop down from the forks of the Malheur. During years of good water supply, the fish reach 20 inches. The signed gravel road leads north from the west edge of Juntura. Warm Springs Reservoir, whose dam forms the productive tailwater reach discussed in this chapter, offers fair to good prospects for bass and panfish.

Restaurants and Accommodations

The only nearby lodging and restaurant is the Oasis Motel/Café in Juntura (541-277-3605). The Oasis is ideally located for those fishing the Malheur: 17 miles to the south lies Riverside Wildlife Management Area while Highway 20 picks up the river just east of town. Always call ahead for motel reservations, especially during the fall when the Oasis fills up with chukar hunters. Undeveloped camping space is available at Riverside WMA, at a few wide spots along the highway below Juntura, and at Chukar Park, located a few miles northwest of Juntura on the road up to Beulah Reservoir.

Author's Tip

Nowhere between Riverside and Juntura is the Malheur heavily fished. Still, the drive-in wildlife management area provides easy access and just a few anglers can tie up the mile or so of water therein. My favorite tactic is to access waters farther downstream in the canyon by parking on the rim above and hiking down. To pursue this strategy, you will need the Bureau of Land Management's $4 map that shows land ownership. The map is titled *BLM Burns District, North Half* and it is available at the district office in Hines (541-573-4400).

Conehead Crystal Bugger

Favorite Fly

Conehead Crystal Bugger

HOOK	3XL streamer, No. 4-6
TAIL	Marabou
BODY	Krystal chenille or similar
HACKLE	Saddle hackle palmered through body
RIB	Fine wire
HEAD	Metal cone
COLORS	Black, purple, olive, white

Fast Facts

Malheur River

LOCATION	Southeastern Oregon
WATER TYPE	Canyon-bound tailwater river
PRIMARY GAMEFISH	Rainbow trout
BEST TIME	Spring and fall for brief periods
BEST FLIES	X-caddis, No. 14; Parachute Adams; various attractor-style nymphs; weighted Woolly Buggers or similar streamers.
EQUIPMENT	5- to 6-weight rod; floating line
CONDITIONS	Fishing is typically restricted to spring and fall, so expect cold nights and cool to warm days. No fresh water available.
DRIVE TIME	From Bend: 3½ hours From Portland: 6-7 hours From Boise: 3 hours

DIRECTIONS   Follow Highway 20 east from Bend or west from Ontario. When you reach the tiny town of Juntura (east of Burns and west of Vale) turn south at the west edge of town on a gravel road pointing the way to Riverside. After about 17 miles, you will reach the river crossing at Riverside Wildlife Management Area.

Local Fly Shops

KIGER CREEK FLY SHOP
120 NW Circle Drive
Hines, OR 97738
541-573-1329

B & B SPORTING GOODS
Highway 20 & Conley Avenue
Hines, OR 97720
541-573-6200

Area Fly Shops

IDAHO ANGLER
1682 S. Vista Ave.
Boise, ID 83705
208-389-9957

STONEFLY ANGLER
625 Vista
Boise, ID 83705
208-338-1700

INTERMOUNTAIN ARMS & TACKLE
900 Vista Village Center
Boise, ID 83705
208-345-3474

BEAR CREEK FLY SHOP
5521 West State Street
Boise, ID 83703
208-853-8704

Contacts

OREGON DEPARTMENT OF
FISH & WILDLIFE
Malheur Watershed District Office
237 S. Hines Blvd., P.O. Box 8
Hines, OR 97738
541-573-6582

CHAPTER 19

CHOPAKA LAKE

Dry-Fly Action for Big Rainbows

Mention *Callibaetis* mayflies, or Speckled-Wing Duns and many Washington fly anglers gaze off into the distance daydreaming about great days on what might well be the state's premier stillwater fishery. Chopaka Lake enjoys legendary status in the Evergreen State, like Hosmer Lake in Oregon or Henry's Lake in Idaho. This scenic mountain lake offers such superb spring and summer mayfly hatches that it ranks with the premier attractions for the "hatch chasers" among us.

Chopaka occupies a narrow, timbered draw in the Okanogan National Forest, just a few miles south of the Canadian border. The lake's fertile waters support fast-growing rainbows planted periodically by WDFW. These fish enjoy a rich banquet of all the usual stillwater prey items. The *Callibaetis* mayflies are heavily preyed upon during the April through September hatch. So reliable is this hatch that on still days, dry-fly action is virtually assured. That's what keeps most of us coming back to Chopaka, despite the long drive. Few things in trout fishing compare to 3- or 4-pound rainbows gulping down mayflies on the flat waters of a beautiful lake.

Many years the mayfly hatch begins by the time the lake opens in April. Otherwise, expect strong hatches by mid-May. The hatches continue through mid-summer. Often the late-summer hatches are rather sparse, fleeting affairs, but autumn brings renewed mayfly action. What's more, the fall season offers a respite from the crowded weekends of spring and early summer.

May and June mark the peak of the hatch, so expect those weekend crowds to be rather substantial. Despite the assemblage of anglers, the crowds here prove entirely social because so many people come for the same reason—to fish the mayfly hatch. Chopaka veterans are easy to identify. They get twitchy around 11 a.m., anticipating the ensuing hatch. Some head out early in the morning to warm up with a little *Chironomid* fishing, but they keep an eye peeled and a change of fly at hand.

On many occasions I've simply waited around my shoreline camp, sipping coffee and enjoying a leisurely breakfast until I see the first mayfly duns appear. Then I grab the rod and head for the near-shore shallows where large trout soon begin rising. Sometimes I fish a Pheasant Tail Nymph for the first half an hour or more until the duns hatch in adequate numbers to get things moving. My strategy is nothing unique. Many other hatch chasers employ the same method, waiting and watching and enjoying a cup of coffee.

During the hatch you can certainly catch fish by wading or walking the shore-line, but generally Chopaka requires a float tube, pram, or pontoon, and many times I've watched a virtual flotilla of such craft assemble on the lake's placid waters. Chopaka's crowds—when they occur during the spring—are comprised almost entirely of like-minded, well-behaved fly fishing enthusiasts who have arrived from all over Washington.

Nearby Fisheries

Blue Lake

Chopaka Lake rests high above the scenic Sinlahekin Valley. About fifteen miles south from the Chopaka turn-off, on the west side of Sinlahekin Road, Blue Lake offers another productive rainbow trout fishery. Rainbows here reach 20 or more inches and the reservoir commands a beautiful view of the surrounding mountains. No formal facilities exist, but camp space is available.

Accommodations

Owing to the time and trouble required to reach Chopaka, most anglers camp right at the lake. Ample space awaits most of the time, but the first few open week-ends draw big crowds. Arrive during mid-week to get a good camp spot and bring along your own firewood or, better yet, camp stove. Despite the infamous "Chopaka Grade," some anglers drive in with tow trailers or even large RVs. Be forewarned, how-

CHOPAKA LAKE

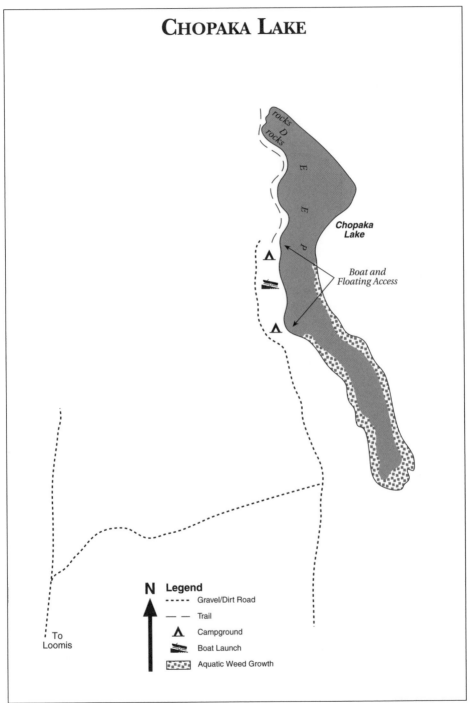

rocks
D
rocks

E

E

P

**Chopaka
Lake**

*Boat and
Floating Access*

N

Legend
- - - - Gravel/Dirt Road
— — Trail
⚠ Campground
Boat Launch
Aquatic Weed Growth

To
Loomis

ever, that the rugged road to Chopaka begins and ends with the insanely steep, mile-long grade that can eat radiators on the way up and chew up brakes on the way down.

One lodging option lies just a few miles from Chopaka, on the east shore of Palmer Lake. The Chopaka Lodge has three units and is located at 1995 Loomis Highway. Make reservations well ahead of time by calling 509-223-3131. Two other lodges are located around Spectacle Lake, about halfway between Chopaka and the jump-off town of Tonasket. Spectacle Lake itself contains stocked rainbow trout. Rainbow Resort (509-223-3700) and Spectacle Lake Resort (509-223-3433) serve the area. On your way to Chopaka (from Hwy. 97 and Tonasket) you will drive along the north shore of Spectacle Lake. In a pinch, you can always make the half-hour run up to Oroville for motel space (Camaray Motel, 509-476-3684 and Red Apple Inn, 509-476-3694). Tonsket also has a Red Apple Inn (509-486-2119).

Author's Tip

During summer, when the damsels hatch, paddle over to the southeast shoreline where extensive weed beds offer dense concentrations of damsel nymphs. Attach 14 to 18 feet of leader to a floating line and fish a slightly weighted damsel nymph pattern against the edges of the weeds. And hold on tight. Sometimes, on this same margin of the lake, Chopaka offers dry-fly damsel fishing, perhaps the most explosive and exciting form of stillwater angling.

A beautiful Chopaka Lake rainbow.

Callibaetis Sparkle Dun

Favorite Fly

Callibaetis Sparkle Dun

HOOK | Dry-fly, No. 12-16
TAIL | Z-lon or Antron strands
BODY | Light tan or light gray dubbing
WING | Deer hair, upright

Fast Facts

Chopaka Lake

LOCATION | Northeastern Washington
WATER TYPE | Natural mountain lake
PRIMARY GAMEFISH | Rainbow trout
BEST TIME | Spring and fall
BEST FLIES | Patterns for *Callibaetis* mayflies, *Chironomids*, damsels and leeches.
EQUIPMENT | 5- to 6-weight rod; floating line and sinking lines.
CONDITIONS | Highly variable mountain weather with frequent spring rain storms. Steep gravel road (Chopaka Grade) can be hard on vehicles, especially RVs and boat trailers.
DRIVE TIME | From Seattle: 5-8 hours depending on route

DIRECTIONS   Follow I-5 north to the Highway 20 exit at Burlington. Then head east up the Skagit River and over the North Cascades. Follow Highway 20 east all the way to the town of Okanogan. Then turn north on U.S. 97 and head for Tonasket. At Tonasket, turn left at the signed intersection, crossing the Okanogan River, and then turn north on Loomis-Oroville Road. About 20 miles later you will arrive at Loomis and the east edge of the scenic Sinlahekin Valley. Continue northwest from Loomis to a signed left turn (Toats Coulee Road), which crosses the valley and then head a short distance south to the signed right turn heading up Chopaka Grade. Set your odometer at the bottom of the grade. Once you negotiate the steep grade, watch for the second major right turn (at a Y-intersection) at the five-mile mark. Take the downhill fork to your right and descend a couple miles to the lake. If you are leaving Seattle via I-90 east bound (Highway 20 over the North Cascades often is still closed for the winter when Chopaka opens in April), turn north on Highway 97 just west of Ellensburg and take the route through Wenatchee and north to Okanogan. If wintry weather assaults Blewett Pass on this route, forget about it and continue east on I-90 to the Columbia River and turn north on SR 281 to Quincy and then northwest on SR 28, which will catch up with U.S. 97 at Wenatchee.

Local Fly Shops

MAZAMA TROUTFITTERS
48 Lost River Road
Mazama, WA 98665
360-573-9383

WORLEY-BUGGER FLY COMPANY
811 4th Parallel
Ellensburg, WA 98926
888-950-3474

BLUE DUN FLY SHOP
960 Valley Mall Parkway, Suite A
East Wenatchee, WA 98802
509-884-4070 and,

BLUE DUN FLY SHOP
135 S. Sherman
Spokane WA 99202
509-884-4070

SILVER BOW FLY SHOP
1003 East Trent Avenue
Spokane, WA 99202
509-483-1772

Contacts

WASHINGTON DEPARTMENT
OF FISH & WILDLIFE North Central Washington
Region 2 Office
1550 Alder Street NW
Ephrata, WA 98823-9699
509-754-4624

CHAPTER 20

LAKE LENORE

Trophy Cutthroat in the Desert

I'll admit that my first Lake Lenore experience was less than memorable. In fact, I was rather disappointed, not in the fish or the fishing, but in the hordes of anglers lined up along the lake's narrow northernmost beach, half of them obviously not really caring whether they snagged the spawning-season cutthroat cruising the shallows and a high percentage of those "anglers" trying specifically to snag fish.

I have issues with the idea of fishing over spawning fish or those about to spawn, yet Lenore's Lahontan cutthroat only go through the motions, so to speak. They cruise the shallows, staging like fish about to spawn, but they don't actually reproduce in the lake. So I suppose I really don't care that fly fishers line up elbow to elbow on Lenore's narrow north shore and target these fish. But snagging is a different matter, and I saw a lot of purposefully foul-hooked trout that spring day back in the '80s.

Luckily, however, my quest to find some solitude led me to the eastern and southern shoreline of this geologically stunning desert lake where I soon learned why this far-away fishery ranks among the state's most popular stillwater destinations. The cutthroat are all big. You don't catch any small fish, unless you count the 16- to 18-inch

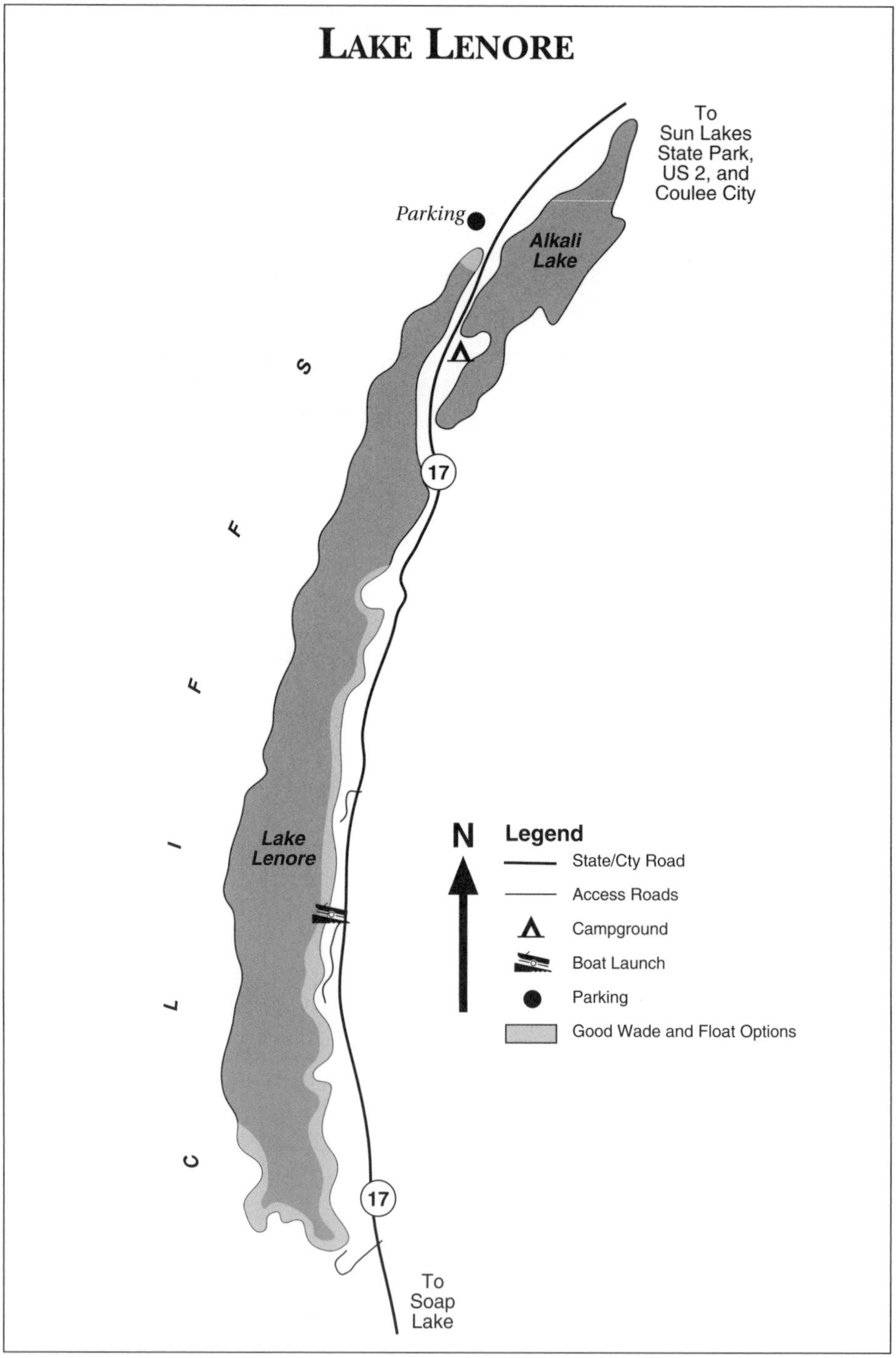
Lake Lenore
To
Sun Lakes
State Park,
US 2, and
Coulee City
Parking
Alkali
Lake
S
17
F
F
I
Lake
Lenore
L
C
17
To
Soap
Lake
N
Legend
State/Cty Road
Access Roads
Campground
Boat Launch
Parking
Good Wade and Float Options

© Wilderness Adventures Press, Inc.

trout termed "shakers" by anglers who seek the lake's 5- to 10-pound trophy-size versions of these beautiful Lahontan cutthroat.

Moreover, the sheer dimensions of the place inspire wonderment. I frequently find myself staring up towards the towering rims of Lower Grande Coulee, trying to imagine the dramatically violent geologic and climactic events that left in their wake this impossibly rugged landscape. Lake Lenore's cutthroat don't demand early morning fishing, yet I always awaken before dawn just to witness the oft-spectacular explosions of color cast upon the rimrocks by the sun's first, tentative attempts to repel the desert chill.

Lake Lenore's highly alkaline waters were devoid of fish until the Washington Department of Wildlife undertook an experimental planting of Lahontan cutthroat from Nevada. Supremely adapted to just such waters in their native range in the heart of the Great Basin, these cutthroat proved the perfect match for stark and stunning Lake Lenore. By the mid-1980s, Lenore had become one of eastern Washington's top destination fisheries, thanks not only to the fast-growing cutthroat trout, but also to the WDFW's decision to manage the lake for very limited harvest.

Few secrets remain about Lenore. It draws huge crowds of fly anglers during popular spring weekends. The congregation gathers at the north end on such weekends and you can join the party if you must. If you share my desire to avoid the madhouse, simply seek the far less pressured waters around the remaining shoreline. At 1,700 acres, Lenore offers plenty of room to stretch your legs. Also, consider an autumn visit to Lenore, as late as mid-November. By mid-October, the summer heat is a fading memory, the cutthroat are in great shape and you can enjoy a huge lake virtually devoid of other anglers.

Either way, your first visit is likely to be memorable, if not for the big, beautiful Lahontans, then certainly for the remarkable desert scenery dominated by the precipitous steeps left over after the great floods followed the retreat of the last ice age. Today, these massive eastern Washington desert canyons are called coulees.

Fishing Lake Lenore

Lake Lenore's cutthroat enjoy abundant forage in the form of all the usual stillwater trout foods. High on the list are *Chironomids*, which hatch profusely during spring and early summer. Just as significant are scuds, *Callibaetis*, damsels, water beetles, leeches and dragonfly nymphs. Dense midge hatches sometimes stir the trout into selective feeding, but rarely are these fish so persnickety as rainbows might be on nearby waters like Dry Falls Lake.

Most of the time, especially during early spring and autumn, anglers can expect reasonable success with basic attractor flies, including Woolly Buggers, leech patterns, Carey Specials and Zug Bugs. On those occasions when the trout demand a more technical approach, *Chironomids* are generally the culprit. Stillwater specialists in eastern Washington virtually invented the idea of dead-drifting *Chironomid* pupa patterns under an indicator. I've seen this method employed more in eastern Washington than anywhere else in the West—and for good reason. It works.

"Bobber fishing" in this manner often leaves much to be desired in terms of action. That's my personal objection to the technique. I don't question its effectiveness nor its legitimacy, but I've bored myself to tears a few times employing it. Certainly that sense of boredom vanishes the instant a 5-pound trout jerks the indicator under water, so I can appreciate Greg Thomas' take on the subject, especially during March, when bitter cold weather tests my resolve: "...it allows one hand to remain in a warm pocket while the other hand braves the elements," says Thomas.

My last March trip to Lenore certainly tested my resolve. I grew up in the terrible cold of eastern Idaho's high-elevation Rocky Mountain winters, so when I tell you it was cold, you can take my word for it. Basically, my resolve lost. A bright sun made no headway against the late-winter chill and I had long since quit casting and stripping flies because each time I did so, the guides collected water and froze solid. I opted for a suspended midge pupa fished below an indicator on a long leader. The first fish came within minutes and fought gallantly despite the cold water.

Ever popular in spring, Lenore's north shore attracts lots of anglers and lots of fish.

Within 15 minutes I had hooked and landed three big cutthroats. Actually, that's not quite accurate—the fish hooked themselves because I had both hands buried deep in my armpits under a heavy coat. The rod rested atop my float tube deck and each time the indicator disappeared, I struggled to free my hands in time to do anything about it. By sheer happenstance, each fish held on of its own accord.

But with each ensuing fish, my enthusiasm dampened considerably owing to frozen fingers. My trusty 6-mm neoprene waders threatened to fail me. How many times had these old 6-mills kept me toasty on late-winter duck hunts? Lake Lenore in March should have been a cakewalk compared to a frozen marsh in January, but I was freezing.

Trolling was the answer. I'd just tie on a Woolly Bugger and troll back to the warming confines of the truck. I didn't even bother switching lines; I just chopped off the midge pattern, removed the indicator and secured a big olive Bugger to the end of my 18-foot leader. Then I kicked like mad for shore only to have one of those pesky cutthroats grab the fly before I had reached cruising speed. I landed and released an 18-inch fish and resumed my beeline for the bank. Another and then another trout came to the Bugger. I landed and released both before hitting shore. I hooked and lost one last fish as I was standing in the shallows reeling up the line.

Perhaps the best 30 minutes of fishing I had ever enjoyed on Lenore and I couldn't take another minute of it.

Restaurants and Accommodations

A couple of crude camping areas are located along the east shore of Lake Lenore, which is paralleled by State Route 17. The best campground in the area is just a few miles north at Sun Lakes State Park. During the busy spring weekends, head straight for the state park before going fishing. If you wait, you may arrive to find all the camping spots occupied.

Area Lodging

Available south at Soap Lake and to the north at Coulee City:

Lake Motel, Soap Lake, 509-246-1611
Notaras Lodge, Soap Lake, 509-246-0462
Royal View Motel, Soap Lake, 509-246-1831
Tolo Village Cottage, Soap Lake, 509-246-1512
Tumwater Lodge, Soap Lake, 509-246-1416
The Inn At Soap Lake, 509-246-1132
Ala Cozy Motel, Coulee City, 509-632-5703
Blue Top Motel, Coulee City, 509-632-5596
Lakeview Motel, Coulee City, 509-632-5792
Main Stay B&B, Coulee City, 509-632-5687

My favorite restaurant in the vicinity is the Mexican joint in Ephrata, called Tequilas and located at 916 Basin Street (509-754-1306). Don't worry about reservations, just drive down when the evening fishing ends. Also in Ephrata, at 33 Basin Street, Tortellini's Italian works for a pasta fix if you're so inclined (509-754-6265). If you're looking for a brief respite from the wind and a decent steak dinner, try Don's Restaurant in downtown Soap Lake (509-246-1217). You can run up the road a few miles and let someone else cook breakfast at Dry Falls Café, located at the junction of Highway 2 and SR 17 north of Dry Falls Lake.

Author's Tip

I've frozen my butt off at Lenore on several occasions, spring and fall, but the late-autumn fishing is well worth the price of admission, not only at Lenore but also up the road at Dry Falls. Wait until late October, bundle up, and head for the Grand Coulee. While you're there, choose a still day and try your luck along the east shoreline of Banks Lake, off State Route 155. I've had some good float tube action near the park at Coulee City, but more remote reaches await farther north.

Favorite Fly

Olive Carey Special

HOOK	Wet fly, No. 4-8
TAIL	Natural or dyed-olive pheasant rump fibers
BODY	Olive-green chenille
COLLAR	Pheasant rump, natural or dyed olive

Olive Carey Special

Fast Facts

Lake Lenore

LOCATION	Eastern Washington, north of Moses Lake
WATER TYPE	Large, highly alkaline natural lake
PRIMARY GAMEFISH	Lahontan cutthroat trout
BEST TIME	March-May and October-November (Lenore traditionally opens March 1, but during severe winters, ice cover may remain until the first week or so of the month)
BEST FLIES	A full array of standard stillwater flies, including midge, *Callibaetis*, damsel, and leech patterns.
EQUIPMENT	6- to 7-weight rod; floating line, intermediate line, Type III sinking line.
DRIVE TIME	From Seattle: 4 hours From Portland: 5 hours From Boise: 6-7 hours
CONDITIONS	Frequent cold weather and high winds during spring; equally frequent perfect weather, though cool, during autumn. Only unimproved camping and launches around the lake.
DIRECTIONS	From Seattle, follow I-90 east past Ellensburg and turn north on SR 283 heading toward Ephrata. Continue through Ephrata and north to Soap Lake on SR 17, which reaches Lake Lenore's southeast corner just a few miles north of Soap Lake. From Portland, follow I-84 east and cross the Columbia on Highway 97 at Biggs. Head north, following Highway 97 past Yakima and up to I-90. Turn east and follow directions as above. From Boise and points east, follow I-84 north and west to Hermiston and cross the Columbia on U.S. 395 heading to Tri-Cities. Continue north through Tri-Cities on 395, then take the SR 17 exit heading north-by-northwest towards Moses Lake and Othello. State Route 17 takes you all the way to Lenore.

Local Fly Shops

WORLEY-BUGGER FLY COMPANY
811 4th Parallel
Ellensburg, WA 98926
888-950-3474

BLUE DUN FLY SHOP
960 Valley Mall Parkway, Suite A
East Wenatchee, WA 98802
509-884-4070

GARY'S FLY SHOP
1210 West Lincoln
Yakima, WA 98902
509-457-3474

CLEARWATER FLY SHOP
417 West First Street
Kennewick, WA 99336
509-582-1001

Area Fly Shops

SWEDE'S FLY SHOP
17419 139th Avenue NE
Woodinville, WA 98072
425-487-3747

CREEKSIDE ANGLING COMPANY
1660 Northwest Gilman Blvd. #C-5
Issaquah, WA 98027
425-392-3800

KAUFMANN'S STREAMBORN
1918 4th Avenue
Seattle, WA 98101
206-448-0601

REI-PORTLAND
1798 Jantzen Beach Ctr
Portland, OR 97217
503-283-1300

REI-SEATTLE
222 Yale Ave. N
Seattle, WA 98109
206-223-1944

PATRICK'S FLY SHOP
2237 Eastlake Avenue East
Seattle, WA 98102
206-325-8988

ORVIS SEATTLE
911 Bellevue Way NE
Bellevue, WA 98004
425-452-9138

AVID ANGLER FLY SHOPPE
17171 Bothell Way NE, Ste. A130
Lake Forest Park, WA 98155
206-362-4030

Contacts

WASHINGTON DEPARTMENT
OF FISH & WILDLIFE
North Central Washington -
Region 2 Office
1550 Alder Street NW
Ephrata, WA 98823-9699
509-754-4624

SOAP LAKE CHAMBER
OF COMMERCE
509-246-1821

DRY FALLS LAKE

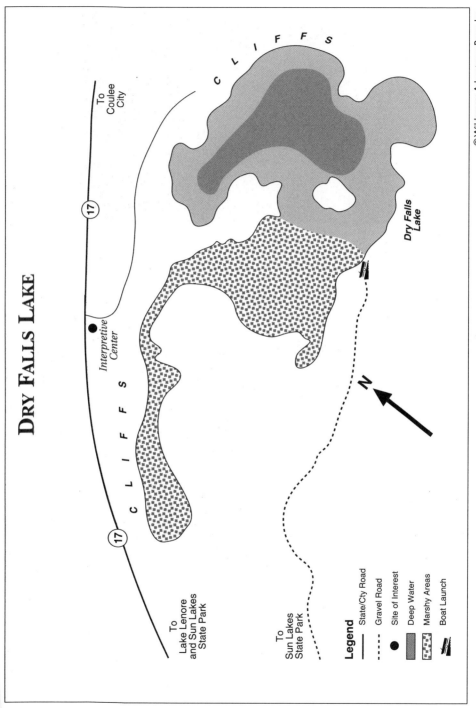

Legend

	State/Cty Road
	Gravel Road
●	Site of Interest
	Deep Water
	Marshy Areas
	Boat Launch

To Coulee City

17

Interpretive Center

CLIFFS

CLIFFS

Dry Falls Lake

N

To Lake Lenore and Sun Lakes State Park

17

To Sun Lakes State Park

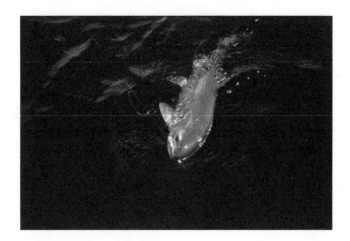

CHAPTER 21

DRY FALLS LAKE

Scenic Splendor and Hard-Fighting Rainbows and Browns

"Awesome. Just awesome," she commented.

A long time ago, too far in my past to even bother with names, we stood atop the observation pullout high above Dry Falls Lake. My old blue-and-rust Ford was about to embark on another term of tailgater parties and impromptu road trips at the university. This trip to eastern Washington qualified as the latter. At least I'd had the foresight to toss in two float tubes, two fly rods and a willing co-ed.

Truly it was—is—an awesome sight. Dry Falls Lake and its attendant massive basalt cliffs once created monstrous waterfalls on the ancient Columbia when the mighty river carved out the Grand Coulee. How the falls must have roared, echoing out across the land.

Many centuries later, the falls fell silent as the climate changed, the river settled into a new and quieter course. Left in her wake was the Grand Coulee and a series of ancient lakes, mere shadows of their former magnificence. Among these was

Falls Lake, a circular basin shadowed by huge, looming abutments. Little imagination is required to envision the precipitous escarpments in their former role as cascades for mountains of water rushing towards the southwest.

Dry Falls is extremely fertile, offering an abundance of every imaginable stillwater trout food. Its planted rainbows and browns grow quickly, although not to enormous size. Typically, they span 14 to 20 inches. Rainbows outnumber browns, but browns grow larger owing to longer life expectancy.

I had no need of explaining all that to my blond companion that day back in the early '80s. Within 20 yards of the launch, five minutes into her first ever fly fishing expedition, she was fast to a big trout—even big by Dry Falls standards. With a little coaching from me she landed the fish, a brute of a brown trout weighing about five pounds. "Awesome," she repeated, admiring the trout as I held it in the net. I never landed her, but then that's not particularly relevant to the story.

What is relevant is the fact that Dry Falls continues to rank among the best of Washington's stillwater big-trout factories. It is also one of the most popular. I love the place, but so too do an awful lot of other folks. I learned the hard way to avoid mid-spring weekends. Some years ago I was fishing Dry Falls on a Friday during April. By late afternoon the dust cloud began well down the access road. That dust cloud continued unabated until caravans of vehicles has filled every available, and every imaginable, parking space at the lake. The pattern repeated itself the next morning.

The fish didn't seem to care and a lot of them felt the sting of the fly hook that weekend. Dry Falls always seems to yield a few nice fish, even under less-than-ideal conditions. Rainbows outnumber brown trout perhaps ten to one. Both species occasionally top 20 inches, but they average a fat, strong 16 to 18 inches, growing fast on a diet rich in *Chironomids*, *Callibaetis*, damsels, and all the other usual suspects.

When you visit Dry Falls, bring your camera. The stark landscape is as much a draw as the fishing. I once decided to explore the rugged badlands out behind Dry Falls, so I laced up the hiking boots and headed east very early one morning. I walked right up on a bobcat, watched two owls chasing one another low across the sagelands, and found a variety of colorful wildflowers waiting to absorb the warming rays of sunrise.

Also bring your full arsenal of stillwater flies. Expect daily *Chironomid* hatches. Mayflies hatch from mid-spring until September and damsels hatch in droves by late spring. In the absence of obvious feeding patterns by the fish, many anglers fish *Chironomid* patterns suspended under an indicator. The tactic works perfectly on Dry Falls. If you find this method lacking in action, head for the deeper water and fish attractor-style wets on a sinking line. My favorite combination is a Woolly Bugger or leech pattern trailed by a beadhead Zug Bug, Prince or Pheasant Tail Nymph.

Restaurants and Accommodations

The towns of Soap Lake and Ephrata lie within easy reach of Dry Falls. Both communities offer several dining options as listed in the Lake Lenore chapter. Soap Lake lies about 20 miles south of Dry Falls. Also, Dry Falls Café is located just a few miles north of the lake, at the SR 2/SR 17 junction. The café opens at 7 a.m. and offers hearty breakfasts that are a welcome warm-up before the morning's fishing down at Dry Falls. You can also fill up your tank and stock up on supplies at the adjacent mini-mart (fishing licenses are available here).

Follow SR 2 east from Dry Falls Café, cross Dry Falls Dam, and you arrive at the little town of Coulee City. Turn north on SR 155 and you drive the scenic east shoreline of Banks Lake. Forty minutes later you arrive at the diminutive community of Grand Coulee, which offers a great little Mexican restaurant called La Presa (509-633-3173). The expansive menu offers just about anything you could want in authentic Mexican fare and all of it good. La Presa is open daily for lunch and dinner.

Sun Lakes State Park, covering a total of 4,000 acres, offers the only camping close to Dry Falls (camping is not allowed at the lake, which is included in the state park). The large campground can fill quickly on prime weekends, so drop by and select a campsite before you drive the few miles back to Dry Falls Lake. You can reserve a site through the Washington State Parks Department by calling 888-226-7688 or online at www.parks.wa.gov/reserve.asp.

If you prefer motel space (often preferable during the early spring and late fall when nighttime temperatures might dip well below freezing), Coulee City offers several options. The town lies at the east end of Dry Falls Dam, which backs up sprawling Banks Lake.

Area Lodging

Ala Cozy Motel, Coulee City, WA, 509-632-5703
Blue Top Motel, Coulee City, WA, 509-632-5596
Lakeview Motel, Coulee City, WA, 509-632-5792
Main Stay B&B, Coulee City, WA, 509-632-5687

Author's Tip

Nearly half of Dry Falls Lake is comprised of weedy, super-fertile shallows. During the *Callibaetis* hatch, try heading for this part of the lake and watch for rising trout in shallow water. The shallow half of the lake is difficult to fish when the wind blows, but on still days it offers the unique challenge of casting to risers and to visible cruising fish.

Favorite Fly

Black Chironomid Pupa

HOOK	Curved-shank wet-fly hook, No. 12-18
TAIL	White Antron
BODY	Black thread and black V-rib material
THORAX	Peacock herl
GILLS	White Antron
HEAD	Metal bead

Black Chironomid Pupa

Fast Facts

Dry Falls Lake

LOCATION	Eastern Washington, north of Lake Lenore
WATER TYPE	Natural desert lake
PRIMARY GAMEFISH	Rainbow trout and brown trout, 14 to 26 inches
BEST TIME	Spring and fall
BEST FLIES	A full array of standard stillwater flies, including *Chironomid, Callibaetis,* damsel and leech patterns.
EQUIPMENT	5- to 6-weight rod; floating and sinking lines. Float tube, pontoon or pram required.
CONDITIONS	Often windy; dusty access road turns gooey after hard rain storms, which occur infrequently.
DRIVE TIME	From Seattle: 4 hours From Portland: 5½ hours

DIRECTIONS   From Seattle, head east on I-90. From Portland, head east on I-84 and then north on Highway 97 until you reach I-90. Follow I-90 east, past the Columbia River and then northeast to SR 283, which continues northeast toward Ephrata. At Ephrata, head north on SR 17 towards Soap Lake. Continue past Soap Lake and Lake Lenore and then watch for the turn-off into Sun Lakes State Park. Drive through the park, following the signed route to Dry Falls Lake. No camping is allowed at Dry Falls, but ample campsites await at the state park. However, make sure to get a campsite before you go fishing. These sites fill up fast on spring weekends.

Local Fly Shops

WORLEY-BUGGER FLY COMPANY
811 4th Parallel
Ellensburg, WA 98926
888-950-3474

BLUE DUN FLY SHOP
960 Valley Mall Parkway, Suite A
East Wenatchee, WA 98802
509-884-4070

CLEARWATER FLY SHOP
417 West First Street
Kennewick, WA 99336
509-582-1001

GARY'S FLY SHOP
1210 West Lincoln
Yakima, WA 98902
509-457-3474

ORVIS SEATTLE
911 Bellevue Way NE
Bellevue, WA 98004
425-452-9138

REI
222 Yale Ave. N
Seattle, WA 98109
206-223-1944

AVID ANGLER FLY SHOP
17171 Bothell Way NE, Ste. A130
Lake Forest Park, WA 98155
206-362-4030

Area Fly Shops

SWEDE'S FLY SHOP
17419 139th Avenue NE
Woodinville, WA 98072
425-487-3747

CREEKSIDE ANGLING COMPANY
1660 Northwest Gilman Blvd. #C-5
Issaquah, WA 98027
425-392-3800

KAUFMANN'S STREAMBORN
1918 4th Avenue
Seattle, WA 98101
206-448-0601

PATRICK'S FLY SHOP
2237 Eastlake Avenue East
Seattle, WA 98102
206-325-8988

ORVIS SEATTLE
911 Bellevue Way NE
Bellevue, WA 98004
425-452-9138

REI-PORTLAND
1798 Jantzen Beach Ctr
Portland, OR 97217
503-283-1300

REI-SEATTLE
222 Yale Ave. N
Seattle, WA 98109
206-223-1944

AVID ANGLER FLY SHOP
17171 Bothell Way NE, Ste. A130
Lake Forest Park, WA 98155
206-362-4030

Contacts

WASHINGTON DEPARTMENT OF
FISH & WILDLIFE
North Central Washington
Region 2 Office
1550 Alder Street NW
Ephrata, WA 98823-9699
509-754-4624

SOAP LAKE CHAMBER
OF COMMERCE
509-246-1821

The North Umpqua—a spectacularly beautiful river with remarkable fish.

CHAPTER 22

THE NORTH UMPQUA RIVER

Steelhead Water of Legend

A sinking line carried my Orange Heron into the green-tinged depths of the North Umpqua's Upper Boat Pool. A cross-stream cast allowed time for the fly to sink before coming taut and swinging slow and deep through the cold March flow. The third such cast met with a violent surge and I was fast to a winter steelhead that I was sure would go 15 pounds.

In an instant the fish "went over" and headed for places downriver. I splashed clumsily ashore to seek better footing to battle this beast, whose initial run had cleaned me of 100 feet of running line and a fair shake of backing—with no sign of capitulating.

Scrambling over cobblestone, I reached Lower Boat about the same time the fish reached Upper Kitchen and I figured I'd better stand my ground here or risk losing this fine steelhead to a sharp reef of bedrock. An unanticipated rushing leap sounded like a bowling ball being tossed in the water, and this just as I had recovered a few feet of backing. Off the fish went again; still I held my ground. My fly line seemed unreasonably distant when the fish finally began to yield.

Then it was a simple matter of bringing her in—taking up line when she rested and giving in to her increasingly short bursts. I finally worked her to the beach, a beautiful wild hen; not so big as I had thought, but still a solid 12 pounds of perfectly proportioned nickel-bright steelhead. The barbless 3/0 hook popped free as I steered the fish into the frogwater and she glided back into the greenish waters of the fabled North Umpqua. A steelhead to be cherished always, for despite the high flows of spring, she took an elegant fly on this most elegant of rivers.

I sat on the bank for a time, just watching the river glide by, it's powerful presence forging a path over water-worn bedrock. A few months from now, I'd be back on these pools, casting a dry line for the North Umpqua's more famous run of summer steelhead. I'd likely be joined in my pursuit by fly anglers drawn from all over the world.

Steelhead fanatics flock to this vibrantly beautiful river. They come to test their skills not only against the North Umpqua's remarkable fish, but also against this unique and demanding river. It's rich history features a litany of famous anglers past and present, among them Clarence Gordon who founded the North Umpqua Lodge, which catered to fly anglers during the middle of the 20th century.

His lodge was located across the river from the mouth of Steamboat Creek, and Gordon and his contemporary anglers named most of the pools on that reach of the

Fishing the Camp Water.

North Umpqua. The Boat Pool was so named because its calm waters allowed a row-boat to ferry visitors back and forth between the road on the north bank. The Kitchen—always a coveted run—was visible from the lodge's dining hall.

Ward Cummings, another prominent figure in North Umpqua lore, guided for the lodge and Gordon. Together, the two men accounted for several well-known and beautiful North Umpqua steelhead flies. The Cummings Special and the Black Gordon remain popular flies on the river, at least for anglers with an appreciation for the North Umpqua's storied past.

Eventually, Gordon moved his operation to the north bank where it evolved into Steamboat Inn under the ownership of Frank and Jeanne Moore, who purchased the lodge in 1957. Moore, Gordon, Cummings, and several others formed a group called the Steamboater's Club. The Steamboater's remain to this day the watchdog of the North Umpqua. It was this group that in the 1950s, convinced the game commission of the need to create a fly-only zone on the river. The fly-only regulations have survived in the form of a 31-mile-long sanctuary set aside for fly fishing.

Years later, the Moores sold Steamboat Inn to current owners Jim and Sharon Van Loan. Steamboat's luxurious accommodations and exceptional dinners have earned widespread acclaim.

Timing the Runs

Summer steelhead arrive in the fly water by early summer. During good years, mid- to late July offers fair fishing. Fish numbers continue to climb through August and September—usually the peak time on the river. Strong runs total 10,000 or more fish. Like most steelhead rivers, the North Umpqua draws a crowd when reports circulate of a voluminous summer run.

As the number of summer fish climbs, the water level drops. By late August, the river reaches its lowest flows of the year. Hot weather often brings a lull in the action, but lucky be the angler who encounters one of those rare August freshets, which usually awaken the steelhead for a time. Low water continues through September and usually well into October. The arrival of the first big rains of autumn spells an end to the low water. Despite increased flows, fishing often holds up into November.

The North Umpqua's winter steelhead run peaks from February through early April. The river's winter steelhead average larger than do their summer-run cousins, with 12- to 15-pound fish being common. During a good year, the winter run exceeds 6,000 fish, all of them natives. About half of the winter fish spawn in Steamboat and Canton Creeks and as many as 20 percent spawn upstream from the famed Camp Water near the confluence with Steamboat Creek. By April, one begins to see steelhead holding on shallow gravel bars in pairs and small groups. These fish are spawners and etiquette dictates that they be left to their business, undisturbed by anglers.

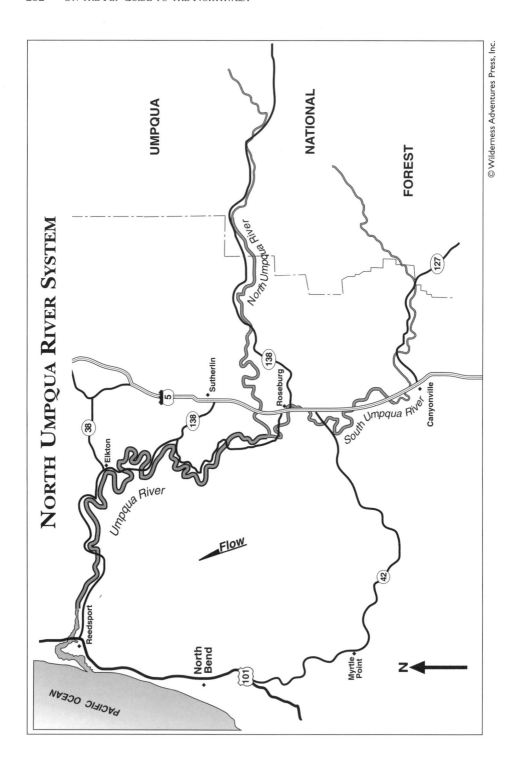

NORTH UMPQUA RIVER SYSTEM

UMPQUA

NATIONAL

FOREST

North Umpqua River

Umpqua River

South Umpqua River

PACIFIC OCEAN

Reedsport

Elkton

North Bend

Myrtle Point

Sutherlin

Roseburg

Canyonville

Flow

N

38

5

138

138

127

42

101

© Wilderness Adventures Press, Inc.

North Umpqua River
Headwaters to Steamboat

Mt Thielsen Wilderness

NFD 1414

FR 60

E Lemola Lake Road

Lemola Lake

NFD 999

To Crater Lake

NFD 600

138

Lake Creek

Basket Butte Road

Flow

NFD 680

Thorn Prairie Road

Clearwater Falls

Loafer Creek

Umpqua Hot Springs

FR 34

Clearwater River

Deer Creek

Toketee Reservoir

138

Soda Springs Powerhouse, mile 65

Slide Creek

Toketee Falls

Boulder Creek

Fish Creek

Steelhead fishing ends here (no fish passage above)

Copeland Creek

Mile 60

Calf Creek

Mott Bridge

Limpy Creek

Steamboat, mile 50

FR 36

Steamboat Creek

138

Parking

Panther Creek

Legend

N

State/Cty Road	River Site
Primary Forest Road	Wilderness
Other Roads	Dam
Campground	Major River
Boat Launch	Minor River/Creek

© Wilderness Adventures Press, Inc.

© Wilderness Adventures Press, Inc.

NORTH UMPQUA RIVER
STEAMBOAT TO SOUTH UMPQUA CONFLUENCE

Mott Bridge

Steamboat Creek

Campwater

138

Steamboat Inn, mile 50

Cougar Creek

Cougar Creek

Thunder Creek

Fish Creek

River

Blue Heron Fly Shop

Susan Creek State Park

Idelyd Park

Honey Creek

Mile 40

138

Rock Creek Hole; flyfishing only waters from this point upriver,

Rock Creek

Umpqua

Lone Rock Bridge

Lone Rock Boat Ramp

Colliding Rivers, mile 30

Little River

Glide

Whistlers Lane

Huntley Creek

Cooper Creek

(prime water begins here)
Whistler's Bend Park

North

Road

Sunshine Road

138

North Bank Road

Mile 20

To Sutherlin

Mile 10

5

Clover Creek

Roseburg

To Grants Pass

99

Page Road

Wilbur-Garden Valley Road

Garden Valley Road

Umpqua River

Mile 0

Flow

Legend

N

‖‖‖‖	Interstate
▬▬	State/City Road
───	Primary Forest Road
───	Other Roads
✈	Air Service
▲	Campground

⚓	Boat Launch
●	River Site
☐	Bridge
▬▬	Major River
───	Minor River/Creek

Throughout the winter season, the North Umpqua runs higher than during the summer and fall. Breaks in the rainy weather cause the water to drop into fishable shape while heavy storms can swell the river to unruly proportions, sometimes for days on end. Local anglers have the advantage as they can head for the river when she drops into shape. Traveling anglers might plan a week for the North Umpqua, arrive with high hopes and then find the river swollen over its banks for the entire time. Under certain conditions, the river can jump six or eight feet overnight, and during wetter-than-average winters the North Umpqua might offer a scant handful of fishable days.

As with winter steelheading anywhere, timing is everything. Before venturing to the river, anglers should check with Blue Heron Fly Shop (541-496-0448), whose owner Joe Howell can look out his front window to check the water conditions. The fly shop is located a short distance downstream from the lower boundary of the North Umpqua's 31-mile fly-only reach.

Flies and Tackle

In most respects the North Umpqua is a physically demanding river. In many places, you must scramble down a steep highway embankment to get to the water. Then there's the wading. The North Umpqua's slippery bottom demands cleated boots, and a wading staff is a good idea. If you're new to this water, well, quite frankly you can expect some of the most challenging wading of your career. Much of the river features submerged bedrock reefs of all sizes and shapes. They make for difficult footing, although many pools allow for minimal wading. During late summer, many anglers opt for shorts or pants rather than waders, but the cleated boots remain an essential item.

Seven- to 10-weight rods are ideally suited to this large river, where steelhead range from 5 to more than 20 pounds. Both single-hand and Spey-casting rods have their place on the river. Recent regulatory changes on the fly water dictate the use of floating lines and unweighted flies during the summer season, making the North Umpqua the last bastion of aesthetically pure, classic fly rod steelheading. Sinking lines are allowed during the winter season.

Many anglers, myself included, prefer classic-style flies. My favorite patterns include the Spawning Purple, Purple Matuka, Black Gordon, Cummings Special, Brad's Brat, and Skunk. Spey-style steelhead flies are also popular, and I especially like them for winter fishing. The simple elegance of the Spey-style seems perfectly suited to a river whose storied pools have enthralled generations of steelhead fly anglers.

During summer and fall the North Umpqua also offers excellent prospects for dry-fly steelheading. Skating flies are best, with many different patterns proving their worth each season. Dry-fly enthusiasts should look for glassy tailouts and gliding runs.

North Umpqua Logistics

State Highway 138 departs Interstate 5 at Roseburg and heads east into the Cascade Mountains. Soon it begins to parallel the North Umpqua, following the river's winding course past the tiny towns of Glide and Idleyld and into the fly-only section. Steamboat Inn sits above the famed Camp Water. Anglers and travelers alike converge at Steamboat for breakfast, lunch, and a spectacular dinner (reservations required). Just upstream from Steamboat Inn, Steamboat Creek flows in from the east. A short distance above the confluence, historic Mott Bridge crosses the river and leads to the parking area for the Camp Water and its famed pools, which include Sawtooth, The Station, The Boat Hole, The Kitchen, The Fighting Hole, and many others.

Upstream from the Camp Water begins the so-called Upper River—another 15-plus miles of prime steelhead water gouging out a precipitous forested canyon. Highway 138 continues upstream, following the river closely most of the way. Pullouts along the highway provide the primary access to the North Umpqua, although Mott Trail, which follows the far bank, allows for foot access in many reaches of the river.

Blue Heron Fly Shop (541-496-0448) is a must stop for North Umpqua visitors. Always congenial, Joe and Bonnie Howell offer all manner of tackle and flies for the river, along with all the information you could want and usually a few great stories for the lucky angler who corners Joe at the right moment. Open since 1982, the shop is located across the highway from the river, just downstream from the fly boundary. A big hand-painted sign announces the driveway on Hargis Lane. Their informative website is located at www.wanweb.net/bheron.

Steamboat Inn

Steamboat Inn is one of the Pacific Northwest's most renowned destinations for fly anglers. For many years the lodge has catered to steelhead enthusiasts visiting from all quarters. The Steamboat Inn dinners remain nothing short of a memorable experience, due to the inherent historic elegance of the dining room itself and to the exceptional cuisine served in traditional courses and accompanied by superb wines.

Dinner is served nightly during the summer and on winter weekends. The festivities begin in the library with aperitifs and appetizers amid an exceptional collection of angling titles. From there, guests migrate to the dining room where dinner is served family style at massive wood-slab tables. The fare is extraordinary and arrives in courses highlighted by a perfectly prepared main course, which varies from night to night. The evening concludes with Steamboat's scrumptious desserts.

A huge summer steelhead from the North Umpqua.

You needn't stay at the lodge to enjoy dinner. Individual dinner is $37 by reservation (wine and gratuity extra).

Many of the great recipes from Steamboat Inn are captured in two cookbooks written by Sharon Van Loan and manager Patricia Lee. The original book is titled *Thyme and the River* and the sequel is titled *Thyme and the River Too*. Both are available through the lodge.

Steamboat Inn offers several lodging options, ranging from riverfront cottages to ranch-style guest houses. All feature first-class décor and amenities. Prices range from $135 to $250 per night. The Inn properties are located adjacent to the North Umpqua's most famed and popular steelhead pools, collectively known as the Camp Water and located about 39 miles east of Roseburg.

STEAMBOAT INN
42705 North Umpqua Highway
Steamboat, OR 97447
541-498-2230; 800-840-8825
www.thesteamboatinn.com

Restaurants and Accommodations

Accommodations on the North Umpqua range from luxurious at Steamboat Inn to rudimentary in the form of numerous clean and convenient campgrounds scattered along the river. Several motels are located along Highway 138 from Glide to Idleyld, including Dogwood Motel (541-496-3403) and North Umpqua Resort (541-496-0149). Also, west of Idleyld lies the Steelhead Run Bed & Breakfast. Built in the 1930s on five riverside acres, this cozy B&B ranges from $65 to $110 per night, depending on which cottage is rented. Contact Steelhead Run at 541-496-0563 and check out their website at www.steelheadrun.com.

Roseburg offers lots of eateries, but only a few really good ones. I'm partial to the southernmost of the Mcmenamin brothers' many brewpubs, this one called Roseburg Station and situated at the historic old railway station on SE Sheridan Street. The food is typical Mcmenamin's pub cuisine but the beer, as always, is top flight. Nearby is the Village Bistro, a great little spot for an outdoor summer breakfast and also a nice stop for lunch or dinner (500 SE Cass/541-677-3450). Los Dos Amigos runs two Mexican restaurants in Roseburg, the downtown version offering the better atmosphere. Also downtown is Umpqua Brewery as well as DeNino's Wine Bar & Italian Deli, both located on Southeast Jackson Street.

Nearby Fisheries
South and Mainstem Umpqua

Should you tire of the steelhead pursuit on the North Umpqua, head for the South Umpqua near I-5 or the mainstem Umpqua to the west. Here you will find slower flows and a dense population of smallmouth bass. Most span a mere 8 to 12 inches, with a few reaching 18 or more inches. But they are numerous and aggressive and a lot of fun on a light rod. A float tube, pontoon, or drift boat is useful, but lots of bank access is available at certain points along the main roads, including Highway 138.

For the ultimate fly angling experience on the mainstem Umpqua, check out Big K Guest Ranch, which offers lodging in 20 separate cabins along with fine meals and guided fishing on a lengthy reach of the river. Big K guides adhere to the lodge's catch-and-release policy, which results in more large smallmouth here than on any other stretch of the river. Guests at Big K can also enjoy horseback riding, sporting clays, guided hunts, and other amenities. As of this writing, rates are $225 per night, including breakfast and dinner. Guides are extra. Contact Big K at 800-390-2445 or visit their website at www.big-k.com.

The Umpqua National Forest offers many high lakes where float tubers can pursue smallish brook trout, rainbows, and cutthroat. On your way east to the North Umpqua, stop in at the U.S. Forest Service offices in Glide, where you can obtain all the appropriate maps. Oregon Department of Fish & Wildlife operates its southwest regional headquarters out of Roseburg, with the offices located on the north side of the highway just east of town. Visitors can stop in to obtain information about fishing in the region.

Nearby Attractions and Activities

A spectacularly beautiful river, the North Umpqua's rapid decent down the Cascade Mountains reveals a precipitous timber-cloaked canyon whose upper reaches offer many stunning waterfalls. Upstream from the fly water, signs point the way to several of these spectacular falls. Picturesque Diamond Lake sits along Highway 138 near the top of the Cascades summit, and bold and rugged Mt. Thielson invites hikers of at least moderate skill and conditioning to attempt her rewarding, sentinel-like summit.

For anglers and non-anglers alike, the Mott Trail offers a wonderful opportunity to explore the far bank of the verdant North Umpqua River. My favorite reach of the trail, and one of the least-used segments, begins at a trailhead on the south bank just below Marster's Bridge, downstream from Eagle Rock Campground. This part of the trail leads several miles down to the Calf Creek Bridge, just upstream from Horseshoe Bend Campground. During autumn, with the maples painted crimson, orange, and yellow, this trail offers stunning views of the river, often from high above its banks. The Mott Trail continues all along the river throughout the fly-only section.

Wine enthusiasts might as well plan a day off from fishing to tour the Umpqua Valley's diverse array of wineries. Sturdy reds predominate. All eight of the region's wineries are located west of Interstate 5. Three are easily visited south of Roseburg, beginning with La Garza and Girardet (Exit 119 off the freeway) and ending with Abacela. Call to make reservations at the latter (541-679-6642). Northwest from Roseburg you can drive a tour route that takes you to three wineries as well. Champagne Creek Cellars offer regular daily tasting room hours while DeNino Estate requires a phone call to make visiting arrangements (541-673-1975). You can also taste DeNino wines at their wine bar/deli in downtown Roseburg at 404 SE Jackson Street. Henry Estate Winery, lies to the north at the little town of Umpqua. Pick up a winery tour map online, at any of the wineries, at just about any western Oregon chambers of commerce or visit www.winesnw.com.

Should you find yourself wandering west down the mainstem Umpqua toward the beautiful Oregon coast, be sure to pack a camera with a long lens and stop by the Dean Creek Elk Preserve. A few miles east of Reedsport, the elk preserve offers an up-close view of an impressive herd of Roosevelt elk. During the fall, you'll find plenty of bulls adorned with massive antlers. They are fully protected on the preserve and quite accustomed to the onlookers who spy them through binoculars from the observation decks.

Author's Tip

The fly water on the North Umpqua River can get a little crowded on prime sum-mer weekends. If you find too many people working the popular runs and pools, try moving downstream below the fly-only deadline. Lots of fish stack up in and move through parts of the river from Deadline down to Glide. Local roads provide access, but in places you must knock on doors to get landowner permission. The reward is uncrowded water.

Favorite Fly

Cummings Special (Ward Cummings)

HOOK	Salmon/Steelhead wet fly, No. 1/0-6
BUTT	Golden yellow silk or wool yarn
BODY	Claret wool yarn
RIB	Gold oval tinsel
HACKLE	Claret
WING	Brown bucktail
CHEEKS	Jungle cock

Cummings Special

Fast Facts

North Umpqua River

LOCATION	Southern Oregon, east of Roseburg
WATER TYPE	High-gradient steelhead river
PRIMARY GAMEFISH	Summer and winter steelhead
BEST TIME	July-October for summer steelhead; February-March for winter steelhead.

BEST FLIES	Classic and Spey-style steelhead flies
EQUIPMENT	8- to 9-weight rods, floating lines; sinking or sink-tip lines for winter fishing.
CONDITIONS	Pleasant summer weather; winter/spring weather ranges from cold and dry to very wet. The river flow increases rapidly with heavy rainfall; tricky wading requires cleats or cleated boots.
DRIVE TIME	From Portland: 4 hours From Seattle: 7 hours From San Francisco: 9 hours
DIRECTIONS	Follow I-5 to Roseburg and depart the freeway at Exit 1, then follow the signs toward Diamond Lake, following SR 138 some 30 miles up to the lower end of the fly water.

Local Fly Shops

BLUE HERON FLY SHOP
109 Hargis Lane
Idleyld, OR 97447
541-496-0448

STEAMBOAT INN
42705 North Umpqua Highway
Steamboat, OR 97447
800-840-8825

SURPLUS CENTER
515 SE Spruce
Roseburg, OR 97470
541-672-4312

NORTHWEST OUTDOOR SUPPLY
435 SE Jackson
Roseburg, OR 97470
541-440-3042

Guides

RIVER WOLF GUIDE SERVICE
(Larry Levine)
541-496-0326

NATIVE RUN FLY FISHING
(Steve Bonner)
541-474-0018
www.nativerunflyfishing.com

Contacts

OREGON DEPARTMENT OF
FISH & WILDLIFE
Southwest Regional Office
4192 North Umpqua Highway
Roseburg, OR 97470
541-440-3353

ROSEBURG
CHAMBER OF COMMERCE
541-672-2648

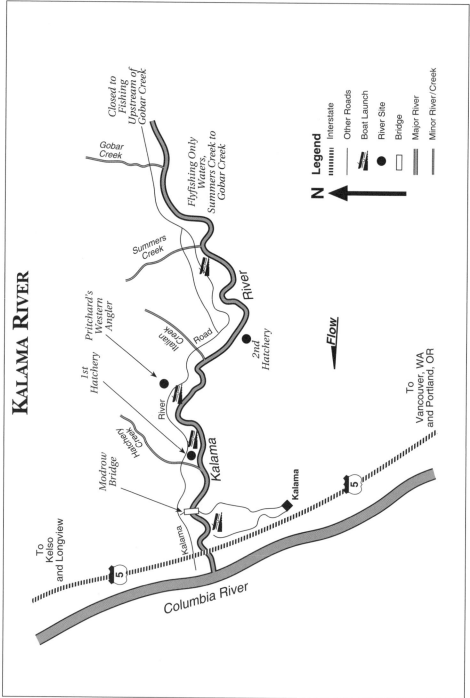

KALAMA RIVER

Closed to Fishing Upstream of Gobar Creek

Gobar Creek

Flyfishing Only Waters, Summers Creek to Gobar Creek

Summers Creek

River

Pritchard's Western Angler

1st Hatchery

Italian Creek

Road

2nd Hatchery

Hatchery Creek

River

Modrow Bridge

Kalama

Kalama

To Kelso and Longview

5

Kalama

Kalama

5

To Vancouver, WA and Portland, OR

Flow

Columbia River

N

Legend

Interstate
Other Roads
Boat Launch
River Site
Bridge
Major River
Minor River/Creek

© Wilderness Adventures Press, Inc.

CHAPTER 23

THE KALAMA RIVER

A Northwest Fly Angling Tradition

Cloud cover in western Washington is nothing unusual considering the temperate climate that dumps 50 to 80 inches of rain per year along the I-5 corridor. Cloud cover in western Washington during late July—now that raises eyebrows, at least within the steelhead angling fraternity. Two days of cloud cover had passed already by the time I headed for the Kalama River, but a third day dawned gloomy and gray, offering ideal conditions for pursuing summer steelhead on the river's clear pools.

I expected company. Weekends tend to draw crowds on Washington steelhead streams, at least when the fish are "in." Rumor suggested the fish were indeed "in" on the Kalama. Much to my surprise, the fly-only water was packed with anglers while the lower river offered plenty of open pools—only one angler occupied the famed Red Barn Hole, easily identified by its namesake, a big red barn perched along the road opposite the river. Heading back downstream a ways, I picked a length of river devoid of other anglers and planned to fish my way down through three promising pools. Before I'd fished out the first of these, the Kalama had cast her spell on me.

Heavily timbered banks reflected in its glassy pools, the river beckoned each gentle cast and I reveled in the way the floating line jumped out over the pool, straightened across the flow and delivered my Spawning Purple pattern into the emerald depths. I meticulously managed each cast, steering the fly slowly across the flow in a classic wet-fly swing.

Not a single fish rewarded my efforts that evening, a fact that weighed little on my mind. I had landed Kalama steelhead in seasons past and would earn still more in days forthcoming. But on this cloudy July evening I knew I had fished well, and I quietly enjoyed the knowledge that in fishing well I had demonstrated respect for this gem of a river and its anadromous inhabitants. Indeed, on a fabled stream like the Kalama one might report that "the fishing is good," but I'd rather hear you say, "I fished well today."

The Kalama long ago earned its place among the Northwest's best steelhead fly waters. Its fly-only section, sometimes called "the Holy Water," is one Washington's most popular destinations for summer steelhead fly fishing. Despite the occasional crowds, most of the time anglers find plenty of elbow room on the fly-only water, which stretches for miles from Summers Creek upstream to Forest Road 6420 below Kalama Falls. The fly water is home to native steelhead. Most of the hatchery fish are captured at the hatchery and recycled through the lower river. The entire upper river is closed during April, May, and June to protect spawning salmonids.

Below Summers Creek, the lower river offers lots of easy access despite extensive private property along the banks. Luckily, Kalama River Road follows closely above the river, offering pullouts for parking and easy access to productive stretches of river. The reach from Summers Creek downstream to Mudrow Bridge (the lowermost boat ramp) covers about 12 river miles.

The Kalama offers plenty of boat access, but by July the water is low enough that a drift boat seems like overkill. Besides, at low water, boaters must exercise extreme caution or risk denting the boat on countless exposed rocks. During the winter-run season, when the Kalama nearly doubles its flow, a drift boat allows access to the far bank and allows anglers to fish waters unreachable by foot. The most popular winter drifts begin either at the Red Barn Hole or a little farther downstream across from Prichard's Western Angler (a tackle shop/store located along the river) and run down to Mudrow Bridge (about 4 miles).

The winter steelhead run peaks between late January and March, with larger native fish arriving during the latter part of that time frame. The summer fish, meanwhile, trickle into the river as early as May. Most summer steelhead arrive between June and mid-August and good fishing continues through mid-autumn. Kalama anglers tag 1,200 to 3,000 summer fish annually—strong numbers for a comparatively small river.

An easy-access river, the Kalama runs directly under Interstate 5 north of Vancouver, Washington. Depart the freeway at Exit 32, just north of the town of Kalama. Turn east and follow Kalama River Road all along the river's north and east bank. Prichard's Western Angler (360-673-4690) is located about 5 miles east of I-5. Call for current reports, winter or summer. Other regional fly shops include The Greased Line Fly Shoppe in Vancouver (360-573-9383), whose staff keeps tabs on current conditions on southwest Washington's steelhead streams, including the Kalama, Lewis, Wind, and Washougal.

Regardless of what the reports might say, the Kalama's decades-long consistency speaks for itself. Winter and summer, steelhead negotiate the waters of this visually stunning little river. So when the clouds arrive during summer or when the colored leaves herald autumn or when winter skies clear during March, plan a day or two for one of Washington's favorite fly-rod steelhead streams.

Fishing the Kalama River

Fly anglers use assorted tactics on the Kalama's summer-run fish. Weighted flies and sink-tip lines are especially popular on the lower river where steelhead, exposed to constant fishing pressure, often seek shelter in 3- to 6-foot-deep riffles with heavy chop and lots of boulder cover. Nonetheless, many veteran anglers still fish the Kalama—both the lower river and the fly water—with traditional floating lines and classic flies. A few seasons ago I arrived at the Red Barn Hole only to find three fly anglers already working their way down through the run. I watched for a while, noticing that the first two anglers were fishing weighted flies while the third fished some sort of skating dry fly. Sure enough, the dry-fly angler rose a steelhead even after the first two flyrodders had already worked through the run. With steelhead, you never know.

The Kalama offers water for all manner of tactics. The river's summer fish will take skaters, especially in the glassy tailouts through the gorge and in other pools left undisturbed on any particular morning or evening. The Kalama's low, clear summer flows offer anglers the opportunity to look for fish. Should you spot a fish in shallow, smooth water, sneak up from above and try a skated dry fly first. One thing about dry flies and steelhead—you'll never take a steelhead on a skater unless you make the effort.

Traditional hairwing flies account for lots of Kalama steelhead. Popular patterns include such classics as the Purple Peril, Green-Butt Skunk, Muddler, Del Cooper, and Kalama Special. In *Steelhead Fly Fishing and Flies*, author Trey Combs relates that Mooch Abrams developed the Kalama Special for searun cutthroat and that "his friend, Mike Kennedy, used the fly to such advantage on Washington's Kalama River that it became known as the Kennedy Special."

Winter steelhead require different tactics due to the high, cold water. Most anglers fish high-density sink-tip lines or shooting tapers coupled with short leaders. The alternative is to fish weighted flies with a floating line and long leader. Many anglers enjoy the opportunity to fish elegant Spey-style or marabou flies during winter and such flies are well suited to the Kalama's cobblestone tailouts. Weighted flies, such as Comets, fish well on the river's boulder studded runs. Prichard's Western Comet was designed for such purposes.

Accommodations

The town of Kalama, immediately adjacent to Interstate 5, has convenient lodging for anglers fishing the river. Kalama River Inn offers plenty of space, but call ahead, especially on weekends (360-673-2855). Kalama has grown into a destination for antique hunters, and the town's eight antique malls represent about 250 dealers.

Choosing a fly for the Kalama.

drops and clears quickly, leaving elegant cobblestone pools that beg a swung fly. The East Fork is a river for all seasons.

My latest venture to the East Fork, a late-summer journey for the river's super-spooky low-water steelhead, resulted in not a single such fish. Yet my efforts hardly went unrewarded: A robust 16-inch cutthroat pounced on a black Muddler, and I remember thinking how unique an experience to find this remarkable searun native so far from the Pacific. Old-timers sometimes talk of the cutthroat runs in the Lewis River, but so few searuns are there now that this was the first I had ever taken from the East Fork.

I pondered my one-fish outing from the umbrella-shaded confines on the patio at Mcmenamin's on the Columbia, one of the more recent additions to the Mcmenamin brother's brewpub dynasty now boasting 52 establishments and growing. That's the other thing I love about the East Fork: You can fish most of the day away, stow the rod and waders, and still make happy hour in Vancouver or Portland. It's a great half-day escape, especially between mid-summer and mid-autumn and again on any given weekday during March, when the big native winter steelhead arrive.

Despite the river's proximity to the sprawling Portland-Vancouver metro area, the East Fork seems many hours distant from the city sprawl. Its shallow lower canyon skulks in the deep shade of a dense canopy of Douglas fir, maple, and alder. At times the paved access road dips close to the water, offering tantalizing glimpses of classic steelhead pools. Otherwise, tracts of private property hide the East Fork from view. Along the way, you will find a series of beautiful waterfalls, all of which are worth a visit with camera in hand. The first of these is Lucia Falls, which in local terms separates the "Lower River" from the "Upper River."

Anadromous fish navigate these falls, but boats can't. Hence the floatable section of the East Fork begins at Lewisville County Park, where a cobblestone launch awaits at the park's far east end. The takeout is just a few miles downriver at Daybreak Bridge. This is a nice, short drift for winter steelhead or early summer fish, but after that forget about it—low water makes for tough going.

The East Fork is small water during the summer; medium-small water during the fishable days of winter. You won't hook dozens of fish in a season here as you might on the Deschutes or Grande Ronde, so the East Fork is not about numbers. If you want high-percentage steelhead water, go elsewhere. The East Fork is more about a beautiful river and a chance to bring a few natives to the bank during the course of the year as you watch the seasons progress.

Accommodations

While the jump-off community of Battle Ground has no lodging options, you can find motel space in Woodland, a busy little town adjacent to I-5 to the east. Woodland also offers many restaurants.

Woodland Lodging

Woodlander Inn, 1500 Atlantic St., 800-444-9667
Hansen's Motel, 1215 Pacific, 360-225-7018
Lakeside Motel, 785 Lakeshore Drive, 360-225-8240
Scandia Motel, 1123 Hoffman, 360-225-8006
Lewis River Inn, 1100 Lewis River Rd., 360-543-4344

Author's Tip

Any East Fork veteran will tell you that the summer steelhead fishing peaks during June and July. However, reasonable prospects await during the dog days of August, especially mid-week when the river is generally, and surprisingly, deserted. During August, the trick is to fish in stealth mode because the steelhead become exceptionally spooky in the low, clear water. Sneak up on the pools, lengthen the leader, and make unobtrusive casts with small flies. When possible, sneak up on the pools and look for fish. Then start in from above after stalking into casting range.

Favorite Fly

Skunk

HOOK	Steelhead wet fly, No. 2/0-6
TAG	Flat silver tinsel
BODY	Black chenille ribbed with silver tinsel
HACKLE	Black
WING	White bucktail or similar

Skunk

*The author with an
East Fork summer fish.*

Fast Facts

East Fork of the Lewis River

LOCATION	Southwest Washington, east of I-5 and north of Vancouver
WATER TYPE	Small free-flowing river
PRIMARY GAMEFISH	Summer and winter steelhead; also king salmon and searun cutthroat
BEST TIME	January through March for winter steelhead; June through September for summer steelhead.
BEST FLIES	Any classic pattern will work. This is a good river for skated dry flies between July and September.
EQUIPMENT	7- or 8-weight rod with a floating line for summer steelhead; 8- to 9-weight rod for winter steelhead.
CONDITIONS	Very pleasant summer and fall weather; wet and cool winters. Good paved road all the way through the fishable water. Day-use parks at the waterfalls.
DRIVE TIME	30 minutes from Vancouver to Lewisville County Park.

DIRECTIONS   Follow I-5 to the Battleground Exit at SR 502 (which becomes NE 219th Street). Follow SR 502/NE 219th east to Battleground and turn left (north) on SR 503 (watch for the signs pointing to Lewisville County Park). The entrance to the park is just past the bridge crossing the East Fork. To access the remainder of the river, continue north a few miles past the park on SR 503 and turn right (east) on Lucia Falls Road, which heads upriver.

Local Fly Shops

THE GREASED LINE FLY SHOP
5802 NE 88th Street
Vancouver, WA 98665
360-573-9383

ANGLER'S WORKSHOP
1350 Atlantic
Woodland, WA 98674
360-225-6359

Area Fly Shops

THE MORNING HATCH FLY SHOP
3640 South Cedar, Ste. L
Tacoma, WA 98409
253-472-1070

COUNTRYSPORT LTD.
126 SW First Ave.
Portland, OR 97204
503-221-4545

STREAMSIDE ANGLERS FLY SHOP
4800 Capital Blvd. SE
Tumwater, WA 98501
360-709-3337

KAUFMANN'S STREAMBORN
8861 SW Commercial Ave.
Tigard, OR 97223
503-639-7004

NORTH COUNTRY OUTFITTERS
6175 NE Cornell Road
Hillsboro, OR 97125
503-615-0555

NORTHWEST FLYFISHING OUTFITTERS
17302 NE Halsey
Gresham, OR 97230
503-252-1529

GORGE FLY SHOP
201 Oak Street
Hood River, OR 97031
541-386-6977

STEWART'S FLY SHOP
23830 NE Halsey
Wood Village, OR 97060
503-666-2471

Contacts

WASHINGTON DEPARTMENT
OF FISH & WILDLIFE
Southwest Washington
Region 5 Office
2108 Grand Boulevard
Vancouver, WA 98661
360-696-6211

CHAPTER 25

THE LAKES OF CENTURY DRIVE: HOSMER, CRANE PRAIRIE & DAVIS

The Stillwater Mecca of Central Oregon

I lived through a classic love-hate relationship during those years when I resided in Bend, Oregon. I loved Bend for its proximity to so many great trout waters. Bend is truly a fly fishing town, as witnessed by the an array of fly shops and by the fact that on any given summer evening its brewpubs resonate with tales of fly angling. But I hated Bend for the guilt it caused me, for during my five years there I probably accomplished about a single year's worth of work. There was just too much fishing immediately at hand.

The spring of 1996 proved the defining example of my lagging discipline. Davis Lake, whose fertile expanse had gone dry during the prolonged low-water years of the early 1990s, sprang back to life after the severe winters of the mid-'90s, bolstered by fresh stocks of Klamath Lake rainbows. Hearing rumors of some monster fish from the previous autumn, Forrest Maxwell and I conferred about our course of action for the spring season. Upon word from me that the road to Davis Lake had opened, Forrest, my long-time fishing partner, then loaded up his big canvas wall tent and headed for Bend. We pitched camp at East Davis Campground on the last day of April and would later move camp to a favorite little secluded site on the far side of the lake.

We broke camp around the first of June. Davis Lake had enthralled us for two months.

Forrest had spent virtually every night there for the entire period, while I commuted back and forth between Davis Lake and my home about an hour away in Bend. Sometimes I'd stay on with Forrest for a couple days, other times for a week. By the time June approached we had caught pounds and pounds of rainbows and had enjoyed Davis Lake at its best. I'll never forget those days when every fish we hooked ran 6 to 10 pounds or the days when the trout went nuts for *Callibaetis* nymphs or the night Forrest rowed completely across Davis Lake under the brilliant glow of the Hale-Bopp Comet.

Meanwhile reports from nearby Crane Prairie Reservoir indicated equally productive fishing for trophy rainbows. I spent a couple days on Crane just after we departed Davis and found freight-train trout eager to smash dragonfly nymphs. By the middle of June, however, the guilt and workload had overwhelmed me. Deadlines had piled up and I had stories to write for editors who were entirely too patient. Thank God they were fly-fishing editors.

I left Bend a year later and I've always missed the place—not so much the town itself as the region it serves; a region rich in diverse fisheries. I return often to fish these waters and I've watched them change over the seasons. During my college days, Davis Lake pumped out huge, strong rainbows. Then I watched it go dry and subsequently spring back to life and prove even better than before. Crane Prairie once boasted awesome hatches of *Callibaetis* mayflies and damsels. Both hatches seem but a mere hint of what they once were. Some attribute the lagging hatches to over-predation by illegally introduced bass. Regardless, the trophy rainbows still roam Crane Prairie, and they remain as hot a stillwater trout as you could hope to find.

I'm certainly not alone in ranking these lakes as central Oregon's chief attractions, for fly anglers quite literally flock to the east slope of the Cascade Mountains south and west from Bend where these remarkable fisheries lay strung along the road known as Century Drive.

The region's splendid scenery rivals that of other western angling destinations like Montana's Paradise Valley or Idaho's Teton Valley. Stunning volcanic peaks of the Cascade Range dominate the skyline to the south of the lakes. Each mountain asserts its own personality. South Sister, Oregon's third highest peak, thrusts its snow-cone summit 10,200 feet into the sky while nearby Middle Sister defines rugged symmetry. The third of the Three Sisters, North Sister, stands stark and bold, its precipitous crags occasionally claiming the lives of would-be climbers. Nearby, all that remains of Mt. Washington's ancient past is a spire-like volcanic core standing guard over timbered slopes.

Mt. Bachelor, looming to the east of Hosmer Lake and streaked with late-melting snow fields well into summer, reigns as one of the Northwest's most popular skiing destinations. The white powder arrives early and remains late into the spring, allowing a lengthy season for skiers of all ability.

Crane Prairie, Hosmer, and Davis are but three of the countless lakes occupying the forested lava lands along Century Drive. Other popular waters include Wickiup Reservoir, South Twin Lake, Elk Lake, and Sparks Lake. But the three headliners are special and their offerings divergent. Shallow throughout, Hosmer Lake is home to landlocked Atlantic salmon planted there for years by the ODFW. Their aerial acrobatics make them a perennial favorite target for countless Northwest anglers who rank Hosmer as a favorite destination. Some huge brook trout inhabit Hosmer as well. Lucky or persistent anglers sometimes hook brook trout up to 25 inches, but most are lost just as fast due to their effective tippet-busting habit of rushing madly into the nearest reed stand.

Sprawling Crane Prairie Reservoir spreads its various arms up old river channels, forming an expansive man-made lake whose fertility yields trophy-class rainbows and a few monster brook trout. Nearby Davis Lake, also a sizable body of water, boasts an even richer broth capable of growing behemoth rainbows in just a few seasons. Unlike Hosmer, Davis Lake's vast surface covers a few deep regions bordering extensive weedy shallows.

All of this great stillwater fishing awaits within an hour of Bend, a town replete with activities, great dining options and a serious fly angling mentality. So convenient is the proximity that I used to sit down for an early breakfast at West Side Bakery, fish the productive mid-morning to mid-afternoon hours at Crane Prairie and by dusk find myself sipping a Mirror Pond Pale Ale at Deschutes Brewery.

Fishing Hosmer Lake

Hosmer Lake is unique among these three spectacular fisheries in that it often fishes well during the early morning and late evening. Likewise, Hosmer's population of damsel nymphs and *Callibaetis* mayflies assure that the magical mid-morning to mid-afternoon window remains the lake's most popular fishing hours.

Comparatively small and shallow, Hosmer is essentially two lakes connected by a narrow channel through extensive reed stands. Atlantic salmon and brook trout cruise the channel, and it serves as the venue for many of the encounters with trophy-class brookies. The main portion of the lake affords ample room for fish and anglers alike. Salmon, often in small schools, abound here. At times they feed along

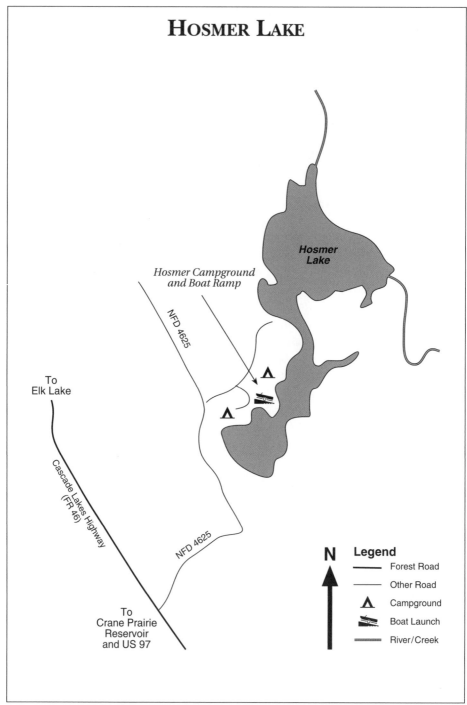

HOSMER LAKE

Hosmer
Lake

Hosmer Campground
and Boat Ramp

NFD 4625

To
Elk Lake

Cascade Lakes Highway
(FR 46)

NFD 4625

To
Crane Prairie
Reservoir
and US 97

N

Legend

—————— Forest Road

———— Other Road

Λ Campground

Boat Launch

River/Creek

© Wilderness Adventures Press, Inc.

the edges, near the reeds, especially when damsel nymphs are on the move during summer mornings.

Hosmer's hatchery-produced Atlantic salmon typically range from 12 to 20 inches and grow at a rate of about one inch per month between May and September. Once hooked, these speedy fish bring the fight to the surface, usually making repeated jumps. They are muscular, streamlined and speckled with large black spots. Far less numerous, Hosmer's brook trout typically range from 16 to 24 inches and only a few fall to fly anglers each year.

You will need a float tube, pontoon, or canoe to fish Hosmer (electric motors are permitted). Shoreline fishing is limited. The lake covers about 200 acres, offering plenty of room to spread out on busy weekends during the summer. If the front portion of the lake fills with anglers, try paddling through the channel until the reeds open up to reveal the remainder of the lake and its stunning view of South Sister, which looms high above to the north.

The *Callibaetis* mayflies hatch throughout the summer, although the density and duration of the emergence varies considerably from day to day. Damsel hatches peak by mid-July and sometimes afford the opportunity to fish adult damsel patterns tight against the reeds. Various caddis draw salmon to the surface, as do *Chironomid* hatches. More often than not, however, Hosmer Lake anglers fish subsurface patterns ranging from small soft hackles and nymphs to leech patterns or streamers.

Immediately adjacent to Hosmer Lake lies a large campground that typically fills completely during summer weekends. For more solitude on this popular destination, try fishing mid-week or wait until after Labor Day when crowds subside.

The South Sister, Oregon's third highest peak, overlooks Hosmer Lake.

Fishing Crane Prairie Reservoir

Crane's surface glimmered in the mid-morning sun, its forest of drowned trees stabbing skyward and abuzz with freshly emerged damsels. The day before I'd hooked some fat rainbows but had also discovered the need for a new damsel nymph, a pattern designed to float so I could fish it just inches below the surface on an intermediate line. That night I sat down at the vice with some dyed-green deer hair and some closed-cell foam. Eventually I arrived at a satisfactory rendition of Crane Prairie's abundant damsel nymphs.

The next step was up to the trout. I had watched some huge rainbows porpoising violently during the heart of the damsel hatch, so I presumed they must have been feeding on nymphs migrating just beneath the surface. Soon my suspicions were confirmed when ever so slowly I was stripping my new floating damsel nymph, using a long leader and an intermediate line when a behemoth rainbow rammed the fly so hard that the tippet snapped on impact. Despite shaking hands, I tied on another floating damsel and steadied myself to keep my hands off the line when the next fish hit. It didn't take long. The next rainbow hit as savagely as the first, but this time I performed better and soon found myself fast to a leaping rainbow of about four pounds.

Those are the fish that make Crane Prairie Reservoir one of Oregon's most popular fly angling destinations. Over the past decade or so, Crane's hatches of *Callibaetis* and damsels seem to have waned compared to the early 1980s when I first began fishing this fertile reservoir. Many people ascribe the problem to a dense population of illegally introduced largemouth bass. Certainly the bass have a negative impact on the trout fishery, yet Crane Prairie remains one of the Northwest's premier stillwater venues for trophy-class rainbows.

Crane Prairie, like its nearby neighbors Davis Lake and Wickiup Reservoir, covers a lot of ground. At full pool, the reservoir sprawls out across almost 5,000 acres. Despite its impressive proportions, Crane averages only about 10 feet deep. During spring and early summer, fast-growing rainbows (along with a few large brook trout and lots of bass) spread out all over the reservoir, feeding around dense weed beds. As the summer settles in, the fish tend to retreat to the various channels—old streambeds reaching around the reservoir like tentacles. The largest of these is the Deschutes Channel, whose original flows were dammed to form Crane Prairie and Wickiup.

Assuming the access roads are passable by its late April opener, Crane Prairie typically fishes well right off the bat. If you intend to fish the opening week on Crane, call ahead to make sure the road is open. During autumn, the reservoir is drawn down, often revealing extensive shallow or even waterless flats. Late summer brings

CRANE PRAIRIE RESERVOIR

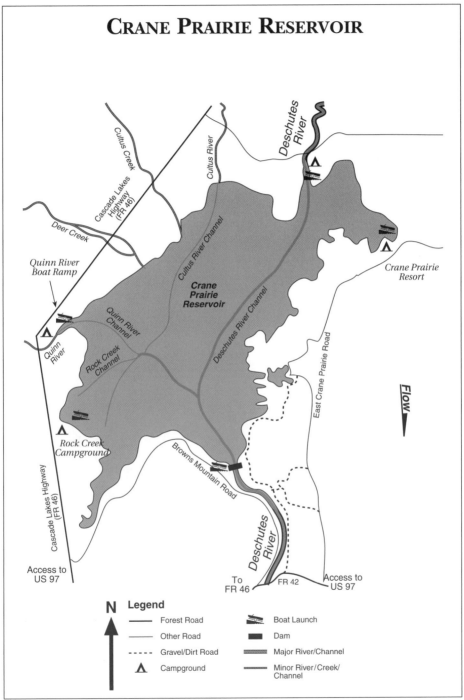

Cultus Creek

Deschutes River

Cultus River

Cascade Lakes Highway (FR 46)

Deer Creek

Cultus River Channel

Quinn River Boat Ramp

Crane Prairie Reservoir

Crane Prairie Resort

Deschutes River Channel

Quinn River Channel

Quinn River

Rock Creek Channel

East Crane Prairie Road

Flow

Rock Creek Campground

Browns Mountain Road

Cascade Lakes Highway (FR 46)

Deschutes River

Access to US 97

To FR 46

FR 42

Access to US 97

N

Legend

——— Forest Road	Boat Launch
——— Other Road	■ Dam
- - - - Gravel/Dirt Road	Major River/Channel
▲ Campground	Minor River/Creek/Channel

© Wilderness Adventures Press, Inc.

a lull in the fishing, but autumn action can be fast and furious for those willing to brave the occasional snow flurries and bitter cold winds.

All the typical stillwater trout foods are present in Crane Prairie, so lots of different fly patterns produce good results. Early during the year, aggressive rainbows feed heavily on scuds, *Chironomids*, mayfly nymphs and other foods. Imitative patterns account for lots of fish but so do various attractor flies, such as Carey Specials and Woolly Buggers. By late spring, damsel and dragonfly nymphs become increasingly evident and imitations often out-fish attractor flies. Crane Prairie's *Callibaetis* hatch is not nearly so dense as it once was, but nymph patterns are still quite effective during the summer months.

Several campgrounds offer convenient access all around Crane Prairie and most include a launch facility. Watercraft is indispensable here, as shoreline fishing rarely produces results. Many anglers use a boat to transport float tubes to the far reaches of the reservoir. To reduce your learning curve at Crane Prairie, call Sunriver Fly Shop to arrange for a guide.

Illegally introduced largemouth bass abound in Crane Prairie Reservoir and Davis Lake, offering a second fishery when trout fishing is slow.

Fishing Davis Lake

Davis Lake is home to some truly huge rainbows. Each year fly anglers land 30-plus-inch trout weighing 10 pounds or more and 4- to 6-pound fish are reasonably common. These fast-growing trout gorge on an abundance of chub minnows, dragonfly and damsel nymphs, leeches, and every other imaginable trout food. Large baitfish patterns and leech patterns account for many of the trophy fish, but from time to time the fish key on damsel nymphs or dragonfly nymphs.

In fact, Davis Lake is one of the best waters I've ever fished for dragonfly action, and the early summer hatch often proves dense enough to trigger selective feeding. Davis Lake spawned my first adventures with floating dragonfly nymph patterns. Two factors converged on me during the early 1980s: I met Brent Snow and I began fishing Davis Lake. Brent was working for the Caddis Fly Angling Shop in Eugene and spent considerable time on Davis and Crane. He had the dragonfly hatch figured out and suggested that I fish the event with floating nymphs and sinking lines—somewhat opposite of the normal arrangement. As strange as the set-up sounds, this method works like a charm.

The idea is to fish the fly on a downward retrieve, as if the insect is dashing for the cover of the weed beds. To achieve this, you fish a large dragonfly nymph pattern constructed of spun deer hair, which is highly buoyant. This buoyant fly is coupled with a sinking or sink-tip line and a long leader. The presentation works like this: After the cast, wait for the line to sink and watch the fly, which will be afloat on the surface. Soon the weight of the sinking line will tug at the fly, usually pulling it underwater. At this point, begin a retrieve comprised of four to six short, rapid pulls on the line. Then pause. During the retrieve, the fly swims almost straight down and during the pause it begins to float slowly upward. The takes are awesome. Fish hit the fly savagely, but you must react quickly to tighten the big arc of line going from rod tip to lake bottom and back up to the fly.

Another option with the floating dragon is to fish the fly in shallow water just off the lava flow using an intermediate line. The lava flow is located on Davis Lake's north end, where many of the largest trout reside. You can anchor a boat right along the flow, but only at the risk of losing the anchor in the rocks below. Generally, a better option is to pull in close and then cast parallel to shore. This is easily done with a float tube or pontoon. If you are fishing by boat, anchor carefully or have one angler handle the boat while the other casts.

All that said, I should admit that few anglers realize the potential for fishing the floating dragon on Davis Lake. Most people fish leech patterns and large streamers. Davis abounds with chub minnows and leeches, so patterns to mimic both prove highly effective. Davis Lake's largest fish feed heavily on the baitfish, which reach eight inches in length. A six-inch-long chub pattern doesn't cast well; so most anglers drag them around on a slow-sinking line, imparting a strip-retrieve if simple trolling proves ineffective. Regardless of technique, large baitfish patterns reign as the most consistent flies for targeting Davis Lake's largest rainbows.

Davis Lake is so fertile that all forms of aquatic trout food are present. I've fished days when only *Callibaetis* nymphs or damsel nymphs seemed to work. Likewise, heavy *Chironomid* hatches sometimes cause selective feeding during the spring.

For many anglers, Davis Lake comprises two distinct fisheries You can target the abundant 14- to 18-inch trout or fish huge flies meant specifically to take huge rainbows. Illegally introduced largemouth bass comprise the lake's other fishery. Despite the inherent threat to the trout fishery, Davis Lake's bass fishery ranks among the state's best. Abundant bass provide lots of opportunity during lulls in the trout action. The bass reside in the weed beds, often in shallow, nearshore areas, and they range up to six pounds or more.

Davis Lake offers three campgrounds, two located on the south end on either side of Odell Creek and a third located on the north end near the lava flow. You'll need a boat, pontoon, or float tube to fish Davis.

Davis Lake.

Derek Fergus with a fine Davis Lake rainbow.

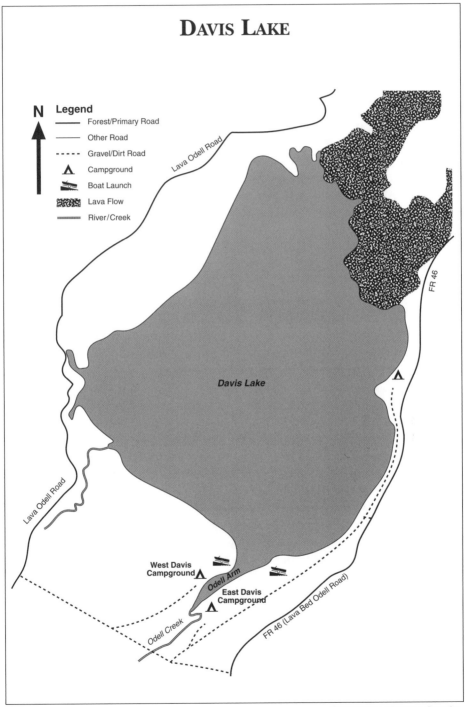

DAVIS LAKE

N

Legend
- Forest/Primary Road
- Other Road
- Gravel/Dirt Road
- Δ Campground
- Boat Launch
- Lava Flow
- River/Creek

Lava Odell Road

FR 46

Davis Lake

Δ

Lava Odell Road

West Davis
Campground Δ

Odell Arm

East Davis
Campground Δ

Odell Creek

FR 46 (Lava Bed Odell Road)

© Wilderness Adventures Press, Inc.

Nearby Attractions and Activities

The Bend area boasts a dozen or so golf courses, so if you're of that persuasion bring your clubs. For details on all the golf options, check out the website of the central Oregon Visitor's Association at www.covisitors.com.

Downtown Bend offers a pleasant contrast to the busy traffic nightmare of nearby Highway 97, which runs the length of the city from north to south. I love downtown Bend, and I'm not alone. When I lived there I couldn't wait for that magical time in the fall when summer tourism died down and the ski season had yet to begin. That was the quiet time when I could share the little coffee houses with a handful of locals or find ample room for a fine ale down at Deschutes Brewery.

Any time of year, however, Bend's quaint downtown district offers something for everyone. Only a few blocks in length and width, downtown Bend mirrors the function of such districts in much larger cities. It is part shopping, part fine dining, part morning coffee and part commerce center. In the space of half a block you can hit the ATM machine, grab a quick beer, have a fine dinner and then secure a cup of coffee. Wine enthusiasts should visit Chelsea Lane on Minnesota Avenue, which stocks a fine array of Northwest and Continental varietals.

The resort community of Sunriver, located just 10 miles south of Bend, offers all manner of accommodations, from numerous rental homes to the well-appointed rooms of Sunriver Lodge. Sunriver has a full range of services, including fine restaurants, and serves as a popular destination for anglers, skiers, golfers, and sun-seekers.

Between Sunriver and Bend along Highway 97, Lavalands National Monument provides a study of the stark and barren lava fields prevalent throughout the region. Nearby, the Oregon High Desert Museum makes a great family outing, complete with historical and natural history displays, all of which focus on Oregon's expansive Great Basin Desert environs. Kids especially gravitate to the live otter and porcupine displays, not to mention the daily live raptor exhibit featuring a collection of indigenous hawks, falcons, eagles, and owls. The museum is located a few miles south of Bend on the east side of the highway. Watch for the signs.

Bear in mind also that skiing on Mount Bachelor lasts well into spring. I've known many Bend-area residents who share an equal passion for skiing and fly fishing. You can fish Davis or Crane during April and still expect good snow on the mountain. Call ahead to check conditions (Mt. Bachelor: 541-382-2442).

Nearby Fisheries

Adjacent to Hosmer Lake on the northern end of Century Drive, Sparks Lake offers good fishing for small brook trout. Shallow throughout, Sparks Lake covers about 700 acres and proves ideal for a canoe. On the south end of Century Drive lies sprawling, 10,000-acre Wickiup Reservoir, home to some of central Oregon's largest brown trout, along with rainbows, kokanee and coho salmon. Wickiup's 14- to 25-inch brown trout are the main attraction for fly anglers. During the fall, the fish feed heavily in the Deschutes Arm, off Gull Point and adjacent to Wickiup Dam. Large streamers and leech patterns prove most effective.

Nearby South Twin Lake and North Twin Lake offer good fishing for rainbows from 10 to 16 inches and both lakes offer some shelter from the high winds that often blow across nearby Davis, Wickiup, and Crane Prairie Reservoirs. Along and near Century Drive, numerous other lakes offer fair to good fishing for brook trout and/or rainbows, including popular lakes like Elk, Cultus, and Lava Lake.

Also located in the immediate vicinity, Fall River offers a chance to test your skills against trout residing in an aquarium-like spring creek. Hatches occur all year and anglers must use stealth, fine tippets, and advanced presentation techniques.

Restaurants and Accommodations

A few blocks off the highway, Bend's diminutive downtown district boasts many fine restaurants. Among my favorites are Hans (915 NW Wall/541-389-9700) and Café Rosemary (222 NW Irving/541-317-0276). Pine Tavern, a longtime local favorite located on NW Brooks (541-382-5581), serves a mean steak. Deschutes Brewery, whose micro-style beer is now bottled and distributed across the region, ranks as the most popular downtown gathering place—expect a line for seating because the brewpub serves up a great dinner—a chalkboard lists nightly specials, which run the gamut from exotic seafood dishes to Mediterranean classics. Deschutes Brewery is located at 1044 NW Bond (541-382-9242). Thai enthusiasts should try Toomies at 119 NW Minnesota (541-388-5590), while Yoko's, next to Deschutes Brewery, serves exceptional sushi and other Japanese fare (541-382-2999).

Bend offers several good Mexican restaurants, but my favorite remains the quaint little Taqueria Los Jalapenos located on Greenwood Avenue east of Highway 97. Recently, Los Jalapenos opened a second restaurant—this one a full-scale dinner house—at 1900 NE Division Street (541-317-2855). Bend's best pizza (arguably) comes from John Dough's at 34 SW Century Drive, just north of Fly-N-Field, one of the city's full-service fly shops. For a hearty breakfast, I'm a sucker for West Side Bakery & Café at 1005½ NW Galveston.

Such a brief accounting hardly does justice to Bend's exceptional eateries. After all, the region boasts several dozen fine restaurants of all descriptions. Likewise, lodging options are nearly limitless, ranging from budget motels to extravagant lodges. Consult Bend's Chamber of Commerce for complete details (541-382-3221). Forest Service campgrounds occupy scenic locations throughout the Century Drive area. Many of these campgrounds fill quickly during weekends. For that matter, if you plan to stay in Bend, make reservations ahead of time because the city can completely sell out on summer weekends. Several nice (and spendy) hotels are located along Century Drive on the west side of town, offering convenient access to the Cascade Lakes. Other motels and hotels are strung along Highway 97 through town. As I often have my bird dog in tow, I frequent the inexpensive, clean and dog-friendly Rodeway Inn (3705 N Hwy 97/541-382-2211).

Other Bend Lodging

Bend has at least 50 various hotels and motels, including:

Bend Holiday Motel, 880 SE Third, 541-382-4620
Bend Riverside Motel, 1565 NW Hill, 541-389-2363
Cimarron Motel, 437 NE Third, 541-382-7711
Courtyards at Broken Top, 61999 Broken Top Drive, 541-318-4238
Hampton Inn, 15 NE Butler Market Rd., 541-388-4114
Mount Bachelor Village Resort, 19717 Mt. Bachelor Drive, 541-389-5900
Phoenix Inn, 300 NW Franklin, 541-317-9292
Pine Ridge Inn, 1200 SW Century Drive, 541-389-6137
Red Lion Inn, 1415 NE Third Street, 541-382-7011
Scandia Pines Lodge, 61405 S. Hwy. 97, 541-389-5910
Shilo Suites, North Hwy. 97, 541-389-9600
Super-8 Motel, 1275 SE Hwy. 97, 541-388-6888
Westward Ho Motel, 904 S. Hwy. 97, 541-382-2111

The community of Sunriver, 10 miles south of Bend, offers a variety of rental houses and other upscale accommodations. This large, planned community is conveniently located for anglers headed to the high lakes—so much so that two fly shops reside here. For information about lodging in Sunriver, call the Chamber of Commerce (541-593-8149). Also, Crane Prairie Resort, conveniently situated right on the reservoir, features nice, wooded RV spots and campsites. The resort also offers rental boats, a store, gas and a tackle shop. For more details or to reserve a camp spot, call the resort at 541-383-3939.

Author's Tip

Nobody is particularly happy about the bass illegally introduced into Crane Prairie and Davis Lakes. But the bass are apparently there to stay, so why not enjoy them when trout action hits a lull. Look for bass in the shallow, weedy margins of both lakes. In the reed stands at Crane and along the lava flow at Davis, bass can be tempted into smashing poppers and divers. Otherwise, try Woolly Buggers and Zonkers.

Favorite Fly

Diving Damsel

HOOK	Tiemco #200 or similar, No. 8-10
TAIL	Olive-green marabou fibers
BODY	Olive-green marabou wrapped on shank
RIB	Fine wire
WINGPAD	Tuft of marabou
COLLAR	Dyed-green pheasant rump
HEAD	Small metal bead

Diving Damsel

Fast Facts

The Lakes of Century Drive

LOCATION	Central Oregon, west and southwest of Bend
WATER TYPES	Fertile, shallow lakes and reservoirs
PRIMARY GAMEFISH	Davis Lake: rainbow trout, 14 to 30-plus inches; large-mouth bass
	Crane Prairie Lake: rainbow trout, 14 to 30-plus inches; largemouth bass; a few brook trout, 14- to 20-plus inches

PRIMARY GAMEFISH	Hosmer Lake: Atlantic salmon, 12 to 20 inches; brook trout, 14 to 24 inches.
BEST TIME	Davis Lake: Late March or early April through ice-up in November
	Crane Prairie Lake: April-July and September-October
	Hosmer Lake: June-July and September
BEST FLIES	All the standard stillwater patterns work well at times, as a wide range of insects are present on these lakes.
EQUIPMENT	5- to 7-weight rod; floating line; sink-tip or slow-sinking line. Float tube, pontoon, or boat required.
CONDITIONS	Cool mountain weather early and late in the season. Frequent afternoon winds. Very nice camp grounds around each of the lakes; good boat ramps at all lakes.
DRIVE TIME	From Bend: Within one hour From Portland: 4 hours From Eugene: 4 hours From Boise: 6 hours
DIRECTIONS	To reach Hosmer Lake from Bend, simply follow the signs to Mt. Bachelor and then continue past the ski resort on Century Drive until you reach Hosmer. This route loops past Hosmer and Elk Lakes and turns south leading to Crane Prairie, Wickiup, and Davis Lake. Faster routes to Davis and Crane Prairie begin at Sunriver. From the north continue south through Bend on Highway 97 to the Sunriver exit or Fall River Road, both of which turn west off the highway and join South Century Drive and lead west to the reservoir.

Local Fly Shops

FLY-N-FIELD
143 SW Century Drive
Bend, OR 97701
541-318-1616

THE PATIENT ANGLER
55 NW Wall Street
Bend, OR 97701
541-389-6208

THE FLY BOX
1293 NE 3rd
Bend, OR 97701
541-388-3330

DESCHUTES RIVER OUTFITTERS
61115 South Highway 97
Bend, OR 97702
541-388-8191

THE HOOK FLY SHOP
Sunriver Village Mall, Building 21
Sunriver, OR 97707
541-593-2358

SUNRIVER FLY SHOP
Sunriver Business Park
Sunriver, OR 97707
541-593-8814

Area Fly Shops

THE FLY FISHING SHOP
67296 E. Hwy. 26
Welches, OR 97067
503-622-4607

NORTHWEST FLYFISHING
OUTFITTERS
17302 NE Halsey
Gresham, OR 97230
503-252-1529

STEWART'S FLY SHOP
23830 NE Halsey
Wood Village, OR 97060
503-666-2471

CLACKAMAS RIVER FLY SHOP
12632 SE McLoughlin, Ste. 200
Portland, OR 97222

RIVER CITY FLY SHOP
11429 Scholls Ferry Road
Beaverton, OR 97008
503-579-5176

BUFFALO CREEK OUTFITTERS
91 State Street
Lake Oswego, OR 97034
503-675-3082

VALLEY FLYFISHER
153 Alice Street S.
Salem, OR 97302
503-375-3721

CREEKSIDE FLYFISHING SHOP
345 High Street S
Salem, OR 97301
503-588-1768

FLY COUNTRY OUTFITTERS
3400 State Street, Ste. G-704
Salem, OR 97301
503-585-4898

NORTH COUNTRY OUTFITTERS
6175 NE Cornell Rd.
Hillsboro, OR 97124
503-615-0555

COUNTRYSPORT LTD.
126 SW 1st Ave.
Portland, OR 97204
503-221-4545

SCARLET IBIS FLY SHOP
2319 NW 9th Street
Corvallis, OR 97330
541-754-1544

Area Fly Shops, continued

THE CADDIS FLY ANGLING SHOP
168 West 6th
Eugene, OR 97401
541-342-7005

HOMEWATERS FLY SHOP
444 West 3rd
Eugene, OR 97401
541-342-6691

Guides

Contact area fly shops for additional guide opportunities.

SUNRIVER GUIDES & OUTFITTERS
541-593-8247

CASCADE GUIDES & OUTFITTERS
541-593-2358

Contacts

OREGON DEPARTMENT
OF FISH & WILDLIFE
High Desert Regional Office
61374 Parrell Road
Bend, OR 97702
541-388-6363

BEND AREA CHAMBER
OF COMMERCE
541-382-3221

SUNRIVER AREA CHAMBER
OF COMMERCE
541-593-8149

DESCHUTES NATIONAL FOREST
541-383-5300
www.fs.fed.us/r6/deschutes

Crane Prairie trophies.

CHAPTER 26

EAST LAKE

Float Tubing a Volcano

It was one of those last-minute deals. Shannon had a day off from the fly shop and at his prodding we left Bend at 10 a.m. bound for East Lake. An hour later I was fast to a 3-pound brown trout that had inhaled a fly intended for the lake's average-size rainbows and Atlantic salmon. By day's end, we had done more than our share of damage to the 'bows and salmon, and I'd be hard pressed to decide whether one good brown trout or several dozen foot-long acrobats topped the day.

East Lake, along with its sister, Paulina Lake, occupies an old volcanic caldera. East Lake's multi-species fishery attracts serious attention, yet fly anglers never accumulate in the numbers typical of Crane Prairie Reservoir or Hosmer Lake just an hour to the northwest. Moreover, this thousand-acre mountain gem ranks among the most scenic of all the central Oregon destination fisheries. Certainly the famous stillwaters of Century Drive offer larger rainbows (Davis and Crane) and larger

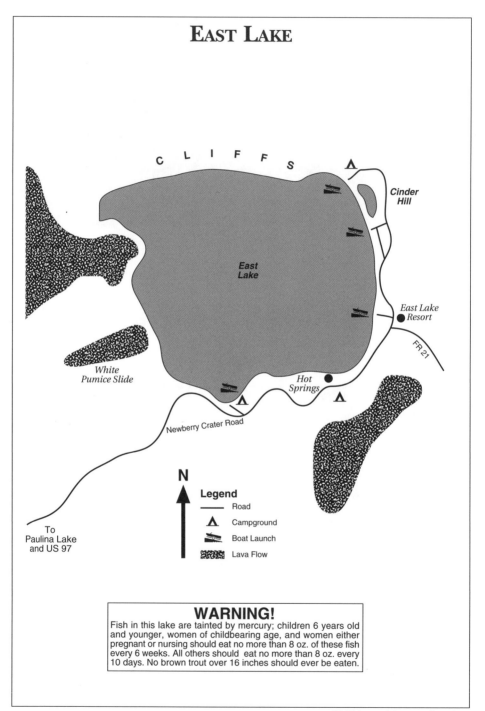

EAST LAKE

C L I F F S

Cinder Hill

East Lake

East Lake Resort

FR 21

White Pumice Slide

Hot Springs

Newberry Crater Road

To Paulina Lake and US 97

N

Legend
- —— Road
- ⚠ Campground
- 🚤 Boat Launch
- ▓ Lava Flow

WARNING!

Fish in this lake are tainted by mercury; children 6 years old and younger, women of childbearing age, and women either pregnant or nursing should eat no more than 8 oz. of these fish every 6 weeks. All others should eat no more than 8 oz. every 10 days. No brown trout over 16 inches should ever be eaten.

© Wilderness Adventures Press, Inc.

salmon (Hosmer), but none of these popular lakes boasts a better *Callibaetis* mayfly hatch than East Lake and none save Wickiup Reservoir can boast a trophy brown trout fishery.

The *Callibaetis* hatch throughout the summer, appearing virtually every day between June and September. Caddis, *Chironomids* and flying ants (along with other terrestrials) provide additional dry-fly opportunities. Planted rainbows and salmon feed heavily at the surface during the hatches and are easily taken on wet flies during non-hatch periods. Most of these fish range from 10 to 14 inches. Older fish reach 16 inches. Much deeper, less fertile, and 2,000 feet higher than the Century Drive fisheries, East Lake cannot grow fish nearly as fast. Also, despite recurring mercury warnings, East Lake is essentially a put-and-take fishery. The rainbows and salmon just don't grow much beyond 16 to 18 inches.

East Lake's trophy-size brown trout comprise an additional fishery, one that attracts a small, secretive group of fly anglers during the fall. These beautiful, long-lived browns, planted by ODFW, reach 20 pounds or more. Typical specimens run 14 to 24 inches. They feast on the lake's population of illegally introduced chub. The browns make up only a small percentage of the catch throughout the summer, but spawning urges and foraging prospects lure them to the nearshore shallows from mid-September through October.

Anglers targeting big brown trout should fish streamer patterns on sinking lines. Look for nearshore drop-offs and either troll the fly or retrieve with a fast, two-hand strip. Float tubers can work the edges along the south half of the lake near the campgrounds and launches. One favorite reach stretches from the East Lake Campground east along the shoreline to Hot Springs. Boaters have the option of motoring across to the roadless north shore, another favorite and productive area for autumn brown trout angling.

Accommodations

East Lake Resort (541-536-2230) offers all services, including rental cabins and rooms, an RV park, café, store and boat rentals. The 14-footers rent for $40 per day (add $5 for weekend days) from mid-May through late September. Consult their website at www.eastlakeresort.com.

Included within the Newberry National Volcanic Monument, East Lake has three nice campgrounds—East Lake, Hot Springs and Cinder Hill—offering a combined 162 sites. Nearby Paulina Lake offers another four campgrounds.

The closest town, LaPine, is about 30 minutes away, on Highway 97. LaPine offers several average restaurants and several motels, all situated along the highway: Best Western (541-536-5730), Lampliter Motel (541-536-2931), West View Motel (541-536-2115) and Highlander Motel (541-536-2131).

An East Lake brown trout.

Nearby Attractions and Activities

The Newberry Volcanic National Monument stretches from Benham Falls on the Deschutes River west of Bend southeast through Lava Butte and its accompanying visitor's center and all the way down to the Newberry Caldera, home of East and Paulina Lakes. The monument encompasses some 50,000 acres of lava flows and related geologic features, with 100 miles of hiking trails to explore. Among the more interesting sites are the Lava Cast Forest, Lava River Cave, and Big Obsidian Flow.

Big Obsidian Flow is located adjacent to Paulina and East Lakes and is one of Oregon's most recent geologic events. The flow formed about 1,300 years ago when more than 170 million cubic yards of obsidian and pumice erupted from a vent in Newberry Volcano. The Lava Cast Forest and the Lava River Cave are both located north of the caldera and accessed via Highway 97 near Sunriver. Lava River Cave stretches more than a mile underground, making it the longest known uncollapsed lava tube in Oregon. The signed access road turns east off Highway 97 about 12 miles south of Bend. The cave is open (for a small fee) between May and September.

Lava Cast Forest offers a mile-long interpretive trail through the lava flows, high-lighted by tree molds created when the molten lava surged through a pine forest more than 6,000 years ago. The site lies east of Highway 97 at the Sunriver exit on Road 9720. The volcanic monument offers a visitor's center at Lava Butte just south of Bend.

Another worthwhile stop is the High Desert Museum, located about four miles south of Bend. This unique museum offers a wide variety of indoor and outdoor exhibits focusing on the natural and cultural history of the high-desert West. The museum is open daily throughout the year.

Author's Tip

By October, few anglers remain at East Lake and yet this is the best time for fly anglers to pursue big brown trout with streamers. The fish hang out in the nearshore shallows, perhaps prompted by their natal urge to seek spawning habitat. East Lake Resort officially closes around September 30. However, if you head for East Lake during October, go to the resort and find one of the few remaining employees—generally they leave a few rental boats at the marina while they busy themselves with winterizing.

Favorite Fly

Brown Zonker (for brown trout)

HOOK	Streamer hook, No. 2
BODY	Mylar tube, epoxied
THROAT	Brown hackle
WING	Brown rabbit strip

Brown Zonker

Fast Facts

East Lake

LOCATION	Central Oregon, about 45 minutes south of Bend
WATER TYPE	Large, deep high-mountain lake
PRIMARY GAMEFISH	Rainbow trout, Atlantic salmon, brown trout
BEST TIME	May through October
BEST FLIES	For *Callibaetis* adults: Parachute Adams, Sparkle Dun, CDC Mayfly Dun, No. 12-16; Pheasant Tail Nymph, Prince Nymph, Zug Bug, No. 10-12; Carey Special, No. 6-10; Woolly Bugger, No. 6-8.

BEST FLIES	For brown trout: Olive/gold Zonker, Grey Ghost, Woolly Bugger, Deceiver, or other streamer patterns, 3-5 inches in length.
EQUIPMENT	Watercraft; 5- to 6-weight rod; floating and sinking lines.
CONDITIONS	Warm days, cold mornings, frequent afternoon winds; summer thunderstorms.
DRIVE TIME	From Bend, Oregon: 45 to 60 minutes
DIRECTIONS	Follow Highway 97 south from Bend to the signed turn-off heading east about 15 miles to East Lake and Paulina Lake.

Local Fly Shops

FLY-N-FIELD
143 SW Century Drive
Bend, OR 97701
541-318-1616

THE PATIENT ANGLER
55 NW Wall Street
Bend, OR 97701
541-389-6208

THE FLY BOX
1293 NE 3rd
Bend, OR 97701
541-388-3330

DESCHUTES RIVER OUTFITTERS
61115 South Highway 97
Bend, OR 97702
541-388-8191

THE HOOK FLY SHOP
Sunriver Village Mall, Building 21
Sunriver, OR 97707
541-593-2358

SUNRIVER FLY SHOP
Sunriver Business Park
Sunriver, OR 97707
541-593-8814

Guides

SUNRIVER GUIDES & OUTFITTERS
541-593-8247

CASCADE GUIDES & OUTFITTERS
541-593-2358

Contacts

OREGON DEPARTMENT
OF FISH & WILDLIFE
High Desert Regional Office
61374 Parrell Road
Bend, OR 97702
541-388-6363

DESCHUTES NATIONAL FOREST
Newberry Volcanic National
Monument
541-383-5300
www.fs.fed.us/r6/deschutes

LAPINE CHAMBER OF COMMERCE
541-536-8410

CHAPTER 27

THE ROGUE RIVER

Historic Steelhead Water in Southern Oregon

Oregon's scenic and legendary Rogue River is one of the most revered of steelhead streams. Many fly anglers have cast their way to notoriety on the Rogue's rugged waters. Among the Rogue's celebrities, none were more famous (or infamous if you were to ask the locals) than Zane Grey, who first visited the Rogue during 1919 (bringing with him the Golden Demon, which became a standard steelhead pattern in the Northwest). Enamored with the river, Grey established a cabin on the Rogue, becoming just one of many famous people who have sampled the treasures offered by this remarkable watershed.

The Rogue is most famous for its "half-pounders," a steelhead of unique life history that is also found in California's Klamath and Eel Rivers. These fish begin life as any other steelhead, living in the river for a couple of years until the migratory urge starts them on their journey to the Pacific. Most make the downriver journey during April and May, like any other summer-run steelhead smolt. Then comes the unique aspect of their journey: Whereas typical steelhead remain in the ocean for one, two, or three years, the half-pounders head back upriver in the fall of the same year, having spent only a few months at sea.

As a result of their short stay in the fertile ocean, the half-pounders span only 12 to 16 inches on their return to the river. Despite their small stature, these little steelhead pack a punch born of their "toughening up" days in the saltwater. After a few weeks in the river, the half-pounders tend to revert to trout-like behavior—at least until the following spring, when most return once again to the ocean. Here their life story takes another twist. Some half-pounders return to the ocean for the second consecutive spring and then re-run the river again that fall, this time as 14- to 20-inch steelhead. Others remain a full year or more at sea before returning as mature fish of 20 to 36 inches.

Most Rogue River summer steelhead derive from half-pounder stock. The little guys are legitimate half-pounders; the medium-size fish were half-pounders last year and the occasional 12-pounder was a half-pounder two or three season back. Not all the fish share the half-pounder life history—the Rogue offers some standard-issue summer steelhead that range from 5 to 15 pounds on their return from the ocean.

Half-pounders dominate the fishery of the Lower Rogue, but as one progresses upriver, the Middle Rogue becomes the haunt of all steelhead. You might very well hook a 12-inch steelhead and a 12-pound steelhead on the same day. Often the Rogue's 16- to 22-inch steelhead predominate in the autumn catch on the Middle Rogue; other days you catch a dozen or so 13-inchers and one or two of the 3-pounders.

On the Upper Rogue, meanwhile, the half-pounder run peters out; most of these little fellows remain in the Middle Rogue, thus making the Upper Rogue the domain of the midsized fish. A long way from the ocean, the Middle and Upper Rogue's steelhead often behave and feed like trout, and many fly anglers use trout nymphing tactics to catch them.

The Upper Rogue

For many seasons the Upper Rogue from McGregor Park to Gold Ray Dam was one of the most productive and least-known steelhead rivers in the state. Local anglers enjoyed fine steelheading without the national attention that draws seasonal crowds to the Northwest's better-known rivers. Such secrets are hard to keep in the angling world, however, and in recent years the Upper Rogue has gained regional prominence for its runs of salmon and steelhead and in particular for its fly fishing opportunities.

Water levels, as dictated by releases from Lost Creek Reservoir, determine the extent and availability of the steelhead fishery on the Upper Rogue. A modest run of mature summer steelhead arrives in the upper river between June and August. They typically range from 20 to 28 inches in length. Some years, though, high water during the summer allows for only limited opportunity on these steelhead. During years of low to moderate summer flow, the fishing can be decent and on the heels of this early run arrives the autumn influx of summer steelhead.

These smaller fish, mostly one-salt adults, arrive between August and November. A few sexually immature half-pounders make it this far and span 12 to 16 inches, but the run offers a majority of adult fish whose extra time in the ocean allows them to reach sexual maturity and reach lengths that commonly range from 18 to 22 inches. These small and medium-sized steelhead feed more actively in fresh water than do the typical steelhead found in other rivers. Thus, anglers often fish for them by drifting nymphs and egg patterns. Traditional patterns fished on the swing still account for plenty of fish for those who prefer such aesthetic pursuits.

Water levels on the Upper Rogue tend to drop as summer and fall progresses. Optimal flows range from less than 1,000 cfs (cubic feet per second) to about 1,500 cfs. Rarely will the river reach these low flows during summer, but fly anglers can take steelhead from the Upper Rogue even when the water runs above 2,000 cfs. At high summer flows, expect to fish sinking and sink-tip lines. Floating line/classic fly enthu-

The Upper Rogue is host to a sizable run of 18- to
24-inch summer steelhead.

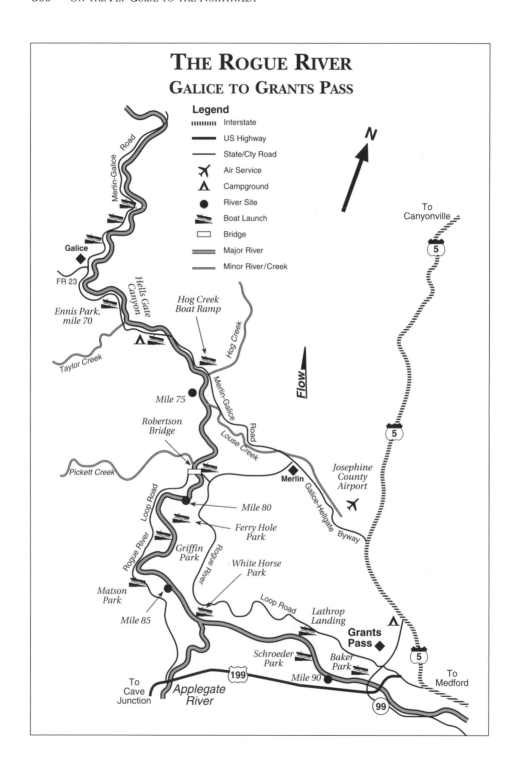

THE ROGUE RIVER
GALICE TO GRANTS PASS

Legend

⊥⊥⊥⊥	Interstate
—	US Highway
—	State/Cty Road
✈	Air Service
⛺	Campground
●	River Site
	Boat Launch
▭	Bridge
▬	Major River
▬	Minor River/Creek

N

Merlin-Galice Road

Galice

FR 23

Hells Gate Canyon

Ennis Park, mile 70

Taylor Creek

Hog Creek Boat Ramp

Hog Creek

Mile 75

Merlin-Galice Road

Louse Creek

Flow

To Canyonville

5

5

Robertson Bridge

Pickett Creek

Merlin

Josephine County Airport

Loop Road

Rogue River

Mile 80

Ferry Hole Park

Griffin Park

Rogue River

White Horse Park

Galice-Hellgate Byway

Matson Park

Mile 85

Loop Road

Lathrop Landing

Grants Pass

5

Schroeder Park

Baker Park

Mile 90

To Medford

To Cave Junction

199

Applegate River

99

siasts should wait until autumn and enjoy the added bonus of the long catch-and-release season mandated by the game commission.

Access to the Upper Rogue begins downstream from Lost Creek Reservoir. The so-called "Hatchery Ramp" is the first of many launches on the upper river. The first quarter-mile of river below the hatchery is closed to fishing. From here, Highway 62 follows closely along the river about 10 miles down to the community of Shady Cove. Below Shady Cove, bank access is limited to a handful of parks and bridges. Twenty-eight miles in length, the Upper Rogue is best accessed by drift boat.

One mile downstream from the hatchery, Casey State Park is a popular launch for trips down to Rogue Elk Park (three miles) or Shady Cove (nine miles). Next in line is Takelma Park, four miles below Shady Cove, then Dodge Bridge, four miles below Takelma Park and situated on the west bank off Rogue River Drive near the junction with Highway 234. The last take-out is Tou Velle State Park on the north bank, seven river miles below Dodge Bridge. To reach Tou Velle, follow SR 234 towards Gold Hill and watch for the Table Rock Road turn-off.

Below Gold Ray Dam, the river flows more or less along Interstate 5 for about 15 miles. Access is difficult in this area and good fly water minimal, making the so-called "Upper Middle Rogue" rather unpopular with the fly fishing crowd.

The Middle Rogue

Its precipitous, rocky canyon cloaked in fir, pine, and oak, the Middle Rogue surges through deep bedrock-lined pools and over rugged jumbles of cobble from Savage Rapids Dam down to Grave Creek. This reach of the Rogue is especially noted for its run of half-pounders. Typical specimens range from 13 to 16 inches in length. Yet their recent return from the ocean is evident in their classic steelhead appearance: bright silver on the sides with a distinctly delineated darker back. Also evident is the strength they gain from their few short months feeding in the ocean.

They make a fine fly-rod fish and have enamored several generations of Rogue River anglers. Often these half-pounders travel in schools, so should you hook one you can expect others to occupy the same pool or run.

Those same adult steelhead that travel to the upper river must first pass through the Middle Rogue, so more often than not you are fishing over adult steelhead as well as half-pounders. Some years abound with 20-plus-inch steelhead. In other years the smaller half-pounders dominate the autumn fishing.

The Middle Rogue, more than 40 miles long, offers a mixture of road-accessible access and boat-only access. The first 15 miles below Grants Pass offer about 10 public access points, most with boat ramps. About 20 miles below Grants Pass, the Middle Rogue assumes a new character as the canyon deepens. An urban river in and around Grants Pass, the Rogue finally assumes a wilderness character as it enters

Fishing the Middle Rogue during October.

rugged Hells Gate Canyon. Beginning above Hells Gate, at Hog Creek Ramp, the Middle Rogue offers another 10 ramps, with the Grave Creek Launch being the end of the line for trips from above and the beginning of floats through the "Wild Rogue" section. From Galice to Grave Creek, plenty of bank access awaits along Galice Road.

The Lower Rogue

Beginning at Grave Creek, the Lower Rogue runs some 60 miles before reaching the Pacific Ocean at the town of Gold Beach. The upper half of this section is road-less, accessible only by foot or boat and includes some awesome rapids, which make the Lower Rogue very popular with whitewater enthusiasts. Splash-and-giggle crowds are dense here during the summer.

Only experienced oarsmen should make the 33-mile run from Grave Creek to Foster Bar on the Wild Rogue section. Included are nine Class III rapids, three Class IVs, and one Class V in the form of Rainie Falls. Obviously, this is expert-only water. Interested parties must obtain a permit from the Forest Service (541-479-3735). The permits are available on a lottery basis for non-commercial users. Also obtain the

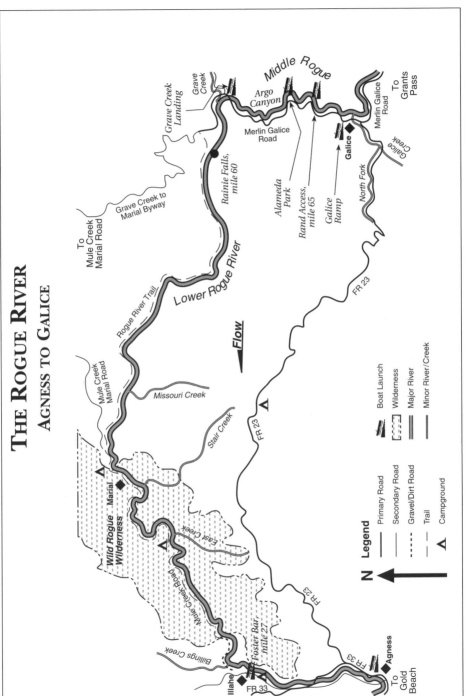

The Rogue River
Agness to Galice

THE ROGUE RIVER
GOLD BEACH TO AGNESS

© Wilderness Adventures Press, Inc.

The Lower and Middle Rogue is renowned for its "half-pounder" steelhead, immature fish that return after only a few months in the Pacific.

floater's guide from the Forest Service and consult any of several good books, including *Oregon River Tours*, by John Garren (Garren Publishing, 1991). All that being said, your best bet is to hire an experienced guide for a camp trip down this awesome stretch of river. Check with Morrison's Lodge or with Oregon Guides & Packers.

A good trail system follows the north bank of the river from Grave Creek to Foster Bar, allowing hike-in access to lots of good steelhead water. You can also access the lower end of the roadless section by jet boat. They are allowed as far as Blossom Bar. Several lodges cater to anglers on the Lower Rogue, including the following: Black Bar Lodge (541-479-6507), Marial Lodge (541-474-2057), Half Moon Bar Lodge (541-247-6968), Clay Hill Lodge (800-228-3198) and Paradise Lodge (541-525-2161).

Below the roadless section lies some good half-pounder water from Illahe to Agness and below. However, much of the river in this section is quite slow and featureless by fly fishing standards. The road from Gold Beach on the coast leads along the south bank to Agness, crossing the mouth of the Illinois River.

Fishing The Rogue

Rogue River steelhead often become active feeders after a few weeks in the river. They eat the river's abundant stonefly nymphs, mayfly nymphs, caddis larvae and various other menu items. Sometimes they rise for dry flies. On the Upper or Middle Rogue you might one day hook 8 or 10 steelhead on dead-drifted nymphs only to find the river seemingly devoid of feeders a day later. So you switch to the classic down-and-across wet-fly swing and hook three fish in an evening. Seemingly, there exists no logic in the behavior of these steelhead. That fact alone reminds us that they are indeed steelhead, no matter how trout-like they might act from time to time.

In any event, no one would argue that the Rogue's small and medium-sized steelhead often behave like trout and that many of them feed while in the river. This allows you to pick your poison, so to speak. Those who enjoy nymphing are assured reasonably consistent success, as are those who prefer the more traditional steelheading tactics. All manner of nymph patterns and classic steelhead wet flies are used to good effect by the river's steelheaders. Among those classic wet flies are quite a few designed on and for this river. Some have familiar names, such as the Rogue Red Ant and Juicy Bug. Because the fish run small by steelhead standards, most anglers fish flies in sizes 6 through 10.

The Upper and Middle Rogue both feature lots of classic riffle-and-run water along with well-defined pools. The river also offers abundant reef rock, which creates complex holding water in places that might otherwise prove unappealing to steelhead. Some of the water is wadeable and some not and a lot depends on flows. In short, the Rogue offers every conceivable type of steelhead holding water, from deep pools requiring sinking lines to foot-deep tailouts where steelhead are attracted by spawning salmon.

The salmon redds deserve special mention. Steelhead hold below and among spawning salmon in just a foot or two of water, feeding on eggs and on dislodged nymphs. For better or worse, many anglers target steelhead around the salmon redds. If you feel that you must fish around the spawning salmon, take great care to avoid wading on the redds or disturbing the fish. These wild salmon deserve our respect and those guides and anglers who exercise all due care can enjoy fast action on Rogue steelhead. Just use good judgment.

Ultimately, the Rogue reveals many personalities. If you lack the time to figure things out on your own, then hire one of the many good fly fishing guides operating on the river.

Pulling Flies on the Rogue

Years ago, Rogue River guides devised a simple and effective method of dealing with the Rogue's many unwadeable reaches and the many neophyte anglers that booked fly fishing trips on the river. Often called the Rogue River Twitch or referred to as "twitching flies," the technique requires little skill on the angler's part. The client takes up a position at the downstream end of a Rogue-style drift boat and either casts or shakes the line out over the river. Then he or she simply holds onto the rod and adds a twitch of the rod tip every few seconds to enliven the fly.

Nothing could be easier for the angler. For the guide, however, "pulling flies" requires constant attention at the oars because the boat must back down the river slower than current speed and usually slide back and forth from left to right. In the hands of a dedicated guide, pulling flies means a hard day's work on the oars. I've marveled at the way Ray Slusser, when called upon to do so, can back a boat through a long steelhead run, effortlessly gliding the boat left and right and left and right all the way through.

Guide Ray Slusser looks on as his client
fishes through a classic steelhead run.

An obvious concession to anglers lacking in casting ability, the "Twitch" has come under fire in recent years as a technique lacking integrity. Certainly a seasoned fly angler will be disappointed if he or she ends up with a guide who pulls flies just out of sheer laziness, and such guides are out there.

Nonetheless, I see pulling flies as a reasonable way to allow first-time anglers to enjoy the hard pull of a Rogue steelhead. The best guides on the river—men like Ray Slusser—are perfectly able and willing to teach you how to cast and how to swing a fly and how to read water. They prefer anglers experienced enough to wade and cast. But such is not for everyone, and guides on the Middle Rogue get a lot of clients more adept at splash-and-giggle summer fun than at fly casting. In addition, the Middle Rogue offers lots of water too deep or too treacherous for wading. So the angler who pulls flies through these midriver slots gets to fish such water.

Along with the development of the Rogue River Twitch came the ensuing popularity of double-hook flies. They ride true in the water and hook fish convincingly. For the Rogue's small steelhead, however, the classic Rogue doubles probably belong in a shadow box rather than in the river. They can tear up a fish rather seriously. Nonetheless, these double steelhead flies retain a unique style and character, one that should remain alive in the annals of fly tying history.

*Guests converse in the cozy confines of the
historic Morrison's Rogue River Lodge.*

The Holy Water

As if its steelhead fishery were not enough, the Rogue offers a unique and productive fishery for large rainbow trout. The so-called "Holy Water" is formed by the tailwater below Lost Creek Reservoir and extends downstream a scant half-mile or so toward the fish hatchery. Its fertile waters produce a succession of fine hatches throughout the year.

The most widely anticipated hatch is the May-June emergence of Salmonflies. The insects hatch mostly during the morning, but the evening ovipositing flights can prove an awesome sight. So intense is the hatch that the Holy Water draws big-time crowds when the hatch peaks. To avoid these crowds, fish mid-week and fish the lower end of the reach or wait till later in the year and fish the caddis hatches or the sporadic mayfly hatches.

Spring creek tactics pay dividends on this heavily-fished water. Use long, light tippets and downstream presentations. The rainbows typically run 14 to 18 inches with a few over 20 inches in length. Some of the area's top steelhead guides also guide the Holy Water.

Morrison's Rogue River Lodge

The last week of October arrived with the promise of rain and on the wings of such promise arrived a drenching deluge whose pounding cadence drowned out all other sounds. Bright maple leaves, awash in yellow and orange, proved no match for the heavy onslaught and down they tumbled under the pelting rain, littering the walkway leading to the entrance of Morrison's Lodge, where the windows glowed quietly like inviting beacons against the dark, lonely night.

Inside the rustic old lodge, dancing tendrils of flame cast their warming shadows across beams of pine, whose aged golden grain had silently witnessed a half-century of angling lore in stories told and retold by visitors to this historic rampart on the banks of the Rogue River. Even now the guests awaiting dinner sit by the grand old stone fireplace, swapping tales of the day's events on the river.

Lloyd Morrison built the lodge in 1945 at a time when essential construction materials were difficult to come by. A guide and lumber mill worker, Morrison's clients included residents from nearby Grants Pass as well as friends from far-away San Francisco. All had to traverse the brutal 15-mile road from Grants Pass to enjoy the friendly confines of Morrison's Lodge and the world-class fishing for steelhead and salmon.

Then as now the cozy dining room served hearty meals before and after the guided fishing expeditions. On this night, as on any other, the practiced skills of Morrison's kitchen staff stole the show with an exceptional display of classically prepared fare, served in traditional courses and accompanied by fine Northwest and California wines. Earlier in the year, seated outside on the spacious deck, Morrison's guests would have savored every bite while taking in a panoramic view of the river a hundred yards away. But autumn brings the rain—and the steelhead. By October the massive log walls form bulwarks against the autumn chill.

Indeed, the autumn crowd at Morrison's is comprised mostly of anglers while the summertime guests arrive with more varied outdoor interests. Morrison's staff includes experienced fishing guides and skilled whitewater guides. Among them is my long-time friend Ray Slusser, whose intimate knowledge of the river and its history ranks him among the most highly regarded oarsmen on the Middle Rogue.

River trips begin early. After a king-sized breakfast, anglers meet their guides for a crack at the Rogue's steelhead and salmon. It is the former, though, that draw the fly angling enthusiasts. Tonight's guests linger long after dessert, sipping red wine and talking of the things that occupy the minds of fly fishers. Likely these topics have changed but little in 50 years: fine fly rods and favorite flies, memorable steelhead and revered pools, imported shotguns and unruly pointing dogs, far away destinations and waters close to the heart, fishing partners now and those alive in memory. To these latter, anglers should always drink a toast and no doubt many a glass has been raised in such honor over Morrison's lively dinner tables.

In 1964, B.A. and Elaine Hanton purchased Morrison's Lodge and moved in with their three young children, Mike, Michelle, and Mark. They moved in just in time for the infamous flood of 1964, which ravaged the property, turning the cottages into piles of ruble. With the help of a disaster loan they rebuilt the property and repaired the main lodge. Additions continued as business grew over the years and now Michelle acts as general manager, her graceful attention to detail evident in all the lodge's offerings.

The Middle Rogue's prime steelheading season begins during September and lasts until Morrison's Lodge closes for the season in November. Make your reservations well in advance. Morrison's offers ample space, but this is a popular place on a popular river. Expect the best of what this river offers, for Morrison's reigns as the premier historical fly fishing lodge in the Northwest. Each well-appointed room features a fireplace or wood stove—amenities whose comforts compete for your favor with the tree-shrouded grounds and the old lodge itself.

On this late-autumn night Morrison's fulfilled an oft-repeated scene, for among the guests was a new devotee to fly angling whose first fly rod fish was a wild steelhead. To this we toasted over an elegant dinner, the October rains forgotten behind a fortress of smooth-hewn logs.

Morrison's Rogue River Lodge serves exceptional meals.

MORRISON'S ROGUE RIVER LODGE
8500 Galice Road
Merlin, OR 97532
800-826-1963
www.morrisonslodge.com

Morrison's offers fall fishing packages that include lodging, meals, and guided fishing. You can choose anything from a 2-day fishing package for $730 to a 5-day package for $1,600. The daily lodging rate as of this writing is $160 for double occupancy and includes nightly hors d'oeuvres, a fabulous four-course dinner, country-style breakfast of gargantuan proportions, and packed daily lunches. To get there, exit the freeway at Exit 61 (Merlin) and follow Galice Road 12½ miles to the lodge, which sits beside the river on your right as you approach from the east. Airline service is to Medford Rogue Valley Airport. Alaska-Horizon flies into Medford from Portland; United flies into Medford from San Francisco and Los Angeles.

Restaurants and Accommodations

Home to about 20,000 residents, Grants Pass offers ample lodging and dining options. Try Wild River Brewery (595 NE E Street) for microbrewed beer, gourmet pizza, and other pub-style fare. Another personal favorite is La Burrita Mexican Restaurant, located on SE 7th Street near the river. Huge, tasty burritos and superb fajitas highlight La Burrita's authentic fare. Popular dinner houses include Hamilton House (1936 Rogue River Hwy./541-479-3938), R-Haus Restaurant at 2140 Rogue River Highway (541-474-3335) and Yankee Pot Roast at 720 NW 6th Street (541-476-0551). For the best deli-style sandwiches in town, visit Millie's, where third-generation owners bake fresh buns daily. Millie's is located at 731 NE 7th Street.

Grants Pass and the surrounding communities offer a variety of lodging options, ranging from lodges like Morrison's to nice B&Bs and plentiful motel space. Weasku Inn (5560 Rogue River Hwy/541-476-6873) was originally built in 1924 and remodeled just a few years ago. Weasku offers riverside cabins and rooms in the lodge.

Motels in and around Grants Pass range from the easy-access venues like Super-8 (541-474-0888) and Redwood Motel (541-476-0878) to fanciful inns overlooking the water, such as Riverside Inn (541-476-6873) or Hawthorn Inn and Suites (541-472-1808). Just south of Grants Pass, right along the freeway, Motel Del Rogue offers nice, convenient riverside lodging.

Additionally, the Rogue Valley area offers plenty of camp space at several nice riverfront parks. Rogue Elk Park, on Hwy. 62 a few miles east of the little town of Trail, includes a nice campground open between April 15 and October 15 (541-774-8183). Valley of the Rogue State Park (541-582-1118) lies adjacent to I-5 between Grants Pass and Medford.

If you are specifically visiting southern Oregon to fish the upper river or the Holy Water, stay in Shady Cove, a small community located on the banks of the Upper Rogue. Shady Cove offers four motels: Edgewater Inn Motel (541-878-3171), Maple Leaf Motel (541-878-2169), Royal Coachman Motel (541-878-2481) and Two Pines Bunkhouse (541-878-2511). RVers can stay at Flycaster's RV Park (541-878-2749) or Rogue River RV Park (541-878-2662). A dozen-odd restaurants line the main street through Shady Cove.

Though not particularly close to the river, the historic Wolf Creek Inn offers luxurious dinners and eight quaint, well-appointed guest rooms. Dinner is served nightly from 4:30 till 7 p.m. Be sure to make reservations (541-866-2474). The original tavern was opened in 1883 and the current inn has been beautifully renovated and preserved. Wolf Creek is located 20 miles north of Grants Pass at Exit 76 off I-5.

Nearby Attractions and Activities

Many opportunities exist to entertain the entire family in the Rogue River country, beginning with the river itself. Anyone with an appreciation for wild places will enjoy a float trip down the Middle Rogue or the tumultuous Wild Rogue from below Grave Creek. Float trip guides are numerous in the area. Guests of Morrison's Lodge can arrange guided float trips through the lodge. Otherwise, contact the chamber of commerce in Grants Pass. Jetboat tours are equally popular and are conducted by Hellgate Jetboat Excursions (541-479-7204) and Jet Boat River Excursions (541-582-0800).

If you have an extra day to explore, head east for Crater Lake National Park, named for the spectacular natural lake that fills the crater of Mt. Mazama, the ancient volcano whose violent eruptions spread ash all over western North America 7,000 years ago.

Wine enthusiasts should make time to visit the Rogue Valley's fine wineries, most of them located south near the quaint and busy town of Ashland, home of the famous Oregon Shakespeare Festival. Among my favorites are Weisingers Vineyard (541-488-5989), Ashland Vineyards & Winery (541-488-0088), and Valley View Vineyards (541-899-8468).

Downtown Ashland is a required stop if you're spending time in southern Oregon. The community caters to the tourist and artisan alike, offering unique shops of all descriptions and countless dining and nightlife options. Fine dining can be found at such popular restaurants as Cucina Biazzi (541-488-3739), Beasy's on the Creek (541-488-5009), Chateaulin (541-482-2264) and Winchester Inn (800-972-4991). Among the fun bars are Siskiyou Brew Pub, Standing Stone Brewery, and Rogue Brewery. The Oregon Shakespeare Festival offers ongoing plays from mid-February through October. By the time steelhead season hits the Rogue in September, you can enjoy downtown Ashland and the plays without the overwhelming summer crowds (for tickets to the plays, call 541-482-4331). While you're there, check out the Schneider Art Museum at Southern Oregon State College.

Also in the general area, albeit 85 miles west of Ashland, is Oregon Cave National Monument. For a nominal fee, visitors can take the guided tours through the remarkable marble caverns. This national monument is located near Cave Junction on Highway 46. Tours run March through November. Meanwhile, *Golf Digest* rated Eagle Point Golf Course as the nation's third "Best New Affordable Public Course" in 1997 (541-826-8225).

Author's Tip

If pressed for time, hire a guide for your excursion to the Rogue. If you prefer to wade and cast rather than pull flies, make sure your guide knows of your preferences ahead of time. Should you find yourself in the Rogue River area during late spring or summer, consider hiring a guide for spring chinook salmon fishing. You won't be fly angling, but you might very well hook a mint-bright salmon of 15 to 30 pounds. You can keep hatchery-born salmon, and no salmon offers better table fare than fresh "springers."

Favorite Fly

Golden Demon

HOOK	Salmon/Steelhead wet fly, No. 6-8
TAIL	Golden pheasant crest
BODY	Gold oval tinsel
HACKLE	Orange
WING	Brown bucktail or squirrel tail
CHEEKS	Jungle cock (optional)

Golden Demon

Fast Facts

Rogue River

LOCATION	Southern Oregon
WATER TYPE	Large river with moderately steep gradient
PRIMARY GAMEFISH	Summer steelhead; also winter steelhead, chinook and coho salmon
BEST TIME	For summer steelhead, July through December on the upper river and September through November on the Middle Rogue.

BEST FLIES	Both classic steelhead and salmon patterns work well, along with standard trout patterns.
EQUIPMENT	5- to 8-weight rod; floating line and high-density sink-tip line.
CONDITIONS	Seasonal rains generally begin during November, so September and October are usually quite nice in the Rogue Valley. Many well-maintained riverside parks are located throughout the valley.
DRIVE TIME	From Portland: 4-5 hours From Eugene: 2-3 hours From San Francisco: 7-8 hours From Seattle: 7-8 hours
DIRECTIONS	Follow I-5 to the Merlin exit (a few miles north of Grants Pass) to reach the Middle Rogue and Morrison's Lodge. Continue down Galice Road, past Morrison's, to reach the end of the road at Grave Creek. To reach the Upper Rogue, continue south on I-5 past Grants Pass.

Local Fly Shops

NATIVE RUN FLY SHOP
324 Redwood Highway
Grants Pass, OR 97527
541-474-0090

SILVER SEDGE FLY SHOP
325 Galice Road
Merlin, OR 97532-9703
541-476-2456

MCKENZIE OUTFITTERS
1340 Biddle Road
Medford, OR 97504
800-704-5145

ASHLAND OUTDOOR STORE
37 Third Street
Ashland, OR 97520
541-488-1202

Guides

RAY SLUSSER, 541-476-8047
STEVE BONNER, 541-474-0018

DAVE CARNEY, 541-582-2236
DENNIS NAGEL, 541-862-2531

Contacts

OREGON DEPARTMENT
OF FISH & WILDLIFE
Rogue Watershed District Office
1495 E. Gregory Road
Central Point, OR 97502
541-826-8774

GRANTS PASS CHAMBER
OF COMMERCE
800-547-5927

Guide Darc Knobel (left) lands a trophy for his guest.

CHAPTER 28

ISAAK LAKE RANCH

Private Waters on the High Plateau

I'll just admit it up front: among the perks for a veteran outdoor writer are the frequent invitations to visit and fish private waters. I've entertained my share of such invitations, many from pay-to-play lakes, most of which, quite frankly, don't interest me too much. I'm all for trophy-sized trout, but I like my fish to look wild—at least to some extent—even if they are of hatchery origin. Unfortunately, many pay-to-play lakes operate on the "hog pond" mentality wherein "management" consists of growing big, fat, malformed finless wonders in a cement tank and then tossing them into a fertile lake so they can grow a little more. Charge a hundred bucks a day and listen to customers boast about the 10-pounder they just landed.

Call me jaded, but I just don't do the hog-pond thing, and I've never played the "trade-a-trip-for-an-article" game. But I'm damn glad I accepted the invitation to check out Isaak Lakes Ranch. Managed by George Cook, the well-known regional manufacturer's rep for Sage Fly Rods, Ross Reels and other product lines, Isaak Lake Ranch straddles a lonely plateau in the wide-open windswept expanse of eastern Washington's coulee country. For nearly two decades, Cook has striven to produce what certainly ranks with the best of the West's pay-to-play stillwater destinations. His fish have fins.

Rather than raise big pigs and dump them in the lake, Cook plants Kamloops-strain rainbows, along with a few brown trout, at six to nine inches in length. They grow up in the lakes. So fertile are the ranch's two lakes, that within a year and a half these single-digit planters reach lengths in excess of 20 inches. They feed on a diet rich in scuds, or "freshwater shrimp," a food source that Cook calls the "key to the party."

Of course these super-rich lakes also teem with all the other typical stillwater trout foods, including damsels, *Callibaetis* mayflies, *Chironomids*, water beetles, and leeches. The limitless food source assures rapid trout growth, and planting the fish as youngsters assures that they attain a beautiful, well-proportioned physique. But planting the fish as juveniles is only part of the equation that has helped Isaak Lake Ranch become so successful that 85 percent of its anglers are repeat customers.

Cook also manages the lakes on a carrying-capacity basis. "These lakes," says Cook, "have a carrying capacity of about 100 fish per acre based on available food" and on particular environmental factors. The upper lake, which Cook terms the "numbers lake" or "opportunity lake" is stocked with 95 to 105 fish per acre. The average rainbow caught spans about 19 inches and a few approach 28 inches. Catch rates are higher in the upper lake than in the lower lake, which is stocked at a rate of 55 to 65 fish per acre of water. Although a 20-inch fish from the upper lake is nothing to sneeze at, the lower lake is the "trophy lake," where a fat 22-inch fish is average and where trout to 30 inches are taken each season.

When I visited Isaak Lake Ranch, the lower lake seemed well-populated with 22- to 25-inch trout, each one so perfectly colored and proportioned that I found myself reminiscing about those good old days on the public reservoirs of eastern Idaho, where similar fish honed my fondness for stillwater fishing. Those southeast Idaho trout reservoirs suffered the occasional setback from a hot, dry summer or a long, cold winter. From time to time, the same two extremes occur in eastern Washington and to a large measure predicate Cook's management strategies. "We are acutely aware of our seasonal limitations," Cook says.

"Our management scheme is not just to attain maximum growth rates in the fish, but more importantly to ensure a high survival rate during the seasonal extremes. We want a bigger fish faster, but we also want a greater number of big fish within the population," Cook explains. "In other words, we make sure our management program fits with the reality of the environment."

Cook also manages pressure on the fishery through very limited opportunity. Only 6 to 10 rods per day are allowed on a total of 105 acres of water and fishing is allowed only four days per week. Isaak Lake Ranch runs its season from March 25 through June 10 and again in the fall, from September 15 through November 10. With such limited pressure on the lakes, anglers are assured an untrampled, quality experience. "Every day is like opening day," says Cook.

Cook told me recently that "Dry Falls Lake (a public fly-only fishery less than an hour away) gets more pressure the first five days of the season than we get all year."

I've seen the opening-week crowds at Dry Falls and, as I replied to George, I'd bet Dry Falls gets more angler-use hours in its first *three* days than does Isaak Lake Ranch during its entire season.

Because fishing pressure is so tightly controlled, anglers should book their day or days as far ahead of time as possible. But you won't find any brochures or websites about Isaak Lake Ranch. After all, when 85 percent of your clients are repeat customers, you don't need any advertisements. To book a trip to the lakes, call George Cook (243-833-0288) or his head guide Darc Knobel (509-884-4070/509-754-4536).

Author's Tip

The upper lake at Isaak Lake Ranch is managed more for numbers than for trophy-class fish, but some real bruisers do inhabit the lake. The far corner of the lake seems the best place to consistently find the 22- to 26-inch fish that reside here. It's a modest journey and the back side of the lake also boasts a thoroughly wild feel, with an abundance of birds and spring wildflowers. Be sure to bring a float tube or pontoon boat when you visit Isaak Lakes.

Favorite Fly
Beadhead Soft Hackle Zug Bug

HOOK	2XL wet fly hook, No. 10-12
TAIL	Partridge hackle fibers
BODY	Peacock herl
RIB	Fine silver or gold oval tinsel
COLLAR	Partridge hackle
HEA	Metal bead

Beadhead Soft Hackle Zug Bug

Fast Facts

Isaak Lake Ranch

LOCATION	Mansfield Plateau, west of Banks Lake in eastern Washington
WATER TYPE	Private fee lake available only by reservation
PRIMARY GAMEFISH	Kamloops-strain rainbow trout and a few brown trout
BEST TIME	Open March 25-June 10 and September 15-November 10
BEST FLIES	The usual arsenal of stillwater flies produce here. These include scud patterns, Woolly Buggers, damsel nymphs, *Callibaetis* mayfly patterns, Carey Specials, Zug Bugs, Prince Nymphs, Pheasant Tail Nymphs and *Chironomid* patterns.
EQUIPMENT	5- to 7-weight rod; clear intermediate line is perhaps most useful, but so too are sink-tip, Type III sinking lines and floating lines. Some form of watercraft is needed, especially on the upper lake.
CONDITIONS	Expect afternoon winds following sunny, pleasant mornings. No formal facilities.
DRIVE TIME	From Seattle: 5 hours From Portland: 6 hours From Spokane: 3 hours From Boise: 6-7 hours
DIRECTIONS	Consult with George Cook or Darc Knobel for specific directions to the ranch.

Local Fly Shops

BLUE DUN FLY SHOP
960 Valley Mall Parkway, Suite A
East Wenatchee, WA 98802
509-884-4070

Guides

DARC KNOBEL
509-884-4070 or 509-754-4536

GEORGE COOK
243-833-0288

CHAPTER 29

GRINDSTONE LAKES
Oregon's Premier Private Stillwater Fishery

Private "pay-to-play" lakes have sprung to life all over the Pacific Northwest, offering anglers a desirable combination of big fish and lightly pressured waters. That combination, of course, comes at a price. These fee lakes run the gamut from hog ponds to well-managed fisheries boasting long-standing reputations for providing top-flight fish and superb fishing.

Among this latter category are the Northwest's two premier exemplary pay-to-play ranches: Oregon's Grindstone Lakes Ranch and Washington's Isaak Lakes Ranch.

Grindstone Lakes occupy a sagebrush plateau in the heart of central Oregon, some 100 miles east of Prineville. The ranch offers five different spring-fed lakes, ranging in size from 25 to 55 acres. All are about 25 feet deep and rich in aquatic weeds that harbor dense populations of scuds, damsels, water beetles, *Chironomids*, mayfly nymphs, snails, leeches, and every other conceivable stillwater trout food. As a result, Grindstone's rainbows grow fast and fat. The fish range from two to eight pounds, averaging three or four pounds. Thirty-fish days are a cinch for experienced anglers, but even beginners can expect good action.

Rustic, lakeside accommodations await at day's end. A 50-year-old block ranch house occupies a slight rise above the largest lake and includes three bedrooms, two baths, one shower, and hot and cold running water. Located in the heart of a huge private ranch, Grindstone's lightly trod, semi-wilderness setting assures that the lakes serve as an oasis for wildlife.

To maintain the high-quality fishing, Bill Beardsley, who manages Grindstone Lakes, allows only 5-weight and heavier rods and no hooks larger than size 6. Likewise, he urges heavy tippets so trout can be played and released quickly. The Grindstone fly list includes all the usual suspects, from Woolly Buggers and damsel nymphs to *Callibaetis* and *Chironomid* patterns.

Most anglers book their Grindstone trips through fly shops in Oregon. Generally, these shops have specific dates reserved well ahead of time and most offer package trips complete with guided service, meals and sometimes transportation. For current information and to check on shops with reserved dates at Grindstone, call Beardsley at 541-480-6308 or check with area fly shops. Three Oregon shops are perennial visitors to Grindstone: Creekside Flyfishing Shop in Salem (503-588-1768), Scarlet Ibis Fly Shop in Corvallis (541-754-1544) and Trophy Waters Fly Shop in Klamath Falls (541-850-0717).

Author's Tip

Four-wheel-drive vehicles are a must for driving to Grindstone Lakes and guests are required to meet at the ranch gate at specified times in the afternoon and evening of the first day of the trip. Fill your float tube (and your gas tank) in Prineville so you can begin fishing immediately when you get there the first evening.

Favorite Fly

Olive Krystal Bugger

HOOK	3XL streamer hook, No. 6, 8
TAIL	Marabou with a little Krystal Flash
BODY	Krystal chenille or similar
HACKLE	Saddle hackle ribbed with wire

Olive Krystal Bugger

Fast Facts
Grindstone Lakes

LOCATION	East-central Oregon
WATER TYPE	Private fee lakes
PRIMARY GAMEFISH	Rainbow trout
BEST TIME	Spring and fall
BEST FLIES	Woolly Buggers and leech patterns; *Callibaetis* mayflies, *Chironomids*, damsels, scuds, and leeches.
EQUIPMENT	5- to 7-weight rod; floating line, clear intermediate and full-sinking lines. Also bring a float tube or pontoon boat and a warm sleeping bag.
CONDITIONS	Access road is rough and requires four-wheel-drive during wet weather. Guests must arrange to meet Beardsley at the locked ranch gate.
DIRECTIONS	For specific directions to the ranch, consult with fly shops that arrange trips or call Bill Beardsley at 541-480-6308. The drive to Grindstone follows the Post-Paulina Highway east from Prineville and the turn-off to the ranch is at milepost 65, about 10 miles past Paulina.

Area Fly Shops

CREEKSIDE FLY FISHING SHOP
345 High Street S.
Salem, OR 97301
503-588-1768

SCARLET IBIS FLY SHOP
2319 NW 9th Street
Corvallis, OR 97330
541-754-1544

TROPHY WATERS FLY SHOP
800 Klamath Avenue
Klamath Falls, OR 97601
541-850-0717

The McKenzie River
Ben and Kay Dorris State Park to Willamette Confluence

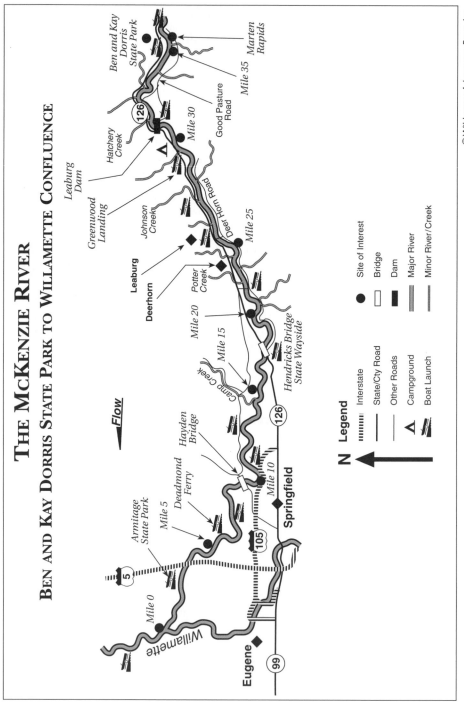

Ben and Kay Dorris State Park

Marten Rapids

Mile 35

Good Pasture Road

Mile 30

Hatchery Creek

Leaburg Dam

Greenwood Landing

Johnson Creek

Deer Horn Road

Mile 25

Leaburg

Potter Creek

Deerhorn

Mile 20

Mile 15

Camp Creek

Hendricks Bridge State Wayside

Hayden Bridge

Deadmond Ferry

Armitage State Park

Mile 5

Mile 10

Springfield

Mile 0

Eugene

Willamette

Flow

N

Legend

Interstate	Site of Interest
State/Cty Road	Bridge
Other Roads	Dam
Campground	Major River
Boat Launch	Minor River/Creek

CHAPTER 30

THE McKENZIE RIVER

Western Oregon's Best Trout Water

One of Oregon's most famous trout streams, the beautiful McKenzie River begins its westerly journey high in the Oregon Cascades. Its clean, cold flows emanate from porous lava flows near Clear Lake, south and west from the Santiam Summit where Highway 20 crosses over the crest of the mountains. Many miles below, the pastoral Willamette Valley tames this tumultuous mountain torrent, and it is in the river's lower reaches that the McKenzie realizes her full potential as a wild trout fishery.

From its confluence with the Willamette River north of Eugene upstream through Springfield to Hayden Bridge, the McKenzie is managed for wild rainbow and cutthroat trout. This lower reach of the river is not stocked with hatchery trout. The remaining stretches of the river, all the way up to Paradise Campground, are traditionally stocked rather liberally with put-and-take rainbows. Despite its immense beauty, the river upstream from Leaburg Dam offers little excitement for the fly angler conditioned to a steady diet of blue-ribbon trout streams.

*An angler plies the water of the Lower
McKenzie River.*

The Lower McKenzie, which begins below Leaburg Dam, offers the better fishery for serious fly anglers. The lengthy run from Leaburg down to the highway crossing at Hendrick's Park includes lots of water largely inaccessible to anglers afoot. The same holds true below Hendrick's Bridge. Thus, most serious McKenzie anglers ply their favorite water with the aid of a drift boat. As you progress downstream from Leaburg Dam to Hayden Bridge, hatchery-produced rainbows become increasingly scarce and wild rainbows increasingly common.

Below Hayden Bridge, the river skirts the north side of Springfield before crossing under I-5 at Armitage Park. Foot access is good at Armitage Park and at a few other places in and around Springfield, but a drift boat still gives an advantage. Armitage Park offers the last take-out on the McKenzie, but many anglers float from Hayden or Armitage down to the mouth of the McKenzie and then down to the Willamette River, taking out at Hileman Landing off Beacon Road north of Santa Clara.

The rainbows share the lower river with abundant native cutthroat trout. The cut-throat rarely reach 20 inches, but 15- to 16-inchers show up regularly. These beauti-fully-marked cutthroat are native to the Willamette Basin, and it is likely that rainbows were native as well, although decades of hatchery plants have confused the genetic picture. Cutthroat become increasingly common downstream from Springfield.

Most of the wild rainbows run 8 to 14 inches in length. However, the Lower McKenzie holds lots of 16- to 20-inch wild trout. The river's wild rainbows exhibit the coloration of a redband trout from the waters of central and eastern Oregon. Consequently, they are called "McKenzie redsides." You cannot fully appreciate the number of big trout in the lower river until you stumble upon the right hatch at the right time. The largest fish reside in deep, hard-to-fish water, and you can fish all day without finding a trout of more than 14 inches.

On the other hand, should you encounter a strong hatch under low-light condi-tions, you might very well find dozens of 16- to 20-inch redsides feeding along the banks in two feet of water. And the Lower McKenzie offers several hatches that bring out the big fish.

The first of these strong hatches is the March Brown mayfly emergence of late winter and spring. The March Browns (*Rithrogena morrisoni*) emerge at midday and the strongest flights occur during warm, overcast weather between late February and mid-April. Robust mayflies, the March Browns are easily imitated by No. 12 and 14 sparkle duns or comparaduns. Some anglers fish soft hackle patterns during the hatch, sometimes attaching these below a dry fly.

Blue-Winged Olives appear around the same time as the March Browns, but the early hatches of these tiny mayflies lack predictability. Later in the spring, warm, over-cast weather usually prompts a good midday *Baetis* hatch somewhere on the river. Small black stoneflies and brown Willow Flies (early black stoneflies) emerge spo-radically between February and April. A few Golden Stoneflies and a few Salmonflies appear during May and June.

Perhaps the best hatch for luring big fish to the shallows, the McKenzie Green Caddis (*Arctopsyche grandis*) begins its annual emergence during late April before peaking between late May and mid-June. These large caddis (size 8-10) feature a remarkable iridescent green body under slate-gray wings. Often they emerge at dusk, a time when large trout feed at the surface with abandon. Dry caddis patterns work just fine, but if you seriously want to target the river's trophies, fish a pupa pattern just under the surface film.

Also during June, the lower river offers its least appreciated big-fish hatch: Green Drakes. These huge, bright-green mayflies hatch for just a few days, but should you happen upon one of those days you will be rewarded with exceptional dry-fly action. Warm, cloudy—even drizzly—days are best.

The McKenzie River

Headwaters to Ben and Kay Dorris State Park

By mid-summer, the hatches switch to evening affairs and include Pale Morning Dun mayflies, Pale Evening Dun mayflies, and the aforementioned Blue-Winged Olives, along with many caddis varieties. Also included are sparse hatches of one of the most beautiful of all the mayflies, a member of the *Epeorus* clan whose brilliant yellow body and wings make the insect glow atop the water. Summer evenings often reveal compound hatches/spinner falls consisting of two or more mayfly varieties, several types of caddis, and a handful of Little Yellow Stoneflies and Golden Stoneflies.

From mid-July through late August—the hottest part of the summer—the water drops to its lowest levels. Spinner falls and hatches occur almost exclusively around dawn and dusk. Caddis activity this time of year accounts for some phenomenal rises right at dark. On certain gravel bars, a dozen or more 14- to 20-inch rainbows begin rising in just a foot or two of water along the banks.

During mid-autumn, the season winds down with a hatch of October Caddis. These giant, orange-bodied caddis require No. 6 flies. Sometimes the evening hatch stirs good surface activity; other times sparse hatches escape unnoticed by the trout.

The Lower McKenzie offers a nice mix of predictable, anticipated hatches and good general all-purpose dry fly and wet fly action. Certainly you can plan a trip to coincide with a specific hatch, but bring all your fly boxes. Changing water levels and weather conditions often alter the hatch schedule, especially during the spring. Be flexible in your plans and in your choice of tactics.

The middle reaches of the McKenzie.

McKenzie Summer Steelhead

From the moment my cleated boots gripped the slippery cobble I enjoyed that weird "fishy" feeling. A golden-hued sunrise had ushered in this September day, a day not appreciably different than any other except that the yellow-trimmed maple leaves hinted that this would be my last day of the season on a favorite summer steelhead river. Soon the upriver dam would release its autumn flow and I would be walking the high ridges for blue grouse and casting pretty flies across the North Umpqua's legendary pools.

But this day would end my season here in the valley. With each September comes this day, a day when I string the rod in an unhurried reflective mood, fondly contemplating the season now ending. Always this day is tinged with regret born of a longing for more misty summer mornings when the *swish-swish* of the fly line seems to echo out across the river in perfect harmony with the water ouzel's melodious chorus and the song sparrow's excited scoldings; more warm evenings when extravagant sunsets trace tendrils of scarlet across the summer sky.

This morning had passed pleasantly as I cast across three elegant pools before noon. I had not a fish to show for my efforts, a fact that weighed very little on my mind, for I had covered the water well; I had fished the pools gracefully. With steelhead, fishing well means something—these remarkable fish deserve a certain reverence earned by their rite of passage, their unique, unlikely journey from fresh water to salt water to fresh water once again.

That September morning I had fished well. Now I was simply fishing because it seemed the thing to do, the best way to enjoy the sunny afternoon warmth that would eventually surrender to the magical last hour of daylight that heralds so many connections between summer steelhead and steelhead anglers. I enjoyed each cast, watching the narrow loops jump out over the water and unfurl across the flow. I had chosen for my fly the Maxwell's Purple Matuka, that locally-renowned fly devised by my fishing partner and one of only a handful of patterns in which I entrust my fortunes astream.

I two-stepped the pool and fished down into the deepening lower reach when finally a heavy resistance snapped the line taut. The fish was well hooked. He had taken the fly mid-swing and likely had the point buried deep in the hinge of his jaws. Despite the relative improbability of this midday, sun-on-the-water hook-up, I was not the least surprised, even by his impressive proportions. He battled gallantly, first dredging the depths and running deep into the hole below and then springing skyward in a series of tailwalks. Through it all I handled him gently, but when the thrashing subsided I leaned hard into him, steering him shoreward. I would not yield ground; instead I trusted my heavy tippet and soon had a magnificent buck by the tail.

Cradling the fish underwater, his head upstream, I admired this remarkable creature, a two-salt steelhead born in a hatchery yet thoroughly wild in all other respects. Reluctant to release the moment, I kneeled down beside this powerful, magnificent steelhead, turned his head slightly and looked into his lively eye. Then I freed him as he had freed me. My season was now over. I unhitched the fly, dried it, and clipped it back into my battle-scarred Wheatley. Then I sat beside the river for a time, watching the breeze ripple the cottonwoods. I sat there until the sun dipped below the trees. Next season was half a year distant, but already the river and its steelhead beckon my return, for lucky are we fly anglers who reside in this valley, where an introduced run of hatchery summer steelhead migrates into the clean, clear flows of the Upper Willamette tributaries.

*Forrest Maxwell
with a McKenzie
summer steelhead.*

Hatchery Success

The Upper Willamette Basin essentially comprises that area of the drainage upstream from Willamette Falls at Oregon City. Prior to the construction of the flood-control dams on the river's major tributaries, the Willamette Valley was one big flood plain. During the wet season, the whole valley flooded and Willamette Falls proved negotiable to anadromous fish, including native winter steelhead and chinook salmon. But during the summer, when the valley dried out, the falls halted upstream migration. Historically, rivers above the falls never had native runs of summer steelhead.

Enter the Oregon Department of Fish & Wildlife and the Skamania-strain summer steelhead that have proved ideally suited to hatchery operations around the Northwest and the Great Lakes region. In 1969, ODFW made the first summer steelhead plants in the Willamette's tributaries. Two years later, 2,310 fish returned, the first-ever summer steelhead run in the Upper Willamette Valley. An important new fishery was born. A significant local economic impact resulted from this new fishery, for the number of large summer steelhead streams in Oregon had just doubled to include five rivers in the state's most populous region.

The 1990s heralded a time of significant change in the management of these waters. Paramount to new management strategies was the potential Endangered & Threatened Species listing of native stocks in each drainage. In 1996, stocking of hatchery smolt was halted on the Malolla and Upper Clackamas Rivers; planting of hatchery trout came to an end on the North Santiam and other drainages, leading to widespread rumors that the summer steelhead program was ending throughout the valley.

For now, though, ODFW plans to continue stocking hatchery summer steelhead in the McKenzie River, along with the North and South Santiam Rivers and the Middle Fork Willamette. District Biologist Steve Mamoyac cautions that "every year the potential for change (in the management of the fisheries) is very real."

Fishing the Summer Run

Flagship river among the Willamette's tributaries, the McKenzie's fame as a trout stream is well documented. Yet its summer steelhead fishery ranks with the state's best during years of strong runs. The 1997 catch totaled almost 2,000 fish. Moreover, the McKenzie—from Leaburg Dam downstream to Springfield—surely remains one of the valley's most beautiful waterways, coursing through pastoral farmlands and timbered slopes.

Access begins below Leaburg Dam, where several productive steelhead runs await. Boaters have the advantage and can choose from any of several float trips. The uppermost drift (the dam down to Greenwood Lane or Lower Greenwood) draws the most users, but also includes lots of perfect fly water. The river's gradient lessens as you progress below Leaburg, so the best steelhead runs are along the upper half of this entire segment; as you approach the outskirts of Springfield, long, broad, comparatively featureless cobblestone flats characterize the river.

Chris Daughters, owner of the Caddis Fly Angling Shop in Eugene, suggests fly fishers learn the location of the launch sites and then choose drifts based on distance and preferred water type. The launch sites are as follows, with mileage given from the uppermost ramp below the dam: (1) Leaburg Dam—0 miles (2) Greenwood Lane—three miles (3) Lower Greenwood—four-and-a-half miles (4) near Leaburg Store—seven miles (5) bridge at Deerhorn Gold Course—eleven miles (6) primitive launch at Partridge Lane—fifteen miles (7) Hendrick's Bridge Wayside —nineteen miles.

Because the fishery peaks during the height of summer when water temperatures are at optimal levels, anglers are afforded the luxury of fishing floating lines throughout the duration of the run. Peak fly fishing occurs from early July until mid- to late September. During years with strong runs (or early runs), anglers can expect to hook fish by early June. Likewise, even after the flows increase during autumn, fly anglers take plenty of fish. Sink-tip and sinking lines prove more effective at high water, but the same swung-fly methods apply.

The major newspapers in the valley carry the fish counts at Willamette Falls or anglers can simply call for a recorded message listing daily and cumulative counts (503-657-2059). The mid-1980s spoiled many of us. The runs were huge and catch rates robust. In 1986, 40,719 steelhead crossed Willamette Falls; 36,940 arrived in 1988. Shortly thereafter, numbers returned to normal, and during the 1990s the run averaged 12,526 fish annually. Those fish passage numbers get a boost when ODFW recycles steelhead on the river, trapping them at Leaburg and then releasing them at points downstream.

Even though the three-fish-every-evening days of the 1980s are gone now, sufficient numbers return to allow for productive fishing. Learn a few good runs on the McKenzie and you will hook steelhead with regularity.

Restaurants and Accommodations

With a population of more than 100,000 people and a major university, Eugene boasts many unique and exceptional restaurants and has no shortage of lodging options. If you're visiting the Northwest and would like to immerse yourself in our brewpub culture, Eugene offers several options: The Mcmenamin brothers operate three pubs in Eugene. The most extravagant of these is the North Bank, situated immediately adjacent to the Willamette River on the northwest side of the Coburg Road Bridge. Mcmenamin's High Street Pub occupies an old house downtown and the 19th Street Cafe resides on the corner of 19th and Agate.

Among the Mcmenamin's ales are their renowned Hammerhead, Terminator Stout, Ruby Ale and numerous IPAs. The food is pub-style. For a different flavor in microbrewed beer and a step up from pub-style food, try Steelhead Brewery on 5th Avenue or the Wild Duck on 6th Street. Eugene's most unique brewpub menu is found at West Bros. Bar-B-Que, located downtown on Olive Street.

Should you find yourself in Eugene during the breakfast hour, don't miss the chance to try The Glenwood, whose two locations serve hearty and healthy fare to legions of dedicated fans. The Campus Glenwood occupies the corner of 13th and Patterson just west of the university while the second Glenwood is located on Willamette Street on the way out to 24th Street.

Meanwhile, if you're looking for a fast, filling and tasty Mexican lunch, head for Burrito Boy on Franklin Boulevard. Some of the city's best Italian food comes from Beppe & Gianni's, down the street from the19th Street Mcmenamin's (541-683-6661). They specialize in raviolis, offering casual, comfortable high-end dining.

Fine dinner fare in Eugene tours the globe, ranging from the remarkable and popular oriental cuisine at Ocean Sky to the continental selections and fine desserts at Café' Zenon (898 Pearl Street/541-343-3005). The city's most remarkable cuisine may well come from Adam's Place at 30 E. Broadway (541-344-6948), but many other great choices await, from the wonderful Marche' (296 E. 5th/541-342-3612) to the popular, trendy Café Navarro (454 Willamette Street/541-344-0943). Such a brief list barely scratches the surface.

To the east, across I-5, lies the town of Springfield, gateway to the McKenzie River. Highway 126 heads up the river, leading through several small, riverside communities replete with services for travelers. Ike's Lakeside Pizza in Leaburg is a popular stop, as is Mom's Pies along the highway in Blue River. Other choices include Rustic Skillet in Blue River and Tina's Lucky Logger in Walterville. Likewise, if you prefer to stay overnight on the river rather than in the city, you can choose from a variety of options.

Area Lodging
Eagle Rock Lodge B&B, Vida, 541-822-3630
Heaven's Gate Cottages, Vida, 541-822-3214
McKenzie River Inn, Vida, 541-822-6260
Riverside Inn & Restaurant, Vida, 541-896-3218
Wayfarer Resort, Vida, 541-896-3613
Sleepy Hollow Motel, Blue River, 541-822-3805
Woodland Cottages, Blue River, 541-822-3597
Drift Inn B&B, Blue River, 541-822-3286
Marjon B&B Inn, Leaburg, 541-896-3145
McKenzie River Trout House B&B, 541-896-9819

Nearby Fisheries

The mainstem of the Willamette River flows through the city of Eugene and offers easy-access fishing for cutthroat, rainbow, and whitefish. March Brown mayflies hatch on the Willamette between February and April. The best fishing begins downstream from Eugene, north of Santa Clara, but time-pressed anglers can enjoy fine rises within Eugene's city limits. Access is good, with several parks and other public easements, both in Eugene and downstream below Santa Clara.

Nearby, the tailwater section of the Middle Fork Willamette offers another steelhead opportunity. Its catch rate rarely compares to those of the other rivers, but the river is substantially shorter than other streams. Access begins at the Pengra Boat Ramp below Dexter Dam. A five-mile drift ends at Jasper Bridge and the ramp at Clearwater Park is another four miles down. Primary access to the river is from Jasper-Lowell Road on the north bank. Middle Fork anglers averaged about 400 fish per year between 1986 and 1997.

Upstream from Dexter Reservoir, the Middle Fork comprises one of western Oregon's best trout streams. Hearing that, you might just rush on down there only to encounter high water seemingly devoid of fish. So I'll add that the Middle Fork is one of western Oregon's best trout streams when the water drops to fishable levels between late spring and mid-autumn. Summer hatches can be profuse and the Middle Fork offers wild rainbows, a few stretching to 20 inches.

While the Lower McKenzie offers the best action for dedicated fly fishing enthusiasts, the uppermost reaches of the river also host populations of wild trout. Most are small rainbows averaging eight or nine inches in length, but they reside in the most picturesque of settings. The upper river, between Clear Lake and Carmen Diversion Reservoir, features two large, elegant waterfalls. Small in stature, this part of the McKenzie is nonetheless powerful and assertive. Fishing here is not for the faint of heart nor frail of body. Trails follow both banks above Carmen Reservoir, and Highway 126 takes you to the upper river.

Nearby Attractions and Activities

The Eugene-Springfield area offers ample activity for anglers and non-anglers alike. One event of special interest is the annual Eugene Fly Tyers Expo, held at the Lane County Fairgrounds on the second or third Saturday each March. Sponsored by the Oregon Council Federation of Fly Fishers, this popular event features more than a hundred fly tyers demonstrating all manner of flies, from bass bugs to Atlantic salmon dressings. For information about the event, contact the Eugene fly shops.

The University of Oregon includes an impressive natural history museum. Also, if you're in Eugene during the appropriate seasons, try to get tickets to a Duck football game at Autzen Stadium or a basketball game at esoteric McArthur Court, affectionately known as "The Pit." The university's long and rich track & field tradition assures that each spring and summer world-class athletes will compete at the Prefontaine Classic and other major track events. On a like note, the city offers many running and hiking trails, including those on popular Mt. Piscah, also the location of an impressive arboretum.

Numerous city parks, including ever-popular Alton-Baker Park located along the Willamette River, offer quiet respite during Eugene's pleasant summers. Eugene's Millrace is a quiet waterway that winds through town. Canoe rentals are available across Franklin Boulevard from the university. For a more heart-racing experience, you can always hire a white-water guide for the middle reaches of the McKenzie River.

Shoppers can enjoy everything from 5th Street Market to Valley River Center. The former features everything from small local artisans to major-label clothing stores, along with unique restaurants and just about everything else you could want under one roof. Valley River Center is the classic mall scene. The Hult Center, located downtown next to the Hilton, serves the city as a venue for all manner of shows, concerts and other events.

The McKenzie River is as popular with whitewater enthusiasts as with anglers. Various whitewater guides offer many kinds of expeditions. Call Jim's Oregon Whitewater (541-822-6003), Oregon Whitewater Adventures (541-746-5422) or Adventure River Center (541-822-3888).

Author's Tip

During the summertime hatch of the McKenzie Green Caddis, look for the best action to occur in fairly shallow water close to the banks. The traditional pattern for this hatch (listed below) fishes great, but many trout prefer emergers just below the surface. To fish a deadly two-fly rig, add a foot of tippet to the bend of the hook on the dry fly and attach a No. 10 Green Sparkle Pupa. At the end of each drift, skate the fly slightly. The rainbows often grab the subsurface pattern just as it begins to swing on a taut line.

Favorite Trout Fly
McKenzie Green Caddis

HOOK	Dry-fly, No. 8-10
TAIL	Deer hair
BODY	Bright peacock-green yarn or dubbing
HACKLE	Grizzly through body
WING	Natural gray deer hair
COLLAR	Grizzly hackle

McKenzie Green Caddis

Favorite Steelhead Fly
Spawning Purple

HOOK	Alec Jackson Spey hook, Nickel, No. 1.5-5
BODY	Fluorescent flame red floss
WING	4 or 5 segments of purple marabou
HACKLE	Purple
CHEEKS	Jungle cock
COLLAR	Dyed-orange guinea

Spawning Purple

Fast Facts

Lower McKenzie River

LOCATION	Southern end of the Willamette Valley in western Oregon
WATER TYPE	Freestone trout and steelhead river
PRIMARY GAMEFISH	Rainbow and cutthroat trout, summer steelhead
BEST TIME	March through September
BEST FLIES	A wide range of hatch specific flies and attractors
EQUIPMENT	5- to 6-weight rods for trout (8-9 for steelhead), floating lines; drift boat if possible.
CONDITIONS	Pleasant summer weather; late winter and spring weather ranges from sunny and fairly warm to very wet.
DRIVE TIME	From Portland: 2-3 hours From Seattle: 5 hours From San Francisco: 10 hours
DIRECTIONS	Follow I-5 to Eugene and depart the freeway at Exit 1, then follow Highway 126 east up the McKenzie.

A McKenzie rainbow taken on an egg pattern during the winter.

Local Fly Shops

THE CADDIS FLY ANGLING SHOP
168 West 6th
Eugene, OR 97401
541-342-7005

HOMEWATERS FLY SHOP
444 West 3rd
Eugene, OR 97401
541-342-6691

Area Fly Shops

SCARLET IBIS FLY SHOP
2319 NW 9th Street
Corvallis, OR 97330
541-754-1544

VALLEY FLYFISHER
153 Alice Street
Salem, OR 97302
503-375-3721

CREEKSIDE FLYFISHING SHOP
345 High Street S.
Salem, OR 97301
503-588-1768

FLY COUNTRY OUTFITTERS
3400 State Street, G-704
Salem, OR 97301
503-585-4898

Guides

DEAN HELFRICH & SONS
541-747-8401

TIGHTLINE GUIDE SERVICE
541-896-3219

CARR'S WILD TROUT ADVENTURES
(Colin Carr)
541-548-0765

MCKENZIE RIVER
GUIDES ASSOCIATION
541-896-3348

Contacts

OREGON DEPARTMENT
OF FISH & WILDLIFE
Springfield Field Office
3150 E Main Street
Springfield, OR 97478-5800
541-726-3515

MCKENZIE RIVER VALLEY
CHAMBER OF COMMERCE
541-896-3330 or 800-318-8819

Fly Shops of the Northwest
OREGON

FLY SHOP	ADDRESS	PHONE/WEBSITE
Ashland Fly Shop	123 Central Ave. Ashland, OR 97520	541-482-1430 www.ashlandflyshop.com
Ashland Outdoor Store	37 N. Third Street Ashland, OR 97520	Local: 541-488-1202 www.outdoorstore.com
Salmon Republic, Inc.	3292 Leif Erikson Dr. Astoria, OR 97103	503-325-7587
River City Fly Shop	11429 SW Scholls Ferry Rd. Beaverton, OR 97008	503-579-5176
Deschutes River Outfitter	61115 S. Hwy. 97 Bend, OR 97701	541-388-8191 888-315-7272 www.deschutesriveroutfitter.com
Fly & Field Outfitters	143 S.W. Century Dr. Bend, OR 97702	541-318-1616 www.flyandfield.com
The Fly Box	1255 NE 3rd St. Bend, OR 97701	541-388-3330 800-411-3330 www.flyboxoutfitters.com
Patient Angler Fly Shop	55 NW Wall St., #B Ste. 1 Bend, OR 97701	541-389-6208
Camp Sherman Fly Shop	Center of Main Rd. Camp Sherman, OR 97730	541-595-6711
Williamson River Anglers	Hwy 62 & Hwy. 97 Chiloquin, OR 97624	541-783-2677
Great American Tackle	16122 SE 82nd Dr. Clackamas, OR 97015	503-650-2662
Riverwire	534 NW 4th St. Corvallis, OR 97330	541-753-1808
Scarlet Ibis Fly Shop	905 NW Kings Blvd. Corvallis, OR 97330	541-754-1544 800-593-8814
Stonefly Angling Shop	1137 E. Main Street Cottage Grove, OR 97424	541-942-3474
Caddis Fly Angling Shop	168 West 6th Ave. Eugene, OR 97401	541-342-7005 800-231-7005
Home Waters Fly Fishing	444 W. 3rd Ave. Eugene, OR 97401	541-342-6691
McKenzie Outfitters Fly Shop	475 Valley River Ctr. Eugene, OR 97401	541-343-2300
Anderson Custom Rods	1976 Foots Creek Rd. Gold Hill, OR 97525	541-582-4318
Native Run Fly Shop and Outfitter	324 Redwood Hwy. Grants Pass, OR 97527	541-474-0090 www.nativerun.com

Northwest Flyfishing Outfitter	10910 NE Halsey St. Gresham, OR 97230	503-252-1529 888-292-1137 www.flyshopnw.com
B&B Sporting Goods	Highway 20 & Conley Ave. Hines, OR 97738	541-573-6200
Kiger Creek Fly Shop	120 NW Circle Rd. Hines, OR 97738	541-573-1329
Gorge Fly Shop	201 Oak St. Hood River, OR 97031	541-386-6977 www.gorgeflyshop.com
Blue Heron Fly Shop	109 Hargis Lane Idleyld Park, OR 97447	503-496-0448
Joseph Fly Shoppe	203 N. Main Joseph, OR 97846-0698	541-432-4343 www.josephflyshoppe.com
Parker Rod & Gun Rack	7364 South 6th Street Klamath Falls, OR 97603	541-883-3726
Trophy Waters Fly Fishing	800 Klamath Ave. Klamath Falls, OR 97601	541-850-0717
Four Seasons Fly Shoppe	10210 Wallowa Lake Hwy. La Grande, OR 97850	541-963-8420 www.4seasonsfly.com
Numb Butt Fly Co.	308 North Highway 25 Madras, OR 97741	541-325-5515 888-248-8309 www.numb-butt.com
Deschutes Canyon Fly Shop	599 S. Hwy. 197 Maupin, OR 97037	541-395-2565 www.flyfishingdeschutes.com
Deschutes Angler	504 Deschutes Ave. Maupin, OR 97037	541-395-0995
Mckenize Outfitter's	1340 Biddle Rd. Medford, OR 97504	541-773-5145
Silver Sedge Fly Shoppe	325 Galice Road Merlin, OR 97532	541-476-2456
Fisherman's Shack	9465 Airlie Road Monmouth, OR 97361	541-838-6395 www.fishermanshack.com
Fisherman's Marine Supply	1900 SE McLaughlin Blvd. Oregon City, OR 97045	503-557-3313
Blue Mountain Anglers	1847 Westgate Pendleton, OR 97801	541-966-8770 800-825-1548
REI	222 Jantzen Beach Ctr. Portland, OR 97217	503-283-1300
Countrysport Limited	126 SW First Ave. Portland, OR 97204-3501	503-221-4545 800-597-4946 www.csport.com
Kaufmann's Streamborn	8861 SW Commercial Ave. Portland, OR 97281-3032	503-639-7004 800-442-4359 www.kman.com
Fisherman's Marine Supply	1120 N. Hayden Meadows Dr. Portland, OR 97217-7546	503-283-0044
Fin N' Feather Fly Shop	785 W. 3rd St. Prineville, OR 97754	541-447-8691

Central Oregon Outdoors	1502 SW Odem Medo Rd. Redmond, OR 97756	541-504-0372
Northwest Outdoors Supply	435 SE Jackson St. Roseburg, OR 97470	541-440-3042 www.northwest-outdoors.com
Surplus Center	515 SE Spruce Roseburg, OR 97470	541-672-4312
Valley Flyfisher	153 Alice Ave. South Salem, OR 97302	503-375-3721
Creekside Flyfishing Guide & Outfitter	345 High St. SE Salem, OR 97301	503-588-1768
Fly Country Outfitters	3400 State St. G-704 Salem, OR 97301	503-585-4898 888-326-4347
McNeese Reel Co., Inc.	1170 Merlin Ct. NW Salem, OR 97304	503-375-6288 800-458-4305
The Fly Fisher's Place	151 W Main Ave. Sisters, OR 97759	541-549-3474 www.flyfishersplace.com
Walterville Fly Shop	39297 McKenzie Hwy Springfield, OR 97489	541-736-1239
Steamboat Inn	42705 N. Umpqua Hwy. Steamboat, OR 97447	541-498-2411 800-840-8825 www.straightlinesport.com
The Hook Fly Shop	Building #21 Sun River Mall Sunriver, OR 97707	541-593-2358 www.hookfish.com
Sunriver Fly Shop	56805 Venture Lane Sunriver, OR 97707	541-593-8814 www.sunriverflyshop.com
The Guide Shop	12140 Wilson River Hwy. Tillamook, OR 97141	541-842-3474 www.guideshop.com
Tillamook Sporting Goods	2207 Main St. Ste. B Tillamook, OR 97141	503-842-4334
Stewart's Fly Shop	23830 NE Halsey St. Troutdale, OR 97060	503-666-2471
The Fly Fishing Shop	67296 E. Hwy. 26 Welches, OR 97067	800-266-3971 www.flyfishusa.com

WASHINGTON

Hook Line & Sinker	3507 A 168th St., NE Arlington, WA 98223	360-651-2204
Auburn Sports and Marine	810 Auburn Way N. Auburn, WA 98002	253-833-1440
Kaufmann's Streamborn	15015 Main St. Bellevue, WA 98007	206-643-2246
Orvis Company Store	911 Bellevue Way, NE Bellevue, WA 98004	425-452-9138
H & H Outdoor Sports	814 Dupont St. Bellingham, WA 98225-3103	360.733.2050 www.hhanglers.com
The Guide's Fly Shop	3960 Meridian Bellingham, WA 98226	360-527-0317

Yeager's Sporting Goods	3101 Northwest Ave. Bellingham, WA 98225	360-733-1080
Diamond Sports Shop	30848 3rd Ave. Black Diamond, WA 98010-9767	604-533-9290
Swedes Fly Shop	16826-119th Place NE Bothell, WA 98011	406-487-3747
Holiday Sports	10776 Mary Lane Burlington, WA 98233	360-757-1221
River Run Anglers	3946 Tolt Ave. Carnation, WA 98017	425-333-4446
Bruce's Fly Shop	1136 20th Ave., Space 6 Clarkston, WA 99403	509-758-8179
Red's Fly Shop	Yakima Canyon Rd. Ellensburg, WA 98926	509-929-1802
The Evening Hatch	105 East Lexus Lane Ellensburg, WA 98926	509-962-5959
Worley-Bugger Fly Co.	306 S. Main, #3 Ellensburg, WA 98926	888-950-3474 www.worleybuggerflyco.com
The Mad Flyfisher	2020 S. 320th St. Ste N Federal Way, WA 98003	253-945-7414 www.madflyfisher.com
Greywolf Angler	275953 Hwy. 101 Gardiner, WA 98382-8722	360-797-7100
Backcast Fly Shop	720 Simpson Ave. Hoquiam, WA 98550-3610	360-532-6867
Creekside Angling Co.	1660 NW Gilman Blvd., C-5 Issaquah, WA 98027	425-392-3800 www.creeksideangling.com
Prichard's Western Angler	2106 Kalama River Rd. Kalama, WA 98625	360-673-4690
Clearwater Fly Shop	417 W. First Ave. Kennewick, WA 99336	509-582-1001
Shoff's Tackle Supply	214 W. Meeker Kent, WA 98032	800-521-0714
The Fly Fisher	5622 Pacific Ave., #9 Lacey, WA 98503	360-491-0181
The Avid Angler	17171 Bothell Way NE, Ste A130 Lake Forest Park, WA 98155	206-362-4030 www.avidangler.com
Ace Hardware and Sport	1736 Front St. Lynden, WA 98264	360.354.2291
Ted's Sport Center	15526 Hwy 99 N. Lynwood, WA 98037	425-743-9505
The Fly Smith Outfitters	1515 Fifth Street Marysville, WA 98270	360-658-9003
Mazama Fly Shop & Troutfitters	48 Lost River Rd. Mazama, WA 98833	509-996-3674
Skagit Anglers	315 Main St., #G Mt. Vernon, WA 98273	360-336-3232
The Fly Fishing Corner	275 W. Cornet Bay Rd. Oak Harbor, WA 98277	360-675-3635

Critter's Outdoor World	5274 Outlet Dr. Pasco, WA 99301	509-543-9663
Bay Street Outfitters	130 Harrison St. Port Angeles, WA 98366	360-224-6962
Quality Fly Fishing Shop	2720 E. Hwy. 101 Port Angeles, WA 98362	360-452-5942
Swain's	602 E. First St. Port Angeles, WA 98362	360-452-2357
Waters West	219 North Oak St. Port Angeles, WA 98362	360-417-0937
Port Townsend Angler	940 Water St. Port Townsend, WA 98368	360-379-3763
Hawk's Poulsbo Center (Fly Shop)	19424C 7th Ave. NE Poulsbo, WA 98370-7526	360-779-5290
Northwest Angler Fly Shop	18804 Front St. Poulsbo, WA 98370	360-697-7100
Sportee's	16725 Cleveland St. Redmond, WA 98052-4464	425-882-1333
Barrier Dam Campground	273 Fuller Rd. Salkum, WA 98582	206-985-2495
On the Fly	10002 Aurora Ave N., # 2246 Seattle, WA 98133-9347	206-528-0428
Outdoor Emporium	420 Pontius Ave. N. Seattle, WA 98109	206-624-6550 www.outdooremporium.com
REI	222 Yale Ave. N. Seattle, WA 98109	206-223-1944
Salmon Bay Tackle	5701 15th NW Seattle, WA 98107	206-789-9335 www.salmonbaytackle.com
Kaufmann's Streamborn	1918 4th Ave. Seattle, WA 98101	206-448-0601
Patrick's Fly Shop	2237 Eastlake Ave. E. Seattle, WA 98102	800-398-7693
Chuck's Fly Shop	1206 36th and L Place Seaview, WA 98644	360-642-2589
The Outdoor Sportsman	1602 N. Division St. Spokane, WA 99207-2421	509-328-1556
The Sport Cove Fly Shop	5727 E. Sprague Ave. Spokane, WA 99212-0828	509-535-7681
Blue Dun Fly Shop	135 S. Sherman Spokane, WA 99202	509-838-3474 www.bluedun.com
Silver Bow Fly Shop	1003 E. Trent Ave. Spokane, WA 99202	509-483-1772 800-732-7815 www.silverbowflyshop.com
White's Outdoor	4002 E. Ferry Ave. Spokane, WA 99202	509-535-1875
R.R. Tackle and Fly Shop	109 E Woodin Rd Sunnyside, WA 98944-9278	360-837-2332
Morning Hatch Fly Shoppe	3630 S. Cedar St. Tacoma, WA 98409	253-472-1070

Toutle River Tackle	428 Moore Rd. Toutle, WA 98649	360-274-6276
The Greased Line Fly Shoppe	6200 Capital Blvd. Tumwater, WA 98944	206-352-5161
The Greased Line Fly Shoppe	5802 NE 88th St. Vancouver, WA 98665-0941	360-573-9383
Blue Dun Fly Shop	960 Valley Mall Pkwy.,#AE. Wenatchee, WA 98802	509-884-4070 www.bluedun.com
Hooked on Toys	1444 N. Wenatchee Ave. Wenatchee, WA 98801	360-663-0740 www.hookedontoys.com
Angler's Work Shop	1350 Atlantic Woodland, WA 98674-1000	360-225-6359 www.anglersworkshop.com
Swedes Fly Shop	17419 139th Ave NE Woodinville, WA 98072	425-487-3747 www.swedesflyshop.com
Gary's Fly Shoppe	5110 Tieton Dr. Yakima, WA 98908	509-972-3880 www.garysflyshoppe.com

WESTERN IDAHO

The Idaho Angler	1682 S. Vista Boise, ID 83705	208-389-9957
Intermountain Arms & Tackle	900 Vista Village Center Boise, ID 83705	208-345-3474
Stonefly Angler	625 Vista Boise, ID 83705	208-338-1700
Bear Creek Fly Shop	5521 W. State Street Boise, ID 83703	208-853-8704
Twin River Anglers	534 Thain Street Lewiston, ID 83501	208-746-8946
Castaway Fly Shop	3620 North Fruitland Couer d'Alene, ID 83816	208-765-3133
Fin and Feathers Fly Shop	1816 1/2 Sherman Ave. Couer d'Alene, ID 83816	208-667-9304

Sporting Goods Stores
-With Fly Fishing Equipment -
OREGON

STORE	ADDRESS	PHONE
Bi Mart	2272 SE Santiam Hwy, Albany, OR 97321	541- 926-6026
G.I. Joe's	2000 SE 14th Ave., Albany, OR 97321	541-967-3260
Bi Mart	5975 SW 185th Ave., Aloha, OR 97007	503- 649-6550
Bi Mart	2280 Ashland St., Ashland, OR 97520	541- 482-8510
Bi Mart	700 Campbell St., Baker City, OR 97814	541-523-1680
Bi Mart	4750 SW Western Ave., Beaverton, OR 97005	503-626-5070
G.I. Joe's	3485 SW Cedar Hills Blvd., Beaverton, OR 97005	503-644-9936
Gart Sports	2780 SW Cedar Hills Blvd., Beaverton, OR 97005	503-644-9800
Bi Mart	351 NE 2nd, Bend, OR 97701	541-389-5505
G.I. Joe's	63455 Highway 97 North, Bend, OR 97701	541-388-3770
Lorings Lighthouse	554 Chetco Lane, Brookings, OR 97415	541-469-2148
Bi Mart	20000 SE Hwy 212, Clackamas, OR 97015	503-558-1415
Gart Sports	8658 SE Sunnyside Rd., Clackamas, OR 97015	503-786-9900
Bi Mart	550 S. 4th St., Coos Bay, OR 97420	541-269-9220
Bi Mart	2045 N. 9th, Corvallis, OR 97330	541-752-7156
Bi Mart	100 Gateway Blvd., Cottage Grove, OR 97424	541-942-9101
Wallowa Outdoors	110 S. River St., Enterprise, OR 97828	541-426-3493
Bi Mart	4780 Royal Ave., Eugene, OR 97402	541-463-1789
G.I. Joe's	1030 Greenacres, Eugene, OR 97401	541-343-1666
Bi Mart	4310 Hwy. 101, Florence, OR 97439	541-997-2499
Sportsman Sp. Gds.	249 Highway 101, Florence, OR 97439	541-997-3336
Bi Mart	3225 Pacific Ave. , Forest Grove, OR 97116	503-357-0244
Bi Mart	230 Redwood Hwy., Grants Pass, OR 97527	541-479-8365
G.I. Joe's	700 NW Eastman Parkway, Gresham, OR 97030	503-667-3126
Bi Mart	2800 Northeast Hogan, Gresham, OR 97030	503-661-2366
Old Pine Sports Shop	Hwy. 86, Halfway, OR 97834	541-742-4036
Bi Mart	200 South 1st Place, Unit 1, Hermiston, OR 97838	541-567-6493
Bi Mart	2075 SE Tualatin Valley Hwy, Hillsboro, OR 97123	503-640-3737
G.I. Joe's	7280 NW Butler Rd, Hillsboro, OR 97124	503-846-1514
Bi Mart	3862 River Rd. N., Keizer, OR 97303	503-371-6711
Bi Mart	1920 Washburn Way, Klamath Falls, OR 97603	541-884-1751

Bi Mart	2510 Adams, La Grande, OR 97850	541-963-2166
G.I. Joe's	17799 SW Boones Ferry Rd, Lake Oswego, OR 97034	503-635-1064
Bi Mart	2680 S. Santiam Hwy., Lebanon, OR 97355-3200	541-258-8040
Bi Mart	4157 NW Hwy. 101, Lincoln City, OR 97367	541-994-3194
Bi Mart	1575 South Hwy. 97, Madras, OR 97741	541-475-1394
Oscar's Sprtng Goods	380 SW 5th Street, Madras, OR 97741	541-475-2962
Bi Mart	1635 South Baker, McMinnville, OR 97128	503-472-8466
Bi Mart	990 Biddle Rd., Medford, OR 97504	541-772-3466
G.I. Joe's	2370 Poplar Dr., Medford, OR 97504	541-772-9779
G.I. Joe's	15600 SE McLoughlin Blvd, Milwaukie, OR 97222	503-653-5616
Bi Mart	514 West Main, Molalla, OR 97038	503-829-4888
Bi Mart	444 Pacific Avenue South, Monmouth, OR 97361	503-838-0547
Bi Mart	2900 Haworth, Newberg, OR 97132	503-538-0631
Bi Mart	2131 Newmark, North Bend, OR 97459	541-756-7526
Bi Mart	2283 S.W. 4th Ave, Ontario, OR 97914	541-889-2141
Bi Mart	1813 Molalla Ave, Oregon City, OR 97045	503-657-3085
Bi Mart	901 S.W. Emigrant, Pendelton, OR 97801	541-276-7850
Bi Mart	12321 Northeast Halsey St, Portland, OR 97230	503-257-3007
Bi Mart	4315 SE Woodstock Blvd, Portland, OR 97206	503-771-1001
G.I. Joe's	3900 SE 82nd Ave, Portland, OR 97266	503-777-4526
G.I. Joe's	1140 N Hayden Meadows Dr., Portland, OR 97217	503-283-0318
REI	1798 Jantzen Beach Ctr, Portland, OR 97217	503-283-1300
Bi Mart	2091 NE Third, Prineville, OR 97754	541-447-0391
Prineville Sprtg Goods	346 North Deer, Prineville,OR 97754	541-447-6883
Bi Mart	1727 S.W. Odem Medo Rd., Redmond, OR 97756	541-923-7220
Bi Mart	1381 N.W. Garden Valley Blvd., Roseburg, OR 97470	541-672-6771
Bi Mart	2155 Lancaster Dr. NE, Salem,OR 97305	503-588-3211
G.I. Joe's	275 Lancaster Dr. NE, Salem,OR 97301	530-364-3366
Gart Sports	2717 Lancaster Dr. NE, Salem,OR 97309	503-315-2255
Sportsman's Warehouse	1260 Lancaster Dr. SE, Salem,OR 97305	503-589-0800
G.I. Joe's	16685 NW 12th Street, Sherwood, OR 97140	503-925-0700
Bi Mart	5744 Main St., Springfield, OR 97478	541-687-7637
Bi Mart	1701 Shaff Rd., Stayton, OR 97383	503-769-6439
Bi Mart	833 E. Central Ave., Sutherin, OR 97479	541-459-0541
Bi Mart	3300 W. 6th St., The Dalles, OR 97058	541-298-1155
Bi Mart	13500 S.W. Pacific Hwy., Tigard, OR 97223	503-624-0103
Bi Mart	25126 Jeans Rd., Veneta, OR 97487	541-935-0902
G.I. Joe's	9805 Boeckman Rd., Wilsonville, OR 97070	503-682-2242
Bi Mart	1600 Mt. Hood Ave., Woodburn, OR 97071	503-981-2101

WASHINGTON

Big Mouth John Tackle	PO Box 8, Aberdeen,WA 98520-0902	360-533-0143
Gart Sports	1101 Super Mall Way, Auburn,WA 98036-6739	253-735-7447
Oshman's	1101 Super Mall Way, Auburn,WA 98001	253-735-7447
Gart Sports	44 Bellevue Way NE, Bellevue, WA 98004-5916	425-456-0600
Sports Authority	15600 NE 8th Street, Bellevue, WA 98008	425-747-6112
Bi Mart	608 E Mountain View Ave, Ellensburg, WA 98926	509-925-6971
Gart Sports	505 SE Everett Mall Way, Everett, WA 98208-3252	425-347-8988
John's Sporting Goods	1913 Broadway, Everett, WA 98201	206-259-3056
G.I. Joe's	35020 Enchanted Pkwy. S., Federal WA 98003	206-927-2943
Olympic Sporting Goods	190 Forks Ave South, Forks,WA 98331	360-374-6330
Outdoor Sportsman	3809 S. Linke Rd., Greenacres, WA 99016	509-328-1556
GI Joe's	1185 NW Gilman Blvd, Issaquah, WA 98027-5322	425-712-9200
Gart Sports	908 N Colorado St # C, Kennewick, WA 99336-7617	509-783-7801
Birdie's Northwest Tackle	23212 172nd Ave. SE, Kent,WA 98042-4715	206-854-4470
Bob's Merchandise	1111 Hudson St., Longview, WA 98632-3158	360-425-3870
GI Joe's	19800 44th Ave W, Lynnwood, WA 98036-5112	425-712-0900
G.I. Joe's	19310 60th Ave West, Lynwood, WA 98036	425-712-9200
Sports Authority	5824 196th Street SW, Lynnwood, WA 98036	425-771-1301
Tri-State Outfitters	1224 S Pioneer Way, Moses Lake, WA 98837-2347	509-765-9338
Oak Harbor Hardware	150 S.E. Pioneer Way, Oak Harbor, WA 98277	360-679-3533
Puget Sound Sport Center	527 Devoe St. S.E., Olympia, WA, 98501	206-943-4867
Bi Mart	11912 N.E. Fourth Plain Blvd., Orchards, WA 98662	360-944-5432
Phil's Sporting Goods Inc.	3806 W. Court St., Pasco,WA 99301	509-547-9084
GI Joe's	4423 South Meridian, Puyallup, WA 98374-1203	253-841-1510
G.I. Joe's	120 31st Ave., Puyallup, WA 98374	253-445-8090
REI	222 Yale Ave. N, Seattle, WA 98109	206-223-1944
Kitsap Sports	10516 Silverdale Way NW, Silverdale,WA 98383	360-698-4808
Gart Sports	15118 E Indiana Ave, Spokane, WA 99216-1832	509-891-1500
Gart Sports	9620 N Newport Hwy, Spokane, WA 99218-1221	509-466-2100
Sportsman's Warehouse	14014 East Indiana Ave, Spokane, WA 99216	509-891-1900
Brock's Sporting Goods	North 2104 Division, Spokane, WA 99207	509-328-9708
Gart Sports	9620 N. Newport Hwy., Spokane, WA 99218	509-466-2100
Bi Mart	110 West South Hill Rd, Sunnyside, WA 98944	509-839-0781
Gart Sports	1905 B S 72nd St, Tacoma, WA 98408-1240	253-572-9900
Sportco	4602 20th St E, Tacoma, WA 98424-1926	253-922-2222
Sports Authority	4104 Tacoma Mall Blvd, Tacoma, WA 98409-7203	253-471-0262

Bi Mart	11912 NE 4th Plain Rd, Vancouver, WA 98682-5526	360-944-5432
GI Joe's	13215 SE Mill Plain Blvd, Vancouver, WA 98684	360-253-2420
G.I. Joe's	13215 B SE Mill Plain, Vancouver,WA 98684	360-253-2420
Bi Mart	780 Grant Rd. East, Wenatchee, WA 98802	509-884-1141
Bi Mart	1649 Plaza Way, Walla Walla, WA 99362-4324	509-529-8840
Bi Mart	3003 Addy St, Washougal, WA 98671	360-335-9700
Bi Mart	309 S 5th Ave, YakimaWA 98902-3548	509-457-5175
Bi Mart	1207 N 40th Ave, Yakima, WA 98908-9456	509-457-1650
Chinook Sporting Goods	901 S. 1st St., Yakima,WA 98901-3401	509-452-8205

Sources of Information
Oregon

River flows, Oregon: http://water.usgs.gov/or/nwis/current/?type=flow

Oregon Deptartment of Fish and Wildlife: Headquarters

2501 SW First Avenue
Portland, OR 97207
503-872-5252
www.dfw.state.or.us/

Regional Offices

NORTHWEST Regional Office
17330 SE Evelyn Street
Clackamas, OR 97015
503-657-2000

SOUTHWEST Regional Office
4192 North Umpqua Highway
Roseburg, OR 97470
541-440-3353

HIGH DESERT Regional Office
61374 Parrell Road
Bend, OR 97702
541-388-6363

NORTHEAST Regional Office
107 20th Street
La Grande, OR 97850
541-963-2138

Local Offices

SOUTH WILLAMETTE
Watershed District Office
7118 NE Vanderberg Avenue
Corvallis, OR 97330-9446
541-757-4186

NORTH COAST
Watershed District Office
4909 Third Street
Tillamook, OR 97141
503-842-2741

NEWPORT Field Office
2040 SE Marine Science Drive
Newport, OR 97365
541-867-4741

SALEM Field Office
4412 Silverton Road NE
Salem, OR 97305-2060
503-378-6925

SPRINGFIELD Field Office
3150 E Main Street
Springfield, OR 97478-5800
541-726-3515

ROGUE WATERSHED
District Office
1495 E. Gregory Road
Central Point, OR 97502
541-826-8774

GOLD BEACH Field Office
742 Airport Way, P.O. Box 642
Gold Beach, OR 97444
541-247-7605

JOHN DAY WATERSHED
District Office
73471 Mytinger Lane
Pendleton, OR 97801
541-276-2344

BAKER CITY Field Office
2995 Hughes Lane
Baker City, OR 97814
541-523-5832

ENTERPRISE Field Office
65495 Alder Slope Road
Enterprise, OR 97828
541-426-3279

JOHN DAY Field Office
P.O. Box 9
John Day, OR 97845
541-575-1167

KLAMATH WATERSHED
District Office
1850 Miller Island Road
Klamath Falls, OR 97603
541-883-5732

MALHEUR WATERSHED
District Office
237 S. Hines Blvd., P.O. Box 8
Hines, OR 97738
541-573-6582

LAKEVIEW Field Office
101 N "D" Street, P.O. Box 1214
Lakeview, OR 97630
541-947-2950

ONTARIO Field Office
3814 Clark Blvd.
Ontario, OR 97914
541-889-6975

PRINEVILLE Field Office
2042 SE Paulina Highway
Prineville, OR 97754
541-447-5111

THE DALLES Field Office
3701 W 13th Street
The Dalles, OR 97058
541-296-4628

Other Oregon Offices

OREGON STATE PARKS DEPARTMENT
800-551-6959 (information)
800-452-5687 (reservations)
www.oregonstateparks.org

OREGON GUIDES & PACKERS
ASSOCIATION
531 SW 13th Street
Bend, OR 97702
800-747-9552
www.ogpa.org

Washington

River flows, Washington: http://water.usgs.gov/wa/nwis/current/?type=flow

Washington Department of Fish and Wildlife: Headquarters

Olympia Office (Main Office)
360-902-2200
www.wa.gov/wdfw

Visitor Information

NATURAL RESOURCES BUILDING
1111 Washington St. SE
Olympia, WA 98501

MAILING ADDRESS:
600 Capitol Way N.
Olympia, WA USA 98501-1091

Regional Offices

EASTERN WASHINGTON
Region 1 Office
8702 North Division Street
Spokane, Washington 99218
509-456-4082

NORTH CENTRAL WASHINGTON
Region 2 Office
1550 Alder Street NW
Ephrata, Washington 98823-9699
509-754-4624

SOUTH CENTRAL WASHINGTON
Region 3 Office
1701 South 24th Avenue
Yakima, Washington 98902-5720
509-575-2740

NORTH PUGET SOUND
Region 4 Office
16018 Mill Creek Boulevard
Mill Creek, Washington 98012-1296
425-775-1311

SOUTHWEST WASHINGTON
Region 5 Office
2108 Grand Boulevard
Vancouver, Washington 98661
360-696-6211

COASTAL WASHINGTON
Region 6 Office
48 Devonshire Road
Montesano, Washington 98563
360-249-4628

Other Washington Offices

WASHINGTON STATE PARKS
360-902-8844 (information)
888-226-7688 (reservations)
www.parks.wa.gov/reserve.asp

INDEX

A

Allan Diversion Dam 221
Alvord Desert 126
Alvord Hot Springs 126
antique malls 266
Armitage Park 332
Ashland, OR 319
Asotin, WA 14
Aspen Ridge Ranch 67
Atlantic salmon 277, 279, 290, 295, 299, 342

B

Baker City, OR 139
Baldwin Saloon 45
Beaver, WA 82
Bend, OR 275, 277, 286
Benham Falls 298
Beulah Reservoir 219, 224
Big K Guest Ranch 258
Big Obsidian Flow Trail 298
Blitzen River 125
BLM Burns District, North Half Map 224
BLM campsites 14
Blount, Tim 120
Blue Heron Fly Shop 255
Blue Lake 228
Blue Mountains 16, 219
Blythe-Chukar Lake Chain 101
Bonner, Steve 62, 66
Bowman Dam 157-158, 162
Brownlee Reservoir 133-140
    Brownlee Reservoir Map 134
Burns, OR 119, 211

C

Calawah River 78
Camp Sherman Store 152
Camp Water of the North Umpqua 251, 257
Canton Creek 251
Cape Alava 83
Cape Flattery birdwatching 83
Carmen Diversion Reservoir 341

Cascade Mountains 99, 259
Cascade Range 199
Central Oregon Visitor's Association 286
Century Drive 288
Chickahominy Reservoir 203-215
    Chickahominy Bird Festival 211-212
    Chickahominy Camping 209, 212
    Chickahominy Reservoir Map 204
Chiloquin, WA 59
Chopaka Lake 227-233
    Chopaka Grade 228
    Chopaka Lake Map 229
Clallam Bay/Seiku area 83
Class IV rapids 39
Clear Lake 331, 341
Collier Park 59-60
Columbia Basin 16, 104
Columbia National Wildlife Refuge 104
Cook, George 323, 325
Crane Prairie Reservoir 277, 280-282
    Crane Prairie campgrounds 282
    Crane Prairie Reservoir Map 281
    Crane Prairie Resort 288
Crater Lake National Park 319
Crooked River 147, 157-164
    Crooked River Dinner Train 162
    Crooked River Map 159
Cultus Lake 287
Cummings, Ward 251

D

Dalles, The 45
Daughters, Chris 339
Davis Lake 275-277, 283-284
    Davis Lake campgrounds 284
    Davis Lake Map 285
Dean Creek Elk Preserve 259
Deer Creek 184
Denio, Nevada 126
Deschutes Channel 280
Deschutes National Forest 300

Deschutes River, Lower   33-45
   Deschutes River Access   42
   Deschutes River Canyon   24
   Deschutes River Map, Lower   34
   Deschutes River Map, Upper   35
   Deschutes River Steelhead   41
Deschutes River, Middle   165-171
   Middle Deschutes River Maps   166
Dexter Reservoir   341
Diamond Lake   259
Donner & Blitzen River   125
Dry Creek Campground   43
Dry Falls   99
Dry Falls Lake   235, 241-246
   Dry Falls Lake Map   242

E

East Fork of the Lewis River   269-274
   East Fork Lewis River Map   270
   Lucia Falls   271
   Lewisville County Park   271
East Lake   295-300
   Newberry Nat'l Volcanic Monument   297
   Newberry Caldera   298
   East Lake Campground   297
   East Lake Map   296
   East Lake Resort   297
Eerkes, Dan   101
Elk Lake   277, 287
Ellensburg, WA   32, 117
Elwha River   89-97
   Elwha River Map   90
   Lower Elwha   95
   Middle Elwha   92
   Grand Canyon of the Elwha   91-92
Enterprise, OR   14
Ephrata, OR   238
Eugene Fly Tyers Expo   342
Eugene, OR   340

F

Fall River   287
Fields, OR   119, 126
Fish Lake   125
Fisher Road Bridge   46
Flemming, Steve   53
Float Tubing a Volcano   295
Foley Station   16-17
Foly Waters   168
Fortson Hole   184
Foster Bar,   311

Frenchglen, OR   127
   Frenchglen Brew Fest   127
   Frenchglen Hotel   124
   Frenchglen Mercantile   126

G

Garren, John   311
Ginkgo Petrified Forest State Park   115
Glacier Peak   197
Glasso, Syd   81
Glide, OR   256, 258
Gold Creek   221
Gordon, Clarence   250
Gracey   81
Grand Coulee   241
Grande Ronde River   7-21
   Grande Ronde River Maps   9-11
Grants Pass, OR   318
Grave Creek   308, 319
Grey, Zane   301
Grindstone Lakes   327-329

H

Halfway, OR   141
Harney County Museum   211
Harney Lake   211
Harpham Flats   43
helicopter fishing   125
Hell's Canyon   136
Heller Bar   14
Hellgate Jetboat Excursions   319
High Desert Redband Trout Cowboy Camp   125
Hogan, Dec   42
Hoh Humm Ranch B&B   82
Hoh, Sol Duc, and Bogachiel Rivers   75-87
   Hoh Rain Forest   84
   Hoh River Map   76
   Sol Duc and Bogachiel Rivers Map   80
   Sol Duc Guest House   82
   Sol Duc River Lodge B&B   82
Hood Canal   89
Hosmer Lake   277-279
   Hosmer Lake Map   278
Hosmer, Crane Prairie & Davis Lakes   275
Howell, Joe   255
Huff, Mac   18
Hurricane Ridge   95

I

Idleyld, OR   256
Inn at Eagle Crest   169

Isaak Lake Ranch   323-326

J

Jet Boat River Excursions   319
jet boats on the Rogue River   311
John Day River   48-53
Johnson, Walt   181
Juniper Lake   125
Juntura, OR   219

K

Kalama River   263-268
   Kalama River Holy Water, the   264
   Kalama River Map   262
Kalama, WA   266
Kennewick, OR   14
Klamath Marsh   59
Klickitat River   46-48
   Klickitat Glacier   46
   Klickitat Gorge   48
   Klickitat River Map   47
Knobel, Darc   325

L

Lake Aldwel   95
Lake Chelan   199
Lake Lenore   233-240
   Lake Lenore Camping   237
   Lake Lenore Map   234
Lake Ozette   83
Lakes of Century Drive   275-292
Lapine Chamber of Commerce   300
LaPine, OR   297
Newberry Volcanic National Monument
   298
Largemouth bass fishery   108
Lava Cast Forest   298
Lava Lake   287
Lava River Cave Trail   298
Lavalands National Monument   286
Leaburg Dam   332, 338
Lenice, Nunnally and Merry Lakes   113-119
Lenice Lake   114-115
   Lenice, Nunnally and Merry Lakes Map
   112
Lewis River   265
Little Imnaha River   18
Little Three Creeks Lake   153
Lonesome Duck Flyfishing Cabins   66
Lost Creek Reservoir   305, 315
   Hatchery Ramp   307
   Rogue Elk Park   307

Lost Creek Reservoirk cont.
   Takelma Park   307
   Shady Cove   307
   Casey State Park   307
Love, J.D.   81
Lower Rogue   308-311
Lyle Hotel & Restaurant   48

M

Macks Canyon   41
Madras, OR   44
Makah Cultural Museum   83
Malheur Lake   211
Malheur River   217-227
   Malheur River Map   216, 218
   Middle Fork Malheur   219
   North Fork Malheur   219
   South Fork Malheur   219
Mann Lake and the Steens Mountains   119-131
   Mann Lake Camping   121
   Mann Lake herpetology   121
   Mann Lake Map   118
   Mann Ranch   121
Maupin, OR   43
Maxwell, Forrest   275
McKenzie River   331-345
   McKenzie River Map   334
   McKenzie summer steelhead   336
Mcmenamin's   271, 340
Meseberg, Levi   108
Methow Valley Inn   199
Metolius River   147-157
   Head of the Metolius   153
   Lower Metolius River Map   150
   Upper Metolius River Map   146
Michael's Divine Restaurant   89
Mickey Hot Springs   126
Middle Deschutes River   165-171
   Middle Deschutes River Maps   166-167
Middle Sister Peak   276
Minam, Oregon   18
Morrison's Rogue River Lodge   315
Moses Lake, WA   108
Mother's Day Caddis   25, 27
Mott Trail   259
   Red Barn Hole   263
   Marster's Bridge   259
   Horseshoe Bend Campground   259
   Calf Creek Bridge   259
Mount Bachelor Skiing   286
Mt. Bachelor   277

Mt. Higgins House   184
Mt. Mazama volcano   319
Mt. Piscah   342
Mt. Vernon, WA   198

N

Narrows, The   211
Neah Bay, WA   83
North Cascades National Park   197, 199
North Fork of the Stillaguamish   181-188
    Stillaguamish River Map   183
North Twin Lake   287
North Umpqua River   197, 249-261
    Camp Water   256
    Fighting Hole   256
    Kitchen Pool   249, 251
    Lower Boat Pool   249, 251
    Mott Bridge   256
    North Umpqua Logistics   256
    North Umpqua River Maps   252-254
    Sawtooth Pool   256
    Upper Boat Pool   249
    Steamboat Creek   250, 256
Numb-Butt Fly Company   44
Nunnally Lake   113

O

O'Sullivan Dam   109
Oasis Resort & Restaurant   44
Odell Creek   284
Olympic National Park   84
Olympic National Park Campgrounds   94
Olympic Peninsula activities   83
Olympic Peninsula Steelhead   75
Oregon Cave National Monument   319
Oregon City, OR   338
Oregon Department of Fish & Wildlife   18,
    21, 120, 219, 259, 338
Oregon Deptartment of Fish and Wildlife:
    Headquarters   351
Oregon High Desert Museum   286
Oregon River flows website   351
Oregon River Tours   311
Oregon Shakespeare Festival   319
Oregon's Great Basin Desert   286
Oroville, OR   230
Othello, WA   108
Owhyee Dam   141
Owyhee River   141-145
    Owyhee River Map   142
Oxbow Reservoir   136

P

Paulina Lake   295, 297-298
Pendleton, OR   14
Phone Company Restaurant   140
Pine Creek   141
Port Angeles, WA   95
Potholes Reservoir and the Seep Lakes
    99-113
    Potholes Reservoir   107
    Potholes Reservoir Map   98
Powder River   136
Prineville Reservoir   157, 162
Private Stillwater Fishery, Grindstone Lake
    327
Private Waters on the High Plateau   323
Probasco, Steve   101

Q

Quail Lake   100
    Quail Lake Map   102
Queets River   78
Quillayute River   77

R

Rainie Falls   308
Rainy Pass   199
Ramp, Marlon   66
Richland, OR   136
Riley, OR   211
Riverside Wildlife Management Area   219,
    221
Rogue River   301-321
    Eagle Point Golf Course   319
    Holy Water, the Rogue's   315
    Middle Rogue River   307-308
    Pulling Flies on the Rogue   313
    Rogue River "half-pounders"
    Rogue River steelhead   312
    Rogue River salmon redds   312
    Rogue River Map   303-304, 309-310
    Upper Rogue   302
        McGregor Park   302
        Gold Ray Dam   302
    "Wild Rogue" section   308
Roseburg, OR   258
Ross Lake   197
Rotenone poison   104

S

Santiam Summit   331
Sauk River   189
    Sauk River Map   196

Schneider Art Museum   319
Seep Lakes Camping   108
Seep Lakes   104-108
   Blythe Lake   106
   Goldeneye Lake   106
   Heron Lake   106
   Janet Lake   106
   Pillar-Widgeon Lake Chain   106
   Soda Lake   106
   Susan Lake   106
   Warden Lake   106
   Seeps Lakes Map   105
Shaniko, OR   44
Sherar's Falls   43
Silver Creek Valley   211
Sinlahekin Valley   228
North Sister Peak   276
Sisters, OR   152
Skagit and Sauk Rivers   189-202
   Sauk River   189
   Sauk River Map   196
   Skagit and Sauk Wild & Scenic
   River System Map   197
   Skagit River   189
   Skagit River Map   191-193
   Skagit Valley   198-199
Skykomish River   173-180
   Skyhomish River Map   172
Slusser, Ray   314
Smeraglio, John   44
Snake River   133, 138
   Snake River Canyon   136
Snively Hot Springs   141
Snow, Brent   158, 283
Soap Lake, OR   244
South Sister Peak   276
South Twin Lake   277, 287
South Umpqua River   258
Sparks Lake   277, 287
Spectacle Lake   230
Spring Creek   60
Staples, Brad   42
Steamboat Inn   256
Steelhead waters   2, 7, 177, 179, 182, 260,
   336, 344
Steens Mountain Recreation Map   126
Steens Mountains   120
Stonefly Time   39
Stonehouse Canyon   121
Summers Creek   264
   Mudrow Bridge   264
   Red Barn Hole   264

Sun Lakes State Park   244
Sun Mountain Lodge   199
Sunriver, OR   286, 288
   Sunriver Fly Shop   282
   Sunriver Lodge   286
Suttle Lake   153

T

Table of Contents   v
Thief Valley Reservoir   141
Thyme and the River Cookbook   257
Thyme and the River Too Cookbook   257
Timing the Runs   251
Tonasket, OR   230
Travel Introduction   1
trout
   wild rainbow trout   18, 23, 31, 96
   Dolly Varden   197
   wild redband trout   69, 125, 163
   redband trout   157, 219
   Kamloops-strain rainbows   324
   wild Rainbows   59, 157
   Lahontan cutthroat trout   120
   trophy-size brown trout   297
   redsides   38, 41, 53, 168, 333
Trout Creek   42-43
Trout Creek Mountains   125
Troy, OR   14
Tudor Lake   121
Twisp, WA   199

U

Umpqua River, *see North and South*
Umpqua National Forest Lakes   258
Upper Hampton Lake   103
Upper Klamath and Agency Lakes   69
   Upper Klamath & Agency Lakes Map   68
Upper Willamette Basin   338

V

Vancouver, WA   265
Vantage, WA   115

W

Wallowa Range   143
Wanapum Dam   115
Warm Springs Dam   219
Warm Springs Indian Reservation   43
Warm Springs Reservoir   217, 224
warmwater fisheries   133
Washington Department of Fish & Wildlife
   21, 104, 190, 235

Washington Department of Fish and
  Wildlife: Headquarters 353
Washington River flows, website 353
Washington's Blue-Ribbon Gem 23
Washougal River 265
  Red Barn Hole 265
Wedding Rocks petroglyphs 83
Wenaha Wildlife Management Area 18
whitefish 157
whitewater 39, 308, 316, 342
whitewater permit 308
Wickiup Reservoir 277, 280, 287
Wildhorse Lake 125
Willamette Falls 338
  fish counts 339
Willamette River 332, 341
Willamette Valley 331
Williamson River and Klamath Country
  59-69
  Williamson River Club at Crystalwood
  Lodge...64-65
  Lower Williamson 63
  Upper Williamson 67
Wind River 265
wineries 30, 95, 259, 319

winter steelhead fishing 81, 95, 195, 251,
  264
wintertime fisheries 169
Winthrop, WA 199
Witzel, John 125
Wizard Falls Hatchery 149
Wood River 70-73
  Wood River Map 71
Worley, Steve 27

Y

Yakima Indian Reservation 46
Yakima River 23-33
  Yakima River campgrounds 28
  Yakima Canyon 30
  Yakima River Map 26
  Yakima River, lower half fishery 29
  Yakima Train Depot Restaurant 28
  Yakima Valley wine country 30
  Canyon Section of the Yakima 24
Yamsi Ranch 67
Yellowjacket Lake 212
Youngers, Rich 42

Z

Zeller's Resort 15

FISHING DIARY

The next pages will provide a space
to collect your thoughts after a day on the
water. The "useful symbols" are meant to
aid in quickly logging key features and
events, while the "notes" section allows
ample room for any additional
information. Keeping an accurate diary
will take the guess work out of a repeat
visit and, in turn, make you a better angler.

Good Luck!

-Wilderness Adventures Press, Inc.

FLY FISHING DIARY

Date	Water Fished	Conditions		Fish Caught
		Weather	Water	
Useful Symbols	HD-Headwater CF-Confluence MO-Mouth ↑-Upstream ↓-Downstream	S-Sunny C-Cloudy R-Rain SN-Snow WY-Windy	CL-Clear OC-Off Color N-Normal (Flow) HI-High LO-Low	RB-Rainbow BN-Brown BT-Bull BR-Brook CT-Cutthroat ST-Steelhead MW-Mtn.Whitefish LB/SB- Large & Smallmouth Bass

Hatch Observed	Notes (i.e. time of day, flies used, fishing pressure)	Pg. #

BAT- Callibaetis spp BWO-Blue-winged Olive PMD-Pale Morning Dun MFY-Mayfly DF-Damselfly LC-Leech
CAD-Caddis TRC-Trico MDG-Midge STN-Stonefly HOP-Grasshopper SN-Sculpins EMG-Emerger SF-Spinner Fall
TW-Tailwater SC-Spring Creek FS-Freestone PW-Pocket Water CB-Cutbank

NOTES

NOTES

FLY FISHING GUIDE SERIES

If you would like to order additional copies of this book or our other Wilderness Adventures Press guidebooks, please fill out the order form below or call **1-800-925-3339** or *fax 800-390-7558.* Visit our website for a listing of over 2000 sporting books—the largest online: **www.wildadv.com**   *Mail To:*

Wilderness Adventures Press, Inc., 45 Buckskin Road • Belgrade, MT 59714

☐ **Please send me your quarterly catalog on hunting and fishing books.**

Ship to:

Name_____

Address_____

City_____State_____ Zip_____

Home Phone_____Work Phone_____

Payment: ☐ Check ☐ Visa ☐ Mastercard ☐ Discover ☐ American Express

Card Number _____Expiration Date_____

Signature_____

Qty	Title of Book	Price	Total
	Saltwater Angler's Guide to Southern California	$26.95	
	Saltwater Angler's Guide to the Southeast	$26.95	
	Flyfisher's Guide to the Florida Keys	$26.95	
	Flyfisher's Guide to Colorado	$28.95	
	Flyfisher's Guide to Idaho	$26.95	
	Flyfisher's Guide to Michigan	$26.95	
	Flyfisher's Guide to Montana	$26.95	
	Flyfisher's Guide to Northern California	$26.95	
	Flyfisher's Guide to Northern New England	$28.95	
	Flyfisher's Guide to Oregon	$26.95	
	Flyfisher's Guide to Pennsylvania	$28.95	
	Flyfisher's Guide to Washington	$28.95	
	Flyfisher's Guide to Minnesota	$26.95	
	Flyfisher's Guide to Utah	$26.95	
	Flyfisher's Guide to Texas	$28.95	
	Flyfisher's Guide to New York	$26.95	
	Flyfisher's Guide to Virginia	$28.95	
	On the Fly Guide to the Northwest	$26.95	
	Total Order + shipping & handling		

Shipping and handling: $4.99 for first book,
$3.00 per additional book, up to $13.99 maximum